ALSO BY ALICE WALKER

Fiction

The Third Life of Grange Copeland

In Love & Trouble:
Stories of Black Women

Meridian

The Color Purple

You Can't Keep a Good
Woman Down: Stories

To Hell With Dying

The Temple of My Familiar

Finding the Green Stone

Possessing the Secret of Joy

The Complete Stories

By the Light of My Father's Smile

The Way Forward Is with a Broken Heart

Now Is the Time to Open Your Heart

Poetry

Once

Revolutionary Petunias and Other Poems

Good Night, Willie Lee, I'll
See You in the Morning

Horses Make a Landscape
Look More Beautiful

Her Blue Body Everything We
Know: Earthling Poems

Absolute Trust in the Goodness
of the Earth

A Poem Traveled Down My
Arm: Poems and Drawings

Collected Poems

Hard Times Require Furious
Dancing: New Poems

Taking the Arrow Out of the Heart

Nonfiction

In Search of Our Mothers'
Gardens: Womanist Prose

Living by the Word

Warrior Marks

The Same River Twice:
Honoring the Difficult

Anything We Love Can Be
Saved: A Writer's Activism

Pema Chödrön and Alice
Walker in Conversation

Sent by Earth: A Message from
the Grandmother Spirit

We Are the Ones We Have Been
Waiting For

Overcoming Speechlessness

The Chicken Chronicles: A Memoir

The Cushion in the Road: Meditation
and Wandering as the Whole World
Awakens to Be in Harm's Way

ALSO BY VALERIE BOYD

Wrapped in Rainbows: The Life of Zora Neale Hurston

GATHERING
BLOSSOMS
UNDER FIRE

THE JOURNALS OF
ALICE WALKER
1965–2000

EDITED BY VALERIE BOYD

SIMON & SCHUSTER

NEW YORK   LONDON   TORONTO   SYDNEY   NEW DELHI

Simon & Schuster
1230 Avenue of the Americas
New York, NY 10020

First Simon & Schuster hardcover edition April 2022

SIMON & SCHUSTER and colophon are registered trademarks of Simon & Schuster, Inc.

For information about special discounts for bulk purchases, please contact Simon & Schuster Special Sales at 1-866-506-1949 or business@simonandschuster.com.

The Simon & Schuster Speakers Bureau can bring authors to your live event. For more information, or to book an event, contact the Simon & Schuster Speakers Bureau at 1-866-248-3049 or visit our website at www.simonspeakers.com.

Interior design by Carly Loman

Manufactured in the United States of America

10 9 8 7 6 5 4 3 2 1

Library of Congress Cataloging-in-Publication Data

Names: Walker, Alice, 1944– author.
Title: Gathering blossoms under fire : the journals of Alice Walker 1965–2000 / edited by Valerie Boyd.
Description: First Simon & Schuster hardcover edition. | New York : Simon & Schuster, 2022.
Identifiers: LCCN 2021047979 (print) | LCCN 2021047980 (ebook) | ISBN 9781476773155 (hardcover) | ISBN 9781476773179 (ebook)
Subjects: LCSH: Walker, Alice, 1944—Diaries. | Authors, American—20th Century—Diaries. | African American women authors—Diaries. | Social reformers—United States—Diaries. | LCGFT: Diaries.
Classification: LCC PS3573.A425 Z46 2022 (print) | LCC PS3573.A425 (ebook) | DDC 813/.54 B 23/eng/20211015—dcundefined
LC record available at https://lccn.loc.gov/2021047979
LC ebook record available at https://lccn.loc.gov/2021047980

ISBN 978-1-4767-7315-5
ISBN 978-1-4767-7317-9 (ebook)

For Belvie, Joan, and Sue,
my human angels,
and for my brother Curtis,
who was a child.

—ALICE WALKER

WHILE LOVE IS UNFASHIONABLE

While love is unfashionable
let us live
unfashionably.
Seeing the world
a complex ball
in small hands;
love our blackest garment.
Let us be poor
in all but truth, and courage
handed down
by the old
spirits.
Let us be intimate with
ancestral ghosts
and music
of the undead.

While love is dangerous
let us walk bareheaded
beside the Great River.
Let us gather blossoms
under fire.

—ALICE WALKER

CONTENTS

INTRODUCTION

BY VALERIE BOYD

"I am amazed at myself. Once more I am warming up to write," the twenty-four-year-old woman wrote in her journal. The date was July 18, 1968; the place was Jackson, Mississippi. "How incredible in some ways it is to thirst for pen and paper," she continued, "to need them, as if they were water."

That young woman was Alice Walker. And through her prodigious talent—as a novelist, short story writer, poet, and essayist—she would go on to become one of the most celebrated authors in modern history.

On her epic journey from sharecropper's shack in rural Georgia to cultural icon, Walker has been a faithful diarist, chronicling her sprawling, complex life in more than sixty-five journals and notebooks spanning some fifty years. In 2007, she placed those journals—along with hundreds of other documents and items from her personal archive—at Emory University's Stuart A. Rose Manuscript, Archives, and Rare Book Library in Atlanta. The journals, as well as certain business and financial files, are embargoed from the curious eyes of scholars, journalists, and fans until 2040.

Now, however, Walker has decided to publish a volume of selected entries from her journals. In *Gathering Blossoms Under Fire*, she offers a passionate, intimate record of her development as an artist, human rights activist, and intellectual. She also intimately explores—in real time—her thoughts and feelings as a woman, a writer, an African American, a wife, a daughter, a mother, a lover, a sister, a friend, a citizen of the world. The journal entries traverse an astonishing array of events: marching in Mississippi with other foot soldiers of the civil rights movement, led by Martin Luther King Jr., or "the King," as she called him; her marriage to a Jewish lawyer, partly to defy laws that barred interracial marriage in the 1960s South; an early miscarriage; the birth of her daughter; writing her first novel; the trials and triumphs of the women's movement; erotic encounters and enduring relationships; the ancestral visits that led her to write *The Color Purple*; winning the Pulitzer Prize; being admired and maligned, in sometimes equal measure, for her work and her activism; burying her mother; and her estrangement from her own daughter. The personal, the political, and the spiritual are layered and intertwined in the revealing narrative that emerges from Walker's journals.

Gathering Blossoms Under Fire is organized by decade—from the 1960s to the early days of the twenty-first century. In this way, the book shows us a woman becoming herself. Many women readers—and readers of all genders—will find themselves reflected in these pages, as Walker chronicles every major life event imaginable: marriage and divorce; becoming a parent; teaching herself to write a novel; her road to financial stability; friends and lovers gained and lost; and finding God—or "Great Spirit," as she calls the divine—in herself and in nature.

As editor of this volume, I have retained Alice Walker's original spellings, punctuation, and dating styles, even when inconsistent, to stay true to her original journal entries. I also have sought to be as inconspicuous as possible, to make myself your invisible friend, leaning in only occasionally to whisper an important fact, clarification, or recollection in your ear: *Hey, you remember this person, Alice's boyfriend from her teenage years. Ah yes, this movie came out in 1976, to critical acclaim. Oh, you know Langston Hughes—the legendary poet of the Harlem Renaissance. And, yes, this person seeking a favor is the same person whose bad behavior you remember from fifty pages ago.* These contextual notes aim to serve the larger narrative, to quietly inform you, dear reader, so that you can stay with the story.

Walker sometimes journaled in more than one notebook at a time, offering parallel versions of the same events, with one version full of detail and the other a quick summary. Occasionally, she might return many years later to a half-finished notebook from a previous decade, picking up a thread of thought and moving forward from there. For clarity and ease of reading in this volume, I have compiled the journal entries chronologically, regardless of the notebook in which they were entered.

Gathering Blossoms Under Fire is a workbook for artists, activists, and intellectuals. It is a primer for people of all ages who wish to live free lives. It is both a deeply personal journey and an intimate history of our time. And for all of us whose lives have been touched—and often changed—by Alice Walker's work over the past five decades, this book is a gift.

In fact, the wide-ranging pages you're about to read here all started with a gift. The cover of the brown faux-leather journal was adorned with a gold border, and the gold-foil lettering proclaimed its purpose: MY TRIP, it said.

Alice Walker was grateful to receive the travel diary from her friend, Cecile Ganpatsingh, a classmate from British Guiana. Alice had just finished her first year as a student at Atlanta's Spelman College, where she'd arrived in 1961 from her small, segregated hometown of Eatonton, Georgia. She brought with her "three magic gifts" from her mother: a suitcase, a sewing machine, and a typewriter. At Spelman, Alice and Cecile had become sister activists, joining several classmates—along with history professors Howard Zinn and Staughton Lynd—in various protests and pickets for peace and civil rights. Now, Alice was on her way to the Youth World Peace Festival in Finland.

At eighteen years old, she had crossed the Georgia border only once—to visit an aunt and uncle one Christmas in Cleveland, Ohio. For that trip, Alice had boarded a Greyhound bus. This trek—with stops in Helsinki, Glasgow, Amsterdam, and Hamburg—would mark her first time on an airplane. Cecile wanted to present her friend with a gift to mark the occasion. In the front cover of the diary, she noted the date—*July, 1962*—and offered these words:

To: Dearest Alice

Here's wishing that your trip will be memorable.

Fondly,
Cecile Ganpatsingh

When Alice Walker returned from her trip at the end of August, the diary was tattered from use. She wrote in it almost daily, commenting on everything she encountered—the cute, charming waiters; the welcoming, curious glances from strangers; the idea of communism itself—with enthusiasm and wonder. In one entry, she chronicled how she usually spent her days on this life-changing journey:

A TYPICAL DAY:

Up at 7:00 for a continental breakfast

Caught bus for the city at 7:30

Attended morning colloquiums and seminars (mostly about disarmament, American imperialism and Russian Communism)

Had lunch with one of the 120 delegations

I usually ate with the Bulgarians, the Cubans or Finns

After lunch attended either an outdoor sports match or some cultural event. (For example, I saw both the Russian ballet and the Peking opera.)

Around 3:00 we went to delightful inter-delegation meetings.

At 5:00 we could either have dinner with another delegation or we could ramble around the city and surrounding countryside. I learned to ride a motorcycle (a jauwa) because they are very popular in Finland.

At 6:00 we took a bus back to our living quarters where we changed clothes to go to inter-delegation or island parties. (Finn. is a land of islands and on each small island there is a park with an outdoor dancing floor—we could watch fireworks or just relax and listen to Finnish music.)

At 11:00 we came back to our living quarters for the night. IT WOULD STILL BE VERY LIGHT OUTSIDE so that it was hard to go to sleep. So, for at least an hour or so we'd talk. (Some of the Americans were very far left, some not as far left, and the rest— just curious.)

To add to this wonderful schedule—I was given bouquets of flowers practically around the clock. This was mostly because the Finns thought that I was Cuban or else a freedom rider. (I was ashamed that I had not been to jail.)

DO YOU DANCE, DO YOU SING? WELL, YOU MUST BE A
  FREEDOM RIDER?
WE SHALL OVERCOME. Congratulate the freedom fighters of the
  south. (Heard it sung in many languages.) Requested of us.

Near the end of her travelogue, in a late August 1962 entry, the budding young writer and activist wrote, "Although I was only in Europe for about a month I know that my life will be different because of it."

She added: "Never again will any Russian or any Cuban or any other nationality of people be my enemies just because they are what they are. Strangely enough, during the past crisis [the Cuban Missile Crisis in October 1962] I have been more worried about the Cubans and the Russians than about myself. Most of all I've learned that there is so much difference between the people and their governments that one cannot any longer hate indiscriminately."

After Walker's trip to Europe, she returned to Spelman but quickly became frustrated with "bad courses, bourgeois teachers and classmates," as she noted in one journal entry. She soon transferred to Sarah Lawrence College in Bronxville, New York. Her journals pick up again in earnest during the summer of 1965, when she visited the South, and Kenya, before her final semester as a student at Sarah Lawrence.

Walker returned to the South in 1965 with some trepidation—but with great determination to participate in the Black freedom struggle. After a short stay, she left for several months of eventful travel in Africa, then headed back to Sarah Lawrence for the fall. There, at age twenty-one, she became restless for the challenges of the real world. "There are times when I feel too old to be among these people at Sarah Lawrence," she confided to her journal. "I can no longer discuss Viet Nam with 'bright' girls who want to reconcile their feelings about the war to their violin music. The deaths of VietNamese children weigh too heavily on me for that."

By June 1966, she was ready to commit herself to the movement, despite the tug of her own work as a blossoming writer. "I have not left yet for Mississippi and feel so much anxiety about leaving my work that it seems almost absurd for me to go at all," she lamented in June 1966. "But something draws me there, although I have no illusions about how much good I can do."

Amid the pickets and protests in the South, young Alice found something she had not been looking for: love. And she found it in the unlikeliest of places—at Stevens Kitchen, a soul food restaurant on Farish Street in Jackson, Mississippi.

She had just arrived in Jackson, she recalls fifty years later, "having been squired from the airport in a blue convertible" by Henry Aronson, an attorney with the NAACP's Legal Defense Fund, which was then run by Marian Wright, the first Black woman attorney in the state. The restaurant was next door to the Legal Defense Fund office, and many of its staffers—including a young Jewish law student, Melvyn Leventhal—regularly took their meals there. "I glared across the room at the white people eating in 'our' restaurant," Walker recalls, "and locked eyes with a very cute guy. Oy vey."

Though the journals are oddly silent on the details of their courtship, Alice and Mel were soon inseparable. "We started dating after a few sorties into the Delta where we integrated hotels and restaurants, which often meant staying up all night in anticipation of being run out by the KKK," Walker remembers half a century later. "We read the Bible and I liked his Song of Solomon."

The relationship lasted beyond that hot Mississippi summer. "We dated as we did our work, but 'dating' wasn't happening much (too dangerous) until we returned to NYC and Mel finished his last year at NYU. I had a place on St. Marks Place but stayed mostly in his dorm room, which we fixed up with a writing desk, first thing."

A few months before graduating from NYU Law School, Mel told Alice he wanted to return to Mississippi and the social justice work that made her fall in love with him in the first place. "I loved Mel because he was passionate about justice and he was genuinely passionate about me," she sums up.

"If we were going back to Mississippi, then we'd be going as husband and wife," Alice decided. "There was a long tradition of white men having Black mistresses in the South. That was not going to be my path. So I proposed to Mel, and he happily obliged. Apart from our love, it was important politically for us to be legally married."

On March 17, 1967, the couple enlisted two allies to stand up with them as witnesses—Carole Darden, Alice's best friend from Sarah Lawrence, and Mike Rudell, Mel's best buddy from NYU Law. They said their vows in the chambers of New York City Family Court judge Justine Wise Polier. "She married quite a few Movement folk," Walker remembers. "We paid her with a bunch of pink tulips."

Not everyone was supportive of the marriage. Distraught over her son's union with a *schvartze* (a Yiddish slur for a Black person), Miriam Leventhal sat shiva, mourning Mel for dead. Unbowed, the couple took another bold step that summer, Alice recalls: "We moved to Mississippi where interracial marriage was illegal."

In her journals from the 1960s—mostly spiral-bound notebooks in primary colors—Alice Walker confided her thoughts and feelings on the passionate, tumultuous decade. In the entries excerpted in Part One: Marriage, Movement, and Mississippi, the young student, activist, and writer covered a lot of geographical ground, moving from the Sarah Lawrence campus in New York to Atlanta and other parts of her native Georgia, where she worked with a student faction of the Southern Christian Leadership Conference (SCLC); to Kenya and Uganda, for a study-abroad program; then to Mississippi, where she further immersed herself in the civil rights movement, and where she met Mel. Throughout her travels, the budding writer blossomed on the page, beginning a lifelong practice of writing first drafts of poems, short stories, and eventually whole novels in her journals. And this is where our story begins.

PART ONE

MARRIAGE, MOVEMENT, AND MISSISSIPPI

THE 1960s

June 1, 1965[1]

Today is my parents' anniversary. They have been married thirty-two years. That seems so long to live with someone and still enjoy being with them occasionally. . . .

. . . Charles[2] is always like a prisoner let out of confinement, stalking here and there, running—sometimes I think from Charles. I love him as I would have loved my brothers if they had been more affectionate. Yet more too, because we always love our friends more dearly than our relatives; friendship is a matter of choice, a commitment to love another person who is unlike you, unrelated to you in any way.

A letter from Marian Wright[3] agreeing with Charles that it would be good if I went to Mississippi. I wonder if I will be able to overcome my nausea about the South (the murders, the fear) if I have someone invincible like her to look up to and to follow around. People have called me brave so often that I almost believe it—if fear is brave I am brave.

Have put the thousand dollars from Charles in the bank along with my own measly three hundred. I am curious to know how long this will last and feel at present that it might well last forever as I feel no need of anything. Most of my clothes I want to give away. It seems ridiculous to keep dresses one doesn't even like.

---

1   In June 1965, when this entry was written, Alice Walker was a twenty-one-year-old student at Sarah Lawrence, a prestigious liberal arts college in Bronxville, New York. At this point, most of her writing consisted of well-received college papers, poetry, short stories, and journal entries. Yet she was beginning to think of herself as a writer. Her first book, a poetry collection called *Once*, would not be published until 1968.

2   Charles Merrill, son of Charles E. Merrill, a founder of Merrill Lynch & Co., the stock brokerage and investment banking firm. Merrill was an educator and philanthropist who supported historically Black colleges and founded the Commonwealth School in Boston in 1958. He and Walker became friendly while she was a student at Spelman College after she turned down a Merrill scholarship.

3   Marian Wright (later Edelman) was an attorney for the NAACP Legal Defense and Educational Fund in Mississippi and the first African American woman admitted to the Mississippi Bar. In 1973, she would found the Children's Defense Fund as a voice for poor, minority, and disabled children.

I must stop fooling myself that certain people can mean more to me than they can. It is not fair to them to lead them on and one's togetherness with one's self is too precious to interrupt with outsiders who bring no spiritual food. As to why we fritter away our lives on acquaintances of no real value I have no idea, except that it is a waste of which many weak hearts are guilty.

I have written a little yesterday and today and the feeling of being able to create something out of blank paper and vapory thoughts is good. I want now to reach a level of patience and precision which I have not had in my other stories. I must also read some more authors and see how they handle dialogue, as dialogue for me is very Tom Wolfe, which is to say, wooden.

June 13, 1965[1]

Orientation (SCOPE, summer student faction of SCLC, Southern Christian Leadership Conference) was one long conversation. Sometimes with one person, often with five, ten, or three hundred. I flew to Atlanta (late) having missed both bus and train and wanting tremendously to get in on every part of the week-long discussions. For the first time in my life Southern accents (the airline hostesses) did not cause my heart to beat faster either in fear or disgust. The slow, nasal voices, accompanied by rather congenial though not quite spontaneous smiles came only as a surprise. I could even understand the charm of them, which Northerners often profess. Two hours in the air from Newark and I am in Atlanta . . . "Where progress always has the right-of-way." Seeing old familiar words, hearing them rolled over the tongue, through the nose and over the lips, realizing once more the peculiar glare and penetration of the heat—fighting an urge mainly because of the heat to get on another jet and go back to New York where the day before had been cool, the accents usually clear and precise—except those from the Bronx, Brooklyn, Queens.

The Atlanta skyline was like a stranger glimpsed again after several days

---

1 In this entry, AW, now a student at Sarah Lawrence College in New York, chronicles her return to the South—and specifically to Atlanta, where she'd attended Spelman College before transferring to Sarah Lawrence.

have passed. I noted the newest buildings with some curiosity but no feeling. The Atlanta I knew began on Hunter Street—the southern portion of the Negro section.

From the bus I could see the historic spire of Morris Brown—the oldest Negro college in Atlanta—rising from its hill, visible from numerous points about the city. Its spire visible to all, its body hidden like a tree root, deep in the soil of the Negro community. Off the bus I ran into many arms and kisses from old friends—all met at one time or another during the past five years—on walks, marches, pickets, etc. All over the North and South. "Brother!" and "Sister!" followed by all kinds of swings in the air—all accompanied by a freedom song in the background, "This Little Light of Mine," I believe, let me know that I was finally in "the Movement" and that what this one had here in the Delta that the ones in the North did not was "soul!" Even while restrained by the usual "ick" of registration I felt more or less home and comfortable with the kind of soldiers I had volunteered to work with. That was the first day.

Monday morning began with grits—

Tuesday Night, June 29, 1965, Liberty County, Georgia

Tonight two hundred members of the Liberty County community attended a mass meeting at the Dorchester Cooperative in Mid-Way. They came to hear reports on the Liberty County Headstart program, the recent upsurge of racial unrest and demonstrations following the arrest of a local schoolteacher on what protesters termed a "made-up" charge. Part of a long chain of harassment of Negroes. The community was told about the serious injury done one of its young citizens, 14 years old, by local Gainesville whites. Johnny Lee Jones is in danger of losing an eye or perhaps both his eyes after being cornered in a poolroom where his father worked by a group of whites. Local Negroes say they know the whites involved and that they are not "youths of about 14 years of age" as local papers and the local sheriff claim. They say that the two chief attackers are both probably in their thirties. No arrests have been made.

The main speaker at the meeting was Rev. B.J. Johnson of Atlanta, Georgia, who told Liberty Countians that they have shamefully misused the power of their ballots if such an example of racial violence as occurred after the demonstration could take place. He demanded that the people take into consideration the lack of protection provided for them and their children by local police and officials when they go to the polls to vote next election time. Liberty County is unique, he said, in that it has more Negroes on the books (registered) than whites, yet the Negroes have not got a single representative on the board of county officials. The mood of the crowd was bewildered and indignant. Several young people expressed concern and anger as regards the corrupting methods used by county officials in the Negro community in order to buy votes at election time.

Undated[1]

Things have fluctuated here between extreme boredom and intense, often dangerous excitement. I managed to get two friends of mine in the Chatham County jail for a night, as well as huge, ridiculous fines for "traffic violations," and so consider that time has not lain too heavily on my hands. We've been doing night demonstrating—sitting down ("in") on the porch of the Georgia state patrol. Hit slightly by a bottle and several rebel yells ending in "Nigger"—accompanied by the usual crowd of onlookers including many "pride of the Souths" using dirty words and making obscene gestures. Somehow I'm always mildly surprised when women carry on so.

One of the most rewarding people I've met is an eighteen year old boy who is about as brave (rather empty "brave" is, but still useful) as I've ever seen anyone be and still live down here. Recently whites attempted to frighten him by pulling alongside his jalopy and aiming a .38 at him. He stared them down. He had led all the demonstrations in this county and the amazing thing about him is that he is how he is—willing to argue, to march, to fight back, naturally—and that he doesn't even know any real swear words! You probably can imagine how hard it is to be a man in the South if you're Negro—but he is, I hope, an indication that all that other is going to be changed—and the South will rise again—but as a nation of men

---

1 This undated entry is actually a draft of a letter to a friend, addressed as "Dear Michael."

(like him) and not a lot of finky little Confederate flagwavers who don't know Sherman from Grant.

Another exciting experience has been my roommate, a girl from Philadelphia whose mother is a raging anti-integrationist. I've read one of her letters to C. and consider her quite pathetically mad; and very, very sick and out of step with the world—and her own daughter. C. tells me, however, that her mother's beliefs (that Negroes are all preoccupied with sex, they all use filthy language, they all want to marry white wives, they all have lice and worse) is more or less typical of a large segment of the (white) population....

... The rest of the people here I like. It is not easy to leave (I'm leaving tomorrow). They are such open, aware, people. Some of them are very young and yet they know things that old men and hotheads have all missed.

Undated[1]

Haiku ... Beautiful
And unexpected
Like the friend
One sees maybe
Once a year

Who can say
I am
African
American
Indian

---

1   Throughout the years, AW would use her journals as a place to write first drafts of poems, short stories, and parts of novels, including her most celebrated book, *The Color Purple*. Some of those entries are included in this volume (as they appear chronologically in the journals) to reflect the unexpected delight of stumbling upon such entries, and to illustrate how Walker's writing life and personal life are always intertwined.

When the next minute
he may be
a butterfly?

July 28, Nairobi Bus Station

"Beware of Pick Pocket" reads a black block-lettered sign over the back entrance to the bus station in what I suppose is the slum section of Nairobi. The front opens on a shabby street compared to the other streets in Nairobi. There are no flowers on _____ street, only a scrubby shrub or two settled rootedly but thinly in red, washed out dirt. Unlike the airport in Nairobi, which is modern, stylish and colorfully chic, the bus station is decidedly down-at-the-heels.

The cold is quite a surprise—July and August are the winter months and I suppose it is close to fifty degrees outside the bus now. What is interesting though is cold weather not withstanding flowers bloom in happy, extravagant profusion.

Undated[1]

I have been reading Tolstoy and wondering how one comes to true honesty with oneself and at which point honesty becomes exaggeration. For a month or more I have known I could be classified with that 10th of the world's women who are capable of being completely sensual. What will develop I cannot imagine but I feel very little fear and a great deal of curiosity.

It seems to me that sex has become a barrier and a taboo when in actuality I cannot see that the complete act in terms of moral value is any worse than a kiss that is meant. In either case one follows in practice the closeness one feels in abstract. This is naïve—because there are more possible serious consequences after sex than after a kiss.[2]

I have at last established a certainty which has meant a great deal to me

---

1 AW wrote this undated entry during a visit to Africa, where she traveled by bus from Nairobi, Kenya, to Kampala, Uganda, and spent significant time living with a Ugandan family.
2 AW wrote this last sentence later, in red ink, as a kind of critical commentary on the previous paragraph.

to know. I do not want _____ for a husband. As a sexual partner this is still the only man who satisfies me but two minutes after climax I am irritated at such petty things about him that I know my "love" to be completely sham—I must say we irritate each other for I get a kind of crazy pleasure from tormenting him.

He can't change what he is (white, middle class American) any more than I can change what I am now (Black middle class American). It is interesting how I always felt I loved him because he wanted me to love him and also because he was so tender and easygoing with me in spite of my "ambitions."

What am I really? And what do I want to do with me? Somehow I know I shall never feel settled with myself and life until I have a profession I can love—teaching Dickinson and Donne to crew-cuts would suit me somewhat. Marriage is not even a possibility for me at the moment—though there are three suitors excluding David who've asked to marry me. "Princeton" would never do for a husband. He has traveled all over the world but it has made him spattered rather than wide. Some day he will live in a house with Japanese rugs and perhaps a swimming pool and probably in Atlanta. I cannot talk to him long—he finds everything I say fascinating to the nth degree and I find most of what he says irrelevant. I've been in bed once with him after drinking too much to keep from having to hear his repetitions but regretted it so much that I made myself quite sick. There is (I learned from this experience) a limit beyond which one must not push sex if there is to be enough good about it to make it worth having. One should never give one's self out of drunkenness, pity, contempt, curiosity only, or passion only. There must somewhere be about a sexual liaison a spot of cleanliness, of joy and exuberance. There is nothing more sodden and unforgiveable than the giving of one's body and the closing off, simultaneously, of one's mind.

—

There is a question whether I am with une enfant or not—there is every possibility, yet I spend my days thinking or trying to think of other things. In case I am I have set about a very logical plan to be executed when I am in N.Y. It boils down to abortion or adoption—in that order.

There was a time when I would not have considered either. And I wonder what price civilization pays for sophistication. I've never really objected to abortion on moral grounds—I do not believe in an afterlife or that abortion is murder and I do believe that a person has the right to decide what he will or will not have inside his own body[1]—but it has always seemed such a stupid necessity when one is old enough and "sophisticated" enough to know what one is doing.

A *Sketch of the Girl*

In her, sensuality and curiosity were evenly balanced—if precariously so. It was a natural occurrence that she would be introduced to a man or see one who appealed to her and right away plan a rendezvous in her head. She had no religious inhibitions about sex itself and no moral scruples about having it when she really felt like it. Consequently she had sampled the native sex product in a number of countries including Africa and Russia and had had offers and enticements from men as intense as the young Israelis and as persistent as the Arabs. To her, sex was not to be taken lightly, however. She put a great deal of herself into it. This is to say that only once when she had had too much to drink had she slept with someone who she did not enjoy in some other, finer way. The medium of her relationships could be expressed in her sexual and otherwise attachment to her art teacher, aged fifty or so, whom she enjoyed intellectually and whose love-making interested her only in the sense that it was a continuation of his peculiar brand of stimulation. It had a certain logical appropriateness about it which she found comfortable and steadying and infinitely reassuring. It was with him that she felt sure life would go on and on forever—and to the rhythm of his unhurried, tolerant drive.

For the most part her choice of sex partners was haphazard. There was among her lovers an extremely young college freshman whose attraction was that he was unspoiled and largely impotent. She liked sleeping with him because at best he made a sort of childlike lover to her and immediately fell asleep, his hand clasping one of her breasts—his curly hair hanging in his eyes. Unfortunately he was Jewish and had a most ethnic taste for garlic

---

1 AW had an abortion once she returned to New York; she recalls that medical professionals withheld anesthesia.

and onions and she had to plan her visits carefully so as to coincide with his fish day. As her affection for him grew the more she began to worry about becoming a Mother image, what with his never wanting to make love with the light on and all—so she dropped him after less than a month.

> I wonder what will happen?
> Why did I feel so nauseous?
> Who would understand?

—

I wonder if my friend in Boston would lend me $600 for unexpected and unexplainable "debt."

Pregnancy in Africa seems obviously a curse—all the pregnant women look so miserable. Damn the rule making missionaries anyway!

—

It is a constant amazement to me that as far as I know I have no conventional morals—but I'm sure that I love truly—those that I love at all.

Recently I have been toying with the idea of beginning to formulate my own Philosophy—not Philosophy of the Absurd, etc., but a Philosophy based on Curiosity—yet, what all would such a Philosophy involve, except a degree of insensitiveness and dauntlessness.

Undated[1]

Why is it we always feel embarrassed by what we write? Is it because writing is such tangible evidence of the follies committed in our minds? Words do not usually leave a trace; most people do not listen to them earnestly enough.

People tell me that to love hopelessly i.e., someone who can never belong to you legally, is to love stupidly. I don't believe it. To be able to love at all

---

1 This entry was written in fall 1965, after AW had returned to Sarah Lawrence College to continue her studies following several months of international travel.

seems wondrous to me—besides I don't think of ownership when I think of love. Is that last sentence a bit trite?[1]

There are times when I feel too old to be among these people at Sarah Lawrence. I can no longer discuss Viet Nam with "bright" girls who want to reconcile their feelings about the war to their violin music. The deaths of VietNamese children weigh too heavily on me for that.

———

To be twenty-one is to be like no other age. It is the age of consent and freedom, yes—and the feeling of being gently abandoned by one's mother.

I can understand how people can joke about suicide. It is such a personal matter that anyone who doesn't understand it as the victim does finds it funny.

If I died tonight a great many people would want an answer to the question—why? No one would consider that I probably wanted to. That's the problem with people—they are not stoic enough to consider death a possibility.

———

It seems essential to me that the artist <u>loves</u> to make love. I could not bear a merely contemplative artist for he would not know beans about the skin he's in nor the soul he's wrapped around. Love tortures and causes us to shriek but in the end it feels out the cloudy folds in our souls and finds a new dimension. It seems to me "Death in Venice" makes this point—or tries to.

I tend to agree with whoever said that Socrates was a goaty old nuisance! One either loves him or hates him—& I don't love him.

Nietzsche says that Philosophers shouldn't marry & usually don't.

Some people would not consider Curiosity a legitimate basis for a Philosophy of Action—yet I wonder if perhaps it isn't the foundation of <u>any</u> Philosophy?

---

1 AW wrote this sentence later, with a blue marker, as critical commentary on the previous sentence.

—

I want to write a story about a black bourgeois woman who is the incarnation of all the imitated white bourgeois values—and how she is trapped by the rigid and archaic socialities she has learned and cherishes. She is lonely, but still hangs on to morals and ways of acting that the West abandoned years ago—except they didn't teach her that and she doesn't know. To her:

1. Sex only in marriage—consequently both sex <u>and</u> marriage miss her.
2. In college she felt the student had no right but the right to study—active thought missed her.
3. She was taught to revere her country—revolution repulsed her so she voted for the very people who hated her.
4. She believed in the "good" of material accomplishment, she surrounded herself with accumulated stuff which made her "settled" i.e., immovable.

How to convey sympathy for this "creature" & contempt for the values she holds . . .

Schopenhauer—"Music & tears, I can hardly tell them apart."

11/10/65
Today I finished a story of which I am proud. "The Suicide of an American Girl." Everyone who reads it is struck by Ana's suicide. None of them apparently have been so near death they've become aware of its close proximity to life.

I tried to explain my concept of suicide in a person's life—it seems to me one of the <u>choices</u> in a person's life.

If one is to have freedom to live one must be granted freedom to die—all it takes is an overcoming of the morals of Christianity which make people belongings of God, not belongings of themselves. If there is to be free will at all it must accept suicide. For as long as man has free will suicide is within his range of possibility.

* * *

I have been close to death a few times and I've tried to remember how I acted with the knowledge that tomorrow the sun will shine without me—did I pray, did I think of people I love, did I feel very afraid?

If my mother were not alive I would have no fear of death. Or my fear of death would be moderate. But as it is I cannot bear that she should see me, her baby, dead. She, being a Christian, would just be able to think what <u>she</u> did wrong. Her own "sins" would be magnified in her eyes and she would know despair. And all the while, she would, of course, be innocent. I do not like a philosophy which would make all guilty.

Nov. 12

I had a very weird dream last night—it was about civil rights and students & Westchester housewives & I was to shoot a duel—Indians came through the river chained together looking exactly alike. I howled like a dog when I saw them, no one else paid them the slightest attention. I woke up with my heart aching and tears practically in my eyes.

I wonder if it would be possible for me to write a story that is essentially a love story which ends happily?

Am very tempted to write a novel about a couple of guys very much like David[1] and myself. The theme I think would be on the girl's (Negro) inability to do anything but constantly try to "overcome"—Her goals, he (white) feels are bourgeois and he has abandoned them long ago; still they are important to her and what her whole being is aimed for. The man feels education unimportant after college (but is this because he doesn't like <u>going</u> to school & is having trouble getting in?) She has no trouble with her studies or with school and so enjoys it thoroughly—it is hard for her to consider her learning and wanting to learn more <u>bourgeois</u>. They part because she wants what she calls her own work (art) in addition to wifedom. He feels threatened by her talent, etc. & knows he cannot keep his dignity with a "smart" wife.

I have thought often of my mom's story about how she married

---

1 David was AW's beau at the time; she struggled with ambiguous feelings about a future with him because of differing views on race and class.

Daddy—I wonder if there is enough to it for me to work on. Essentially it is the "same <u>old</u> story."

It is only those things I do which I can find no explanation for and don't understand that I enjoy writing about.

<u>Is it possible to create out of happiness?</u>

June 2, 1966

The autobiography of Billy Holiday[1] has moved me very much, perhaps because she was such an honest broad and so very game. I am not sure I like her singing as much as I like her, but it is of such a distinctive quality one cannot imagine anyone else sounding like her. Is this genius?

June 3, 1966

Who cares to write stories "with punch?" Not I. Also I wonder if I could develop into an existentialist writer—actually I'm not sure what that means. An existentialist <u>person</u> understands the world is perhaps ending, and badly, and resolves to live a moral life anyhow.

I suppose I myself am an existentialist as much as I can understand its definition. All those months at Sarah Lawrence studying Camus, and Sartre, and it's still rather vague—it would seem that whatever I wrote would probably be existential, doesn't it? And yet it is not. I should probably become better acquainted with the potential of the short story. Right now I would like to do a story in the fashion of Ambrose Bierce. He is very much like Poe to me, even more terrifying, perhaps. Certainly more haunting than Ray Bradbury, whose stories I must also reconsider.

June 8, 1966

Another march, in the tradition of Selma, to sweep Mississippi[2] this week and next. Dr. King, interviewed by some reporter from Philadelphia, sounds

---

1 Singer Billie Holiday's 1956 autobiography *Lady Sings the Blues* was coauthored by William Dufty.

2 AW was still in New York, having finished her studies at Sarah Lawrence College the previous winter. Here, she is anticipating a return to Mississippi to rejoin the civil rights movement.

extremely tired from walking fifteen miles yesterday. I guess I should buy myself some comfortable shoes . . .

June 10, 1966
Anna Karenina, page 154

"I think . . . that if there are as many minds as there are heads, then there are as many kinds of love as there are hearts . . ."

June 11, 1966

I will talk today (if I do not forget my appointment) with the <u>fact</u> people about my experiences at Spelman.[1] Recently I've begun to wonder what I really know . . . for my criticism was administered without love—with anger and some contempt. Bad courses, bourgeois teachers and classmates aside, it was there that I met Howie, Staughton, Charles—and lovely Connie.[2]

It is really true that we must be careful what we wish for—we will probably get it. Though my life has moved slowly and crookedly it moves of its own will (mine) in the direction of my wishes. In some sense this is frightening—but since I shall never wish to be the president's wife there is not much danger.

June 27, 1966, New York City

I have not left yet for Mississippi and feel so much anxiety about leaving my work that it seems almost absurd for me to go at all. But something draws me there, although I have no illusions about how much good I can do. I would like to go with Marian and Henry[3] out through the woods and across those flatlands, going out so smoothly into the horizon.

---

1 AW was being interviewed by *Fact* magazine, an American quarterly in circulation between 1964 and 1967.

2 These are all friends—including Howie, aka Howard Zinn, then a Spelman history professor—whom AW met during her otherwise dissatisfying experience as a student at Spelman, before she transferred to Sarah Lawrence.

3 Marian Wright and Henry Aronson were attorneys for the NAACP Legal Defense Fund. "They represented black people who challenged the violently enforced segregation and dehumanization of people of color in Mississippi," Walker would recall. "Marian was the only person I 'knew' in the state, because she'd also attended Spelman College. We'd never met."

The Upper East Side after the Lower East Side: too much glass, new cars, skinny girls and money. One must, I imagine, get used to both cleanliness and money and the fact that they are likely to make one sterile and sweet smelling, like a bar of soap.

July 3, 1966, En route to Jackson, Mississippi

A fat cloud, shaped like an airplane, tries to compete with our jet—a gust of wind, a bit of sun—pouff, its tail gone, its wings gossamer wisps, falling whitely, like arms. The blue Atlantic, stretching outward endlessly, islanded by banks and hills and mountains and flatlands of clouds—and perhaps peopled by a blue and white race who dive in and out of sea and sky, glittering as they laugh and jump, like jeweled buttons.

From here I can see the king of one cloud island, whiter among his subjects and with pigs' ears and a snout. His stomach spreads across his entire kingdom.

A string of clouds makes strange shadows on the mountains, stretched out beads with sun between them, like a necklace.

Jackson, an example of a surprise. How afraid I am to say I like it. Tut, Doris, Laura, Marian—Melvyn.[1] I do like it though because people are mainly doing what they want or what they feel has to be done—in the interest of people who care—and of those who do not.

August 1966

A dream terrified me this afternoon. I had come back (to Georgia) and told my family about Mississippi—the beauty of Mississippi Negro bravery—the beauty of the people kicked off their land and the founding of the co-ops where people learn to sew and make themselves useful citizens with another trade than farming (sharecropping). I had my mother practically in tears. I cried myself throughout. I remember a feeling of wanting them to fully un-

---

1   All were colleagues in the civil rights movement in Mississippi. Melvyn Leventhal was a new friend, a Jewish law student working with the NAACP Legal Defense Fund.

derstand the suffering and deprivation of other Negroes, while we sat around a full table among rosy-cheeked children and well-fed adults. My brothers looked dubious and contented. All that I said seemed not to be trusted. So I cried, my mother looked helpless. My family said nothing, even when I mentioned (a lie) that I had bought clothing for their children from the co-op.

Then I asked my brother to drive me to a local Negro restaurant/tavern as I wanted I think to converse with friends about the possibility of a Movement in our town. He refused, saying that he was out of gas and besides was headed in the opposite direction from where I wanted to go. I said fine, that this was all right, that I was used to walking since being in Mississippi and that he could just let me off at the gas station, which he agreed to do. At the gas station there was a car full of policemen and somehow an argument started which developed into a very heated one when the officers realized who I was. That I had been in Mississippi and perhaps intended to speak to local Negroes—how they knew this I was not sure. My family, all except one brother and my mother, abandoned me and the scene I remember is of my mother and brother standing with me within the circle of policemen. During the earlier squabble they had crushed my ankle with some sort of club and I kept being amazed that it didn't hurt or buckle under as I stood talking to them.

They carried the three of us away in their car, most of their abuse directed at me. We stopped at a church where the sheriff drew his gun and proceeded to brandish it about saying he was going to kill me. After a preliminary paroxysm of terror in which I grappled with him for the gun, I told him to go ahead and knelt on my knees facing my mother who appeared an abstract figure in pink of sorrow, tears, and a wringing of hands. The sheriff and I counted to three in unison, then jumped up at the end of the count. The man with him laughed and said we were both afraid, and he took the gun, at which point I tried again to take it while he twisted it between my legs and tried to pull the trigger while I was astride the gun point. Twisting myself out of his grasp enough to move the gun I aimed it at his back and pulled the trigger only to discover it had no bullets in it—at which discovery he laughed, got the gun in his hands again and proceeded to put in one bullet that looked like a half-used cigarette with gray ash on the end.

At this point my mother intervened although I cannot recall how, and shouted at me to run! run!—which I did, while she struggled with the man who had the gun. Thinking I had hid under the church, they burned it down, but I ran across fields until I came to the home of an old Negro lady with light brown skin and white hair, and wearing a blue dress (whom I had seen at a banquet) who kept me and cared for me until my wounded ankle healed and then she sent me following the North Star, slipping from ice cake to ice cake across the river, a tiny dark-haired baby in my arms. A modern Eliza.[1]

August 1966

A remarkable memory: Today, walking with Eric,[2] we saw a flower pit full of summer flowers all in bloom. I called it "a flower pit" and a memory, long buried, of where I got the expression, came alive. When I was a child at home—when we lived in the country—my mother kept her flowers in a flower pit during the winter. This pit was like an outdoor cellar, rather shallow—I imagine four to six feet deep, and built close against the house for added protection from the wind. Sometimes the pit would get a lot of water in it and for fear of freezing or rotting the flower roots my mother would throw open the doors, or take away the tin or whatever and let the sun in.

The flower I remember best is the geranium. Mama had many different colors, but lots of red and salmon colored. I remember her so well, bending over the pit on cold January mornings after a hard freeze. "I just want to see how my flowers is doing," she'd say, frowning slightly and stepping down into the pit. It is odd how memories come back. Now I recall very vividly

---

1 A heroine in *Uncle Tom's Cabin*, by Harriet Beecher Stowe, Eliza escapes the evils of slavery and her cruel master by crossing the Ohio River in the dead of winter. Alice Walker recalls: "I had many nightmares and anxiety dreams while living in Mississippi, all based very much on reality. Lynchings, 'disappearances,' rapes, bodies found mutilated in the river, assassinations, were a part of life in this poorest state of the Union. Today I understand that the 'tiny dark-haired baby in my arms' was my belief in 'freedom' and in myself, embarking on this journey alone."

2 Eric was a white comrade in Mississippi who was from the North and "who seemed companionable," Walker recalls. "And innocent. A movement type, no doubt: curious, astonished, disbelieving he was still in America."

how Mama used to put up fruits and vegetables and how she was better at it than anybody else in the neighborhood. During harvest she canned countless jars of peaches, blackberries, peas, corn, and beans. Our walls were beautiful with the radiant colors of her produce contained in clear glass jars. Edible jewels surrounded us.

May 18, 1967[1]

I am afraid, worried, distracted, and it is an old-new feeling and quite unshakeable, although for Mel's sake it must be overcome. There was a time when a mother-in-law's shouts, as in a story, would have amused me; now they do not, of course. They fill me with dread for the knowledge that these shouts are unchangeable keeps me from being optimistic about a better future relationship.

I don't think I know everything there is to know, but I do know that I love my husband. This pain each time he pains, sickness even in my body because he feels it, too. My life is double and our lives, one.

We are both nervous, jittery from caring so much about each other.

Undated

Dear Langston,[2]

You have been gone about a month, and I have not felt old-fashioned sad, yet! Now Mel and I are reading your autobiography

---

1   AW was a newlywed when she wrote this entry. Just two months before, on March 17, 1967, she'd married Mel Leventhal, the young lawyer with the NAACP Legal Defense Fund who first appeared in her journals, in a casual mention, in June 1966. Her journals are oddly silent on their courtship. In retrospect, AW believes she didn't write more about this in her journals because she was focused on writing her first novel, *The Third Life of Grange Copeland*.

2   In this undated entry, from sometime in June 1967, AW is addressing Langston Hughes, the legendary American poet, novelist, playwright, columnist, and social activist, who died on May 22, 1967. He had become a friend and mentor to Walker, and he published one of her earliest stories, "To Hell With Dying," in his 1967 anthology, *The Best Short Stories by Negro Writers*.

and getting to know you through it. How I wish we could have heard all of your wonderful stories from your own lips.

Funny, learning about your love, Mary, from a book. I am almost sorry you let her get away. Perhaps you could have starved cheerfully together. Where do you suppose she is now? Married with grown children? Dead too?

I wrote to you the night you died. What a quaint thought—for you are no more dead than I am. You never got the letter and I am sorry. For I was offering our help and telling you in humorous terms about my plight with my mother-in-law. She just don't like us colored people!

Quite frankly, I don't like her either.

You have no idea how ill I've been. And I worry that I will be a nuisance to Mel. Especially because I cry so much and for such varied reasons. I suppose I am "emotional."

I wish so much you were still on 127th street. You were such an honored friend. We wanted so much for you to know our children, and for them to know you. It is hard to believe you were sixty-five; you had almost no gray hair, and you did not look, at your funeral (which Mel and I liked and enjoyed very much) as if you suffered. Unfortunately, you did not look very much like yourself at all. You darkened a lot from when you were young till when we first saw you that night at Lincoln Center.

I have never loved any great old man the way I did you, on such short acquaintance; would you be my friend still—? Wouldn't it be too, too funny if there is a heaven (or hell) and you are there fiddling around with those of your old cronies lucky enough to have made it? Perhaps we'll meet, but if not you are here with us in each and every word you wrote.

Love always and always,
<u>Moi</u>

—

<u>Proverbs 10:15 . . . . A rich man's wealth is his strong city; the destruction of the poor is in their poverty.</u>

My old man (Grange)[1] feels, when he witnesses the love of the Movement participants, that the new millennium for which he has waited (for Ruth) had come—but he goes one day to witness a demonstration and sees the young men beaten by the police. The demonstration goes on and is hailed by everyone as a "success," but he becomes thoughtful, despairing of the future. He knows too well the reciprocity of violence. We have not seen the end of this refusal to love yet, he says to Ruth.

December 4, 1967

A lot has happened since my last entries, easily six or seven months ago. My life is more full than I ever thought it could be. And that is because of my love, not so much my work. Art will always copy life.

My husband has arrived and claimed me forever. He is The One; it is like a fairy tale in its finality—can there be any doubt that, no matter what we will live happily ever after? I did not believe I could become One with anyone—but now I am One. With M.

It seems true that one's dreams might come true if one waits long enough and remains a hopeful virgin at heart.

The novel too is becoming a reality, albeit a slow one. Perhaps I should have stuck with Hemingway's example—stories until the Novel was inevitable. I don't know. Maybe I just write funny. In any case, I think I can see improvement in many themes, stories, "ideas."

Mel and I are independent. No debts yet. I like this. It gives us freedom from people who only come to pry. Sometimes I wonder if we are more or less complicated (our lives) than when we were single. It is such a strange and sometimes fearful comfort: having someone to lean on.

---

1 Grange and his granddaughter Ruth are major characters in the novel Walker had started writing in 1967. It would eventually be called *The Third Life of Grange Copeland*.

December 19

Next week this time I pray I will be home with my dear husband and our Myshkin.[1]

Fiction is not like poetry which is original and real and not ever fiction.

CANE: by Jean Toomer, Boni & Liveright, 239pps.

This work so underestimated I am sure. I must find out how it was received when it first appeared. How much influence it obviously had on R. Wright![2] How free it is in its showing of the Southern loveliness. There is a freshness that is sadly missing in much of black writing today.

Freshness, brevity, universality.

What I really feel ready for is my book of short stories. The novel confuses me. If I am honest.

As much as possible (complete!) my characters must be human in their own natures. Apart from the pressures the white world puts on them. One might have a host of principals, college presidents, even teachers, whose cruelties and limitations of spirit convince them at least that they are free. Free enough so that one might write about them as complete (assuming of course the good in them too) entities in themselves without showing them as malignant outgrowths of the white man's system.

There must be beauty too. A full, untrammeled beauty of individuals living their lives. A beauty rarely glimpsed because oppression, for most of us, blots it out. And yet this is our strength. This beauty gave us what courage and love of goodness we have. It was not the ugly, which merely terrified.

*   *   *

---

1   Myshkin was the couple's dog, affectionately named after Prince Myshkin in Dostoyevsky's *The Idiot*. The author once described the character as "entirely positive . . . with an absolutely beautiful nature." Some consider him an "idiot," but he possesses an emotional intelligence far beyond that of all of the other characters in Dostoyevsky's novel.

2   Richard Wright, acclaimed author of *Native Son* and *Black Boy*.

What I must say: That we have always hurt one another, that the parents do it more than the grandparents—because they are so involved in the creation of a new being for the endurance of the same troubles. That the old must lead the young, not only in teaching the sometimes violent art of self-assertion, but in also giving down a sense of caring, a purposeful inclination to clannishness. We must accept full responsibility for one another as our best heroes and heroines did. Even at gunpoint we must free one another, as Harriet Tubman did, forcing her timorous charges through the swamps.

July 8, 1968

Today I received copies of my book of poems [*Once*].[1] Some first reactions— I don't like the cover, too much like a Borax box. Didn't like my photograph on the back. I look old and tired. Thought the product cheap looking. Later though I felt better. But the poems were written so long ago, and I am so different now. Actually I'm not even the same person.

Giving out copies of the book is pleasurable, as giving is one of the great joys left.

It is good having Andrew,[2] he keeps me from grieving over Myshkin. How could human beings steal a dog from anyone? It is almost like stealing a child. Mel is happier too now that there is another dog in the house.

July 11, 1968

After many months of wondering how I, as a married woman, could continue a personal diary, I found the answer (I think) quite by accident last night. And it happened when a third person, a girl we love, hurt my husband's feelings. Then I realized, as I felt his pain, that he is my personal life and that the true joining has come about between us.

---

1   Published in 1968, *Once*, Alice Walker's first book, showed her to be a young writer of unusual maturity and power. All the poems in this collection were written either in East Africa, when she was there for the summer of 1965, or during her senior year at Sarah Lawrence.
2   The couple's new puppy.

He was hurt because Barbara,[1] our closest friend, still regards him on the nitty gritty level as white. I suppose I'm the only black person who does not. Indeed, we are shipwrecked on the American island, just us two against both black and white worlds, but how it makes our love keen! I am reminded of Voznesensky's poem about pressured lovers being like two shells enclosing their pain but also their intense joy at being permitted by the gods such magnificent, almost heroic emotion.

How I would have been bored as a preacher's wife!

Now that I've found my voice is big enough, occasionally, for two, there is so much to write about that I could not before. There is the growing animosity which blacks in Jackson have towards whites—but not towards the white Mississippi crackers who deserve it, but towards the white civil rights workers who in my opinion do not.

I am thinking now of how Ronnie's head was split open by a young kid up in Bolivar. Ronnie![2] Who has worked his ass off every summer in Mississippi hauling black people to the polls—because he is white and the black kid knew he wouldn't fight back and wouldn't call the police! It is so unfair. And then poor Ted Seaver, beaten to a pulp because he was a more effective organizer than his black "friend." And then there is the black man from Boston who left his family to come work in Mississippi (wife, children; why didn't he "work" in Roxbury, it needs it as much as Mound Bayou?) who threatened to beat up my husband? If he ever tried it I'd want to murder him and there's no question I'd want Mel to press charges. Enough is enough! As far as I'm concerned, as long as Mel works to change this world into a better one he's guilty of nothing. And of course to me there are no white people only white minds. Malcolm learned this, I suspect Baldwin knew it all along. How could my husband be white when we are together trying to make the world fit for our brown babies, our friends who are different colors outside but black by choice?

Barbara objected to Mel's confidence in this country's capacity to re-

---

1 Barbara Greene worked in Mel Leventhal's office and became a good friend to the couple.
2 A young Jewish man who'd traveled to the South to work in the civil rights movement.

press any black uprising. But she and I have said the same thing, made the same dour observation. After all this time though she resents hearing him say it <u>as a white man</u>. And though it is easy to understand her resentment, we are very hurt—was it because we thought that among our small circle of friends we had abolished the concept of color based on skin color alone?

July 15

It is far more difficult to train Andrew than Myshkin. Andrew is also much more nervous, high-strung. He bites much more and his teeth are certainly sharper. But he's growing into a big healthy boy and we're pleased he can gain two pounds in four days. We've had him two weeks today.

How odd it is—I am having trouble writing honestly or well. Could it be because I dared mention to Mel that I might one day publish this journal? And then the things that really have shaken me—Dr. King's death, Bobby Kennedy's death[1]—I can't seem to put in any literary form. I could no more write a poem about the King than I could dance on his grave. And that no doubt says something about my poetry. I believe it is ironic, largely satirical, bent on much which Dr. King was not about. He needed poetry of Tennyson, Matthew Arnold, deep and slow and allegorical—as did Kennedy, strangely—and perhaps, at the other end of the spectrum, Robert Browning.

I wonder if walking those last miles with the King really caused me to lose our baby—or was it my tribute to the man who had made my own life bearable? Funny how I couldn't face then the thought of bringing forth a child in a world where Dr. King no longer lived. How many times I said to Mel "I will stay here—meaning this country—for as long as he can stay." After that, fuck it. And now I feel more than ever the futility of staying here, and yet, where is one to go? How necessary it is for one of our "leaders" to find an answer to just that question. Integration leading to assimilation—everybody becoming a bland if luscious brown—that's repugnant! But sepa-

---

1   Civil rights leader Martin Luther King Jr. was assassinated on April 4, 1968. Presidential candidate Robert F. Kennedy was shot on June 5, 1968; he died the next day.

ratism won't work either—and besides, is one ready to thrust one's life into a possible dead end? Unequivocally not! . . .

. . . Adversity often makes us know what we believe. That is, what we both believe and <u>will stick to</u>.

Have been thinking about James Baldwin and must write him a letter. One loves him, one admires Ellison's one book[1] and therefore him. Spending a night with Baldwin would be fascinating, just perhaps watching him sleep, or, before sleep, brush his teeth, rub a hand across those big eyes. A night with Ellison would probably be like a day with any man and his wife who had a view from their window of the Hudson.

Just looked up a marvelous word—adamantine. Means hard, unbreakably hard, like a diamond.

How hard his business and social life is for Mel! Someone else's name signed to his work, one mean old man keeping him out to poker games and golfing parties! They distrust and dislike him as a white man, as does Barbara, and I don't really blame them. How can I? When I have this earnest distrust of all whites except the ones I've chosen from among the rest and really after much meeting of standards on their part.

The race issue (can one call the cause of so much pain and blood an "issue"?); but anyhow, it has spoiled all our souls here in America. We do not have sweet souls any longer, if indeed, we ever had them.

There is an awful lot of anger in me against anyone who even remotely harms my husband. What a strange and wonderful feeling to be like a mother towards her child. My heart breaks when he is hurt or sad. It is as if an unbearable weight is pressed on me until I see him smile and can believe he is all right. . . .

. . . And now we just about own our house. For a very brief time, surely. And if the draft calls before I am certified pregnant what will we

---

1 This is a reference to *Invisible Man*, the only novel Ralph Ellison published in his lifetime.

do? Go to Canada? Mel hates running which is why, I guess, we're here in Mississippi. I hate this country but that includes being made to leave it. Lord, and I know this is full of hypocrisy—I know you worked for my mother—keep us together. I don't care where we go, just as long as it is together.

If we were out of the South—even in Atlanta—I would be in school. A lazy person must have several degrees to impress other lazy but efficiently bureaucratic people. Even Jackson State, that place from which educated escapees are rare, has the nerve to demand credentials that look good in their catalog. And yet, I can't blame them, they're trying to upgrade their school, their education, and don't know yet they'd have to begin, not in the college but in that crucial place where the sperm hits the egg.

—

There is nothing more despairing to me than the thought of a job. What am I to be then, in functional life?

I am obsessed with the notion of writing my next novel about eight post-Spelman ladies (not a bad title!) Making it revolve around The Suicide of An American Girl. Eight women, eight very different characters, their backgrounds, loves, etc. Revealed on their way to the funeral of Anna.

There could be a basic study of types of black women.

1. The frustrated, frigid spinster
2. The revolutionary white-hater, white-lover
3. The back to Africa one—Anna
4. The rich beautiful/homely one
5. The one on exchange to Finland
6. The Southern bourgeois one
7. The Northern hippie one appalled at the illiteracy of Spelman college students
8. The actress who opts for Paris

July 18

I am amazed at myself. Once more I am warming up to write. How incredible in some ways it is to thirst for pen and paper, to need them, as if they were water. . . .

. . . Making a quilt the old fashioned way, "piecing" it. I wonder if Mama would be surprised. I never cared at all for housework. But making a quilt is not housework. It is art, creation, invention. And it saves money while keeping Sears, Roebuck out of one's bed.

The lady next door thinks I'm smart. Me! And I can see she bends her mind trying to understand why I treat Andrew as if he were a child. They believe, clearly, that one should treat one's dog like a nigger. Poor us, how we pass the cruelty on. But Andrew's job will be to protect me, and in Mississippi only Andrew and my dear husband will do it.

A special delivery letter from the Library of Congress. Amazing. They want to know this and that about ONCE so they can make up catalog cards. I will be in the library! How exciting. Much more exciting than anything else that has transpired concerning the book.

I feel so strange, people really bother me. Almost <u>all</u> people. I begin to understand why Muriel (Rukeyser)[1] once said she <u>hated</u> teaching at Sarah Lawrence. One must feel free as much as possible of other minds sticking, probing, into one's own. My need for privacy seems almost paranoid. But I enjoy people too, occasionally. . . .

. . . I like to love people overwhelmingly, like I love Baldwin. And Baldwin, who simply tries to live, could do so in a castle, with a moat, and with a dozen footmen. I would be ecstatic if it made him happy. For he identifies with <u>the poor in spirit</u> and that is with everybody enclosed in the human condition. . . .

. . . I am bored, I think, with seeing the words black, white, Negro, Col-

---

1   Muriel Rukeyser was a poet and social justice activist who taught at Sarah Lawrence College during AW's time as a student there.

ored. And isn't it sad that my eye can spot "Negro" in a newspaper page without being able to see another single word?

September 2, 1968

Roles reverse in man-woman relationships. First the woman wants the simplicities of home and family (or she does not) while the man wants to explore the world on less than $3.00 a day. Then the woman wants a similar freedom and the man wants security. In young relationships the systole-diastole destroys what is left of dependency and intimacy.

A story that is about the break-up of a young interracial love and how it is not a struggle between black and white but between a bourgeois and a radical view of life. One has had, the other has not had, and <u>wants</u>.

Jackson – Oct '68

On the nights I sit home alone waiting for Mel I realize he is the most important part of my life. And I do not fear him as I have always feared MEN—the only fear I have is that I will hurt him. He is so understanding. Or in any case he tries hard and is gentle, kind. Sometimes I feel like a shrew.

What always amazes me is knowing I can't live without writing. Surely this is odd. How my fingers want a pen in them, my hand likes the feel of paper and notebooks. Sometimes I think my notebook got Mel to take me seriously. "Everybody 'writes,'" he said. He did not know until he saw my notebook that I was married to it.

—

How odd, after so much travel, to land in Mississippi. Definitely <u>not</u> the route Wright and Baldwin took. Mel would like to stay here a long time. So would I if only we could get away two or three times a year. Soon we will have been here a year & a half. I begin to feel like a colonizer.

Our house is lovely. Everything is as much what we like as we can make it. I know we will hate to leave it. The sweetgrass tree outside my window is so gorgeous in the fall!

December 2, 1968

I am very interested in myself. That is a Truth. What are others? That I live, that I love life better than death. That I love beauty, that my husband is the jewel in my crown. That I love hair, lots of it. That the bible was not meant, in its entirety, for me or for black people. That I am vain. That I depend on mirrors. That I am stronger than I have ever shown myself. That I must write. It is as distinct an urge as any of the private ones. That I fear many things. Ideologies. That it takes time for me to grow. That today is my mother's birthday and that I don't know how old she is.

January 2, 1969

The beginning of a New Year. Nixon in power. The Southerners beginning an early bloom. How they hate the Kennedys and poor old Johnson who never could look at the camera straight. Whoever saw his eyes through his glasses and if you saw them weren't they like gray marbles and full of icy woe. I surprise myself liking Johnson just the same, the man has passion. Johnson got his daughters by doing the usual thing—and enjoying it. Nixon got his by sweating, probably clammily. God! How can we live looking at Nixon's face. It is like a Kabuki mask. When he smiles it is like watching a moth approach a flame. I hope we are the flame. He believes a great deal in intelligence. Little does he know that computers can and will replace him. What we need is an irrational good guy. There's no substitute for heart.

Only two and a half months until Mel is 26. If we make it without having to "flee" the country we will be thankful. I still think his draft board has a nerve asking him to [join] the Army. He's already <u>in</u> the army. . . .

. . . I've never said "I don't know," as often as I say it now. Things are so bad, even without thinking of Nixon and his Bonwit Teller family. The Movement as we knew it is dead. The revolution of love has been betrayed. People snap at you now. Blacks and Jews are fighting each other, while the WASPs control and manipulate. Even this view is subject to distortion. The only thing that survives onslaughts of mud is friendship.

People wonder, I suppose, what keeps us here. Beyond the obvious things: Mel's job,[1] the big backyard that lets me write. The quiet neighborhood,

---

1   Mel worked as a civil rights attorney for the NAACP Legal Defense Fund.

the few helpful and genuinely nice people we know. There are few enough of those, that's true. But the "Southern way" among black people is great because kindness to disaster-stricken people, help, aid, fried chicken, is a way of life. If anything should happen to us, concern would be natural, unforced. I like that.

Undated 1969

We must go wherever we are not destroyed in the image of those who hate us. Home is wherever we can live human lives. Remember, it is possible for the soil of one's birth to poison one.

—

What is hard to admit is that for the first time in our marriage I don't feel Mel is capable of empathizing about a thing. He can understand but it is beyond him to feel what I feel when I go through a day as humiliating as this one. Coming here and settling has been a mistake. There is no avoiding the fact that away from the South, at Sarah Lawrence and in New York, I was a different person. More bold, more free, without this feeling of choking. Mel wants me to be what is not in me to be. I know if I had not met him I would not be here now. I surprised myself today, for the first time thinking that had I married a black man we would have had sense enough to know we couldn't live in Mississippi. What is hard for other people to understand is that analyzing the situation is the least helpful. For a scarred soul there is no healing, no cure. I cannot pretend I am unscarred, unbitter. I looked at the back of that cracker bus-driver's head and I hated him and everybody that looks like him. I'm not going to stay here much longer—and all the placating, explaining, courageous talk in the world is not going to make me stay here and be destroyed. I am not Joan of Arc or even Anne Moody[1] and I feel I've had it.

What will this mean in terms of us? For the first time I feel I'm tied to a rock. Not that Mel's a rock—everything around us is a rock. Even the shut-

---

1   Author Anne Moody wrote about her harsh experiences growing up poor and black in rural Mississippi, and her involvement in the civil rights movement, in the acclaimed 1968 autobiography, *Coming of Age in Mississippi.*

ters on the windows! Mel wants to stay here til he makes his mark—am I to stay here til Mississippi makes its mark on me? There are times, it seems to me, when a little selfishness is warranted. And I admit a creeping, growing selfishness. I want to survive. I want to live without choking, without worrying every minute that I'll be hurt. My feelings are precious, at least to me, and just because other people live through vileness and endure doesn't mean I can or will.

What choice is there? And what do I want?

He doesn't really understand—but even if he did it wouldn't help. I am alone.

May 22

Hiram[1] has just called to say he really likes the book! I'm very happy. He tells me he's sending a letter full of "nit-picking" later, but loves the book as it is! Marvelous!

---

1   Hiram Haydn was Walker's editor at Harcourt, Brace & World, and "the book" was the novel AW had been working on, *The Third Life of Grange Copeland*.

PART TWO

THE NATURE OF THIS FLOWER IS TO BLOOM

THE 1970S

Jan. 16, 1970

Tomorrow my daughter will be two months old. She does not seem real to me yet as my daughter. But she is the compact, warm, squirming bundle I love to rouse from sleep—holding her against the warmth of my body so that waking will be pleasant, will not jar her. And her eyes, already when she smiles, a bit mischievous. How she blooms and blossoms day by day. Andrew plops himself down in front of her door. Already he knows he must, as daddy tells him each time he leaves us, "take care of Rebecca—take care of Moma." So tonight he lies in the hall, half a room from each of us.

It is still strange having a baby that is all my own (and Mel's) and I think the amazing thing about one's baby is that you'd love it regardless of the father. Although when you love the father as I do, the love is more perfect, a blanket love, inclusive, warm.

Rebecca—Mel's choice. "Let's name her Rebecca, if she's a girl." But I was sure she would be a boy, Adam. Now I know no other name would have done as well—or so I feel now. First I was a baby myself—& now I know why a mother is a child's one necessity. Then I was a little girl. I had a long spell as young woman, then as woman. 25 before I had my Rebecca. Rebecca is way behind the first children of all my friends. But she should understand that Mel & I took a long time to make up our minds. We wanted to be sure.[1] On the other hand, Rebecca herself makes us sure & would have, I expect, even if she'd come three years ago.

Did I ever write anything here about the pregnancy? Long, with strong bouts of nausea, spitting. Unable some days to face my black literature class. Then, in the middle, better, so to Mexico and a long buying spree. Rugs (para mi nino!)—mostly Mel's buying and the Tamayo[2] which I had to have. I realized during pregnancy how much I love Mel, how glad I was to be carrying

---

1 Alice and Mel decided to have a child partly as a way for Mel to avoid the draft and not go to Vietnam, AW recalls. The couple wanted "to keep our work going in the civil rights movement as well," she says, noting that Mel's legal skills were crucial to black advancement.

2 Rufino Tamayo was a Mexican artist whose colorful paintings depict contemporary Mexican subjects.

his child. Mama says a man like Mel, so full of love, should have 50 children. So actually if we stop at one it will be a poor return. The last 3 months difficult, heavy, lonely. The last few weeks unending. . . . The labor long, hard—36 hours—beginning the day after Mel & I planted roses. Mel in Texas most of the first day, but then with me the rest of the time. How he suffered I guess I'll never really know, but it was very hard for him. And how happy he was when it was over and how he grinned when he first saw Rebecca!

I thought, what a lot we've been through together and how strong & sure I felt about us.

A page at least belongs to Mama, who came & stayed 4 weeks. She did everything for me, for us. How she loved to hold Rebecca against her and folded in those big fat arms. Nights she took her & rocked her all night when she cried. I knew how much my mother loved me by her love & patience with my child. My mother was unflappable, even if she didn't know newborn babies can't perspire!

Mel's mother, here for Thanksgiving, made me more nervous than I needed to be at the time, but she meant well and her help with the washer-dryer was more thoughtful than I'd ever dreamed. Rebecca uses diapers, diapers!

The first month was so rough I felt I couldn't have got through it without Mama—and to think I almost didn't ask her to come! Silly me.

* * *

And now my darling husband is in Greenville & my dear daughter is asleep— old troop de troop. Mama called her "the little trouper." The house is quiet. I am sad we will soon—a year or so from now—be leaving it. We have been, thank God, so happy here, and have planted trees & flowers.

Tonight I had a nightmare & got the gun out. I guess I am afraid. Happiness scares me. I am superstitious. Mel, Rebecca, Andrew, are all that matter to me really—& my Mama. The pussywillow is opening on my desk.

April 11, 1970
Jackson, Mississippi

I guess I really am a queer fish. When I write poems, as I've done at a brisk rate for the past 4 hours, they come to me out of locked rooms—out of nowhere. It is the oddest thing! I feel <u>hot</u>, in the same way I imagine a poker player must feel hot. But what bothers me is my constant bouts of depression. Am I going crazy? What is wrong? Am I simply bitchy? I think I will make an effort to get away for a little while. I feel locked inside myself. I feel cramped. And yet when did I ever have more? Somehow that is the problem. I am insecure or else a raging feminist. I resent so many small things—and god knows I don't <u>want</u> to be picayune.

Hurray! The novel is done—the galleys done, the book jacket already printed (according to Hiram).[1] I cannot believe it—How long it has been, almost three years!

Now I have so many questions going around in my head. Who to send what stuff to. Isn't that a switch?

Who am I? Why did I lose my wedding ring? Why do I go passive & get headachy so often?

---

1 AW had finished her first novel, *The Third Life of Grange Copeland*, and Hiram Haydn was her editor at Harcourt, Brace & World.

Undated

> "At the center of my
> work there is an
> invincible
> Sun."
> —CAMUS

Peaceful days are strange, guilty days. I don't know why this should be. But perhaps it is withdrawal from the world situation, when all you really want to consider is "what shall I cook for supper."

Reading this journal is scary. Like looking back at someone you almost know. But there are good days.

July 4, 1971

Things fall apart long before you hear the crash. Our marriage began to change drastically with the beginning of my pregnancy with Rebecca, or perhaps even before. I felt so alone so often & was. Mel never seemed to realize that I followed him to a wilderness with the reassurance that we would be company for each other. I can say without exaggeration that the past two years have been primarily miserable. Everything I've feared marriage might turn into. I, who love dancing, danced once this year. I, who love traveling, was convinced not to take the trip I needed to California.

But I will be going away soon. I am not sad or even sorry. If I stayed with Mel I'd find myself married to a man whose only reality for me is what other people tell me.

No. Not for me. I must fall in love again. Try again to come alive, to live and grow and be a part of someone who is capable of seeing so much of serious life a joke.

The abortion was so painful I thought (and so did the doctor) I would pass out. I could feel the blood leaving my face and my poor body all in a concentrated flame of pain. Perhaps my love died in that fire. Mel was busy with his brief and I no longer care about Mississippi, or the people who live here.

—

And what of Rebecca? At least she is the only child I will have![1] Thank God for that. I will try to do what is best for her—the old cliché. Neither Mel nor I should have had a child. We're equally unready. Ah, well. Nursery school, then kindergarten, school and then college. With summer camps in between. How heartless I am, people will say. But I am not content with children. Two days with Rebecca, sweet as she is, turns my hair grey.

I keep thinking of this poem that should contain the line "his father built him a house with beams of human ribs." But I can't get beyond the imagery of that line.

Actually, though, for all my grumbling, I love Rebecca and miss her if I don't see her in the morning. I suppose it shows in the way I can't bring myself to let Mama keep her for longer than a week every (so far) two years!

—

I must have faith in myself. And never stay where I do not wish to stay simply because I fear (and I do) the new, the different, the suddenly changed world. To be single again. What will it mean? I am 27. That is not old. It is younger than Susan Sontag.[2]

I must prepare to make a living as well as write.

But it is just I never really made room in myself for the presence of a child. How singleminded & studious I was, how determined always to do what I want! But Rebecca, when she runs up to me and hugs my legs, burying her

---

1 AW chose to have tubal ligation surgery that ended her ability to become pregnant.

2 Susan Sontag was a writer, a white contemporary of AW's, who was already regarded as an influential cultural critic, filmmaker, philosopher, teacher, and political activist.

warm little head against me, is so deeply in my heart it is <u>weird</u>! Especially when, sometimes, I find it almost unbelievable that I actually have a child!

March 2, 1972 / Cambridge, Mass.[1]

I am surprised, no, shocked, that nearly two years have passed since I wrote anything of substance in this book.[2] It has been a time, especially the first year, of watching Rebecca grow. This occupied my attention completely for five or six months. She was more beautiful than she will believe when she is grown up later and reads this. But something began to bring me down. The loneliness of Mississippi, the barrenness—culturally—of Jackson, and Rebecca began to seem an extra arm I didn't know how to use. Mel was away nearly all the time. He has sued half the white folks in the state. And that didn't leave him with much time to be with us. I limped in and out of depression. Violent depression. I always feel I will kill myself before these sessions end. It is very frightening. I wonder if I should try to see Robert Coles.[3] I think I might trust him. And he did write me a couple of sweet notes.

It was easier after Rebecca's first birthday, because then she was at Mrs. Cornelius',[4] down the street part of every day. But I was lonely to the point of screaming & for the first time in a long time I doubted that Mel understood. I doubted his love.

Teaching at Tougaloo[5] helped some. I love the spirit of T. I love its ac-

---

1   AW was doing a yearlong writing fellowship at the Radcliffe Institute at Harvard, in Cambridge, Massachusetts.

2   AW developed a habit, throughout her journaling life, of putting down a notebook midway through, starting another one, then picking up an old notebook and resuming her thoughts where she'd left off. For this volume, however, an effort has been made to organize the journal entries, from various notebooks, in chronological order for more convenient and coherent reading.

3   Robert Coles, psychiatrist, author, and Harvard professor.

4   AW sent toddler Rebecca to a nursery school at the home of her neighbor, Barbara Cornelius, an experienced teacher and civil rights activist, who taught children their ABCs as well as freedom songs.

5   Tougaloo College is a small, historically black liberal arts college near Jackson, Mississippi.

tivist history/movement history, but they can't afford to pay me very much or retain me for very long.

The decision to apply for the Radcliffe Institute fellowship[1] came from both of us. Mel realizes as I do that I have to get away from Mississippi.

A REMINDER TO YOURSELF:

When you are back in Mississippi remember that during the month of February (after you had gotten over the flu you caught while lecturing 5 hours at the Germantown Friends School in Phila.) you were very, very happy. Alone in the house on Linnaean St. Nothing to consider but the part-time course at Wellesley, the class you audited at Harvard, & best of all, your own writing! Don't forget that during this period you wrote 3 stories & began the 2nd novel!

You missed Rebecca but only really felt it when you were worried about her. You missed Mel because he gives you confidence with his love. Alone, you have very little self-confidence. You don't believe you are beautiful, you worry about small imperfections that his kisses would make lovely forever.

You are glad Mel is keeping Rebecca. It allows you to breathe, to be free in a way you have not been for five years.

I have discovered many important things over the year: new friends and <u>A Room of One's Own</u> by Virginia Woolf plus all the incredible black women authors whose lives ended in poverty & obscurity. Of them all I love Zora Hurston best. She had guts & soul & a loud mouth!

March 4

Today I went to Nouveau Riche & bought a purple knitted sweater and at an antique jewelers a Navaho Thunderbird with a turquoise stone. The bird

---

1   In early September 1971, AW began a writing fellowship for the academic year at the Radcliffe Institute in Cambridge. The institute was created to help women with family responsibilities pursue creative or scholarly projects. AW's fellowship included a $5,000 stipend, office space, library privileges at Radcliffe and Harvard, and the opportunity to audit classes at either school.

is silver. The Navaho thunder symbol's very rough. I like it immensely; it is the way I like my jewelry, very rough, of pure earthy elements and preferably old and "primitive." The other pendant is an amethyst also very pretty, of the Twenties the jeweler said. Not as large or as fine as the thunderbird, however.

These little shops around the square are exciting. I like the knitwear and the jewelry and the way there is so much to choose from.

I felt a feeling of relief the other day when I received the other half of my grant (2500) and the 758.00 from Wellesley[1] for the month. I like knowing I can support myself. It is a beautiful luxury to be able to afford, on a whim, a Navaho thunderbird and an amethyst pendant.

I enjoyed talking with the girls from Radcliffe. They are so young, but well-read for freshmen. They do not make me feel old though. Funny that the woman who teaches Black Literature at Harvard drives a white Cadillac & wears a mink coat. Perhaps that is what teaching at Harvard means to her.

A good call tonight from Mel & Rebecca. They will be coming next week. I feel sometimes that I never had them but at other times I can barely restrain a desire to drop everything & go home.

At times I am dismayed that there are things I am afraid to write about in this journal for I know they might be misunderstood.

Back in Jackson
June
I enjoyed giving the convocation address at Sarah Lawrence[2] this year, but finding time to write it proved difficult. I had all those Wellesley papers to

---

1   While doing her Radcliffe fellowship in Cambridge, AW also taught a literature course at Wellesley College, a private women's liberal arts college in nearby Wellesley, Massachusetts.
2   AW delivered the convocation address at her alma mater, Sarah Lawrence College in Bronxville, New York.

grade. Then the packing & the week-end at Bar Harbor with Mel & Gail. What I liked was having a captive audience of mostly women—several of them black—to whom I could relay my own interest in black women writers. I am <u>determined</u> that Zora Neale Hurston, <u>at least,</u> will never be out of print again!

The young man, David Nall, who received the first Alice Walker Literary Award[1] at Tougaloo was the young man who brought short stories to me the day after he was beaten up by white officials in Mendenhall. Which is why I like Tougaloo. Fight for your rights in the day, study & write short stories at night. Fifty dollars is a small gift but somebody once gave me fifty dollars and it made all the difference. Maybe I can give one hundred next year.

The mail just came (Let me describe our mailbox, on this middle-class street. The kind the farmers use, made like a loaf of bread, with a flag that you raise when you're sending mail, only painted black, because I had a can of black spray paint) and I received a $250 honorarium for the Sarah Lawrence Convocation speech. It feels good to get a check for sharing what has become important to you. I don't want to be paid expenses for attending board meetings, however.[2] After all, my value as a member might turn out to be nil. Besides, Sarah Lawrence has given me a great deal.

June 15, '72
Rebecca said today "I can cook soup, and eggs, and <u>win</u>dows!"
　She also said later, while painting at the kitchen table, "A, I, and O." Then "Oh oh, the 'O' is upside down!"

June 19—
Well, Langston, I began your biography in earnest today.[3]

1　This was a $50 literary award that AW established to encourage young writers at Tougaloo College, a historically black institution in Tougaloo, Mississippi, just north of Jackson.
2　AW had been invited to join the Board of Trustees for Sarah Lawrence College.
3　AW was beginning to write a children's biography of legendary poet Langston Hughes, with whom she had become friends not long before his death in 1967.

Aug. 11, 1972

The small biography of Langston Hughes is almost finished. Today I went down to the library (Carver branch) to try to find out when the earthquake occurred in Mexico that frightened Langston's mother. Would you believe there is no record of any earthquake in Mexico City in 1907, the year I surmise Langston was there? He was six years old. Well, perhaps the year was 1909 when there was an earthquake in Guerrero.

Reading Meltzer's book[1] I am struck again by how noble Langston was. God, how we misunderstood him!

—

The librarian insisted on having me sign the new library card "Mrs. Mel Leventhal." I could have killed her. Why is it so hard for people to understand a woman needs her own name?

It is becoming so that I no longer want to use my married name at all. Under any circumstances. Mel is hurt by this. Perhaps he thinks of what other people think. But surely I know him better than that!

The bout in the hospital was not unpleasant. I think, with the several small nagging worries I have, that the operation will make me feel freer. Motherhood, when one wants only really to write, is too heavy a burden. I read Margaret Walker's account of how she wrote Jubilee—over twenty or thirty years—and I think how much more she could have done without four children and her dedication to being a good mother and cook.

Zora Neale Hurston never had children. Neither did Nella Larsen. I understand why. Women have never been able to take their work seriously enough because babies have a way of becoming one's work. This is horrible to me. Whenever I speak to young women I will continue to warn them about marriage with children. Marriage without children could be almost complication free. You could always leave home for a few weeks, or for good.

* * *

---

1   Milton Meltzer, a friend and Hughes collaborator, published a 1968 biography of the poet—for young readers ages 10 and up—called *Langston Hughes*.

The galleys of Revolutionary Petunias seem to me cold.[1] The poems do not have the various fires I felt. I feel a cowardice creeping in, an uncertainty. Why is this? Perhaps I will feel better when I see the book.

On the other hand, the collection of short stories, In Love & Trouble, seems to me good. At least the first section and the newer stories. I especially like "Roselily" and "Crime."

Cambridge—2nd yr. Sept. 23, 1972[2]

Reading <u>Gemini</u> today I was struck by how funny Nikki is![3] And how different her humor is than, say, Langston's. It stops at nothing, which is a kind of courage. I liked the book—which surprised me. But I still feel N. is clever rather than wise, a woman who, for all her rhetoric, probably will never understand that Ayn Rand will forever be incompatible with black people. Perhaps it <u>is</u> wrong, this new fondness we have of weak people—from the weak-minded slave masters on down, or up, depending on your point of view, but it is something rare. And it is indelibly ours. Black.

Oct. 72—What does it mean to be alone, without a man? Is it safe to admit that I'm happier (most of the time) when I am alone? Marriage, in this house, depresses me. But I don't think I felt like this in Jackson last summer. Why is it that I can't remember happiness, only sadness? Why are my feelings about staying married so ambivalent? Do I love Mel enough to stay with him or don't I?

Cuba keeps coming to mind.[4] I wish Mel had given me a better reason

---

1   Partly because of her time at the Radcliffe Institute, AW had managed to complete a second volume of poetry, *Revolutionary Petunias & Other Poems*, as well as her collection of short stories, *In Love & Trouble*.

2   AW had written to Radcliffe officials early in 1972 to request a one-year extension of her residency. "A renewed fellowship," she wrote, "would give me a much-needed sense of freedom and possibility."

3   *Gemini: An Extended Autobiographical Statement on My First Twenty-Five Years of Being a Black Poet*, by Nikki Giovanni, was published in 1971.

4   AW had passed up an opportunity to travel to Cuba because Mel did not want her to go.

for my not going than that he is jealous of Bob.[1] That is the least reason, even if the "worst" had happened. Someday I must feel freer than I do now. My man <u>must</u> understand. How am I to live, to write, if jealousy prevents me from seeing the world?

Perhaps what I am really writing here is that I see the end of us. For I will have none of Sylvia Plath's Bell Jar![2] I wasn't born to live on the equivalent of 500 pounds a year, updated from 1928!

2 Nov. 72—Cambridge

It bothers me that the fact of my S.L. board[3] membership will be on the book jacket of <u>Revolutionary Petunias</u>. Why can't I resign myself to my own triviality, that is, who cares? So what if such affiliations are tacky if used as props. Why not recognize that and get on with it. I am so uncomfortable with "success." So questioning of "approval." But certainly I needn't apologize for being a member of the Board. It is a good experience <u>to have had</u>, like picking cotton.

Curiosity about experience has never deserted me.

A good name for a blues singer

"Blue Mullen"

Undated

Mel says my letter to him about Cuba was mostly "I" this and "I" that. I suppose I am selfish. I <u>know</u> I am. I don't give Mel very much of myself. I can't work up much interest in his work—I'm not jealous of it any longer—but there is my old distrust of the Law. Lawyers. I wish I could feel more.

---

1   Bob is Robert Allen, a Morehouse College graduate and friend of Alice's from her days at Spelman. He and Alice had what she called "an attachment" in the late '60s, before she met Mel. "We had really strong feelings for each other," Allen would recall. "But I was already engaged to someone else."

2   Sylvia Plath's 1963 book, *The Bell Jar*, is an intensely emotional, semi-autobiographical novel about a woman falling into the grip of insanity.

3   A reference to her membership on the Board of Trustees for Sarah Lawrence College, her alma mater.

Feel more positive, more amorous. One day they will prove absolutely that women's bodies are more sensitive than the mind—or rather, that the spirit is willing but the flesh avoids contact.

—

Radcliffe bores me with its invitations to be a part of it—teas, dinners, discussions on women. Wellesley, for the first time, today seemed like a land under water. Unreal.

U. Mass unbearable because only one student so far writes well.

If I write the novels I am considering, under the general title <u>Women of Salt</u>—how many novels am I considering? Three? With The Third Life of Grange Copeland as the foundation. Because of course the trilogy would have to begin with <u>Ruth Copeland</u>.

How I wish I could begin now. Be rid of teaching, lecturing, answering mail. And I really should give up the Board of Trustees. Although after Margaret Schifter's letter—about an older alumna giving $5,000 worth of stock because of my article in the Sarah Lawrence Alumnae News—I feel less useless. Still, it is hard to believe I can offer anything in the business meetings. Figures give me such a headache. And the buying & selling of stock, and the way the room becomes airless & straight-up like a cemetery.

Nov. 11, 1972

Went to a nearby head shop and bought a sensational pipe for smoking. I think it is called a silver duke. It has a long slightly curving stem made of beaten silver (with cordlike silver rings) and a bowl that is wood or clay but dark brown, intricately carved. It is a pipe just right for me. Elegant, lean, silver and wood (or clay). I have been smoking every night, lying on the sofa. I sat up the other night in near-shock because the smoke made me realize how deeply I once loved Bob.[1] How well I had hidden that from myself. I must have died a little when we parted that summer (after our one night together) and he honored his "commitment" to Pam.

---

1   She's thinking of her old flame, Robert "Bob" Allen.

A part of that feeling for him has led me to fall for men who in some way resemble him.

How odd that all that feeling has been buried in me all these years. The smoke brought out other feelings. Sexual and strong and not always heterosexual. I wonder if other women experience this diffusion of sexuality—in their fantasies?

Paula, who visited me this afternoon, at least has the courage to talk about being in love with a girl at Wellesley. And wanting to love her physically. But most women probably deny all such longings, and consider them perverse. I suppose I am no exception—except that instead of thinking them perverse I think that making the fantasies & longings real (to actually have a homosexual relationship) is nearly impossible if one is not driven to it by desire. Curiosity and fantasies do not give one the necessary courage to approach the daughters of bilitis.[1]

As with the deaths of great men, I find I can write nothing, practically, about the Vietnam/American War.—Why don't they call it The American War? More greasytalk, evasive lying. But I send a little money. Maybe one mother's child will eat. All I can say about the war is that the bombs will fall on Washington & New York & Atlanta & Boston someday. I hope the people who voted for Nixon will understand war then. And if I die with the first bomb, that will be good, it will be justice. For I have assassinated no one to stop the war. I have harmed no one, in any way. I have breathed & eaten & made love among murderers without disturbing them. How can I live and do nothing? Nothing <u>real</u>?

---

1   Though AW is using the term here humorously to refer to all lesbians, the Daughters of Bilitis, also called DOB or the Daughters, is thought to be the first lesbian civil and political rights organization in the United States. The organization was formed in San Francisco in 1955 as a social alternative to lesbian bars, where women were often harassed by the police. The DOB sought to educate women about lesbian history and offer support for those who wanted to come out.

Nov. 12, 1972

I have been impressed by the African novelists I've read. Camara Laye[1] is no exception. The Radiance of the King seems to me successful (even though I have not yet finished it) in a way that most novels are not, only short stories. It is a sustained fantasy-parable, yet very real & applicable to the world.

——

Everyone is surprised that Diana Ross is so <u>fantastic</u> in "Lady Sings the Blues." Well, I suppose I am a little surprised. But my praise for her fine job is an embrace of sisterhood I wish I could give her. The horrible things our "poets" have written about her are not excusable. Nikki, Don,[2] others, sought to crucify a woman because of her success & her tacky singing dresses and for her "white" sounding voice & music & for her wigs & for her white husband. But the work Diana did in this movie speaks of her love of Billie Holiday. It is a labor of love and labors of this sort outweigh any number of weird personal choices—certainly outweighs hairstyles & marriage vows.

"Work is love made manifest."

November 28

I sympathize (and more) with the countless women who struggle alone to raise their children. The real heroines must be those legendary women who raise six and seven and eight children all by themselves. Rebecca is good. She does not request much. Just love and a few hours of attention—the love isn't hard to give, but the attention is.

I try, loyally, to defend Mel's insistence on staying in Jackson to work.

---

1 Camara Laye, a writer from Guinea, was the author of *The African Child*, a novel loosely based on his own childhood, and *The Radiance of the King*, described by critic Kwame Anthony Appiah as "one of the greatest of the African novels of the colonial period."

2 Black poets Nikki Giovanni, Don L. Lee (later known as Haki Madhubuti), and others had harshly criticized Diana Ross as a crossover singer, but she found some redemption with her performance as Billie Holiday in the 1972 film *Lady Sings the Blues*, which was nominated for five Academy Awards, including Best Actress in a Leading Role.

But I no longer believe it is fair—and I realize I've felt this way for a long time. Mississippi destroys my good feelings about myself. My consciousness must work overtime just to suppress my instinctual reactions to things. John & Leslie[1] were surprised that going to the movies in Jackson is such a psychic ordeal.

Why am I going back there, then? Is it mainly because Rebecca & the teaching and everything is too much for me alone? That, and the loneliness. Which means I need Mel for myself, I guess. But perhaps this is something I am not to know, for a while.

To rest, to not be distracted, to work. That is what I need. And I need my family to be secure, to be whole.

Perhaps "laziness should be admitted in the clearest terms!"

My mother's birthday, she is sixty. Does not regret any part of her life. Commendable. But is it true?

Dec. 23

Back in Jackson. Being alone all day with Rebecca drives me crazy. I envy Joyce Carol Oates[2] mostly for her free days.

Dec. 27

Watched William Buckley[3] talking on "Contemporary Southern Writers & Literature" with Eudora Welty and Walker Percy. Jerry Ward[4] asked "What about old & young black writers from the South to whom the South is not dead nor homogenized?" He listed some: Margaret Walker Alexander, Er-

---

1   Friends of AW's in Cambridge.

2   By this time, the prolific writer Joyce Carol Oates—a Walker contemporary—had won the National Book Award for Fiction for her 1969 novel, *Them*. She was married but had no children.

3   William F. Buckley Jr., conservative author and commentator, founded *National Review* magazine in 1955. He also hosted a public affairs television show called *Firing Line*.

4   A notable black literary critic, poet, and essayist, Jerry Ward began teaching at Mississippi's Tougaloo College in 1970.

nest Gaines, Alice Walker.—But of course "Southern Writers" are white, by definition. Just as South African and German writers are. And what kind of writer were you, Zora Neale? And you, Jean Toomer?

Dec. 28 or 29th

Mel is what I invariably think of as "a real Jew." Which is to say that although he does not seem remotely like any of the other Brooklyn Jews I've met, he would be quite at home in the Old Testament. He loves justice, like one loves a magnificent misused person. He knows what mercy means— and humility. Characteristically, too, he is also long-suffering. I'm not sure I comprehend, or can completely appreciate this quality, yet.

Dec. 29th

Two copies of Revolutionary Petunias arrived. I like just about everything, I think—but it is always easy to like the looks of anything that is completed. But "midget" should be "giant" and there is at least one other place where a word I changed in proofs was not changed. Why is this? I must ask. Why, I wonder, do I feel so much less emotion when I see the books of poems?

March 30, 1973

To record that I am still alive, in Mississippi. That today was filled with work—on the novel, on the review of June's book on Fannie Lou Hamer,[1] on Mister Sweet's Blues, on my essay about Black Women Writers—which is going too slowly. But whenever I can work and begin the day without a headache I am happy—Mary Helen Washington's review of R.P. helped too.[2]

I must recognize, and soon, that these speaking engagements exhaust me. I stand on a stage with faces looking up and I'm always wondering

---

1   Sister writer and friend June Jordan's children's biography, *Fannie Lou Hamer*, was published in October 1972.

2   In a review in *Black World*, literary critic Mary Helen Washington said that readers of *Revolutionary Petunias* would leave Walker's work "understanding not only the southern Black experience a little better but also understanding better the nature of the Black experience as a whole."

"Why am I here?" because to me, standing on the stage as a speaker turns me into a judge. And I hate judging. I wonder if this is unreasonable? But this hatred of appearing to be a judge causes me, I feel, to seem wishy-washy. Unsure. Yet I feel and believe deeply. It is just that to talk about it is painful.

But the feminist talk at Brown ironically brought me in contact with <u>four</u> black men I like, love, and respect. Ferdinand Jones who popped up with his shy, quiet wife, and Michael Harper who talks & carries on like Langston, Barry Beckham, who is quiet, thin, and with a <u>beautiful</u> loving black skinned wife (this always moves me to almost insane heights of joy. Why? Am I such a hypocrite!?) And then, James Alan McPherson, who didn't know what to do, when I hugged him. He had stuck out his hand—as if this Southern black woman could bear that. I never <u>heard</u> of such shit, to quote Bessie Smith. The story of his that I love, he thought was "a bad story." How funny. We never know about our own work, where it is going, that is. I love him because of that story.

June 16, 1973

I'm glad I wrote "In Search of Our Mothers' Gardens" to read at the Radcliffe Symposium on Black Women, but why did I have to burst into tears in the forum later? The truth is that in a way I am not embarrassed by tears if they are speaking to feeling in life, as opposed to abstractions—which the forum presenters were indulging in. June[1] was wonderful. She hugged me and after Barbara Ann Teer[2] said "You're trying to carry your mother and the weight is too heavy," June said, "But why shouldn't you 'carry your mother,' she carried <u>you</u>, didn't she?" That is perfection in a short response.

It is just that I learn, as I write about her—all our mothers—just how fantastic they were and are. Sometimes I want to write about smashing a white face but it always comes to this: I would rather write about our mothers right up until time to smash, then I'd just smash, and then if I lived to

---

1   Acclaimed Caribbean American poet, essayist, activist, and longtime friend June Jordan.
2   Barbara Ann Teer, an African American writer and producer, founded Harlem's National Black Theatre in 1968.

tell the tale I probably wouldn't even bother to tell it, I'd go back to describing our mother's face. That is why June's poem moved me so:

> "Mama help me to survive
> And help me turn the face
> of history
> to your face."[1]

The other thing is: It is good to read about women like my mother at Radcliffe. It forces reality into the crevices of all those who think Radcliffe is the very top of things when the real top is clearly on the bottom—or was. It will not remain there. With my last breath I will rescue the bottom rung.

I am upset—deeply—about the subservient condition of African women. I wonder how other women feel about this? It certainly helps to make me ambivalent. It is like, just when you're ready to accept the Muslims and agree to believe in their mythology you notice how they treat "their" women. Like slaves and children and fallow fields open for seed. Or looking about for something really revolutionary you check out Baraka's group and find that women's "place" is somewhere behind & far to the left of the throne, or you turn to the RNA and they see women as something they own.[2]

And I wonder if other women or men think about what it will mean to be venerated, protected, saved, and in other words turned into Scarlett O'Hara.

Lord, this is some thick shit Black women must get through.

Undated

June found my review of her book not praise-ful. And I tried to make her understand this: to me, truly, "work is love made manifest." What I love I

---

1   This is a paraphrase of a line from June Jordan's poem "Getting Down to Get Over."

2   The references here are to radical black poet Amiri Baraka, formerly LeRoi Jones, and the Republic of New Africa (RNA), a radical black separatist organization (founded in Detroit in 1968) that sought to establish an independent nation within the United States, composed of the five Deep South states.

labor for, but words that simply praise never seem like love to me. They seem easy. But I guess they sell books.

I must try to sell her book in Mississippi. That will show my very real love for what she has given me.

Aug. 21, 1973

So now I know—it is possible to fall in love (all over again, or perhaps for the first time) with one's husband! Because I am in love with Mel. I am becoming sexually awakened truly for the first time. Liking sex and easy about it. It has probably been hard work over the years for Mel—luckily it was work he enjoyed.

Ruth tells me that Mama says "nothing happened" when she made love with Daddy until after Curtis was born, when she was in her thirties. Perhaps it is true that women develop later than they seem to.

Aug. 21, 1973

I did not return to this notebook to write about the Caribbean cruise in July, but to write my impressions of Eatonville & my hurt & horror at the neglect of Zora's memory as evidenced by her grave.—I still can't write about it. But I must.[1]

Undated

Seeing Zora's grave in its field of weeds[2] made me thankful that I love Mel. All she had, at the end, was her dog Sport. And her "friends." Really just Sport.

---

1   Sometime later, AW wrote the following addendum to this entry: (See essay: "Looking for Zora" 34 pps. But what is wrong with this piece is that it is understated.)

2   AW had traveled to Eatonville and Fort Pierce, Florida, to look for the grave of Zora Neale Hurston (1891–1960), a writer she greatly admired, who had been buried in an unmarked grave, despite a stellar career as the most prolific black woman writer of her generation. Passing herself off as Hurston's niece, AW found the grave in a weed-choked, segregated cemetery and, with her own money, bought a small gray headstone to mark the grave. Because of Hurston's persistent mendacity about her age, AW placed the wrong birth year—1901 instead of 1891—on the marker. Scholars later learned that Hurston had lopped 10 years off her age in a radical act of reinvention that enabled her to finish high school after a decade of "wandering" following her mother's death.

This is what I had engraved on the stone:

ZORA NEALE HURSTON
"A GENIUS OF THE SOUTH"
NOVELIST FOLKLORIST
ANTHROPOLOGIST
1901 – 1960

Undated

When I was growing up (and when I talked to my boyfriend later in college) and heard people say they were afraid to go to Alabama and Mississippi, I was embarrassed for them. Imagine being afraid of being in your own country! Simply to live anywhere with freedom requires a willingness to become an immovable force, except by death.

Dec. 15

Have sold so far:[1]

300 copies to Headstart
and about 25 at The Artisan Shop
and have 25 for Christmas
giving. Plus, had my review
reprinted in local paper and
have had it placed in 4
bookstores & one drugstore.

I liked your book, June. I <u>liked</u> it!

---

1   Here, AW is referring to her friend June Jordan's book *Fannie Lou Hamer*, a children's biography of the Mississippi civil rights activist.

Feb. 9, 1974—My 30th birthday
1443 Rockdale—Jackson

A bright, sunny day. Rebecca woke up singing and puttering around the house. Mel's asleep because his poker game took up all last night. I have felt—all last week—that suicide was just a matter of finding a sharp enough blade. Am haunted terribly by the exposure of myself in the O'Brien interviews.[1] It seems to me I've destroyed something in myself. Something that could only exist in complete privacy. And yet I felt compelled to be honest about why and how I wrote the things I wrote. I guess vanity also plays a part—for I worry that now people will assume I <u>am</u> ugly, and freaky and weak. Of course I am weak. But I also intend <u>not</u> to give up, not to break. I don't like anyone thinking they can pity me. The thought gives me the horrors. If only I could empty my mind of regret, of shame over the exposure. If only I could believe I am not dangerous to myself.

But—back to the 30th birthday. Ruth sent a card. Mama sent a check for $30. It is the kind of gift I had forgotten she loves to give. The check has a picture of her on it and her two gold teeth shine. I also discover that she spells "Lou" "<u>Lue</u>."[2] Why have I forgotten that?

All in all a rotten year. I can't remember a worse one. Mel has arranged to work out of the Inc. Fund[3] office in New York. I have asked Gloria Steinem[4] for $15,000 for 2½ days work a week & 3 months off. This will probably be refused.

I wonder if I will ever be among friends, living a life I enjoy.

<u>Have you forgotten your happiness in Cambridge?</u>

That's true. I must try harder to remember what feeling good <u>feels</u> like.

---

1   This is a reference to an interview with John O'Brien, published in his 1973 book, *Interviews with Black Writers*. Speaking of the childhood incident in which one of her brothers shot her in the right eye with a BB gun, she said: "For a long time, I thought I was very ugly and disfigured. This made me shy and timid, and I often reacted to insults and slights that were not intended."

2   AW's mother's name was Minnie Tallulah Grant Walker; Tallulah was shortened to "Lou" or "Lue."

3   NAACP Legal Defense and Educational Fund, or LDF.

4   Gloria Steinem, a new friend, was cofounder and, at the time, editor of *Ms.* magazine, where AW had become a contributing editor, writing several articles a year.

4/9/74

  As long as I love life
and as long as life continues
to hurt me with its cruelty
its indifference and its beauty
I will write poems.

  Where once I thought
I was ugly
I now perceive myself
to be
a woman to fit my needs
my feet no larger
than my shoe.

4/10/74

I wrote these two "things" yesterday, lying in bed, looking out at the emerald green backyard whose beauty I have taken too much for granted.

  An interesting thing has happened. Since writing about the accident for a public readership I am now able to discuss it almost normally with real people. I can <u>admit</u> to actual people that the fact that my right eye wanders bothers me. And I become more determined than ever to have it straightened! And so, I went into university hospital last week and had two muscles in my eye rearranged, so that now, instead of turning slightly (or a lot) outward my right eye even seems to turn a bit inward, but is mostly straight though bloody as strawberry jam. This simple procedure should make an enormous difference in the way I feel about myself. But there are even more wonderful things to report: My pre-period depression is being helped by Dr. Hickerson's little pills, also my insomnia & tension that always accompanies it. But the <u>best</u> thing is that I went to see Mama a few weeks ago and I told her about the abortion I had in college nearly ten years ago. Women who come of age five years from now will not understand that, loving my mother as I do, the fact that in her eyes I had sinned caused me complete &

utter torment for most of the years since it happened. And both my sisters convinced me my mother would never forgive me: That she would think of me as a murderer. But how little I valued my mother's love & understanding while I believed them. Because not only was she quick to forgive me & tell me of her love for me, she explained her own terror when she knew she was pregnant with my older brother—& she was unmarried. She threw herself down cliffs and against things, trying to dislodge the fetus. But of course, she said, those things are tough. I cried, telling her. I love her so much & I felt at any moment (especially since she is so reverently religious) she would turn away from me. But she turned to me and now I can sleep peacefully again. My mother is not dead to me—which is what I felt all of last year. And I realized that to me my mother's love is more important to me than God's love or forgiveness. For to me, my mother is God.

April 10, 1974

So, to sum up:

1. We are leaving Jackson[1]
2. Rebecca is healthy, bright, pretty and no more trouble to me the writer than Virginia Woolf's madness was to her or the worry George Eliot had that she was living unmarried with a married man. Mel shares the care of Rebecca fairly. He appreciates my work—my only worry is that he may be a poker addict. We love each other, after seven years & one near divorce.
3. My mother knows "the worst" of me and forgives, understands, & loves me.
4. My father is dead. I do not have to pretend a civility I do not feel.
5. I have straightened my eye.
6. My novel is between 1st & 2nd drafts.

---

1 The family was moving to New York, where Mel was to work out of the NAACP Legal Defense and Educational Fund's office.

7. I have accepted a job as an editor of <u>Ms.</u> for $700.00 a month plus $750 per article. (They suggest 4 a year—I think it will be more like 2).

8. <u>In Love & Trouble</u> was the editor's choice of The New York Times last week. And won the Rosenthal Award from the National Institute of Arts & Letters.

9. <u>Revolutionary Petunias</u> was nominated for a National Book Award.

It will be interesting to see if my depressions continue, after all this.

For a Sign Painted Over My Desk:

"Dear Alice,

Virginia Woolf had madness
    George Eliot had ostracism, someone else's husband and did not dare use her own name.
    Jane Austen had no privacy and no love life
    The Bronte Sisters never went anywhere & died young and dependent on their father.
    You have Rebecca—who is much more delightful and less distracting than any of the things above."

May 1, 1974—Last night Mel went out after 12pm to mail off "Looking for Zora" so that Joanne at <u>Ms</u> will get it May 2nd. This was after he had Mrs. Cox retype it—sitting waiting in his office for five hours and proof-reading each page. He looked tired and gray when he stumbled in—but was quite willing to go out to mail it at the downtown P.O. He is a good person and believes in my work. I wish I could be as enthusiastic about his profession as he is about mine.

—

There are some weird characters hanging about the edges of my mind. For example: the very proud, very severe & handsome & <u>clean</u> woman who used to come begging on this street. Her look said clearly: I refuse to work—other than to walk from house to house—for a living <u>any</u> more. Was she someone's maid before? What is the story?

In front of me, over my desk, I have a large lithograph of three watermelon slices by Tamayo,[1] a picture of myself at the age of six (before the accident—a pretty, bright-eyed little girl looks out at me; there is a shyness & a tenderness in that small face) and I have a picture of Mae Poole, my great-great, great grandmother, taken when she was 90. The watermelon helps me. For it means I can love things <u>in themselves</u>, as opposed to becoming hung-up over what other people think about them. My own picture reminds me of my young and tender vulnerability—and causes me to reflect on how that child differs from the woman I have become. I know the accident changed me. Literally, it caused me, in a sense, to close my eyes. Because I did not want people to notice the gray scar tissue that covered my pupil, I stopped looking at them. It is hard for me to look at people directly—strangers, especially—even now. But now that my eye is straight I will train myself to stare. Which privilege the writer, the artist, always has. According to Flannery O'Connor.

I should also record that there have been times when I was <u>glad</u> of the accident. Because it opened me to the awareness of other people's pain.

---

1 Rufino Tamayo was a twentieth-century Mexican artist who focused on paintings, printmaking, and sculpture.

Undated

Essays keep asking to be written, but I must attempt to keep them away until <u>after</u> I've finished the novel:[1] However, for the essay in the form of a letter I must recall the following conversations:

Me: "Of course you know Zora—and all women, especially if they were black—had great problems being a writer."

1. Houston Baker, critic (black) and full professor at the U. of
    Virginia, Eng. Lit:
       "Zora's problem was that Langston Hughes didn't love her."
       [at Baker's home, Charlottesville, Virginia, Apr. 13, 1974]

2. Conversation with Ernest Gaines:
       On my mention of Zora:
       Something to this effect—"You must encounter a lot of
       people who consider your work is a continuation of the
       Hurston tradition."

       Gaines, shrugging "Yes. Every time I speak or read
       somewhere kids come up asking about her." Another shrug.
       "I've never read her."
       (Gaines' deepest appreciation has been for the work of
       William Faulkner)
       Both conversations at Ernie & Linda's in San Francisco, April
       22, 1974

3. Conversation with James McPherson[2] who says "Ellison was
    the first to take us [black literature] beyond protest and purely
    questions of race."

---

1   At this point, AW is working on another novel, a meditation on the civil rights movement.
2   James Alan McPherson was an American essayist and short story writer. He was the first
Black writer to win the Pulitzer Prize for Fiction, for his 1977 collection *Elbow Room*.

"But wait," I say, "Zora's book [TEWWG][1] came out the same year as Wright's <u>Native Son</u> & was already beyond protest and 'purely questions of race.'"

J.M. answers: "I remember how you spoke of her when you lectured up at Brown. But I haven't read her."

4. Turner's[2] comment in his book of "criticism," <u>In a Minor Chord</u>.

"Always she [Zora] remained a wandering minstrel. It was eccentric but perhaps <u>appropriate</u> for her to return to Florida to take a job as a cook and maid for a white family and to die in poverty."

5. The result of all this ignorance and hatred is shown in this statement so often seen in the defensive writing of blacks—male & female:

. . . "the woman is not given a literary description. She is but a shadow in black life, a dreamy substance indeed, romanticized by an aeon of faggots."

—Hart LeRoi Bibbs[3]

"A Diet Book for Junkies"

Surely we must ask ourselves why it is that when most black people think of black women in literature they come up with nothing, i.e. "Mammy" or some welfare prostitute whose only lines are in curses, or with extremely objectionable negatives, like Wright's "Bessie" being beaten to death by Bigger's brick.[4]

---

1   *Their Eyes Were Watching God*, Zora Neale Hurston's best-known novel, was published in 1937.

2   Darwin T. Turner, a Black literary critic whose critique of Hurston was particularly harsh and laced with sexism.

3   Hart Leroy Bibbs was an African American poet, photographer, musician, actor, and artist.

4   A reference to the plot of Richard Wright's novel *Native Son*.

There is not any indication that Larsen's Helga Crane[1] is related to Bessie Head's heroines in <u>Maru</u> or <u>A Question of Power</u>. The work of connecting has simply not been done.

Undated

I am not really a Movement sort of person and have felt guilty about this. It is like this: one half of me yearns to be on the barricades, the other wants only to observe the fight. So I am somewhere in between. A pair of eyes. Only occasionally a fist.

Undated

Perhaps if I "name" the problem at <u>Ms.</u> I can better deal with it. Surely it can't be as simple as color!? But of course color isn't simple. Only a simpleton would think it so. For color is history and society and caste and class—but mainly <u>memory</u>. Not simply my own, but my mother's and my grandmother's and my father's and so forth.

Basically, too, what I want for the world is not what they—American white feminists—want. Or rather, it is not what the majority of editors at <u>Ms.</u> want. I want desperately to be rid of a yearning for the material beyond adequate food, lodging and shelter & clothing. Facing up to my cowardice in this will probably take all the strength I have.

Undated

Today all I thought about was how bored I am in this marriage. How constrained I feel, trying to figure a way to live a life of my own with Mel and Rebecca requiring that I live at least a part of theirs. I can't think now of anything unexpected Mel has said to me in the last year.

---

1 A reference to the protagonist of Nella Larsen's novel *Quicksand*.

1976

Jan. 3, Midnight:

The new year has begun. My daughter's head is on my shoulder. We are friends. We discuss <u>Langston Hughes, American Poet</u>.[1] I love her and feel good.

When her father and I are not close, I feel closer to Rebecca. It is as if showing love continuously to two people produces a strain in me. When my affection is channeled in one direction there seems to be more of it and I am more relaxed about it.

Jan. 5 –

This morning Rebecca went back to school after a 2 wk Christmas holiday. I woke her up. Pressed her through dressing. She's very slow in the morning, but also very talkative and cheerful. I don't know if she's used to having me share her bed. I like sleeping with her. I feel great tenderness near her. When we lie in bed reading or when she is asleep and I see her curls sticking out over the pillow.

She is very maternal. She asks me if I would like to rest my head on her shoulder. I say yes. She puts her arm around me, her hand cupped under my chin, and it is good rest. We have changed places. I think when she is grown up I will be able to rely on her. I will need someone to rely on. She seems a lot stronger than I was at six.

Several hours later after writing letters & working on proofs for Meridian.[2] Rebecca due home any minute from school. I feel eager to see her, to make her welcome. When the doorbell rings, I will rush to the door, pull her in out of the cold, give her a hug, soup, place myself at her disposal for an hour or so. It is because she has been away for six hours that I feel this way. Schools are useful things for writers who are parents.

It is 2:30. On Mondays and Fridays school lets out early. There it is!

---

1   AW's children's book about Hughes, published in 1974.

2   Published in May 1976, *Meridian* is often described as AW's meditation on the civil rights movement. It follows Meridian Hill, a young Black woman in the late 1960s who is attending college as she embraces the civil rights movement.

Undated 1976

In the Brooklyn house on 1st St.[1]

The new novel: Two women who spend several days together for the specific purpose of telling each other everything. Total honesty on these issues & levels:

1. How they feel about men and/or women as partners
2. America & the political establishment, the war
3. Revolution—why they are or are not more active (China, Cuba) The Feminist Movement
4. Children, husbands, life-styles
5. Philosophies, religion, breaks with the past

Can two women be honest with each other?

April 19, 1976

I have had one or two periods of depression in the past two years. Compared to my frequent bouts in Jackson, this is nothing. Only once was bad enough to frighten me. I am full of work, and new friends . . . and travel.

Bob[2] and I—after all these years (he says thirteen)—have finally managed to spend a second night in each other's arms. It is quite true I've always loved him—since Spelman. Even before he was aware of me. Still, he says he fought loving me because of his marriage to Pam.[3] Now he says "Do you believe I love you?" I say "Of course." Because, frankly, why else have we managed to keep in touch with each other all these years?

---

1 AW, now separated from Mel, is living in Brooklyn, New York.

2 Robert Allen, an activist and writer, met AW when he was a student at Morehouse and she a student at Spelman. In the journals, AW refers to him initially as Bob, later as Robert, and occasionally as Roberto.

3 Pamela Parker, a white civil rights and women's rights activist, married Robert Allen in 1965.

June 12, 1976

This whole spring has been devoted to being openly in love with (and loved by) Bob. So intense are our feelings that I'm sure we give the impression of being crazy. I feel such combinations of tenderness, sadness, fear. A lot of fear. And I am only somewhat comforted by the knowledge that he is also afraid. Whenever we make love I cry, flooding him and everything else with my tears. It is as if I'm holding everything I ever wanted in my arms and yet—what? I don't know yet.

—

With B. I always have the feeling he's done (whatever he's doing) it before, that there is a plan of some sort that he's following. Perhaps I am simply suspicious because P.[1] is as involved in our threesome as she can possibly place herself. So whatever happens between B. & me I feel is already shared with P. whether she is present or not.

I find P's sexual interest, her "sisterly love" that dreams of "sharing orgasms," disconcerting. And B's assertion that he would not be bothered if P. & I made love mystifying. I'm afraid I do not even <u>like</u> her, though I have tried to over the years for his sake mainly.

And do I like him? It is hard to give up on someone loved for nearly half of one's life. And yet, as Bob has said, perhaps I mistook him. Assumed he was more than he was. (Apparently this is true, if in fact he is just "an ordinary nigger.")

(I never think of myself that way. To me my life is holy. My spirit God-filled & precious, and my face & body beautiful.)

Always people lose me by pushing me too far. B. has pushed me as far as I'm willing to go. I don't want <u>not</u> to love B. And yet, it seems hopeless, except as a kind of well-intentioned farce involving the three of us. As for his love for me . . . it is often too oblivious of what I am that I see no reason to trust its longevity.

---

1   Bob's wife, Pam.

July 9, 1976

A supremely miserable day. Perhaps one of the most miserable of my life. Last night I told Bob I do not wish to see, talk to or receive letters from him again. He was speechless with surprise and hurt. And well he might be. I love him more, I think, than I have ever loved anyone. But there is nowhere for our love to go, and I refuse to throw away a first rate love on a fifth rate affair. He has been busy making plans for our engagement—so comic! And of course all it means, all it ever meant was he wants me in addition to Pam. While I need someone like Mel,[1] only less boring, to lean on, to turn to in sorrow and trouble and fear, all emotions I feel too frequently with Bob.

But it hurts so much to give him up for good. He has been, in a sense, my last and only hope. Reading his books his mind is so admirable, and I know he is gentle. But what is happening (has already happened) to his soul?

I sense it is being lost, corrupted, led into the darkness. I am not prepared to follow it there. So I lay about today crying, praying to be released from my feelings for him as I would pray to be released from an illness.

What they (B&P) do not see is that they have been using people ("consuming women") between them to enliven their marriage. I think of the other women & lovers they have shared and I call them, to myself, sister-victims. And I wonder if any of those other "victims" fell in love with Bob as I have done. He did not love any of them, he says. And yet, all of that experimentation with other women was supposed to be out of love! Such hypocrisy! And blindness and cruelty! Alas, it is ironic to read how little Bob cares for "monogamy" when he & Pam are probably the most monogamous couple I've ever met. It is true they have sex outside of marriage, but it is always the marriage that endures.

The truth is, I object to my position in this "triangle" on historical as well as personal grounds. I have always tried very hard to accept & care about the white women my black male friends have married or loved. But I real-

---

1 AW and Mel Leventhal are separated at this point, but not yet divorced.

ize I can only accept it if I'm not involved in a deeply emotional way. I too feel it is a rejection—not perhaps of me personally—but of black women. I suppose I also feel less respect for the black man in such a liaison because I am always wondering—Is it really love, or was he too weak to resist the advertising?

With Mel I did not worry about any of this. I thought his choosing me showed excellent sense, because, as a black woman & as myself, I know I am the best that could possibly be offered. I even used to enjoy watching white women try to interest him. They failed.

But with Bob I would never know and therefore never be at rest. And this fact shames me for us as a people because he is the best we have to offer—as a brilliant, handsome, radical young black man—and yet . . . contradictions. Is this what all those "crazies" in the 60s were trying to get us to see? I couldn't listen to them then, because I was trying to build a life with Mel. But they were right in their fears, if wrong in the kinds of pressure they brought to bear on those of us caught in the contradictions of this racist, consumer, capitalistic & most of all manipulative society.

I hope I can look back on this entry sometime in the future when I am recovered and feel nothing more than curiosity that I could have cared so much. How desperately I hope that! At the moment I feel that till the day I die I will love Bob.

November 4, 1976

I am on a plane to Mexico City; from there I will go to Cuba. . . . But first, an update, since diary-keeping has been replaced over the past year by letters to Robert.

Perhaps I might have stayed longer with Mel, in my marriage, if we had followed my suggestion of dividing the house—or, certainly of having separate bedrooms. I grew to resent more and more the intrusion on my mornings of Mel's incompatible habits. Habits no worse than my own, and easily lived with except in such close proximity. The main one: he is "a night person," would sleep till noon. I get a headache if I stay in bed past nine.

So I was leaving for over a year. And moved into the study, then into Rebecca's room.[1]

Then, in January, Robert appeared. I mentioned the impending divorce,[2] and—as I'd hoped—he pursued me in words, as he has pursued me with slightly ambiguous actions over the years.

At first it seemed impossible. I had forgotten what it was about him that had never left me. He seemed somehow debased, debauched; there was about him something diminished and unclear. This I later understood was not simply my imagination. His life has had its other pursuits . . .

In any case, by April we were committed to try an affair. In April in Santa Cruz, we knew we were in love. It has been seven months of the most intense emotion—love, passion, lust, fear, joy—I have ever known. Also despair.

But Cuba. In a way, Cuba connects us. It is an experience I have always wanted for myself, and it is an experience Robert has always wanted (& tried to give me) me to have.

Undated

Huey and Gwen[3]—

Gwen: large, dark eyes. Small build. Intelligent, sharp, not relaxed easily. Huey: Shiny eyes, like a cat, with a slanted cat-like shape. Large. A pointed nose. A lithe body. Seems to drag (slightly) one leg. A magnetic personality. An interesting blend of graciousness and a quality one is aware of as being "claiming dominance." He and Gwen expected me to attack—probably because of the story about his murder of a woman (prostituting to earn money) in Oakland.

---

1 In late 1976, AW moved from the house she and Mel shared in Brooklyn into her own apartment nearby. As with many modern families, Rebecca shuttled back and forth between both parents.

2 Alice and Mel separated in 1976 and officially divorced in December 1977.

3 Huey P. Newton, revolutionary activist and cofounder of the Black Panther Party, had fled to Havana in 1974, along with his partner (later wife) Gwen Fontaine, to avoid prosecution on a charge of murdering a young Oakland woman.

Undated

This is the urban winter. Very mild weather. From 70–80 degrees every day. Nights cool. A breeze constantly passing over the island.

The Cubans range in colors that are incredible, subtle in their different shadings. There are some blondes. Then dark haired blancos. Then creamy ones, then tan, then brown, then—with many, many other lovely shades— that beautiful, luminous black that "covers the bones with light."

Everybody works! In the countryside, on the way to Lenin School, men & women of all ages doing all kinds of work: building, smoothing, pruning, planting—all school age children are in school. Some little ones accompany their mothers. But the sense is of a whole people on the move, making secure the revolution.

July 8, 1977

I keep putting off beginning this journal because the things I must write, must admit by writing them, are hard, even threatening to me. My heart flutters miserably, my breath is unrelaxed. . . .

But, to begin.

My earliest memory of my father is this: I must be between 2 & 3. I am walking but I don't know if I can speak. I am standing on the porch of the house where I was born.

It is not summer, because there are no flowers blooming in the yard. My father comes up to the porch. He is carrying a tin syrup bucket (his lunch box). He is very dark and rotund. He stops before he reaches the steps up to the porch and smiles at me. I must smile back, because he really smiles and laughs, and begins to dance for me. He is doing perhaps the dance called The Black Bottom. His arms go out, and his legs and feet move very fast. With his mobile smiling face, this is very entertaining. I laugh and clap my small hands in delight.

Now it becomes so much harder.

I don't remember when I became aware that my mother was lighter than my father. My father was nearly black, though with a reddish cast to his skin which (this reddish cast) he inherited from his father, a man of brown-red skin & features commonly called "Indian." What I do remember is the value my father placed on my mother's "bright skin." He thought it beautiful and said so. I believe I heard him say more than once that he "didn't want no blackskin woman—" There was always a disparaging joke at the end of this sentence & I have no doubt repressed it.

But I also loved my mother's color. It was part of what made up my mother. She is darkskinned now, she darkened as she aged, and today when I see her I'm always a little surprised, as if my mother, the one I remember from childhood, is hiding somewhere within this darker one.

My father then rejoiced in my mother's light color. She, on the other hand, used to say she liked three things black: a black shoe, a black car and a black man. So they were well suited in their colors. Each having what s/he wanted.

Perhaps if they'd had no children, or if I had been the only child, I would not have been affected by my father's color preference. Since I was a girl, my mother's color preference didn't apply to me.

My eldest brother, Fred, is very dark, and was described as "handsome but dark." I do not know how this affected him. He married a virtually white woman. A woman of pale, almost translucent skin, huge gray-green eyes, and a tubercular cough.

When she came to visit us we wondered at the straightness of her auburn tinted hair, at the lightness of her eyes, and at her skin, which seemed even paler in the summer in Georgia when the rest of us were darker than ever from the sun. She was without character, as we had known it. She flirted with my next oldest brothers, was happy permitting my sister to clean up after her, smoked all the time & over everyone, did not discipline her child . . . But she was forgiven because of how she looked. We were proud to have this woman, this paleness, among us. We never noticed that, in herself, she was unexceptional.

But it is the next of my parents' children, Mamie, who is villain and sister victim of this piece, for she was born with skin even lighter than my mother's.

Mamie was very bright, intellectually, and this caused everyone to assume this smartness came from her color. She was praised for knowing a lot and for not being blackskinned at the same time. Perhaps she grew to believe herself that lightskinned people are superior—which would explain her subsequent rejection of us all.

My father worshipped Mamie. Since M. left home when I was a baby, I have no memory of how she and my father interacted while she was still a young girl. From hearsay later—from Mama, Ruth, my brothers—I learned that she was considered perfect in his eyes, even though there were apparently already signs on her part that she found him embarrassing. Not so much at first because he was black—perhaps not at all because he was black—but because he was poor & poorly educated.

My father rejected my sister Ruth. This was brutally clear. This was not because of her color (darker than Mamie, lighter than Fred, cinnamon) but because of "her ways" which reminded my father of his mother (shot & killed by her lover when my father was 11: she died in his arms, in a pasture, on the way home from church*) and his two sisters, Sally Mae & Daught. Both wild.

So, two sisters. One loved for her color & intellect, the other rejected for her "character." Coincidental that the lighter skinned one was the one loved. The darker the one rejected.

Mid-way between my mother's light & my father's dark, I emerged bright, intellectually, and a pretty child. At the age of two, & even earlier I'm sure, I was confident about my looks. Everyone told me I was "cute" and "sweet"—my mother & sister (Ruth) dressed me beautifully & a line long remembered in our family is this one, uttered to my father who was trying to decide how many of us he could fit into Miss May's car (he was her driver) to take to the circus: "Take me, Daddy. I'm the prettiest!" I was 2.

When I watch Rebecca primping in front of a mirror, or tossing her curls, I think of myself at her age. Confident, even conceited. "Take me, Daddy. I'm the prettiest!"

But this confidence was shattered when I was eight and had the "accident" that cost me the sight of one eye, though fortunately not the eye itself. For six years the gray scar tissue covered the larger part of the pupil, ruining—I thought—my looks. It was during those six years that much new

---

* No. Actually she died a few days later, at home, in bed. [AW's note to herself.]

feeling was born within me. Those six years that made me a human being. Those six years—so unbelievably painful—that made me a writer.

Knowing all this, I ask myself, Would you be willing to go through those 6 years again? And I answer, No.

My fear of rejection was born then.

Two things: when the incident happened, I lied to protect my brother. I said I had stepped on a piece of wire that flew up, hitting me. I did not tell my parents I had been shot.[1] For several days I was delirious with fever. My mother cooked delicious meals that did not tempt me. My father attempted to bring down my fever by making a garland of cool lily leaves which he held around my head—This is the last memory I have of my father touching me with love.—Not until years later did I learn the other act of love: that he had stood on the highway flagging down cars to take me to the hospital— because he was black the cars did not stop. Consequently it was a week before I saw a doctor. By then it was too late.

For the first time, I felt shame for how I looked. I was no longer—in my own eyes—"the prettiest."

It seemed to me my father began to withdraw. And I felt that, though I was a lovely brown which no one could deny, and intellectually bright, I was yet damaged and subject to being rejected. Perhaps it was during this time that I began my own habit of withdrawal, which culminated in my relationship with my father in my fourteenth or fifteenth year when I did not speak to him the whole year.

Each time I think of this I ask myself: Can this be true? You lived in the same house with your father but did not speak to him?

It sounds impossible. But this is how I remember it. I emerged from that year no longer loving him. Hating him, in fact, which was my object, I suppose, all along. If only he had known how to reach me. If only he had stopped my withdrawal before it was too late. If only he had refused me the right to be silent—forced me to talk to him. But he did not.

What else, besides my accident, triggered this? Surely it was my matur-

---

1   She was shot by a BB gun as her brothers played.

ing awareness that my father accepted Mamie's condescending behavior towards him & loved her still because he took such pride in how she looked. This made him seem an idiot in my eyes. At the same time, it aroused the most painful feelings of jealousy and envy. Doubly painful since I did not admire my sister's behavior all the time. Often she was wonderful, but as often she was not; she made my mother cry and made all of us feel inferior. She after all had seen the world & had white friends, even! We knew nothing, it seemed, by comparison.

How hard to bear this: a love for my sister (because of course I loved her very deeply) and envy, jealousy, mixed with censure. For to me she was not perfect as my father seemed to believe. He could not see her as she was, it seemed, which frustrated me—particularly during that period (& there must have been one) when I considered myself a rival for my father's love.

I could not face my father's rejection of me, so I did two things. Began an early rejection of him—finding fault in everything he did (which was unfortunately easy, he did so much that was faulty) and seeing his rejection of me not in terms of myself but in terms of Ruth. I convinced myself, in other words, that I rejected my father not because he rejected me, but because he rejected her. This saved my pride, my sense of myself as worthwhile. It was not, I don't imagine, good for Ruth.

What I internalized from all this, but repressed, was, among other peculiarities, an attraction to light/dark couples (symbols, I now suppose, of my parents) and a tendency to feel rejected very easily by the darker person.

But that is later in the story.

Last night I realized how stupid I have been lugging about my melancholia (which surely must have something to do with Papa's death.[1] Perhaps my soul knows it should be in Georgia saying good-bye to my only grandfather, the only link to so much that I will never be able to connect with again).

I am missing the stories of Papa's life that are being retold in Georgia this week of his funeral. I am also missing the congregation of his descendants, fellow & sister carriers of his blood, his features. His personality & character.

---

1   AW's paternal grandfather, Henry Clay Walker, died on July 1, 1977.

He was such a handsome man! His skin, in its red-brownness, so rich and masculine. His carriage so erect! His eyes so wise.

I liked everything about him except his cruelty toward his wife. I liked especially his name: Henry Clay Walker.

```
1977   Born July 7, 1889
  88   Died July 1, 1977
1889
```

Eighty-nine years. So long!

The blessing . . . He died simply, without suffering.

The Old House
Putnam County, Ga.
July 27, 1977

It is a cool, moist morning after a fine night's sleep. (I am thankful for sleep! For even the most transient calm!) (I am religious. If only I could find a way to regularly worship the natural wonder of the world).

R.[1] was at the airport. Knowing I would be seeing him brought back the backache which I've had, connected to him & my dilemma, for the past seven months. Amazing, this backache! Obviously my body is telling me the love we share is a burden.

I wanted to see him.

I dreaded seeing him.

I looked at him critically. I did not permit my gaze to cover him in gold.

Which raises the question: Did I manufacture him as an object of my love?

We had a drink & talked superficially about . . . his progress towards the Ph.D. & the Port Chicago Project.[2] Rebecca at camp. My helping to raise the first wall of Bertina & Stasia's house.[3]

---

1   Robert, alternatively referred to in the journals as Bob, and occasionally as Roberto.

2   Robert was beginning work on a project about the largest mass mutiny trial in US naval history. On July 26, 1944, in Port Chicago, California, an explosion killed 320 men, 202 of whom were Black. According to historical accounts, more than 200 men then refused to unload any more ammunition, which led to court-martial.

3   Bertina and Stasia are a lesbian couple that AW has befriended.

(Ruth says that Miss Shug gave her "drawers" to Ma<u>ma</u>[1]—Papa's wife: Miss Shug the lover & beloved—who asked for them. Surely this shows, on Ma<u>ma</u>'s part a belief in magic.)

July 27, 1977

Today we went to visit Papa's grave. I felt a distinct need to lie on top of Daddy's grave "to ascertain the view" from the position of his grave. While lying there, listening to the cicadas, crickets & the wind, I felt close to him. I wanted to tell him I was in pain, myself, and confused, myself, and helpless to do other than bear both the pain and the confusion—as he had done. The tears welled up out of my back and I burst into tears. The first tears I have shed for Daddy, five years after his death. I felt better for having shed them, wan, subdued, tired. I am learning more than I ever wanted to know about suffering. What it means to hurt and hurt and to have to trust to Time, and not one's own will, to ease the ache that never is far away.

Then we made the trek through the jungle to Papa's old house. An amazing pilgrimage with Ruth—who'd held me on Daddy's grave in sisterly comforting.

There are times when I am envious of Pam. Feel jealousy. Hate her. Other times I want to ask her to forgive me for ever hurting her. I realize that to me she has never been quite real. She always seemed a peripheral character, pale, small, maniacal & incomplete. Little more than an obstacle to what I wanted. But no doubt she <u>is</u> real. A complete, hurting human being. As far as I know, her pain through all this might be the same—or even more—than mine. At least I've only depended on Bob emotionally & sexually. She is financially dependent on him as well. Perhaps this last dependency makes them closer. He can "protect," she can "depend." There is so much anxiety involved in being independent. Just as there's shame, I think, in being dependent. "We live on what <u>I</u> make," Bob once said with some pride. I am

---

1 AW referred to her grandmother as Ma<u>ma</u> and her grandfather as Pa<u>pa</u>; note this reference to "Miss Shug," her grandfather's lover.

too used to feminists who never talk like that, even if they feel the need to <u>want</u> to be in such a relationship from time to time.

~Rachel & Henry~
<u>A Romance</u>[1]

1. Imagine Henry marrying a woman his family chose for him. Kate. He not loving her. She proceeds to bear his children.
2. He falls in love with someone else. Violently. Inevitably. Miss Shug. She proceeds to bear his children.
3. The wife, Kate, unloved, takes a lover.
4. The beloved, Miss Shug, gets married. Husband takes her away.
5. Henry beats Kate. Kate cannot leave her children. Her lover murders her in a pasture on her way home from church.
6. Henry is left with four small children. Beloved Shug has 2 children, his, but is married & living far away.
7. Henry hears of a man with available daughters. He proposes to hire one to tend his house. The father of the daughters won't hear of this for fear his daughter will be seduced.
8. He proposes that Henry marry Rachel—who is homely, a good worker, has had two dead children. Her only fault: generosity.
9. Henry marries Rachel without loving her. She is a good mother to the children. They grow to adore her. Henry still pines for early Beloved who comes back from time to time—her husband dies.

   Rachel is worked very hard. Never pretty, she doesn't begin to compare with Beloved. Henry uses her sexually. Beats her because he is now tied to her & not with Beloved.

   She endures. She has always loved him. Continues loyal & faithful.

---

1   This is an early outline for the novel, inspired by stories of her grandparents' lives, that would become *The Color Purple*.

10. He takes her for granted. The children grow up.

The relationship changes, now the children are grown.

He realizes he desires <u>her</u>. And that a life with the Beloved is impossible now. They are all getting old.

Rachel, having resigned herself to his not loving her, finds release in church. He sees the church as a rival.

They have been together forty years. He is afraid of losing her. She dies.

———

Plan: To buy a house in Park Slope by the time
my lease runs out/by December 1978.
Christmas – Georgia?
February – East Africa
May – England/Ireland
July/August – MacDowell

———

Arrival – Hugs – Chatter – lunch – a fire in the fireplace – listening to the rain – lovemaking (somewhat speedy but deep and satisfying)—a magnificent orgasm that made me call on God, which amused me even as I heard the words come from my lips "Who me?" I thought. But, as usual, <u>fine</u> sex. Although I forgot to help B. with his. Later, that I forgot how to help him also tickled me.

We lay together briefly—we showered, we smoked (a mistake) & he left for Atlanta & "dinner." Rushed sex definitely is inferior.

———

The Zora Hurston Reader[1] needs some sections on Zora's sojourn among the root workers. The articles read——boringly. They don't show—for the most part—her fiction's attention to detail. But it will be a fine volume.

———

1 AW was compiling a collection of Zora Neale Hurston's writings; it would be published in 1979 by the Feminist Press at CUNY under the title *I Love Myself When I Am Laughing and Then Again When I Am Looking Mean and Impressive*. The title is a quote from a letter Hurston wrote to her friend Carl Van Vechten, in response to some photos of her that he'd taken.

With the Janie Awakening Section from Their Eyes Were Watching God, and the two short stories, the scenes from Tell My Horse, etc.

I feel sometimes that my family and I could not be more strange to each other. And over the past several years, I've felt it especially true of Mama & me. I don't know this new Minnie Lue. She seems a shell. Is it only her religion? But she has also been completely conquered as a black human being—because she believes, indeed, that whites are better. This is painful to see in one's mother. The doting on white persons' compliments, even more than on her own sense of what is good, bad, or beautiful. The sickness of inferiority is everywhere in the family. The use of "nigger" unabated since last time. No concern for how the children will grow up to see themselves.

Undated, August 1977

Ms. $12,000 plus	=	after taxes 9,000
Yale $5,000	=	4,000
		$13,000
Lec. 6,000	=	4,000
		$17,000

I probably earn about $20,000 a year, and that's a lot.

My goal, by Dec. '78, is to have saved $30,000 to pay down on a house!

I'm getting closer to the feeling that this is right and something I want to do.

I feel good, children. After much struggle I do believe I'm catching a glimmer of light ahead!

I feel grateful to—everybody, including God, whom I go around thanking in my head all the time. Agnostic that I pretend I am!

Aug. 23 – Sept. 2

10 days with Robert—more or less.

Seeing him after a long period apart is always startling. Only occasionally is he handsome to me, and at those times his looks are enhanced by some activity in which he is involved: caring for a child, swimming, dancing.

My heart kept its cool except for brief periods of fluttering whenever we smoked grass. Which was fairly often.

But all in all, I passed the test. Not to permit myself to slip into the old pattern of adoration—desire to possess—or to dream about a future for the two of us together. Obsession is, I pray, over.

So the New England tour was a great success. NE as always beautiful, especially Vermont & upstate New York. Bob tender and consummate as a lover. Interesting & valuable as a friend, fairly good as a surrogate parent to Rebecca.

An almost blissful week. Swimming, climbing, and love-making, fucking, screwing, getting it on, loving and being loved. Bob's touch is the most gentle I've ever felt, yet the most assured & firm.

"I love you."

It does not come into my mind or heart to say it as much or with the fervor I once felt—and yet, I feel love for Bob. Perhaps I am no longer in love. And that's a blessing.

I waited last night after he left for some physiological distress. There was momentary slight tension in the shoulders, but I took aspirin and that eased it. Except for this cold & my period, I feel fine.

And assess myself thus:

A woman beginning the Prime of Life—33

with 6 books, all in print,

with health & a healthy, growing, intelligent & beautiful daughter,

$9,000 in savings and $11,000 more to come—

with two excellent part-time "jobs" that pay well.[1]

With time to write, travel, think.

With friends I love & who love me—Bob, Sheila, Mel, June, Judy, Gloria, Joanne, John & Susan, Vincent . . .

---

1 The jobs she refers to here: teaching a course at Yale and serving as a contributing editor to *Ms.* magazine.

My own apartment, in which I can do anything.

Can it be, I am a human being again!

I must devise a prayer to be said to the benign spirit of the universe.

I need to give thanks, to "talk to God"—to be in contact with the force that makes our lives unique through suffering and eventual grace.

September 5, 1977

There are moments when I feel frighteningly alone. It is at these times that I panic. Tense. Fear. It is in these moments too that I recall all the things I may have done that are "not right."

I often wonder, for example, if I was fair to Anais Nin in my "obituary" of her.[1] Perhaps I was wrong about her, self-serving. I probably should not have published the letter she wrote to me. Then there is the fear that Mel is basically duplicitous, not to be trusted. And that I no longer understand how to be on good terms with Rebecca. Then there is living in the city (without a garden). Without frequent contact with the earth I might as well be floating. Then too there is my dissatisfaction with my work and my need to form some sort of objective overview of what I wish to accomplish.

Should I take a leave of absence from Ms or shouldn't I? Will I really be able to cope with buying a house?

One idea that made excellent sense was about publishing my two books—simply to complete the book of poems & get it to Wendy.[2] Then tackle the essays.

I wish I felt closer to Wendy—trusted her more.

Is it all about trust, or the lack of trust?

Perhaps it is myself I don't trust. Perhaps I find myself doing or saying things of which I don't approve.

This is dangerous because so corrosive of self-respect. Hummm . . .

Bob? Even as I held him I wondered who and what I held. Though less

---

1 The obituary, "Anaïs Nin: 1903–1977," was published in the April 1977 issue of Ms., p. 46.

2 Wendy Weil, AW's literary agent.

this last visit than others. What is clear is that my trauma found a catalyst in Bob, but he was not himself the total trauma—as I once thought.

———

A terrible relapse—as bad as Jackson though it didn't last as long as my depressions used to.

Talked it over with Gloria, with Mel, with Sheila. Sheila <u>really</u> helped. She made me reflect on the beginning of the depression . . .

It was when Rebecca told me they'd torn up the rose bushes at the other house.[1] "My" roses. Roses over 50 years old. "They were diseased; weren't blooming," said Mel. They were uprooting <u>me</u>, I felt. The house on Midwood St. meant a lot. The garden was perhaps the part that meant <u>most</u>. In uprooting the roses they were <u>destroying my garden</u>, the metaphor and <u>fact</u> of my existence.

Also, Rebecca stayed with her father and I realized <u>I really needed her</u>. The kitten she gave me ran away. Next day Mel helped retrieve him, crying, from the backyard.

I think dope isn't good for me, that it causes my depression to deepen. Perhaps this is one reason that people who meditate don't smoke.

Sheila thinks I should try to get into a larger place as soon as possible— This makes a lot of sense to me. The apartment is charming but too small.

Sept. 21, 1977

In fact, I am in transition. All moves should, therefore, be cautious ones. The "relapse" was a serious one. I thought of death constantly, as relief. I know very well, however, that death is not what I want <u>this</u> early in life. I love living far too much, and am only too capable of finding and enjoying the next ambition (adventure) 'round the bend. If I can only hang on.

For the past few days I've missed B. Thought often of our trip to New England. The fun we had, the laughter that is ours alone. The swims amid a

———

1   At this point, Mel was living with his new partner, Judy, in the Brooklyn house that he and Alice once shared on Midwood Street. AW was living in a Brooklyn apartment, and they shared custody of seven-year-old Rebecca.

drunkenness of good feeling. Good, creative sex. I've wanted much to call him up. To write more than I have.

And yet, the new me—with backache gone (thank god!)—is holding me to a safer course. So saying: Don't go back to emotional dependence. Don't accept burdens you can't handle. You've suffered enough to last awhile. And so I've not called—I have never liked calling his house—and my letters, though loving (because of course I do still love him), are bright rather than warm.

The truth is I can't forget him. But I've worked sincerely at not doing myself in any further in the relationship. If we are to be loving friends who see each other only occasionally, then I shall stick to an emotional austerity that permits this arrangement to be beneficial rather than painful. The longing I can handle, the pain erodes my sense of worth and my sense of self.

Lectures lined up for the remainder of '77.

2,500	Sanford
200	Germantown
750	Williams
200	Folger
1000	Mercer
$4,650	

Bucknell? That would bring it up to $5000. All for savings. The house.

Soon a year will have gone by. My transitional year from dependence to independence. From a belief in the authority of others to (I hope) a belief in my own authority. If I can continue to grow out of the panic I shall be, continue to be, both grateful and happy.

In this latter period (Aug–Sept.) Rebecca has become more the center of my life than she has ever been. I notice that I respond to her as if she is someone whose feelings I profoundly respect. I am as careful of her as of a friend. In fact, I see her as a friend. And this has happened because she has shown me how little she thinks of being taken for granted. She asserts her right to share time with me alone. Her right to a share of my attention when we are entertaining a guest.

She has made demands!

So far (after two classes) I <u>like</u> being at Yale once a week. It is like a kind of rest. Exhausting as the actual teaching is. It amuses me that I "share" a room with Imamu Baraka.[1] He has it Mondays, I have it Fridays.

My students intimidate me a little, they are so articulate. But they are not <u>writing</u> about much. Their experiences seem to have been thin and boringly ordinary. My mind wanders when I read their work.

Lying on my gorgeous bed looking at Mel (who came to pick up Rebecca) I noticed again his uneasiness, his look of evasiveness. What is he hiding from himself? There have been times when I imagined going back to him—but always, fortunately, I remember I am thinking of a different, younger & more sensitive man than the one now before me.

Mel has never permitted himself to break down, even a bit. So much is feared, repressed. It occurs to me that he has rushed from one care-giver to another. I think he will be much more interesting after he's allowed himself a crisis.

But maybe this isn't all altruism? I'd like it to be. But I've been very, very

---

1 Amiri Baraka, previously known as LeRoi Jones and Imamu Amear Baraka, was an acclaimed, controversial African American writer of poetry, drama, fiction, essays, and music criticism.

angry with him, too. Because ours was a good marriage that needn't have atrophied.

I like <u>Ms</u> better, now that I'm committed to one day a week. One day there, one at Yale, the rest of the time to read, be with friends, an occasional lecture to give me travel & place me among mountains, Fall foliage, etc.

Oct. 3, 1977

Another good session at Yale. A very good decision this was to teach. New Haven is quiet, parts of it quite pretty. Relaxed.

On Saturday a long call from B. He thinks he can come East[1] even sooner than he'd originally planned. I am thrilled. But calmly. It is always momentous whenever I see him, but now I see it is possible to live without him— though I do not choose that option. I love him, finally, with open hands.

I've made up my mind, apparently, to fight my depressions and so, a week before my period I was careful to eat well, rest, get in some pleasant activities—movies, walks, friends—and to take my vitamins religiously, and to take Pamprin—2 pills a day for seven days. Result: no (knock on wood!) depression so far, & my period started today! I feel happy. All day I've walked about gazing at clouds. Loving them. Saying quiet prayers to the Spirit of the Universe, and loving Brooklyn. I may well stay here forever. And today I feel that's okay.

I look forward very much to buying a house!

10/5/77

While in New Haven I thought so much about Pam I had to write her. To explain to her simply that I wish her well & to say I'm sorry if I've hurt her. Throughout, the weight she's been to me is guilt, that I rejected her (phony-baloney offer of love she made or not) and confusion because I felt attracted to her. I like her aggressiveness, the way she wears old clothes.

I <u>seem</u> to feel better for having written. My guilt/memory had caused me to look at every small brown-haired white woman & see Pam.

---

1   Robert/Bob lives in the San Francisco Bay Area.

* * *

It appears I will make about $6,000 in lectures between Oct 13th & December 6th. This is good, because I can put it directly into savings for the house. My goal is to be able to make a $40,000 down payment—which should be possible if I can stick to $10,000 from G. The $11,000 from 55 Midwood, $10,000 I've saved, & $10,000 from lectures & royalties.

If this works out, it means that by September of '78, I can deal!

Looking back over this diary I see I'm concerned about money. It has dawned on me lately that insecurity is one of the biggest killers of art. Somehow the novel, or the next collection of stories, is seen as happening only when I'm in my own house, and managing things okay.

One of the reasons I was/am angry with Mel is that he did not try hard enough to keep me. He disagrees, of course, since "to keep me" he gave up his law practice in Mississippi & moved to New York—which he's always hated. Perhaps that's why he's angry with me! Even though now he is happier here than he was in Jackson.

Oct. 10, 1977

Mel came by yesterday to bring the rest of my clothes from 55 Midwood, to pick up the separation agreement papers and to sit (after I offered) and have a cup of tea. It was remarkably pleasant. He looked better than last time. Not as pale, aged. He is still suffering disappointment that he was not offered the Justice Dept. job.

Head of the Civil Rights Division. He's right—it should have been his. I felt real empathy for him. I told him my plans about the house—he worries that it will prove too great a responsibility. I hope not.

We drank tea. Laughed. Smiled at each other. Spoke of our daughter. When he left he kissed me on the cheek. I kissed him on the cheek. We parted with warm feelings—I suggested he and Judy go to Negril for a week.

Bob called. Happy to be coming East next week-end.[1] Said: "I've already

---

1 Bob still lives with his wife, Pam, in California.

got my ticket in my hot little hand!" What is this we have? A love. A relationship. The most intense of both our lives, I would guess.

Today I came across an old letter of Pam's. She is telling me what she liked and didn't like in Meridian and commenting on my visit to Bob's family in Atlanta with him. 10 months ago I couldn't have read the letter. And it still hurt some. Why? Because Bob is still her husband. He is mine only to the extent that he loves me—and because there are so many things to admire about Pam. Her apparent lack of jealousy, for example. The time she took to think about Meridian & give me her response.

I know that Pam feels rejected by me. As a bisexual, as a woman/white. While I simply want Bob. Not the pair.

I seem to be drifting, in my work. Is it because of my work at Ms & Yale? Is it because of the readings? On the other hand, I've been buying and reading more books than usual. And there is something going on in my head—a new novel is trying to form itself. If I can be at MacDowell[1] for July & August—perhaps I can get on paper a solid outline of what I want. A modern novel, about marriage.

After Thanksgiving – Nov. 25, 1977

A call from Bob . . . we reconfirmed what you, Diary, already know, viz, we love each other. Why is this so? I throw up my hands. We spoke of his mother's visit with me. To eat out with Sheila (at Sheila's) & Frank, & then live jazz . . . Zake's husband, saxophonist David Murray.[2]

At first I'd dreaded the weekend with Sadie,[3] but then, because she is so game, I enjoyed it. Looking at his mother I saw him.

I am truly thankful for my sister Ruth, for Rebecca, so patient & loving overall, for Bob, who has helped me grow up. . . . As well as my low, low blood pressure 90/62!

---

1   An artist residency program in New Hampshire.
2   Zake is the nickname of the playwright and author Ntozake Shange.
3   Bob's mother.

Great Spirit of the Universe I salute you in peace after the battles of this most difficult year of my life.

Dec. 15, 1977

Bob came back with The Story! Of the Port Chicago Disaster. His odyssey South a huge success. He is full of his script. I am full of—the apparent tenacity & growth of our deep caring for each other. As usual, sex/love with him incredible. Three hours of loving pass like minutes. My orgasms deep and intensely shared with this man who says: "I've discovered I'm not empty. That I am full!" So good to witness this, to be part of his growth. His eyes shine. They glow when he looks at me. I am always smiling when he is here.

Dec. 16, 1977

1. Wendy called to tell me Greil Marcus[1] is reviewing the re-issued Grange Copeland for Rolling Stone. Should appear in 3 weeks. Also, about then, in the New Year, G.M. is coming to town and would like us to meet. I say yes. Yes. Recalling that, in the New Yorker last year, he did my favorite (though limited, if long) review of Meridian.
2. She also says the selected essays: In Search of Our Mother's Gardens should do well.
3. I asked her about Bob's screenplay of The Port Chicago Disaster. She says yes, she'll read & if possible send it on or recommend it to the women of the Ziegler Agency on the West Coast.
4. Called Bob & told him this. He is tired, back home. Washing clothes, reading mail. Tending Casey.[2] Happy at hearing this news.

   I feel pleasure that he is pleased.

----

1 A well-regarded white male author, music journalist, and cultural critic, long associated with *Rolling Stone*.
2 Robert's young son with his wife, Pam.

5. We laugh again as we hear each other say: I love you. Who can fathom it? But I think—though I did not say it—he is becoming the man I always thought was there. But I'll be cool on this—because perhaps he isn't.

    <u>Anyway</u>

6. Finally reached the woman, Martha Pitts, who can get me through to Assata.[1] She says, ramblingly, that perhaps Assata can call <u>me</u> on Friday. That I will need a green press card to get inside the prison.

Dec. 20, 1977

It suddenly struck me tonight that I should start making notes for a new novel, one I can work on at MacDowell[2] this summer. And then I realized I'd acted on my deeply felt impulse to limit my external expression to cut out excessive speaking engagements. I canceled the benefit for <u>Heresies</u>[3] and also the panel discussion at Barnard. It felt good to say "No." And to plan—My plan is one reading a month. Nothing during the summer (other than writing & walking & thinking) and this should be quite possible on my <u>Ms</u> salary plus the readings & whatever royalties I receive. What makes the difference is now I've saved up the down payment for a house and have grant money stretching over two years! With such good fortune I should be ashamed not to produce at least a true confrontation with my own mind.

---

1   Assata Shakur, political activist and member of the Black Panther Party and the Black Liberation Army, was convicted in 1977 of murder for the 1973 death of a New Jersey state trooper during a shootout on the New Jersey Turnpike. Her supporters argued that the trial was unfair, as New Jersey law did not require prosecutors to prove that Shakur fired the shots that killed the officer. At this time, she was serving a life sentence at New Jersey's Clinton Correctional Facility for Women.

2   The MacDowell Colony in New Hampshire, the oldest artists' colony in the United States, was founded in 1907 to offer "creative individuals of the highest talent an inspiring environment in which they can produce enduring works of the imagination."

3   Founded in 1977, *Heresies* billed itself as "A Feminist Publication on Art and Politics." The magazine would continue to publish until 1993.

And that, of course, is why I'm so tense.

Tonight, curled up in bed with Rebecca. Me reading <u>The Women's Room</u>.[1] Insight written as trash—good! Perhaps it'll sell! And Rebecca also reading a novel—about witch-watching. Close, warm, good.

She does not seem afraid about Mel going to Washington. Though she seems resentful that he might marry her. (Judy). (Not Washington, D.C.)

I feel hardly anything that he might marry her. How over that all is. Definitely.

Dec. 21, 1977

After taxes my <u>Ms</u> salary is 8,400.00. My rent is

3,600.00

$4,800.00 is what's left for food, clothing, Rebecca.

If I could add another $10,000 each year from lectures & royalties—we'd be okay. More than okay really.

Now I shall lie in bed & read <u>A Fine Old Conflict</u> by Jessica Mitford. Tuscaloosa[2] is asleep on the sofa. The backyard is full of birds chirping, chirping. A damp, chilly day. My period is four or five days off. This means I should start preventative measures against depression. (Have done so.)

Risk makes my back ache. (It's been aching off & on for a year.)

Mel came over last night to bring Rebecca clothes. She'd been wearing the same outfit for three days and stunk. We discussed the Washington move.

He says that, just as I'd thought, our divorce[3] has made Judy more eager to get married. He asked my opinion. I advised a period of time—3-6 months—to reflect. Time <u>alone</u>. He nodded at this but really has already made up his mind. He says his "equivocation" makes him wonder if re-marriage is the right thing, just now.

---

1   Published in 1977, *The Women's Room* is the debut novel by Marilyn French, an American feminist author.

2   The family cat.

3   Alice and Mel's divorce was finalized in December 1977.

Well, for me it isn't, I offer. He says he told Judy to "let him recover" from the divorce, first.

I'm very happy he's quit smoking. He also takes care to tell me he's actually reading stuff that isn't Law. I say Good for Him!

Rebecca is my friend! Becoming more solid all the time. This morning she asked me to awaken her more gently—as if she sleeps more lightly than her father who once slept through a fire & the noise of 4 fire trucks. But I'll try. In fact, if I can only wake up myself, I enjoy kissing her awake.

Dec. 23, 1977

Slept poorly last night but went to bed with big plans for writing a review of Smedley's <u>Portraits of Chinese Women in Revolution</u>.

I like Smedley saying she is not one of those to die for beauty. I certainly feel I could easily die for lack of it. Ugliness, unrelieved, would kill me off quicker than depression, probably.

Part of my sleeplessness is fear of how I shall "get through" the 25th. That huge "family day" across the land. Rebecca will be with her father— I suppose I shall work on the Smedley review now that Assata can't see me until the new year.

Last Christmas was our first alone. But was it really? Probably not.

In any case, meditation, lots of sleep, good eating are in order—along with vitamins, work and reading.

Dec. 24, 1977

Christmas Eve. A bright, sparkling day here in Brooklyn. No sign of depression yet . . . Thanks to the Great Spirit. Of course! "The Great Spirit!" Once again, Native Americans got there before me.

A fine time last night, reading Smedley until four in the morning. Re-reading her splendid autobiographical novel in preparation for doing the review of Chinese Women. So many thoughts churned up by her muscular prose.

*   *   *

My mind seems to have been waiting for this slowed pace I've given myself. It seems to be saying: "Look, look at this! I've worked all this stuff out & I've just been saving it for you!"

I had some wonderful thoughts about bi-sexuality. . . . The problem with sex is that people have gotten used to thinking you have to be "ambivalent" or "committed" "straight" or "gay-lesbian." Either–Or. But nature is much more interesting than that.

Dec. 26

June[1] reminded me of some of the miseries of Christmas last year that I'd blocked: That it was the Xmas she had cancer. It was the Xmas Rebecca & I were in our new little apartment alone. I was not in good shape. I recall that time was hanging rather heavily on my hands. . . . She is so right—what an abysmally painful Xmas season <u>that</u> was! And how different this one is, when I feel a growing trust replacing the fear of solitude.

Dec. 26, 77 after midnight

Mel tells me he is writing a diary! Can anyone doubt divorce is excellent for him!

A.M. 12:30 Jan. 1, 1978

Was I also alone last year on New Year's Eve? It seems to me I was. But it must have been quite different. Tonight I'm reading Gorky's <u>Mother</u>. I also watched "Come Back Little Sheba" on the tube. Some firecrackers went off signaling the New Year & there is still noise far away . . . Tuscaloosa & I are snuggled in together, content.

Perhaps that's the difference. I sip my glass of white wine and consider [in the middle of this consideration Bertina[2] called to wish me Happy New Year!] that another year, a hard, hard year has come & gone, and I survived it. [Bertina just called back to invite me over there—& I'm going. Later, diary.]

---

1 The poet June Jordan, a longtime friend.

2 Bertina is a friend of AW's who has expressed an attraction to her, but Bertina is in a relationship with another woman.

Some dancing, ice cream (why, my diet!) Bertina stealing caresses—this seems to me so childish and untrue. It chills all ardor I might have felt. But it was a pleasant distraction.

I felt quite unmoved, really, beside her. It causes me to wonder—I care for her, but in what way? Am I forcing yet another bi-sexual experience on myself to prove I can be the way I think is "the way people should be"? Dancing with Bertina I thought—Great Spirit, help me—of Robert. And how, dancing with him fills me with such happiness I smile as if my mouth is lost to me.

But mainly I thought of myself—lucky to be among friends who wish me well.

Well, well, **January 1, 1978**! The time has not exactly flown, but in any case, I am still here. I am still here and I have continued with my work. Since that fateful July 17–18 months ago I have published essays, book reviews, a foreword to Hemenway's book on Zora,[1] Anais Nin's obituary, letters to the editor, lectures. I have travelled to Cypress, Greece, Jamaica and suffered & struggled with myself and the politics of those countries every step of the way. I have completed another volume of poems. I am finishing a collection of my essays. I have compiled a Zora Neale Hurston Reader. I have taught Advanced Fiction a semester at Yale. I have continued in pleasant fashion at Ms. I have been invited to read and have accepted, all over the United States. I have given benefit readings. I have left my husband & have been mutually and amicably divorced. I have moved into my own apartment where I have now lived a full year and a month. I have had my failing ear improved by surgery. I have replaced my front teeth. I have made new friends & many new kinds of love. I have contemplated suicide seriously only twice—or perhaps 3 times. I have resolved not to be a suicide because I love life which I know, better than death which I don't, and which I suspect is the ultimate bore.

In this period of my life I have discovered—a major discovery—that

---

1   Robert E. Hemenway's *Zora Neale Hurston: A Literary Biography* was published in 1977, with a foreword by AW.

sex is rightly acclaimed one of the great urges of humankind. That it is in fact incredible & that I have an enormous capacity for sensual pleasures. —I have discovered also that I am alone in the world but that that is the true condition of everyone. That to pity myself because of this, or to fear it very much is to waste energy & time.

Today I am deliberately bringing this notebook to a close, noting briefly what I have elsewhere noted more fully—in the brown leather notebook from Bob & in the blue paisley one from Gloria.

This morning I've been lying in bed with the Times. I woke up this morning, not in the panic that tortured me so many of my mornings last year but with passable calm. I made myself a nice cup of tea. I gazed at myself in the mirror. This is what I saw: A face that still resembles the face I had when I was six. A creamy brown red skin, eyes that are open, a mouth that has known kisses and which loves to kiss. I have decided to seriously diet. I weigh, this morning, 130 1/2 lbs. I will attempt a weight of 122–25 by the end of the month. I do not wish to be thin but voluptuous only in bust & hips. There is an incipient belly I must rid myself of. And, if I am to wear jeans more often—which I like—I must maintain the figure I want in them.

In the Times I read Vincent's letter to the editor in which I and Meridian are mentioned. He calls me one of "our best younger artists." Art may or may not have something to do with age. What moves me is Vincent[1] himself, my friend and more since July 23, 1976.

There is little to be said about Bob (now Robert) that has not been said in the other notebooks. He was on hand when I looked at this apartment after renting it. He was on hand to verify one of the separation agreements from Mel. He and I have continued. Persisted really, almost against our will. Though June might recover from a broken heart in 3 weeks, I discovered my heart to be somewhat more attuned to the slow pace with which I confront everything else in life. I love a man (Robert) with a love that remains largely inexplicable to me. But I no longer suffer on a grand scale. Now I suffer modestly. Mainly loneliness, a yearning for him when we are apart.

---

1   Historian Vincent Harding.

But this diminution of suffering came about through struggle so profound I was forced to rethink my life from the period in my parents' lives before my own biological conception.

Never have I felt the need to deeply question Robert's love for me, only its quality and his sanity.

Our times together have been invariably profound. All anyone could hope of lovemaking, companionship, anxiety and hope.

I am beginning to love another woman. This is still something of a puzzle to me since I do not know how much of it is curiosity & adventurousness on my part (the writer as fool, pursuing the unknown). I am a fool in some ways, but this doesn't make me as indignant as it once did.

I have a cat who at this moment is dreaming underneath my elbow as I write. He comforts me. Perhaps when I am old I will be someone with masses of cats, cows, and other creatures. Flowers, too, of course.

The questions that have occupied this period are: Can I survive & be reasonably happy on my own, supporting myself and Rebecca? Can I live outside of the marriage that gave my life such stability during most of its existence? Can I write even while riddled with anxiety, jealousy, fear of rejection, aloneness; in short, can I assume responsibility for my own life?

And love.

Jan. 4, 1978

At the moment when, exhausted from lugging the groceries up the stoop, I saw the package inside the door, I guessed what it might be. Was it the flatness of the package? Its weight and size when I held it in my hand? Perhaps I felt sure of what it might be coming up the stairs, it in with my groceries. My mind stayed on it while I stowed perishables in the refrigerator. Then I flung myself upon it—thinking for one moment that perhaps it was another of Robert's household gifts. Perhaps another hot plate. (Hot dish holder). But it is this, this book! A beautiful thing that moves me because I realize Robert truly sees me as someone who writes, that he desires to be with me as I write, and he wants it all to be beautiful. Reader, I adore him.

I pray that this book will be filled with as much growth and self-discovery as the other one, but with less pain.

Jan. 5, 1978

For this fine paper I should have a fine fountain pen. Alas, but, so what. I can write. I can see. I have fingers. I love and am loved. Rebecca, working beside me on the bed, is healthy and bright & lovely. I am shapely. Alert. Learning to cook well.

Well. So. Today filled with work glorious work! On the essay "A Child of One's Own."[1] I like what is happening in my writing—I seem to be making a new form that goes this way & that, but with me and History steady in the center.

I called Robert to thank him for the journal. He is delighted with my pleasure, as he always is. <u>Also</u> everything is so sensual between us; a telephone call about work becomes erotic because of our response, not to the words, but to the timbre of each other's voice.

Jan. 6

Just received a second call from Assata Shakur. We discussed her "Birth Journal."[2] She is not pleased with it, wants to rewrite it. I encourage her to write it any way at all she likes, since only then will it be worthwhile for her and valuable to other women. I told her I'd like to visit her in prison but that I don't know exactly "why." I have no "plan." She says I should come, she'd like to see me.

Jan. 14

Yesterday I learned I am to become a homeowner! I accepted the news with some trepidation. All that I've read seems to say I'll save a lot on taxes.

The house! 4 stories, two rooms per floor. Tall & skinny, like a person. I think I should put in a deck in time for spring. And that's all. I can save the

---

1   This essay—about motherhood and work, and the value of having only *one* child—was originally delivered as a talk for a 1979 program at Sarah Lawrence College honoring the poet Muriel Rukeyser, who'd been AW's teacher there. AW would eventually publish the essay in her 1983 collection *In Search of Our Mothers' Gardens: Womanist Prose*.

2   An unpublished manuscript of autobiographical poetry and prose that Assata Shakur was working on in prison.

painting until another time. A deck and an air conditioner on the bedroom floor.

When I'm inside the house, 423A 1st St., I don't feel it is small. It seems small only when I think about it. The bathroom is small. It might be nice to make one of the bedrooms into a bath—with a bidet.

Feb. 3, 1978

Just returned from a week in San Francisco with Robert. Extraordinary trip. . . .

Two interesting visions occurred when we were together: I had a vision of us slaying dragons—back to back, swords flashing. Then off we went to glide down a river in a canoe. My hand trailing in the water.

Then, when I was listening to Stevie Wonder with Robert & hearing the song "As"—"I'll be loving you always" I saw, not Robert or anybody else. Just myself. Alice loving Alice. Kissing Alice. Embracing Alice. Dancing all around the world with Alice. This self-love & self-generated joy continued through other songs.

It is true. I do love myself. I accept myself. I take myself to my bosom. I feel such tenderness for myself, often so lost, confused. Struggling.

When Robert & I sleep together we sleep soundly. I hear nothing. Think of nothing. It is delicious.

Feb. 16, 1978

The day after Mamie's 46th birthday.[1] Ruth called last night to say M. is in terrible shape: no money, no food, ill. According to Ruth she had an attack (of frustration, humiliation) at the Welfare office (!) where she had gone for emergency money after the blizzard. The Welfare people no doubt treated her like they treat all poor people—with condescension & contempt.

Ruth took her food, braving the snow. She said M. lined it all up neatly on the floor & played with it, enjoyed it, like a child.

I am shocked at this word on her condition. I just sent a birthday check

---

1 Mamie and Ruth are Alice's older sisters.

and some Harriet Tubman stamps. I will try to send something often. Although I feel free of her domination—I don't think she could make me cry as easily now as fifteen years ago—I still feel uneasy, somewhat fearful about her. I want us to be on good terms, but not necessarily intimate ones.

Robert arrived Saturday—cheerful, bright, funny. Gone the gloomy stranger of the week before. Our three days together were wonderful. Each day different, each in its own way, delightful.

We talk so much better together now. I know it has everything to do with his trial separation from Pam. I don't feel he is going back to her when he leaves me. He asked me if I thought I'd ever marry again. I said I thought not. That I would like to live with someone, but not ever again as a "wife." I pointed out how society insists on married women <u>being</u> wives, even when the husband doesn't.

We discussed money. I explained to him how bad I've felt—& been encouraged to feel bad <u>by him</u>—when I haven't made less money than him. I told him I had seriously tried to figure out a way to make an unthreatening amount of money so that he wouldn't be upset. That I consider this foolish. After all, I can't promise to always make less money than him or that I'll always make more. I can't <u>promise</u> I'll make any. And I shouldn't have to worry about his feelings or fear his (or Pam's) snide remarks that I am "bourgeois." Where were they when I had no money whatsoever & my family didn't either? They were both looked after by parents with money & good jobs.

Undated

There must have been a moment, sometime, when black men understood black women. However, it is not now. Nor was it in recent memory.

It is that mythical moment however which we must remember, must cherish, if we cherish our destiny as a people, as we cherish our common history & our common children.

Undated

What made me feel better today? I stayed home. I worked. I meditated, briefly. I slept a lot last night and this morning.

Part of my downness is that I don't want to be separated from Rebecca this coming year.[1] A school year is a long time for her to be away.

March 9, 1978

My anxiety must be because of the impending move. And what can I do to make it less?

I am afraid of the move even though I desire it. Because it will mean strangeness, a higher monthly note, $467.06. I am fearful also because I see my money dwindling.

I can't understand why I'm so afraid I <u>won't</u> manage when in fact, my affairs look fine. I feel <u>some</u> terror at not holding onto my job at <u>Ms</u> but I must remember my anxiety over being there, too.

If worse comes to worse the IRS can wait, or I can even take out a loan.

I am in need of love. And loving. With that, all this other stuff would just be—"other stuff." I fear I am falling out of love (love already) with Robert. Yet, to face this is to face a void. And that scares me. Because actually I have thought consistently of Robert for the past 2 years.

He has filled hours, days, months of my life. If he is no longer there, what is?

So what have we got:

1. News about Mamie on welfare & "crazy" from Ruth. Which frightened me because she is my closest model.
2. Tina, 32 yrs. old, killed by pneumonia & her husband, my old classmate, Murl.
3. I owe 5 thou in taxes.
4. I'm taking a leave from Ms.

---

1   Rebecca, now eight years old, has been staying alternatively with AW and Mel, since both parents have been living in Brooklyn. However, with Mel's impending move to Washington, DC, the family has been making plans for Rebecca to spend the school year there with her father.

5. Money is going to be tight.
6. I dread telling Edgar[1] we're leaving.
7. Bad communication with Vincent.[2]
8. Distance problem with Robert.

Good grief! No wonder I'm upset!

Yes. <u>And</u> Rebecca may be going away next year to school in Washington.

On the good side, I got:

1. Travel to the desert with Robert in 3 weeks
   a. To see the Southwest!
   b. Painted desert
   c. The Grand Canyon!
   d. Cacti!

Brings us to April 5th. That's far enough to look. Thank you, Great Spirit. I feel better.

Next day—March 10, 1978.

I <u>still</u> feel better. Was very careful all day not to break the spell.

I told Edgar (by note) that we're moving. A moment of fondness between us on the stairs. He says forget the April rent—my security check will cover it even if my lease isn't over. I thanked him. Said we have enjoyed living here. So that was <u>easy</u>. The forms from the bank that I needed to get a cheaper mortgage are coming from the Bowery. <u>That's</u> good.

Mel tells me the money from the house will not be taxed. That's good.

I have more $ in my savings account than I thought. <u>That's</u> good.

I am due one more payment from Ms.

U. of Mexico is providing $1200.

---

1 Her landlord.

2 She'd hurt her friend Vincent's feelings by criticizing his cologne but felt better after calling to apologize.

U. of Cal at San Diego should come up with an even $1500. The expense money should cover plane fare <u>and</u> car rental.

Amherst has asked me to be Visiting Artist year after next—'79–80. So has Yale. Looks like I really should take this coming year solely for my own work—the time will surely come when I'll have to work for others instead of myself.

An offer from California wouldn't be bad.

Sunday—March 12, 1978

This morning a headache threatened to develop. But I got up, took aspirin, washed dishes, swept, washed my hair. Bought the <u>Times</u>. Mel came by & picked up Rebecca. A bit of warm feeling. But an edge to it. Somehow.

Mainly though I wanted to record that I feel better still. That the depression lasted for about four days. Immediate trigger, my tax bill. But <u>before</u> that, the business with Mamie. The "murder" of Time. The fear of being alone next year.

I feel some anxiety. But that deep well of despair is more shallow tonight.

Last night I felt like praying on my knees. While there I had this insight/help: One reason I should not kill myself is that I enjoy the beauty & wonder of the world/life much more than I could possibly enjoy the nothingness of death.

Death is the ultimate bore.

No grand canyons. No deserts. No great skies & cumulus clouds. No coming of spring.

4 days of feeling rotten. Better, I think, than last September because I faced up to probable causes sooner & didn't lay it on my relationship with Robert.

Still, I must devise a plan for these periods.

March 17, 1978

My eleventh wedding anniversary with Mel!

We're no longer together but it was a good marriage. We were able to do the things we wanted to do.

Some good talks & letters with Robert. He says he misses me and also wants us to be together. I certainly need to be with him. I miss his love & his loving.

But I must plan carefully so as not to erode my independent base.

April 6, 1978

Robert and I have decided to live together! (For a year, in San Francisco, beginning in September.)

We met in Albuquerque on the 30th, after my lecture & reading at the University of New Mexico. Rented a car and began the drive toward San Diego by way of Mesa Verde in Colorado.

Robert is no longer supremely beautiful to me. I seem to love him on another level, a deeper level. When we are together I feel at rest, as if I've come home. He says with me he does not feel lonely.

Our first night: a motel duplex with fireplace in the lower Rockies. I became ill—from the exhaustion of the lecture/reading (which went well, actually), the excitement of seeing Robert, the desert, the mountains, etc.! An indifferently prepared dinner and two and a half ~~bottles~~ glasses! of wine. (Threw up, had diarrhea, plus my period & cramps). Ugh.

Robert was tender, lovingly helping me deal with weakness in knees, swimming in head. Vomit.

Then I fell asleep—woke in the night halfheartedly attempted to make love to him—because we had both looked forward so much to making love—but he said: we need to sleep. And he was right.

We reached Mesa Verde the next day. A wonder of human ingenuity and common sense. A feeling of affection for the Anasazi who built the cliff dwellings. Robert beside me in the sun. Perfect happiness.

Then on toward Arizona and the Grand Canyon. And the desert.

On the way to the G.C. I saw (we saw) a sunset over a smaller canyon, one of the wonders of my life & my favorite sight during the trip. A sky of gold and pink & green, with great & small clouds of blue/gray & huge white. A sun golden & hanging in the huge sky. The canyon, green to the lips, below. Exquisite. We stopped, of course, to see it. To love it with our eyes.

The canyon, though magnificent, did not move me as much. We stayed at a lodge. Made wonderful love most of the night. Slept in each other's arms.

When I sleep with Robert I sleep completely.

The next day, we awakened to snow—dawdled a bit to let the sun and wind clear it away. Then walked—a <u>beautiful</u> walk—around the edges of the canyon. Robert photographing me in various humorous positions. Our mutual fear of our great height affecting us & making hand holding extremely meaningful.

Then on toward the sun & the desert. Miles of desert flowers, rocks—formations of great beauty, whimsy, dignity. Robert beside me in the car . . . I felt at peace, wanting nothing more.

And of course we talked about our future together.

I propose to rent my house for all of next year. Robert and I will find a place together in San Francisco. We will need a minimum of five rooms. A yard and a fireplace. Flowers!

I feel I could well just stay with Robert, indefinitely. But something tells me: keep your house, your furniture. Try the city (SF) & Robert for a year. See how you work there. I think I will love San Francisco. It seems to me I always have—since before I even saw it. But I fear it too. It seems too new to love, somehow. And yet, I have already loved it.

April 14 — Day before taxes.

This week, which I faced with terror, went very well. Why, because I took a no-nonsense no-stall attitude toward <u>work</u>. On Monday I went to Yale to get copies of Zora's photographs for <u>The Reader</u>.[1]

I was trembling inside most of the day from my fear/anxiety over moving, Rebecca, missing Robert, etc. But looking at the photographs of Zora I had to laugh. She is up on somebody's chairs doing a crow dance! They will be perfect for the reader. I want her laughing on the cover, frowning on the back.

Then on Tuesday I worked on the material in the <u>Reader</u>.

---

1   AW refers here to her work on a groundbreaking collection of Zora Neale Hurston's writings, to be published in 1979 by the Feminist Press at CUNY under the title *I Love Myself When I Am Laughing and Then Again When I Am Looking Mean and Impressive*.

Should I include "Six-Bits"[1]—it <u>is</u> sexist. Very. Perhaps I should leave it out. But I want Z. represented fully.

Wednesday I began writing up my notes & drafting the preface. Thursday I polished. Today I worked on "Laurel"[2]—and the week went by!

Now Rebecca & Brenda[3] are away for the weekend. The apartment is quiet. I read, watched television. Meditated. Napped. Earlier I'd called Robert to be sure he was okay. He's hit with taxes—as are we all.

Working on a paper to deliver in Los Angeles in May—where Vincent, he reminds me—will also be speaking.

After all this time, talking to him makes me feel my heart as a distinct organ. Amazing!

Also read next to the last draft of Michele Wallace's book <u>Black Macho and the Myth of the Superwoman</u>. It is a <u>vital</u> book but Michele doesn't take it far enough. Her projections & recommendations need expanding.

Rebecca showed me a book of names in which "Alice" means Truth.

---

1   Hurston's 1933 short story "The Gilded Six-Bits."

2   AW's autobiographical short story about a young Black woman, Annie, who, while working in the civil rights movement in the South, begins a passionate affair with her polar opposite, Laurel, a young man she describes as a "parody of the country hick."

3   Brenda, AW's cousin who has recently moved to Brooklyn from Georgia, has been helping take care of Rebecca, especially when Alice is traveling.

Undated

Have just returned from a lovely walk in the park with Brenda, whom I like. We discussed our parents, which we often do.

Spring is here! The trees are turning green. Etc. I feel eager to be in my own house. To be airing and priming and planting. I feel good about owning a house again.

And I'm not so anxious as I was about money. Perhaps I'm getting used to looking out for myself.

Thoughts of Robert are mild. I miss him and think of him a lot, but I also am alive in other moments.

April 24, 1978

A letter from Robert in which he explains part of his depression of two weeks ago was from anxiety that he had not told Pam of our plans to live together next fall. Now he has told her but he says she has taken it surprisingly well. I don't suppose I'll ever understand them. I worry about Robert's indecisiveness. His slow acquisition of self-knowledge. But on the other hand, the way he has tried to make the break as gentle as possible, his love of Casey,[1] I admire.

A glorious day in Brooklyn. Sun, sky. The big green is coming.

Today I worked on The Zora Reader. Finally faced my own dislike of Zora at different periods in her career. . . . There is a stubbornness in Zora that precluded certain kinds of intellectual experience. She stopped growing.

She fell back on earlier modes of being—they were not "wrong," only odd for the different time she was living in.

Today I am feeling tired but quite happy. I like having my desk overlook the street. I can see the mail person bringing the mail. Today he brought a letter from Robert.

I do like the house. It is entirely charming! My bedroom is dark and cool and quiet.

---

1   Casey is Robert and Pam's young son.

5/12/78

I continue to like the house so much I never want to go out. All day I feel peaceful and abstracted by work & thoughts of work.

I've done very good work on The Reader the past two days. Tomorrow I'll be finished. I've only a morning of typing at the most. I'm beginning to be glad again that I'm doing the Reader . . . and very happy with the way things are going for Zora. She was right to think New York City was bad for the creative spirit. It is—even in my little house I feel the discordant energy of the city. Too many people. Too little space. And yet—to live in New York, what I have is ideal. Enough personal space, beauty about me, a garden.

Robert called this morning. He is going over to look at the apartment Tillie[1] called me about. $300, 2 baths, 3 bedrooms. Furnished.

We can take it, maybe, July through August & August through October. Robert suggested I do my MacDowelling in S.F. So I will plan to move out there in August. So this place would be sublet August–August. A year.

Thank God I'm not in love with my possessions or it would be difficult to leave them.

I will just take Mae Poole and a few other members of the family. Little Alice.[2]

Fortunately, it won't be hard to keep track of my $ records, since I know I only have the Guggenheim plus 3 months of Ms $.

I should plan to spend a week with Rebecca about once every two months.[3]

The minute the reader is out of my hands I must start a file on Rachel & Henry.[4]

—

---

1 Tillie Olsen, the feminist writer, was a friend who lived in San Francisco.

2 Here, AW refers to a photo of her great-great-great-grandmother, Mae Poole, and a photo of herself as a child, at about age 6.

3 The plan is for Rebecca to live with her father in Washington, DC, for the school year.

4 An early working title for the new novel AW is contemplating, based on her grandparents' marriage; ultimately, it will become *The Color Purple*.

Rachel & Henry
A
Story of
Struggle and Love

Undated, mid-May 1978

A reading Tues. night at Bedford Hills, a women's prison. Entirely depressing. Women passive. My cold uncomfortable. Energy level low. A little prison goes a long way with me. I used to think I'd make good use of prison—I'd read & write & study. But I wonder . . . perhaps the knowledge that I'm enclosed would drive me crazy.

Since Brenda has been staying with us I eat much better. I do most of the cooking but knowing that she likes to eat wholesome food helps me prepare it that way & prefer it that way myself.

I haven't eaten sugar in months. And I feel better. Nor have I had coffee. I've had lots of vegetables, fruit, pickles, etc. Oatmeal, which is a great breakfast. Filling & nutritious. Plus, g<u>ood</u>.

Rebecca is making some dinner for herself. Afterward she and I are going to lie in my bed and write stories. Sometimes I feel distant from her. I see a streak of Miriam[1] in her. It saddens me whenever I see it. (Self-centeredness. Vanity. And then too R. looks so much like her). She is coming now—she's eating a sandwich of peanut butter & grape jelly. I tell her she should have milk with it but she declines.

A remarkably pleasant weekend. Bertina came over Friday night for smoke & kisses. Then Saturday night we went dancing. Have I ever had such a good time dancing? Have I ever danced better with anyone? I think not. (Except with, of course Bob—we are just two fools in a class by ourselves). Bertina is upset because I plan to live with Robert next year. I found I didn't know what to say to her. I could not say "No, I will not go off with Robert." I <u>want</u> to go off with Robert.

---

1   Mel's mother.

But the dancing was a wonderful thing. Bertina dances like a devilish angel & she's <u>so</u> beautiful. I've never seen anyone more beautiful. The drawing of her over my mantle (not <u>really</u> her, but her) doesn't capture the liquid quality of her soft black eyes.

We went to La Femme, a lesbian bar & disco. <u>Lots</u> of women having a great time together. Met Olga & Nancy, Bertina's friends. Nancy is Puerto Rican, Olga is Chilean—I like them, especially Olga, a lot. . . .

. . . Bertina & I do a lot of touching: stroking, caressing, kissing on the cheek and neck, the hands, arms. And this is very nice. We are attracted to each other but at some point—we stop. It is as if there is no goal in our lovemaking & we can stop just anywhere. So that I have climaxed only once with her—& I don't think she ever has. I think sex—the abandon of sex—frightens her. She is afraid to let go, to "lose control."

Which is precisely what I am trying to learn to do—lose control. The more I lose, the better.

When I am with her I often fantasize about Robert—primarily, I think, because it is he who taught me what I know about making love. The things I do that give B. such pleasure are things Robert does to me.

Sometimes I think part of my problem in making love to B. is my conviction that making love with Robert is the best—I want to reach the point where I can feel it is all good—which it all is—just different.

5/18/78

Just sold "Goodnight, Willie Lee, I'll See You in the Morning"[1] to Dial for $2,500 advance—that will pay for the bathroom! Fantastic.

Joyce Johnson, my new editor (first woman). Blonde, short hair, round head & face, large gray eyes. Reminds me of the little white girl my mother used to keep, Elizabeth Candler.

---

1   AW's third collection of poetry, published in 1979. Writing these poems of "breakdown and spiritual disarray," Walker says, "led me eventually into a larger understanding of the psyche, and of the world."

5/19/78

Finally there's light, tentative sun! After two weeks of rain.

Mel still has not given me my share of the money from the house—he's waiting for his lawyer to send all the records so he can account for how the money is divided. I figure this: if the house sold for $66,000 & we bought it for 51,000 that leaves $15,000 plus our down payment of 35,000 mortgage or 15,000 + 16,000 = $31,000. 31,000 / 2 = 15,500 of which I already have taken 5,500 = $10,000 left of which I pay an undetermined amount of closing costs, realtor and lawyers' fees—approximately $2,000. Which leaves $8,000 plus $500 approx for dental insurance. Roughly $8,500.

My aim is to have $10,000 left in my savings account, which has only $3,743.35 now.

—

The Boston trip was a tremendous strain—the cold, my reluctance to see Mamie. Mamie turned out to be the right thing to do. She looked the same. Seemed cheerful. Somewhat studied cheerfulness at times. But her health does not seem bad, though she led me to believe it is.

She lives in a place called Windsor Village in Waltham. She has just enough space, a bedroom & study & bath upstairs, a kitchen & large living room downstairs. She gave me a white box that she made as I was leaving.

Among her curios upstairs was a photo print (on a block of wood) of Zora! Most amazing. She had no idea who it was!

I felt entirely calm, entirely grown up with her perhaps for the first time. I enjoyed being with her. I like her humor, her true eccentricity.

The double readings were too much. But a good feminist crowd that I enjoyed.

Boston made me realize anew how filthy N.Y.C. is.

A week from now—if the Lord wills—Robert & I will be together. Right here, in this bed.

—

Anyway, I had a pleasant conversation with Mel. He actually ate & drank something: apple juice & shrimp & teased me—now that we're divorced I make lots of money _and_ blossom into a great cook. How come? I remind him he only ate meat & potatoes, which was not a challenge. We shared an hour with Rebecca who is thrilled to be the star in her school play The Wizard of Oz. She is the Wicked Witch of the West with only one line but with that one line she apparently steals the show. She does not want me to see her—says it would make her nervous. I understand this, though at first I was hurt.

Then, a nice quiet little house to myself. I read more of Nin's 3rd diary,[1] my favorite thus far—or perhaps I am just now beginning to understand her. Many fabulous insights about friendship, love, the need to save a human space when all around us there is bestiality, inhumanity, ugliness and war. I misjudged her, I think, & I am sure to regret it always.

Really in tuned. In tune. With Anais in this third diary. Woke up wanting to read. Read five pages over a cup of coffee. I certainly failed to give her her due. I did what people always do to people who persist in evolving. I tried to pin her in one position of arrested development. Stupid.

—

Am at the end of this one—a good place to record a decision helped along by Anais: I must become more complete, detailed, in my journals. I am guilty of fragmentation. I have written shorthand accounts of events for my own use. But the journals have a further use, I see now, from reading Anais and being helped by her.

Reading Anais makes me happy I am a writer. Happy that it is a part of myself that requires only a pen & paper to exist. Happy that I see the connection between writing and psychoanalysis—which as Anais says is the true string of Ariadne.[2]

---

1   Anaïs Nin began to keep a diary in 1914 at the age of eleven. In 1966, she published the first volume of her diary, covering the years 1931–1934. Six more volumes followed. The published volumes of her diary became popular among young women, making Nin a feminist icon.

2   A reference to the Greek goddess Ariadne and the phrase "Ariadne's thread," a term that refers to solving a problem through an exhaustive application of logic to all available routes. The key element to applying Ariadne's thread to problem solving is the creation of a record—physical or otherwise—of the problem's available and exhausted options. This record is called the "thread," regardless of its actual medium. So, we see in this entry AW's

I love Langston, though he has on occasion disappointed me. I love Zora though she has done the same. I love Toomer's <u>work</u>. I love Anais. Tillie. (Though Tillie is maddeningly insensitive in person). I love Gaines' work. I love Marquez's work. I love the sun. The trees. The sky. Robert, Bertina & myself. Rebecca & the desert. 5/27/78

———

I have completed the blue book. So—back to this one.[1]

May 30, 1978
9:10 a.m.
Waiting for Robert, whose plane was to arrive an hour ago. He intends to make his way here via subway & bus. I am calmer waiting than usual. I've spent the past two evenings with Bertina. I'm sure that has something to do with it.

When I don't see her, I miss her. I miss her voice & her soft eyes and touch. I woke up, washed, dressed in shorts & tee shirt—mauve & navy—subdued—and combed out my curly locks which are looking scrumptious, although I've done nothing to fuss mentally with my hair for the past two weeks. I cannot abide straight hair, yet my own completely un-relaxed kinks drive me wild with frustration. I've broken several brushes & combs. I like my hair the way it is now. Unrelaxed but dried on rollers. This gives me manageability and natural texture—unfortunately the least bit of heat will undo it.

June 2, 1978
A lovely day in my little house. Working in the garden, desultory reading, musing. Robert off to the city to have lunch with Jennifer Lawson and work

---

evolving view of her journals as a keeping of records, like Anaïs Nin's diaries, toward addressing issues or problems in her life.

1   AW often journaled in more than one notebook at a time, sometimes picking up a thread of thought in a notebook that she hadn't used in years. For clarity and ease of reading, the journal entries have been compiled chronologically in this volume, regardless of the notebook in which they were entered.

on research in the library. I feel a kind of detachment. A kind of unreality. I have felt it since he came. There are moments when I feel we truly touch, but they are moments. I no longer feel the intensity I did and I wonder if it is only fear—it probably is. I fear leaving my little white house, my friends. At the same time, I'm eager to explore California. Perhaps I will discover I am a California person.

On the other hand, perhaps not.

What <u>am</u> I feeling?

Motored to Washington with Robert and Rebecca. A good part of the distance asleep from the grass . . . but pleasant and smooth. Dropped Rebecca at Mel and Judy's. Mel now lives in a two story brown rowhouse on a wide street with large elm trees. Near the part that has Mary McLeod Bethune's statue. (On the statue I noticed one of the letters of her name is missing—this is demoralizing. I wondered aloud to Robert if all our statues, stones, etc. have something (a letter) missing).

In the house I annoyed Mel because I saw a quilt someone gave me in North Carolina. It was on a bed in the study. So much of what's in their house is stuff I bought. But so what? This attachment to "my things" is something I don't want anyway—which is one of the reasons I left "our house." So peculiar seeing him with Judy, seated, eating, at "their table." But absolutely no wanting to be in her place. He looked pallid, slug like, sick. I can see the age creeping up on him as it creeps up on us all—except: I was going to write . . . I intend to fight it. But I don't intend to <u>fight</u> it exactly. Just not to give in before I have to.

An interesting evening with Robert. He was disappointed last night that I "cooled off" between foreplay and consummation—while he was changing the record on the record player. I explained the grass made me sleepy. But it ended with lovemaking in any case. I enjoyed it.

What bothered me was that he said "Now I have to start all over again," as if arousing me sexually is work. I think I know what he <u>meant</u>—that he was already <u>so</u> aroused . . . but still my feelings were hurt and I began making love to him for the first time with resentment rather than delirious happiness.

June 23, 1978

Went back to Spelman yesterday with Robert. To pick up his mother[1] but also to go to Giles Hall where we met in Howard Zinn's Russian Literature class. What a great class that was! What a great teacher Howie is! Anyway, the campus is very much changed although center campus is much the same. Lovely. Graceful. Marvelous red brick buildings, old very green & graceful trees. But I felt very distant, as if I'd never <u>lived</u> there, only visited. I thought seeing Spelman again would be painful but—no.

Being here with Robert's mother I understand how successfully she trained him. To be punctual, neat, courteous, and straight. But their relationship seems easy enough, now.

Sadie is much more low key and direct than Miriam.[2] I feel more at ease with her, though seeing her at Spelman brought back a distance . . . Years ago I was rushing to chapel and she was keeping tabs on who was or was not in her seat.

But at last all that is "cured by time"!

June 30, 1978

Georgia in the summer is, above all, hot. For several days now we've existed in a heat wave of temperatures in the high 90s–100s. Miserable weather that causes irritability, restlessness, inertia and stupor all at once. People who live here become used to it—some even profess to like it. I feel imprisoned by it. As if the heat itself closes me in and prevents my moving as indeed it does.

I feel a great deal of tension still which has settled in my back/neck. I can't determine whether this is just my usual response to true bourgeois surroundings or whether it goes deeper. I feel so often out of synch with Robert—as if I don't know him or can't comprehend what he is. Last night at the Chinese restaurant he became angry because each one of us wanted

---

1   Robert's mother, Sadie Allen, was a longtime dean of students at Atlanta's Spelman College, where AW first met Robert, then a student at Morehouse, in a class taught by Howard Zinn.

2   Miriam is Mel's mother and AW's former mother-in-law.

to order a separate dish and not the family style service he thought more interesting and more economical. He threw down his menu & swore & flung himself up from the table & out into the W.C. It seemed so childish we all—his mother, sister, niece, my Rebecca, even Casey—laughed. And yet I felt embarrassed for him because my view is that it didn't matter enough for anyone to feel upset. It seemed to me R. was on edge from the Black Conference he is participating in & in which he has no faith.

He referred to the black people several times as "niggers" in telling me how they wished to "do something <u>NOW</u>!" even though when called upon to do anything <u>NOW</u> no persons were forthcoming.

I thank whatever shapes this universe that I have great respect for Black people even when the intelligentsia is foolish and irresponsible. I know that whereas we may yet become, in fact, "niggers" that is not our heritage. Sadly, I must agree with DuBois that a people who laughs at & ridicules itself can never be great. Perhaps our greatness is in the past.

I feel sorry for R. that he does not respect Black people and therefore cannot respect his own colleagues and peers or of course himself. This lack of self-respect no doubt bodes ill for us as a couple for I don't know how to honor someone who is so lacking in self-respect.

———

My mother's house this time was uncluttered. It had a neat, swept-out look. She has an air conditioner that she uses so rarely she doesn't know how it works. I said: You should use it. She said: But it gives me a cold! Sitting up under it! I said: When you go into your bedroom you can leave it on to cool the whole house. To which she replied:

"But you know those things don't turn corners!"

"What?" I asked.

"A fan will turn a corner," she said. "But not an air conditioner."

It tickled me but made me think again of her wonderfully creative way of speaking. I love her way of phrasing things—I don't know anyone else whose speech is as lively and full of surprises.

I feel homeless. The feeling Robert expressed when he was at my house. No matter how welcoming other persons are there is the sense of being a guest. Where do I not feel that? At Mama's, Ruth's, Sheila's to some extent. I felt very much "the guest" at June's.

What is required is—separate, self-sufficient space for everyone! <u>That</u> solves the problem, I think. Space on different levels or on/in different wings.

Gave Ruth $500 as a house warming (or cooling) gift. In a sense I can't afford it & at times since I gave it I've resented her.

I am made to feel guilty because my life is easier, "more attractive" than hers.

She plays on my guilt effortlessly. She never even asks if I have problems since her troubles are so much greater than mine. I owe her everything she needs to "make up" the difference between us.

In her presence I certainly feel an inequality—but it isn't because I am "famous" (as Robert says) and she is not. It is an inequality of spirits. A train of bad news about everyone one knows depresses me . . . I feel guilty about this, as if I am at fault. I'm not.

What holds us to our brothers and sisters is the good they did us in the past, as children. It is next to impossible to forget the kindnesses done to us by siblings as children.

Mamie made a whirlwind tour of Eatonton, Macon & Atlanta. Was nice to everyone, including Mama and Ruth. This is entirely new & either she is preparing to die or move to Georgia.

I feel I have moved out of my family almost entirely. At times we touch, but mostly we miss. We have always had different aspirations, felt things differently. I felt myself to be rejected when I was no longer "the prettiest." I felt especially rejected by my father. Poor Daddy! Now when I see photographs of him I feel such a rush of tenderness, for his fine, expressive eyes.

—

Robert says Pam fears I will be harmful to Casey because I "hate her and hate white people." White people certainly take themselves seriously, in whatever situation they manage to get themselves, in my view. I don't think I'm capable of harming Casey or any other child except by accident. I can't even be mean to the awful brats on my street in Brooklyn— They've ended up watering my flowers for me, just as the little kids in Eatonton do for my mother.

Admittedly it has been hard for me to think of Casey as Robert's child.[1] But now I see a resemblance & <u>feel</u> Casey is Robert's child. Even if I didn't like Casey (which I do) I love his father too much to wish to harm him.

Perhaps Pam hates me & hates black people—which is the grand tradition of Western White Civilization. It is not in my tradition, as a black woman, to hate children, black, white, yellow, or red. Thank God.

I resented feeling defensive—and especially disliked bringing my work into the discussion. Robert wondered who Pam has been talking to, about me, and hit upon the probability that this new fear of hers comes from her & her friends' reading of my work. I pointed out that one of my concerns in both my novels was the "white" black child & that though an abusive father murders one (his own son) & society kills another (Truman's deserted child) this is not in fact <u>my</u> behavior with <u>my</u> black/white child. That I was commenting less on myself, by far, than on black society & primarily the observable behavior of black men.

I suppose it is the Aquarian in me that is hurt that anyone, for whatever reason, would think I could be a racist or could willfully harm a child.

Of course, white people would make racists of almost anyone.

I am looking more and more like Daddy & Aunt Sally. This is especially true as I become darker. I am now chocolate, as Robert says, and very attractive, I think. Large dark "Walker" eyes, a full-breasted figure, good legs. Fabulous thighs. It's true I've eaten too much cake since I've been here, but when I get back to Brooklyn I'll be too broke to eat much food.

Robert has gone back to Atlanta. It was sad seeing him go. It is true that he was terribly tense in Atlanta & made <u>me</u> tense, but it is also still true that <u>whate</u>ver feelings I have they are more intense with him.

---

1   Though he is biracial, toddler Casey had blue eyes, and his skin color was such that he might be mistaken for white.

July 6, 1978

Woke up this morning after a night wrestling with Rebecca who kicks and carries on in her sleep. The mattress & pillows I bought for this bed alone saved me from being utterly uncomfortable. There is a large, double window by the bed in front of which is an electric fan. My mother, dressed in a vivid pink housedress, was watering her flowers outside. Her hair, her beautiful hair, which I washed & styled yesterday, is like a flower of white silver. She moves from plant to plant steadily, patiently, watering, watering. Sometimes she bent below the level of the window and I could not see her; then I thought—just like that, one day, she will not be anywhere when I look for her. How empty & unfeeling her space will be! I can hardly imagine the world without Mama. And yet, that is exactly what I'm trying to do: imagine the world, my life, without Mama. In her garden now are giant blue and orange hydrangeas and periwinkles (!) and petunias and geraniums and sultanas.

July 10, 1978

Have been very tense since returning to Brooklyn, which, for its part, put on a street face of liveliness & light. But, alas, New York itself, & not simply its taxi drivers, is what I dread. Each time I return to the city I see its shoddiness, its abuse. And then there is its noise, its congestion & dirt.

On the other hand, I have a lovely view of gardens and a small waterfall/ fountain from my window and when I arrived truly expecting the worst, the house was intact. The bathroom looks plausible even if the shower leaks.[1]

I positively dreaded going out to Stonybrook to read—so much so that I expected at any minute to have some fatal accident.

But I arrived, after two changes of trains, still nervous but committed to at least making an appearance. Found it much less awful than anticipated, of course. Wonder if I'll ever learn, in my body, that it is the anticipation of awfulness that is awful. Anyway, read for about 30 minutes, feeling a distance, as usual, between me & the overwhelmingly white audience. From white audiences I feel distant, from black audiences I feel an underlying criticism—but not from everyone, just some people in the audience, and I understand this.

Bertina. When I arrived I found a letter from Stasia[2] who stayed here some days & nights while I was gone.

At times I worry that my friendship with Bertina hastened the breakup between them. But it should be possible to say you like one member of a couple more than you like the other one. That you wish to be firmer friends with one & not the other.

I have felt guilty about my inability to work. Reading Tillie's excellent Silences[3] I wonder what damage has been done to me this past year or two when I have been producing short, perhaps fragmentary or distracting work. For the first time I think of conditions of work, when sharing a place with Robert. I've thought so much of his needs—what of mine?

A room of my own. A desk. Typewriter.

---

1   AW had just had her bathroom renovated at her home in Brooklyn.

2   Stasia was Bertina's partner.

3   First published in 1978 by white feminist writer Tillie Olsen, *Silences* challenged the existing literary canon and explored the various ways that the creative spirit can be silenced in America because of race, gender, and class.

*   *   *

Well. Two more weeks. After which I can begin a five day countdown before leaving. I'm ready. There's so much noise on my street. Cars, children.

It is a charming house still but—I am ready for another life.

July 22, 1978

In two weeks I will be leaving for SF. In one week Mel will pick up Rebecca.[1] Rebecca & I have had moments of incredible love & sweetness—as if we're missing each other already. But, typically, we've also had periods of estrangement—as when she kept wanting me to go bike riding on a hot, muggy day and I had just told her I was hot, tired and had cramps. The wonderful thing about our kind of love is that it stretches over all extremes and remains. And each time I'm grateful & happy & amazed that she isn't more (long-term) angry with me. I am so often a <u>distracted</u> mother (with a one-track mind & an inability to pretend interest where there is none). And of course I hate lying & so won't lie to cover up whatever I really feel. She is a true Scorpio. Self-absorbed, possessive . . . wonderfully generous, loving, loyal. What I like is her sense of humor—if all else fails, she finds a reason to crack-up—& her laugh is loud & dumb & causes people to stare (& laugh) just like mine!

———

Louisa & Bryant[2] like the house. Louisa says if I can let them "slide" a bit they should have no trouble paying the rent. I am to have 3 people[3] in the house (& the baby, of course) without jobs. I try to think what will happen if they can't find work. All I can think is—I'll have to continue to make the mortgage payments on the house, plus pay my share of the rent with Robert in SF.

So far I have $3,000 worth of readings, etc. to do next year. More, I'm

---

1   Rebecca will be living with her father Mel in Washington, DC, for the school year, while AW spends the year with Robert in San Francisco.

2   Friends to whom AW planned to rent her Brooklyn house during her year in San Francisco.

3   AW's cousin Brenda was to share AW's Brooklyn house with Louisa and Bryant.

sure, will follow. On my part there needs to be a commitment to a place (to live) as well as to my writing as the absolutely only work I do. To some extent this already—& has always—been the case. But I see how the constant worry about money, being independent, being "responsible" gets to be a fundamental distraction—and then, when my mind should be only on the novel it is on whether I can get ten readings (at $1000 each) a year.

The truth is, I could probably manage with five readings a year, plus royalties & reprints. Though I castigate myself at times for this worrying over my affairs I am also glad to begin to feel I can <u>manage</u> my own affairs. Perhaps every great learning experience is accompanied by terror, just as being in love is. But perhaps for the next foray into the unknown one will not be so terror struck. That calm that one reaches, that I've achieved on other levels, might even be achieved when it comes to being in charge of my material life.

July 24, 1978

Today is much cooler than yesterday when it was close to 100°. I feel, correspondingly, much less oppressed, much less flat. Called Bertina & Stasia & invited them to dinner Wednesday night. There is still <u>some</u> tension, but there is also my entirely unchanged conviction that they are both extremely <u>good</u> people. As someone said in the sixties about such people "even their errors are correct." There is an innate courtesy in both of them. A kindness & forthrightness I love & admire.

In all this I am, believe it or not, working on my writing. I understand I must have a place, a settled place, for this. New York City is not at all conducive to what I'm planning—a long novel and long short stories, for which I need even longer walks, hikes, camping trips on which I can do nothing but watch clouds & hawks, & an occasional lizard.

I see much more clearly what I'm doing <u>this</u> time to protect & nourish my work. Last time (Mel & Mississippi) I did what I did instinctively. I turned my back on New York—dirty & distracting, hard on the nervous system—and found a good <u>three</u> years of writing near-peace, plus an additional two years' worth of life/material. I chose a man to live with who smoothed the days for me. Sometimes I wonder if anyone could be as supportive of my work as Mel? Can Robert & I be mutually supportive? Since he needs the same kind of smoothing of the way that I did, & do.

The new book of poems GNWL is stronger for Joyce Johnson's suggestions and cutting.[1] I liked her reliance on her feelings, I liked her sensitivity to me. In short, I have enjoyed so far working with her. She is so entirely different from Hiram & Tony. It is as if we are jointly working on something to make it better rather than working on something to make it sell.

July 25, 1978

I am working on the surface. Thinking on the surface of my mind. This is clear after a long afternoon on the beach at Fire Island. The waves, the sand, the sun, the breezes cleared me out & unkinked the knots in my back so that as I lie here early in the morning I am more relaxed than I've been since Georgia.

The city, city life, is only good for that: surface stuff. For real thought is connected in a way to real exercise and exercise requires a suppleness of limbs. In the city one's limbs contract. One's muscles are worried about attack. I think I am reaching what I need to reach to come to a decision re: SF. That I want to move there <u>anyway</u>, that I'm not moving there solely because of Robert.

Today has a lecture/discussion of <u>Meridian</u> at Yale for Michael Cooke's class 11:00. The rest of the week has: Henri, Bertina & Stasia for supper Wednesday. Conference with Joyce Johnson & book jacket designer at Dial, Thursday morning, contract signing at Wendy's office & film viewing (ERA video) at <u>Ms.</u> in the afternoon. Friday, Nan & Quintanta. Painting & cleaning & perhaps some time with Bertina on the weekend.

---

1   This is a reference to AW's third book of poetry, *Good Night, Willie Lee, I'll See You in the Morning*, and her new editor, Joyce Johnson, at Dial Press.

July 30, 1978

Rebecca left yesterday with Mel. She seemed happy to be going. I felt relieved but also bereft, and today I feel the tension that records still another life change. I've been through so many over the past two years. The separation, trip to Cuba, finding an apartment, my struggles with love & Robert & Bertina . . . , house-buying, moving. Now my child gone for a year. After nine years of being with me.

I wanted to ask Mel if he was <u>sure</u> Judy would be good for/to Rebecca. But that would have angered him. It's a normal enough question, though. I needed the reassurance.

Feelings of tension, tightness, a kind of hesitancy about getting started on this new life.

Undated, around August 7, 1978

Arrived in S.F. on Saturday safe and sound. Bob & Casey. Happiness. Joy. That we begin this part of our lives together. To share a life. Children. Adventure. Love.

From the living room window there is a wonderful view of the San Bruno Mountains & houses all over the hills between. It is a beautiful city and Robert has been showing it to me. We went picnicking & to the beach. We can now rest in our silences together.

August 12, 1978

Today, less than a week after my arrival, we are indeed "resting in our silences." And I'd rather not.

The week has been one primarily of strain though with a few breaks of sunlight here & there. I was feeling fine—I think—until Robert let me know he is <u>innately</u> critical of "whoever he lives with." I used a towel instead of hot pads to take a hot dish out of the oven—this annoyed him. He talked a great deal about seeing this as crazy and says it is "his mother <u>in</u> him." I said I had no intention of submitting to crazy criticism from whatever source.

Still, my muscles began to tighten. . . . I thought that throughout our relationship Robert has kept me off balance.[1] That as soon as I feel the ground under our mutual feet, he comes with an earthquake.

Yesterday there was a party for Glory. She's lovely. The party food was salami & ham mostly which I no longer eat. Later I said "I'm hungry."

Robert responded as if I were a child who did not understand I'd just left dinner. "You're <u>hungry</u>?!" "Didn't you eat lunch?" "But we just ate . . . at least <u>I</u> did." And so on & so forth.

Later, went to a wonderful movie: "Heaven Can Wait" with Warren Beatty. Back home, smoke, music, backrub, bed. But no loving. I feel estranged.

Perhaps I should recast my dreams. I think I will continue to like San Francisco, especially once I learn to drive here. I could use the year to get used to things—make new friends . . . make of my relationship with Robert a friendship that will be conducive to this, rather than this "thing" we have that ties me in knots.

After three months we should live in separate places. Since I want to live with someone I can start working on that.

I'm very glad I brought my "family" with me. . . . The photograph of Mae Poole. Myself when I was a child.

Undated

A long, wonderful letter from Jane Cooper & an invitation to honor Muriel[2] on December 9. I would love to do this because Muriel means a lot to me. The effort here will be to give to Muriel the honor she is due without feeding the vanity of her liberalism & the liberalism of the majority of "good white people" who will be at Sarah Lawrence & who see Muriel as their excuse for being.

---

1   Robert worked as an editor for *The Black Scholar*, a journal of Black studies and research based in the San Francisco Bay Area.

2   Poet Muriel Rukeyser was one of AW's professors at Sarah Lawrence, and Jane Cooper was a poet and professor there as well.

August 20 – A bright, <u>beautiful</u> day. The sun is warm, the sky blue and clear except for mantles of fog on the shoulders of the far hills.

Have resolved to transcribe 10 pages a day of the journals at least. Began yesterday. My early entries are stiff, stilted, self-conscious and poor writing. Sloppy thinking. The worst.

<u>But</u> every once in a while there is amazingly useful stuff. All in all, I think I have improved as a human being. I have certainly grown more closely attached to life. I appreciate it & love it more now than I ever did. I call that improvement because learning to accept a gift gracefully is an accomplishment.

Told Robert he is like Felix Unger[1]—picky, petty and undermining. He complained that I "<u>never</u> put anything back into the refrigerator." I said we should move into separate places at the end of October—this to assure the survival of our friendship. I can't respect pettiness. It's so ridiculous. Nor can I hope to work while constantly worrying about the ring around the tub. Etc.

There are other positive things about separating our living arrangement.

Robert and I can see each other several times a week and go on our wonderful rambles together without getting stuck in the "marriage syndrome."

I <u>like</u> SF. I feel it is the most compatible place I've ever lived (2 weeks & visits). I like the climate, the views, the water, the varieties of peoples, housing, life styles, foods.

Perhaps I've found my city.

Undated
A lovely week-end. Yesterday St. Claire Bourne[2] came to breakfast to discuss the film he hopes to make of Robert's Port Chicago Disaster.[3] I liked

---

1 Felix Unger is one of the two main characters in the 1968 movie (and popular 1970s television show) *The Odd Couple*, about mismatched roommates—one fastidious and tidy, the other laid-back and messy.
2 A well-respected independent Black filmmaker.
3 Robert was working on a nonfiction book about the 1944 explosion at the Navy's Port

him immediately. He is tall and deeply brown, with soft black hair growing over his collar and beautiful expressive brown eyes. I felt very drawn to him. (It continues to amaze & delight me that there are so many fine folks in the world.) We hung out together for the entire day. Had drinks at a pub, a walk, a movie and dinner. Robert says it is the sort of thing he'd never do alone. Work is compulsive. But it is exactly the kind of day I most enjoy and by which I can best be seduced from work.

Today I can't seem to get into work. It is a fantastic day. Bright, warm, breezy. Clean. Gloria Steinem is calling to talk about pornography vs erotica. I'm blank on that today.

Calls from Nina and Ms lawyer Nancy Wexler about the "real people & issues" in "Laurel"—that is what is upsetting me, making writing joyless today. Or perhaps it is just that my journal 1965–66 is so juvenile. The writing so poor. So pretentious & labored.

———

Just had an Indian visitation:

He said: It is okay to smoke grass to help you temporarily forget or ease your problems.

But you must go through a time when you engage your problems without the smoke. Otherwise they will not be worked out, only layer on layer like a criss-cross web.

August 25, 1978
Last night Robert arrived home in good spirits (with Casey & ribs) because it appears one of the apartments here might be available soon. He would like to have one because they are perfect in every respect for children & progressive working adults who wish to have some say about where they live.

Chicago ammunition base just north of San Francisco that killed 320 men, 202 of whom were Black ammunition loaders. In the aftermath, the 258 survivors refused to continue loading munitions, and 50 were charged with mutiny and court-martialed. Robert's book would eventually be published, in 1989, as *The Port Chicago Mutiny: The Story of the Largest Mass Mutiny Trial in U.S. Naval History.*

Although I want this for Robert if it is what <u>he</u> wants, I find myself feeling bad. I keep asking myself: why?

Is it because he asked to borrow $8000.00 for the down payment? Of course I said an effortless "No," like a typically large hearted Aquarian.[1] But I was annoyed that he would ask <u>me</u>—disregarding that I have left one house I just bought to live with him. That he is unlivable with. And now he asks that I supply a place for him to live though I have no place of my own.

He is both selfish & oblivious & what concern he has is for Pam & Casey, exclusively.

"Work out an arrangement with Pam," I said, "so you can get money out of your house."

"That's where it is," he agreed.

I feel my love leaking out of me. This depresses me because I've put so much energy into trying to build something. But Robert is not even <u>there</u> for me. His love is like Chinese food. It leaves me hungry even before the meal is over.

I'm sure the problem is that he never learned how to love. Perhaps if he could love anyone it would be me, next to, of course, himself—with whom he is definitely enamored.

—

Ahgh!!

August 29, 1978
Ah <u>so</u>! Well.

An amazing & delightful weekend. I find that if I express my feelings as soon as I know what they are or might be & as soon as I am <u>able</u>, I feel better <u>immediately</u>. It is incredible—& so simple. A good diet & free expression all along would no doubt have saved me from much depression in the past. . . .

Last night, making love to Robert I was amazed (so much amazement

---

1   AW's birth sign.

around here) to look at him & know I love him. The leak has stopped. But why? Because he sees he has problems & is trying to solve them? Because we've decided not to live together & it is a relief to both of us? Because— In the bath I washed his face & body as tenderly as I would bathe a child. His ears, his beard, his nose & eyes.

He takes me to see giant trees, the ocean in the middle of the night, to picnic in the glory of the day. He presents me with the world. The natural world, which I deeply love—& he is part of it.

I have decided to buy into the St. Francis Square apartments. A 3 bedroom two bath apartment is available but the price is $9,000, with a "carrying charge" of $213.00 a month. I have in savings $12,350.00. The way I figure it, the first thing to do is try to put $2,000.00 into savings—more if possible—to make a balance of $5,000.00. Would I feel secure with that amount? Probably not.

Let's see. I'm due:

```
1,125.00 – Wendy/Dial
1,100.00 – Dutch
3,500.00 – Guggenheim
  500.00 – Stony Brook
2,000 – Readings
$8,225.00
```

Let's say $8,000 between now and the end of the year. Of that I could probably put into savings $4,000, bringing my savings back up to $7,000 after the $9,000 purchase. Then I could attempt to reach $10,000 & rest a while. Then: the house in Brooklyn should pay for itself, $545 a month plus 155 applied to my "rent" out here of

```
 213
-155
($58)
```

I would pay per month as <u>my</u> $ for housing, gas, electricity, everything but telephone.

Sometimes this feels like a house of cards. I keep thinking: it can't be as simple as this. Perhaps I'll be royally zapped by taxes.

———

Went to have my eyes checked yesterday—& to buy sunglasses. The s/g should help my headaches. And I feel restored to know my left eye is healthy & holding up. Also bought a lovely, <u>luscious</u> red dress—heavy satin— & some gorgeous scant underwear for me & Roberto. Picked up ticket for my trip to Seattle & Alaska.

I find San Francisco manageable and bright & compared to New York quite unhurried, polite.

9/29/78

3 hour visit from Tillie Olsen.[1] She knows so much & tries to tell it all.

Before that Robert & I "purchased" 15 Galilee Lane #6!

10-3-78

This morning I began moving into 15 Galilee Lane. We picked out 2nd hand furniture from the Salvation Army & Bus Van, which convinced me of the superiority of old furniture—if it is also stylish, well made & cheap. We have a rose colored horsehair sofa & chair set ($245) and a queen size bed ($94) and a white mattress for Casey ($9.50) and a beautiful simple but fantastically <u>heavy</u> wooden table ($145). This afternoon the bureau from the Salvation Army is due which virtually furnishes the place.

———

1 Activist and author Tillie Olsen is best known for her prize-winning fiction *Tell Me a Riddle* and *Yonnondio: From the Thirties*. Her interest in long-neglected women authors inspired the development of academic programs in women's studies. About the influence of her work, AW has said: "As much as I learned from *Tell Me a Riddle*, I learned even more from Tillie's landmark classic and original essay 'Silences: When Writers Don't Write,' which I read while living in Cambridge in the early seventies, raising a small daughter alone and struggling to write myself."

Undated

Casey & I are getting along better now that he realizes I know his mama.[1] I think—in his loyalty to her—he thought he & I couldn't be friends.

Oct. 16, 78

I have been working subconsciously & consciously to rid myself of the Christian-indoctrinated concept of God as a specific white-haired English speaking patriarch as played by Charleston Heston. I'm beginning to succeed. Now when I pray to the Great Spirit I get vast stretches of desert, trees, the infinite sky, bits of cloud, flowers, squirrels, etc. etc. This pleases me tremendously.

Oct. 26, 1978

An interesting evening with NaNa,[2] during which she got me interested once again in meditation. I've been lax—because I've been happily in love (for a change—or maybe not: I've probably had very good luck in love, considering all the fine folks I've loved!) and I've been smoking a lot of dope with Roberto, and am not ready to stop yet.

Anyway, I mentioned to her that I loved Bertina (she had just said her relationship with June didn't work out because they weren't peers)—and I later had this insight: perhaps I chose to love Bertina because she was not a peer & because a successful relationship would be, given our differences, very unlikely.

She was "safe."

11-7-78

Well, tonight I am alone in the apartment, having asked Robert to leave. It's a long story, which I think I must wait to write tomorrow. Tonight I'm tres fatigue.

*   *   *

---

1   Born in 1975, Casey was still a toddler when Robert and Pam separated.

2   An old friend.

The long and short of it is: We went to see a film "Black Britannia" at Berkeley. The film is important, of course, about the racism of the British & the resistance of the Blacks (West Indians). But it is limited by its view of black people as black <u>men</u>. Robert & I attempted to discuss this: He hadn't noticed the sexism particularly. We arrived home & I had lots of mail (& rent checks, for which I'd waited). He watched me opening my letters. I was chattering, happy (because Brenda wrote that both she <u>&</u> Louisa have jobs!)

So after sharing my relief at this I walked around into the bedroom. And then Robert said: "I stood it as long as I could."

"What?" I asked.

"The ring around the bottom of the commode."

"<u>What</u> ring?"

"The one that's been there for a while."

"Well, what is it?"

"Some gunk."

"Gosh, I hadn't even noticed it? What did it look like? What color was it?"

I am brought up short. All my delight changes into a feeling of incompletion, inadequacy. But something rises up in me. At first it is humor. I can't believe anyone would seriously criticize me about cleaning my own bathroom (when I was so happy, especially). I try to see a joke somewhere in it.

He says "I cleaned it" (while I was mindlessly reading mail—people inviting me to lecture, write articles. People sending rent checks). I say "Good for you!"

He says: "It's true that you have a higher level of tolerance for mess than I do."

(He has said this about Pam, actually.) But I don't think about this then.

When I probe him about <u>why</u> he's criticizing my ability to clean my toilet bowl he says: "Don't prod it, it'll come along enough on its own."

"What?"

"My meanness."

Well, the next morning he says he's sorry he hurt me. I spent the night feeling, of course, less than wonderful. In the morning he put his arms around me in bed, but they felt only confining. I got up & went to my study to work.

I cried some. He said he felt awful. I held him. He held me.

In the afternoon I had a five hour lunch with Carole Ellis.[1] And we discussed "our men." A pattern—to which I'd blinded myself—emerged. Of my constant attempts to please Robert & his constant attempts to minimize me. Belittle. Ridicule. Undermine. It occurs to me that on some level, not too far beneath the surface either, he hates me. Is using me. Is exploiting our relationship—& has very few feelings that are positive. His own sense of inadequacy causes him to only fake pleasure at other people's success or happiness.

He is constantly professing what he doesn't feel. <u>That</u>'s why when he says "I love you" it is as a goofy adult would say it to a child. It is not straightforward. Clear. Grown-up. Responsible.

While I am cooking dinner I tell him the relationship is over. I feel nothing but contempt. He pretends he doesn't even understand the significance of his "offense."

I remind him that white America has worked for 400 years to link black women to cleaning toilets & have failed. And he, I say, is not going to succeed either.

He said: "I don't want things to be this way."

I felt nothing. A coldness, an emptiness.

Next day he began removing his things. He also asked me if I'd like to go for a walk. We went to the Japanese gardens. Walking was enjoyable. We walked around the lake. He asked for another chance to be my friend. I said I'd think about it while in D.C.-N.C.-Ga. & Miami. We came back to my apartment & had dinner. Or rather, pieces of cold fried chicken from the earlier ill-fated dinner.

The distance continued within me. He offered to drive me to the airport. I said okay, but that it wasn't necessary & that I did not wish us to become people who exchanged services (his idea of being a friend is to provide services) without essential caring. Love.

---

1   A new friend.

Nov. 14th

In my mother's house in Georgia. In my bedroom. The trip East, so far, has been okay. The Georgetown/D.C. part was <u>fine</u>. Rebecca & I stayed in Henri's[1] flat in Georgetown. Met Richard Sobel & Annie Sobel & their former Civil Rights Law partner. A nice afternoon. Then dinner the next night with Henri, her friend Florence, Karen Wynn, Rebecca & Gloria Steinem.

Gloria as always warm, real, lovely. She gave me, Rebecca & Henri back massages. Wonderful! I gave her a foot massage. Also gave Rebecca a foot massage. A warm, friendly women's evening. Great food (cheesecake!) great talk, music.

Then drove Rebecca back to Mel's house. Gloria to Stan's.

Next morning off to spend the day with Vincent[2] in North Carolina. Good. Though I napped the whole time we were in Ella Baker's house[3]— where he is completing <u>There Is a River</u>. We want to keep our friendship. But wish to include Rosemarie & Rachel & Jonathan. We spoke of San Francisco & how I've grown to love it. I sensed an interest in Vincent for S.F. Rachel would love it.

Then on to Atlanta & Ruth & Mama.

I've felt that romantic love—of which I've been a willing & often deliriously happy victim over the past 2–3 years—distracts us from the direct appreciation of the beauty of the universe. The goodness of life. The joy of simply <u>being</u>.

I looked at the sun. The moon. Trees. Everything. With <u>such love</u>.

---

1 Henri Norris was a friend in Washington, DC, a Black woman attorney whom Alice had first met in Jackson, Mississippi.

2 Respected African American historian Vincent Harding. Rosemarie was Vincent's wife; Rachel and Jonathan, their children.

3 Ella Baker was a civil rights and human rights activist and an influential Black leader whose career—mostly as a behind-the-scenes organizer—spanned more than five decades. Born in 1903, she grew up in rural Littleton, North Carolina, and attended Shaw University in Raleigh. Decades later, she returned to Shaw to help found the Student Nonviolent Coordinating Committee (SNCC).

Nov 18

Yesterday my daughter was nine years old! I called her from her great Aunt Sallie's house in Opa-Locka, Florida. She said she'd had a telegram from Gloria S. and a phone call from Curtis, in Greece. And that there are parties coming up. She sounded happy.

Aunt Sallie looks exactly like Daddy. She has his eyes. I cried most of the first day because she said—when I asked her what Daddy was like as a boy: "I don't remember. You should have asked him." And then. "You're not going to write a book off of me. Understand?" My feelings were hurt. I tried to explain to her that as a writer it is impossible for me to make (keep) the kind of promise she exacted. That I would not write about her or about what she told me. But she didn't understand. She said later, "Don't write anything about me because I don't want to read it." I made up my mind not to pursue the "novel" based on my grandfather's life—but here I am on the plane back to S.F. <u>writing</u> about Aunt Sallie. Not to betray her, as she feared, but because she has been a worthwhile experience in my life.

So: She is 67 years old. A Gemini. Blackskinned. Tall. Large dark eyes. Very attractive. This was very reassuring to me, since I look like her. She is not fat. This was also good to see. She takes care of eight foster children. All black, very black. All quiet, mannerly, except my favorite, the disabled boy, Glen, who is in a rage frequently & disgusted with his smallness & powerlessness.

Aunt Sallie lives in a flat typical Florida house on a lower middle class street. Her yard is full of flowers & trees. She has two dogs. She has a brown station wagon. On the front is a red tag that says "Christ is the Answer." The only music in the house is religious music—and all the children sing religious songs to entertain themselves. It is reminiscent of us, I suppose, in the early 50s.

People like my aunt & her "daughter" Maxine would make ideal revolutionaries. Perhaps all religious enthusiasts would. (They are Pentecostal). I felt that my aunt—somewhat wild in her youth—needed something to stabilize her. To "save" her. So she turned to God, man having failed so dismally.

* * *

Ruth and I struggled through the rough periods of our relationship as we've done for years now. She made a real effort not to talk so constantly about herself. I intend to have a bracelet made for <u>myself</u> that spells <u>Silence</u>. Because I think there is a real danger in talking too much. I think talking robs us of potency the way perfume is robbed of scent when the bottle is left open. I always feel bad, almost nauseous, when I've talked too much. I guess that's where the expression "spilled her/his guts" comes from.

11-22-78

Isn't this the day Kennedy was assassinated fourteen years ago? How time has moved on! . . .

. . . This day for me—& yesterday—brought anxiety. I am in the grip of an anxiety attack. I must devise some way to survive it.

First of all: I am anxious because the things I am writing are so very close to my life & the lives of people I've known that I am afraid for us. In "Stripping Bark From Myself" perhaps I am slowly committing suicide except the suicide is not the quick one I've imagined but one that is simply a withdrawal into myself & out of the world.

I was truly hurt—as by a blow—by Aunt Sallie's desire that I not write about her. Perhaps everyone I've ever written about would have said the same thing, given a chance. But of course they weren't given a chance.

I think I should take a break from writing. Just read for a few months. But can I <u>do</u> this?

As much as I wish to show my appreciation of Muriel, I <u>dread</u> being at Sarah Lawrence & speaking on "Muriel Rukeyser Day." I don't want to see . . . all the generous, liberal ghosts of the past. And I don't want to make the long, stressful flight back East.

A very small royalty check from Monica for <u>Once</u> & <u>The Third Life of Grange Copeland</u>. <u>Grange</u> has sold 845 copies in paper. This nets me $42. I can't believe it. Hardcover sales: 77. Nets me $61.22. Definitely better to have hardcover sales.

<u>Once</u> in paper has sold 145 copies—nets me $7.25.

11-23-78 Thanksgiving Day.

Today Robert, Casey & I are going to Petaluma to visit Carole Ellis, a woman I met in The Black Scholar office and with whom I recently had a revitalizing lunch. She is making Turkey & Broccoli—Robert has made & is taking one of his pies.

We spent a lovely evening together last night in front of the TV, and in bed. We even talked about my feelings now about my writing in a way that relieved me. I really felt he was listening & being neither competitive nor judgmental.

11-28-78

I went downtown today to pick up the copies I had made of the photograph Aunt Sallie gave me. I've pasted a large blow-up above my desk. My parents are <u>so</u> beautiful. I can't get over it. They are so full of <u>substance</u>. They were so poor & yet just looking at them you see the richness, the fully realized selves.

They are more vivid than anybody I've ever seen.

12-28-78

Amazing news. When I was in New York[1]—getting there was another trial without disguise—I wrote 10 new poems! Good ones! And this is how it happened: a voice said, before I wrote each poem—an inner voice, but distinct—"Write . . . so & so . . ." & that would be the first line of the poem.

Sometimes—on all of them actually—I resisted. I'm not, I said. It was relentless. "Write so-&-so." And when I wrote it, the rest of the poem followed!

Isn't this weird?

Life has led me to a breakthrough, I think.

---

1 She was there to attend the event at Sarah Lawrence College, in Bronxville, New York.

Jan. 4, 1979

I began this journal exactly a year ago. With the hope that it would contain less pain, more growth, some happiness. It has been a good year for me. When I have loved & been loved and in which I have grown, had less pain— and first saw The Desert. I <u>love</u> The Desert.

Tonight Roberto & Casey came for dinner—then TV & kisses & then I sent them home. Robert & I are going to try the 3 nights a week together that we had before Rebecca arrived for Xmas.

Another year. What do I want? Health. Good work. Love. Rebecca's happiness & mine, & Robert's. Another visit to The Desert.

A great treasure from '78 was the 1933–34 photograph of my strikingly beautiful & moving parents. Other treasures: Robert's love. Rebecca's love. The return of my work. The 10 poems of December 10th!

I haven't been thinking about $ so much, now that I have this place. Even though carrying charges increased, I still feel I have a bargain.

Plus Ms. wants to buy "at least 4 poems!" says Joanne. So I will be able to pay my American Express bill, & my Mastercharge, & I should put at least $2,000 into savings. February brings $1,250 from the Library of Congress— March, perhaps a reading at Lewis & Clark. April has Albany & Cazenovia & another school.

I am to get the disability insurance from Monarch Life—$500 a month when/if I'm ever unable to work. That could cover rent here, & food. Then I would continue to rent out the Brooklyn house for enough to cover the mortgage, insurance & repairs. And sit tight. Or sit cheap.

<u>Ms.</u> is good for medical insurance.

Lincoln Savings Bank has a policy to cover my death.

I am writing my will. If taxes don't crush me, I'll be in great shape!

(If, of course, I continue to get work.)

Mel & Judy had a baby boy, named Benjamin, on January 1st. Rebecca & I felt bad the whole day—happy for Mel & Judy, of course, but as if we've lost something. And we have. I tried to assure her that her daddy would always love her just the same, but I don't really know this. Mel has a lot of love, but seems most comfortable keeping it in one channel.

I am still thankful I will have no more children. I am perfectly content with what I have.

1-17-79

Robert gives me walks, the moon, pens that write smoothly, in pretty colors . . . he gives me breakfast, rides in the car, trips to visit the ocean, woods, sky. He gives me love that is as vulnerable as my own. This morning, making love, I felt <u>such</u> peace. I love the way he smells. His body has a sweet, clean, fresh smell.

I went today & had something called a "Jheri–curl." It is like a relaxer-permanent except that the hair is curled rather than straightened. It looks <u>very</u> natural—in fact, I would have been happy with more curls.

My aim is to have lots of curly hair again—& the first step is to find a way of helping it grow.

I have worried lately that perhaps essay writing is endangering my fiction. I feel this especially about "One Child of One's Own." As if I'm using up a rich source of fiction-energy. But am I? Nothing but this essay seems likely to come out of the Cambridge/Wellesley experience.

Jan. 24, 1979

The Jheri-curl was a bust. But I like my barber/stylist. She <u>thinks</u> about things—& writes.

I am ready to plant roses, primroses, parsley, basil—Oh! Spring is coming, or I miss my grass. And out here if spring starts in January what a long spring it must be!

I am happy.

2-4-79

Ebony & Washington Post want comments on Michele Wallace's book.[1] An interesting book; not original, really. Most of the things in it have been said before, as Sheila pointed out, & said better.

That she permitted Ishmael Reed[2] on the cover along with us women feminists was extremely opportunistic & shortsighted on her part—& unfortunate. How is anyone to trust someone who wants the blessing of a man who thinks black women are barracudas?

Anyway, I declined to comment—and would have my endorsement off the jacket if I could. Why did I put it there? Pestering from Michele—<u>fear</u> of Michele, whose mother[3] once terrified me on yet another awful panel.

What I find about myself is that black women have terrorized me—all my life. That my sisters are capable of terrorizing me to this day. I have tried to please them because of that. They in turn have rejected me for just that "weakness." Interesting.

I have wanted to hold us together because we are the center of the race—but this has not prevented evil & competitiveness & deformity. Not at all. And that is what I hear in the voices of black women. In the voices of my friends. . . . Presumption, & lack of history.

Quoting myself: When a white liberal tells you (she has never heard what you're saying/writing before) what you are saying/writing has not been "hazarded" before, it simply means she doesn't know your history. That is <u>all</u> it means.

---

1 Published in 1979, Michele Wallace's *Black Macho and the Myth of the Superwoman* harshly critiqued the patriarchal culture of the civil rights and Black Power movements of the 1960s and pondered persistent sexism in the Black community.
2 African American novelist and poet Ishmael Reed, who wrote a blurb for the cover of Wallace's book, was vocal in his criticism of Black women writers who embraced feminism or called out sexism among Black men.
3 The author's mother is acclaimed visual artist Faith Ringgold, best known for her narrative quilts.

2-10-79

Birthday party last night—me, Rebecca, Henri, Florence, Bernice (Reagon)[1] and her friend Amy. A little nervousness at first but we all bumbled along as best we could until the feeling got right. Bernice & I had a chance to talk. I felt we could talk & talk. I have such respect for her. For her work: its integrity, pride. She says: "I don't know what pride is!"

Rebecca & I easy together—she seems changed for the better by the experience of having a baby brother. Mel's son is cute & cuddly and keeps them up every night. . . .

Mel & I talked on the phone to make arrangements for Rebecca.[2] He is unhappy with his job in Washington and thinks a move is in the offing. He says he "moved too quickly" on this, & that he "hadn't thought it through." I, on the other hand, he said, seem to have done a better job of planning.

I said I'd always loved San Francisco. But I don't know if that's what he means. It is true that I've tried to spend time <u>feeling</u> out what I want & don't want. So that I could cut down on the possibilities for regret. But if Robert had been as available as Judy & Washington as near & glorious as San Francisco, I'm sure things would have been very different.

2-23-79

I have been pulling myself out of the dumps with work, exercise—and prayer! My mother wrote me a note for my birthday. In it she said: "Don't forget to pray." It has been a long time since I've prayed & I think I'm praying to God in myself and the Spirit of the Universe. But I prayed, twice, and felt better immediately. Perhaps there's something in humans that <u>needs</u>

---

1   Bernice Johnson Reagon, social activist, singer/songwriter, and scholar, was a founding member of the SNCC (Student Nonviolent Coordinating Committee) Freedom Singers. In 1973, she founded the acclaimed Black women's a cappella ensemble Sweet Honey in the Rock.

2   Rebecca, now nine, has been living with her father, Mel, and his new wife, Judy, in Washington, DC. With the birth of a second child, Rebecca's baby brother, Mel is reconsidering his move to Washington and discussing with AW the possibility of Rebecca living with her in San Francisco when the new school year begins.

prayer. It is good for us maybe, just as talking to ourselves is. Or talking to another.

Today we worked in our separate places. Then got together to watch the sunset on the beach. A magnificent sunset. Really breathtaking & tear making—with the spume of the waves making a screen, as Robert said, across the sun. And birds flying across—& purple clouds.

A young man up the beach applauded—& he was right. The sun puts on quite a show.

But alas, Robert & I had words. He reproached me for not having brought money along, so that he had to spend his entire 9 dollars on dinner.

"Shall I go up and get my money?" (to pay for overdue library books.)

"I guess you'll have to; I don't have any more money."

Now—I have paid for 5 out of six dinners over the past week. I have loaned Robert 500 & The Scholar 2000. I have taken up slack financially willingly in this relationship—& to hear him say, "I guess you'll <u>have</u> to, I don't have any more money" made me want to throw a left hook to his head.

What does it mean? This reproachful tone? It is the husband's tone. Luckily he is not my husband. Eventually he will learn that.

When we came upstairs I paid him exactly what I owed him. I <u>could</u> have requested that he pay <u>me</u> exactly what he owes me.

But I feel a headache coming on behind this. Robert makes me realize that one of the joys of being independent is that you don't have people speaking to you as if you are a dumb wife or an idiot child. At times like this I think: if I were dependent on him he'd think it perfectly okay to speak to me in reproachful tones—to humiliate me. . . .

. . . Today, thank God, was a good one for me. For the most part, my heart remained light & clear; this is a great blessing. I thought some more about buying a car—mainly to drive to the beach. I <u>love</u> the beach. But I should probably wait until after I've paid taxes for the year.

Robert called at 10 to apologize, again, for his reproachful tone. Says he's still upset from talking to Pam's mother who feels he hurt Pam "terribly" by leaving her.

I am getting pretty sick of Pam, I 'spect.

Anyway, I asked him not to beat himself up over it. That life is full of surprises & I slept "blissfully" last night.

I asked him to think of a possible resentment of me because at present I am more financially able than he is. I think there is something in men, programmed in, that makes them resentful of women who can take care of themselves & of men too, financially. But I wouldn't give up my independence for anything. Once dependent you can be spoken to like a dog— & have no place to go.

3/5/79

A long (2 hours) conversation with Mel. I talked, he talked. Both of us about things we find difficult to discuss with other people. . . . The support he gives me for my work is something I <u>deeply</u> miss. He sees & understands its value. He values me. Remembers so many of the things that made me. Langston's "moment of generosity" indelible.

Unfortunately, Langston's comment that I "married my subsidy" also indelible.[1]

Mel always doubted my love, because of that comment.

3-12-79

Something changed profoundly between us when I understood Robert had not defended my essay/forum response to Robert Staples' sexist attack on Ntozake & Michele Wallace.[2]

---

1 Legendary poet Langston Hughes had befriended Alice and Mel early in their marriage, not long before his death in 1967. He became her mentor, her "literary father," as she would recall, and her first publisher, including her short story "To Hell With Dying" in *The Best Short Stories by Negro Writers* (1967), alongside such distinguished authors as Gwendolyn Brooks and Jean Toomer.

2 Black sociologist and scholar Robert Staples harshly critiqued authors Ntozake Shange and Michele Wallace in a piece called "The Myth of Black Macho: A Response to Angry Black Feminists," published in the March/April 1979 issue of *The Black Scholar*. AW wrote a memo to *The Black Scholar* in response. As she put it, "The editors considered the memo both too 'personal' and too 'hysterical' to publish. They suggested change, and I withdrew

He just stood dumbly by, suspended.

I told him I feel he has no convictions—& really, over the long run it is impossible to respond deeply to people who have no depth.

He is very afraid to face himself.

I told him we are all afraid. But to face ourselves without drugs is to attempt to face our authentic selves, not fantasies. And indeed to exist in our own lives. I'm not sure why this is coming now, for him.

I actually feel very distant & find myself thinking of other possibilities. Especially of women—who, compared to men, have a terrific record.

Robert says he may get a job driving a taxi, or in a factory. Or with children. He feels oppressed by the intellectual role he's been in since Morehouse.

3-26-79

A delightful conversation last night with June. She is going to be away the few days I'm in New York. I felt all the old trust and wanted to discuss "trust" and "people's flaws" with Robert. But Maya Angelou had canceled the benefit she was going to give for The Scholar and Robert couldn't respond, except to fear where the conversation would lead. He is very afraid that serious conversation will lead to criticism of him. But I really had in mind a rather abstract discussion that would, possibly, illuminate this swing from trust to distrust back to trust I feel in my intimate relationships.

I told him that his flaws make him more real to me—in a way no one else has ever been quite real. (Perhaps this means other people have fewer flaws—but I don't think so. I think it simply means his are more upfront— & that his "flaws" in a woman would not be flaws at all. But to me they would still be.)

Anyway I felt the old "distance"—but not in a sad way. Though I cried, of course. But then I always cry. I want, I think, to stop this & wonder if I can. Can one stop crying through an act of determination?

---

it." She later published the piece—in which she offers her own measured, incisive critique of Michele Wallace's *Black Macho and the Myth of the Superwoman*—in her 1983 book *In Search of Our Mothers' Gardens.*

My tears are always very near the surface. Any emotion makes them well up & spill over. Grief, yes. Sadness. But also joy, anger, deep sexual feeling.

The sun is moving—or the earth is. I can no longer watch it set from my balcony. And now I notice the 9:00 sun just streaks my desk, whereas before it flooded it.

We went to Polk Street last night for ice cream. A dark, rainy night—but still easy & friendly and simple.

Went to hear Keith Jarrett at the Opera House. Wonderful music. He is very fair skinned. I was really happy to see his dull, kinky hair. I could have kissed it! The audience was 95% white & I kept thinking of how they are absorbing us—our creativity & even our physical selves. Jarrett's children are probably completely white—as Robert's child is.

I felt a great desire to lop off the heads of the whites in the audience.

It was a fine, attentive, music-loving San Francisco audience. But as usual with whites oblivious of the true cost of their pleasure.

When I mentioned my feelings to Roberto he was, I think, disturbed. When he is disturbed he gets clinical (he is studying medical sociology): "What brings on these feelings of wanting to lop off white people's heads?" he asks. I reply "Living in America." But he pretends this isn't an answer.

April Fool's Day 79

I think I know what love is. It is a connection to someone else that can't be broken just because you want to break it. It is a connection of the heart's fibers.

Alice, stop criticizing Robert & stop letting him criticize himself so unmercifully.

Remember the good parts and there are many. Remember, for example, the last few days: the long walk & the sunset—gifts from Robert to take with you back east. The dinners. The baths. Candles. Holding. Know that you love this man. Stop trying to get out of it. Whatever he is, you love him. Period.

Oh.

I want to love and be loved. And I am.

4-5-79

I find refuge in my work. Of course when it isn't coming I am wretched. It will be better too when Rebecca is here. And I will continue to make friends, involve myself with other people.

I'll trust my connection to Robert but I will also protect myself against him. This is the only way I can continue both to live & to love him. Both of which I desire to do.

The novel will not be put off much longer. And that is just as well.

I feel that Robert, who tries so hard to be responsible, fights the fetters of responsibility by attempting to make others be responsible for some of his worst behavior.

I also think I am too much for him—though I've dulled my plumage considerably.

Amazing. Men. Even the most "woman like" wish to be dominant. Wish to "put woman in her place."

4-26-79

And so—the end of this book.[1]

I am writing. I am settling here in San Francisco, which I love. In my co-op, with its petunias red & purple & white on the patio. (& daisies, marigolds, impatiens—my standards). Next week perhaps we will go on our trip to Yosemite. Perhaps not. I thank the universe I have friends & acquaintances who sustain me. The house in Brooklyn is secured. I will spend June in it, fixing it up for new tenants. In July or August Rebecca will join me here. (I have bought a $10,000 money market certificate to help me save against inflation.) And I will continue to put money into my savings account. Especially since I will have no "job" next year. Nothing steady, that is, except the Ms. consultantship. But if I rent out the Brooklyn house, my living expenses, except for food, will be taken care of.

---

1   AW often would summarize her current situation when she came to the end of each individual notebook or journal. This one, a gift from Robert, was a rich brown weathered leather.

I have a pain in my left breast caused by wearing sexy bras. Other than that—I am well—& grateful to be so.

May 1979

Today Mary Helen sent me a <u>Times</u> piece on Toni Morrison.[1] It is really very good. Gives a sense of Toni's moods & resilience & <u>self</u>, which interviews do not always convey. She sold paperback rights to Song of Solomon for over $300,000.00. I've been looking inside myself to see how I feel about this. A little jealous? A little envious? Probably. But on the other hand, it helps that she writes so beautifully—even if I feel her characters never go anywhere. They are created, I feel, so they might legitimately exist. And that's art, for sure, but not inspiration, direction, <u>struggle</u>.

Besides, I have chosen to struggle for peace of mind, the inner spirit, & inner life. And for happiness & peace. And I've started on the path . . . toward the life that works for me. Blessed. Robert loves me & I love him & Rebecca. And life is good. I <u>resent</u> the little flashes of dis-ease when I hear the loud hosannas & the large $ figures. I have everything I need. Why do I feel—when hearing of others' riches—it is not enough? It is no doubt the programming. Always want more than you have. Of everything. More food. More clothing. More praise. More money. And yet, more of all these could not make me more happy. Because I am happy already.

—

St. Clair Bourne came to visit, and I like him. But not as much as I did a year ago when he spent a day with Robert & me. Suddenly there are all these black men who want to visit me, to take me to lunch. It bothers Robert. But I am cool. If Robert & I don't work out—and, as he says, we're working out beautifully—I will have other men in my life. But I would trade all of them for Robert & for the life we're building together.

My class at Berkeley is going well. We've struggled through a number

---

1 "The Song of Toni Morrison," by Colette Dowling, the *New York Times Magazine*, May 20, 1979. AW's longtime friend, literary scholar Mary Helen Washington, sent her the piece.

of black women's slave narratives. I have about 30 students & auditors. Majority black women, which pleases me, and the rest rather sharp white women who seem serious. Many of the women—at least two—are black but could pass for white. They make this a part of their approach to the class.

I like teaching at Berkeley. I like being in the Afro-American Studies department. I like . . . the friendliness of everyone. The sincerity & simplicity. Not at all like Yale, where all the men are honchos. And the women seem so uptight. I even like the bus ride—and have given up the thought of owning a car. What a relief!

June 1, 1979
Arrived 3 1/2 hours ago at 423A First Street, Brooklyn. Amazing that I ever lived here. Astonishing that I ever dreamed I could live very long in Brooklyn. The city of Manhattan shrouded in mist—the Brooklyn streets littered. But on the other hand, I haven't yet been up on Seventh Avenue. Perhaps I should just walk up to the corner store & see what's happening.

—

The world tomorrow was, as usual, better. Went into the city to visit Sheila & JoJo & to see their street fair (block party). Then home, late, where an extraordinary thing happened. One of my new neighbors on First Street, Tod Boresoff, was out sweeping the sidewalk in front of his house . . . we exchanged pleasantries. I mentioned I was open for new tenants—he produced three! And next morning almost before I was up they appeared on my doorstep. Anne, Margaret & Joan. They've been back once since then, to check the space carefully. Will be coming back Sunday with 4th woman.

Spent Tuesday painting the kitchen, which surprised everyone. "You did it yourself?!" I feel good about having done it. Accomplished in a new skill. Now I must paint my bedroom in San Francisco. Something rich. Orange? Cantaloupe (soft, like that).

Louisa & Bryant left the house filthy, full of their junk and crawling with roaches. But Louisa returned the $75 that remained in the repair fund—that's something. I'm pleased they're out. Brenda's floor immaculate. Though she also shared the kitchen, which was disgusting. Food stuck on chairs, the walls. Etc. Etc.

Monday I spent at <u>Ms.</u> Interesting to be there as a guest. It tired me. I <u>do</u> have trouble breathing in New York. It isn't just my imagination.

Seventh Avenue is terrific! I've been enjoying it since the week-end when I was so critical & still comparing Brooklyn to San Francisco. They are <u>entirely</u> different. Each with its own allure. I think I shall offer a two year lease—because, who knows, I may come back to live in my little house after all. And really, in its way, & in its <u>location,</u> it is excellent. Eight rooms – sun deck – fireplace – room for guests. Rebecca. Me. A stoop. 7th Avenue nearby. The city near enough.

Why shouldn't I think in terms of living in New York <u>and</u> San Francisco? Why not, indeed.

Have started meditating again. Like it.

Today, the 6th, thought nostalgically of Robert. Wondered how he is finding Cuba.

Dreamed last night of the 3 of us: me, Robert & Pam. Wanted to write her a letter assuring her Casey is none the worst for his friendship with me for all his whiteness.[1] And her assumption that I would respond to him in a racist way.

House spoken for: 4 young (my age 35) white women have spoken for the house. A 2 year lease, with a 7% increase in rent per year.

June 17, Father's Day
Lying in bed in the Brooklyn house. After a full day yesterday selling books at the 1st Street block party/flea market.

June 21, 1979
I have (with Rebecca's help) boxed up all the things we are moving to San Francisco. Such a lot it seems. The mahogany bedroom set (<u>suite</u>?) and the

---

1   Casey, Robert and Pam's young son, is biracial, but "white" in appearance.

pine bench and the early American book press table & clothes & books & books & records . . .

I feel restless now that the movers are here—even <u>more</u> restless before they came, of course. This little house! I understand now why I bought it. I bought it as a place to store my papers. And the things I hope someday to put into a country house. So—in the basement, I've stored paintings, my Mexican desk, a thousand or so books. (A thousand are waiting near the door for the Salvation Army.) And next to its use as a place for my papers I bought it as an investment <u>and</u> lastly, as a place to live in, should I want to, in New York.

And Park Slope is really the best of New York City to me. A lovely neighborhood, vital but in no way hurried.

Looking out into my garden—a secret place under the huge black walnut—I try to still my anxiety about the movers. Overhead I hear them dismantling the bed & dresser, the washstand. And I feel very nervous. The bedroom set is so old & so heavy & so set in its ways! I cringe at the affront it might feel to be so frequently pulled apart & moved after standing in the same spot for 75 years!

A long letter & cards today from Roberto. Bob. Finally, I can call him "Bob" without hearing Pam's voice saying it too. My guilt about her is abating. I feel close to her at times in spirit. But I do love Robert/Bob. I feel what we have together is special & even though I've pulled back some—seeing that he is not there always to support me—I still feel the greatest delight reading his words of longing and love.

He writes of Mexico City in which, apparently, he spent several days. Then on to Cuba. He wishes we were visiting both places together. So do I! All our lives I can imagine us "touring" in a nice big touring car, driving over oceans, across continents—having a <u>wonderful</u> time together and sharing many nights of passionate & loving love.

We are sharing pyramids. The Olmec's (black) in Mexico. The ancient Egyptians' (black) in Egypt, & the Native American in Macon, Georgia.

Anyway—in the middle of that thought I went up to check on the movers. <u>They broke my antique dresser top & mirror.</u> To <u>smithereens.</u> The lovely mahogany columns & the glass. I couldn't bear to look at first. It was I imagine like being afraid to see a smashed body. I was in shock. But slight shock, to tell the absolute truth. I was happy it wasn't Rebecca. Delighted it wasn't me. Enchanted that it wasn't Robert's plane falling—or any person smashing to earth. But still—such beauty is hard to bear in ruins. It happened because the young Italian in the group—others are Puerto Rican & Black—(The P.R. is brown & lovely, gentle. And with a sense of humor.)—was trying to show me how to get the last slats out of the bed frame & doing it in a showy, macho way.

June 26

And now back in San Francisco. What a relief! Robert met me at the airport, sans flowers, but with many smiles.

I was so tired I literally could not see straight. We came home & piled into bed. In the morning made love—but I still feel out of it. It is midnight & I am still wide awake.

What troubles me: mostly, perhaps, leaving the Brooklyn house empty, with the memory of the burglary (break in of the house—theft of gun & T.V. & turquoise bracelet) the day before I left. The financial over-extending I'm experiencing. Fear over $ in the future. Rebecca to come soon. My work. Robert & this feeling of amicable distance.

Robert says I don't have to pay everything at once. That would help. Also to call tomorrow to get the cost of the moving so I'll be prepared for it.

Meditation is what I need.

July 4, 1979

The best July 4th I've ever had. It started last night with Robert's decision not to go to Atlanta for his family's reunion. I cooked a nice dinner & we watched two Paul Robeson movies on television. Then this morning we devoted to lovemaking. <u>Hours</u>. Bathing & eating & touching & loving. Then a long nap. Rose around two & I made a great lamb gumbo. Then off to the East Bay Hills & a spectacular walk—meadows, plains, lakes . . . magnificent trees. I love California.

Then dinner at a place with pillows on the floor in Berkeley—and a lovely drive home.

Everything mellow. Golden. Warm.
Amazing.

I do not feel like working—& that scares me.
Prolific Writer Attacked by California!
Slows Down!

July 12, 1979

<u>Many</u> feelings of vulnerability about the essay in the August issue of <u>Ms.</u>[1] I thought I was ready for it to be in print—and basically I am. But the talk with Tillie upset me. Started me once again on the inquiry of whether I am being fair to everyone in the essay. <u>Fair</u>. Why do I worry so much about being fair? Because I know right from wrong. And fair is right.

July 13, 79

The lesson of sleepless nights—of which I've had 2 1/2—is that I should not be upset the week before my period. The conversation with Carole Lawrence[2] upset me—she seemed so competitive & self-righteous. Ugh. And I of course brooded & brooded over it for longer than I should have. Luckily I had completed the script before she & I talked. . . .

. . . Anyhow. I will type up "Finding the Green Stone" today and mail it off to Nguzo Saba Films! My curiosity is deeply aroused by the notion of learning something new—and from a black woman! This is incredibly tempting, always. When not threatened they make wonderful teachers—in my experience.

---

1   "*One* Child of One's Own," *Ms.*, August 1979. Reprinted in the 1983 collection *In Search of Our Mothers' Gardens*, this essay discusses AW's belief that women artists should only have one child because more children would hamper independence and creativity. She also discusses many Black women's attitudes toward white feminism.

2   Film producer/writer Carol Munday Lawrence had asked AW to write a script for a film adaptation of her children's story, "Finding the Green Stone." Her production company was called Nguzo Saba Films.

July 26, 1979

Many years after Fidel & Co.'s attack on the Moncada Barracks.[1] A full, good adult day. The movers arrived with my furniture at 7:30. Robert & I had been sleeping all warm & snug. His arms around me. I got up to make coffee for him. (I love to do things for him. Last night I tucked him into bed—he had a stomachache. I kissed his eyes. I coddled & caressed him. I enjoyed it as much as he did. And he did enjoy it. He responds beautifully to being touched.)

Anyway, movers wanted a cashier's check for 1,009.40. So, to the bank. Then unpacking & seeing that the dresser & mirror were fixed. But the bed suffered. Missing bolt. Chips, scrapes. Etc. But tonight—after christening the bed with a "quickie," & going to Oakland to see children's slides celebrating July 26th—I am resting in my big bed once again.

The day has brought much that is good between me & Robert. He helped me so much. Just by being <u>with</u> me. Unpacking boxes. Putting up the stereo. Holding me from time to time. And he finally gave up on going to the office altogether & stayed around to be with me until he went to pick up Casey.

I am so happy with him. His gentleness & fatherliness with Casey— some of which rubs off on me. I am still hungry for fathering! I listen to Robert explain some small wonder of nature to Casey & I am enthralled, and somehow comforted. I tell him that he is like having a daddy.

What will it be like when Rebecca is here?

Whatever it is like—I have had a year I hope never to forget.

August 1, 1979

I believe Mama is to leave the hospital today. She has been there for 2 weeks. I am afraid she will die—and of course she will, one day. On some level, as they say, I am prepared. On another though I am not. I don't want her to be in pain, that's the main thing. She's too good to suffer. Ruth is with her & I'm glad of that. There's no one like Ruth when it comes to sickness.

---

1   On July 26, 1953, Fidel Castro and about 140 rebels attacked the federal barracks at Moncada. The Moncada assault was the first armed action of the Cuban revolution, which triumphed in 1959.

She should have been a doctor or a registered nurse. Then her life would have the dignity her talent deserves.

When there's only enough money, etc. to send <u>one</u> to school, <u>all</u> suffer.

Important reminder for when I'm edgy, jumpy, scared, out-of-sorts, suicidal (though not as graphically & urgently as when I was in my 20s, thank god!): Several days of severe upset beginning with a very <u>bad</u> conversation with Carol Lawrence & carrying through my period, always a tense time (I must remember the dolomite!) and publication of the essay.

The point is, I am all better now. Enjoying being alive. Loving the sun, moon, flowers, stars, Robert's touch as much as ever.

I am learning to trust the return of the "normal." Sleep is necessary. Eating well. Dolomite rather than Pamprin, I think. I should also look into potassium. But the bad times happen & must be got through. And then one regains one's balance.

I must frame my parents' picture, & mine, & put them in the line of anonymous black faces on the wall.

August 2, 1979

A perfectly lovely adult dinner evening with Barbara Christian,[1] Grace ___, & Najuma. I made scampi & noodles & salad. Juice, watermelon. But should have heated the plates.

Anyhow, <u>much</u> good talk & laughter. They stayed from 7–10:35.

We decided that the black male writers we know act like children. And the critics even worse. Like cowboys or something.

—

I sold the walnut dresser & the box springs & mattress. $75. Rebecca's room is all ready for her![2]

I have a teaching job lined up for the winter quarter at UC Berkeley. Lectures at Mills & Stanford.

---

1 Barbara Christian was a feminist author, scholar, and professor of African American Studies at the University of California, Berkeley.

2 After a year of living with her father in DC, nine-year-old Rebecca is joining her mother in San Francisco.

August 13, 1979

Rebecca arrived safely—thank every good spirit of the universe, and even every bad one. She has been here a week & she & I are settling in together. She is more high-key than I. Her talking exhausts me—but she tries very hard not to be too much for me, & I appreciate it.

She & Casey get along better since I've explained that babysitters must at least be <u>aware</u> of their charges.

Robert is resentful of her & jealous—emotions I feel sometimes about Casey. But all in all, we're becoming something like a family.

Robert & I have been seeing each other for—nearly 4 years. Let's see—I've been with him here in SF for one year. Before that, we went to the family reunion together 4th of July 1978. Ah! I can't remember! I just remember loving him very intensely for a very long time—& now I have an answer when I ask myself: Why do I love him? I love his smell. I love the way his body feels. His skin. His chest. I love his touch. I love his vulnerability in argument. I love his deep feelings of sorrow. I love his love of the open. I love the dumb way he holds me, as an animal would hold me, loving but without words. I love his ability to comfort me without words. I love his cooking, washing, cleaning—I love his fathering. I love his shyness.

The other night, Rebecca's 3rd night with us, I said to Robert who asked me what was wrong: "I wish you could converse." He was hurt. He said he did, had been talking. That I forgot. But I said no, he hardly said anything & I wanted always <u>more</u>.

Rebecca came in & thought we were arguing. But then we each turned to her and brought her into our discussion.

Bob explained that I always forget the good parts—that he'd literally come in the house talking about his day's mail. (He had. In a rushed, rather feverish monologue, he'd talked about his mail.) But this was not, I said, conversing!

Rebecca, a budding sage, said: But remember how you always say I'm too talkative & pushy when I talk too much? I think if Bob doesn't feel like talking, & you push him, that that's pushiness!

She is right. It turned out well, our discussion, because although Robert was hurt at first, he saw that I did not want to hurt him, only to express my need of him.

He has been trying to express himself more now, verbally. But his silence is still more eloquent than his speech—except when he's saying something he really wants to say—& <u>feels</u>.

Sept. 10

Am writing a very interesting piece on pornography—it is in the form I seem to be developing: the essay-story. Suits me at this stage, anyway.

Soon Rebecca will be in school for most of the day. I am beginning to enjoy her very much. We're becoming friends though I am frightfully distracted by life outside us, at times. My hatred of so much frightens me because there are times I simply cannot feel <u>beyond</u> it. But I must try, for my own sake.

And so, compañero, the way it is as of September 10th is: the day is gorgeous. My balcony is abloom with flowers. My daughter is healthy. My lover is well & loving . . . My eyes are with me. I see! A miracle in itself. After paying for the furnace I will not owe very much, & mostly on my MC card—which can be paid leisurely.

Food will become our greatest concern—as it has always been humankind's. At the end of 2 years my $2,500 will be worth considerably less. But will at least be a savings account. I will keep the $10,000 "rolling over" to collect whatever interest I can. I will keep the house in Brooklyn. It is worth at least $100,000 on today's wildly inflated housing market. I will keep it in good repair.

15 Galilee house is doing just fine.

After paying for the furnace, and whittling down the MC bill, and allowing for repayment of the loan: I will need to earn at least $500 a month.

Sept. 18, 1979

Told Robert last night that his marriage to Pam hurts me. I should have said: it embarrasses me. I do in fact feel embarrassed by it. "How can you love me & be married to someone else?" I asked. I was amazed at how melodramatic I sounded—but even more amazed that I <u>meant</u> the question.

He asked if I'd be interested in getting married. I said No.

The truth is I am tired of white folks by the time I'm in my house—I don't want them intimately about me anymore. I'm just <u>weary</u> of them. And Casey is hard enough to deal with without having to consider his mother as well.

Ah, but it is <u>so</u> painful. Robert clinging to his marriage as if it is a blanket, me knowing myself well enough to know—I cannot love him as fully as I wish because I can't trust him.

Not completely, as I would love to do.

One thing is clear, as it has been now for some time—this is love. I shudder to think of minimizing it, of not letting it grow.

Nov. 7, 1979

Am annoyed that my neighbor, an English teacher, doesn't know my work—but is reading Toni Morrison whom he compares to Steinbeck & Faulkner. <u>Sula</u> was given to him by a friend he says who asked him to read it and render an opinion. I said I felt <u>Sula</u> was beautifully written but unfinished. Underdeveloped, really. But then I stopped—because I realized reading a black woman writer was quite new to him—but also I just felt weary of it all. The nagging need to feel "successful"—the ups & downs, emotionally, of being "somebody."

Last night, for example, my "talk" at Antioch. Rebecca whispered "There's hardly any black women here." Right. Two out of 20. And the white women—<u>so</u> unconnected to real life. I had, for the first time, the feeling of being "entertainment."

One white woman said "I want to work with Black women, but I'm a separatist. What should I do?"

I told her she should do whatever—as for me though I can't afford the luxury of being a separatist.

A largely lesbian group whose eyes glazed over at the mention of men.

Only beginning the novel will save me for myself.

Nov. 12, Veteran's Day—

In the middle of what may or may not be the beginning of a novel, I started writing this clearly lesbian story. That has been the joy and surprise of the past few days. Just the way it bubbled up. Then, the night after I'd written a scene of two women making love, I dreamed of making love myself to a black man and to a white man. Have I ever dreamed of making love to a white man before? I think not. But this completes the circle, so to speak. The lesbian story seems to have freed my basic human eroticism. Interesting.

Just watched an interview on TV of Jane Fonda in which she emerged as a whole woman—grown-up, responsible, etc. Then there was a second interview conducted by her father—& she became a little girl again. Amazing.

> "Until the connective tissue is broken, I will continue to swallow myself."
> —MICHELLE CLIFF

Profound.

12/6

Last night I dreamed again of Ishmael Reed![1]

He was at my house (some country looking place in the country, with a porch and screen doors). And he had all these (4) children. Little boys.

He was in another room from where I was. And I was in a room talking to someone else, a woman. Anyway, his children came up on the porch & the smallest boy, Malcolm, said something like: "How do I get through this door." And I said, in a mean voice, "Well first you open it." Sarcastic. Waspish. And his face looked hurt. I had hurt his feelings. He went into the room down & across the porch where his father was.

Soon I went into that room, where Ishmael was sitting in a rocking

---

1   Ishmael Reed is an American novelist, essayist, poet, and cultural critic, perhaps best known for his satirical works challenging American political culture, and for his strong critique, during the 1970s and '80s, of Black feminist writers.

chair. I said "Where's Malcolm?" And there he was, near his father. I sat on the floor beside the chair and looked at Malcolm. I said "I sounded mean to you & I'm sorry for that. Please forgive me." And he just looked at me for a second—he looked just exactly like Ishmael in miniature; same round head & cheeks, same sturdy sort of chunky body. But his eyes were the soft, trusting, bewildered, recently hurt eyes of a child.

I opened my arms and he slid onto my lap, putting both chubby arms around my neck and nestling, snuggling close—all under my chin & everything. It felt so good! It was the best, most relaxed part of my sleep.

I think this means I hurt the little child in Ishmael, somehow, and I am sorry. I will try to let him know this.

———

St. Claire Bourne came to the Womanbooks party for Zora![1] It was wonderful to see him. I was excited—but for some reason I can't recall his face. Not distinctly. He says he will be coming here in February.

The party was glorious! Zora grinned the whole evening. So many fine people came: Ruby Dee, Laverne & her two children. [Poet] Howard [Nemerov] & his wife. Suzanne & Joanne from Ms. Marie Brown. Feminist Press folks. Gerald Gladney, Melvin Dixon, Michael McHenry—& on & on. Everything sold out. Amazing. I never felt happier.

Mary Helen[2] was profound and wonderful.

Goodness pays!

I am so happy to be home! Robert & Rebecca met me at the airport—all smiles & hugs and lovely looks. They are both so beautiful.

12-31-79

And so, to end the Seventies . . . Robert and Mary Helen are out in the rain shopping at Japantown. MH is here for the MLA[3] & we've been talking

---

1   A book launch party at NYC's Womanbooks for the Zora Neale Hurston reader that AW edited, *I Love Myself When I Am Laughing*.

2   Mary Helen Washington, a respected literary critic, professor, and friend, wrote the preface to the Hurston reader.

3   Mary Helen Washington was in San Francisco to attend the annual conference of the

non-stop as usual. R & I visited her panel yesterday, when she read her fine work on Nella Larsen. Then too we've gotten book reviews for "Zora"—the Times' review is excellent. The <u>Voice</u> not so good but finally the review had to admit that Hurston's work, especially in "Eyes," is magical. And magic means craft + talent + courage.

My life here is <u>so</u> full & rich—and I've found God! God is the inner voice that speaks up for what is the best/right course to pursue in any situation. It is the voice of the universe as it must have been when all was perfect. "Om," which is harder to hear today because of congested living & noise pollution & the hurried life.

I have cramps today—from doing yoga incorrectly, I think, and it is raining. Still, I am aware of sunshine in my heart. Because I know what love is. And I love so <u>much</u>. My most recurring expression is "I love . . ." Trees. Sky. Colors. Food. Everything that is in harmony with the soul of the universe ("om"). I meditate. I pray, in meditation. I talk to myself & converse with my inner voice. And I understand things . . . what Sojourner Truth meant by "God." The inner voice.

Robert and I are very happy together. I'm amazed by him. He seems to be blossoming and I love the way he loves me & the way he is around the house. He cooks breakfast, straightens up. Shops. We grocery shop together sometimes & it is <u>fun</u>.

Now we three have had lunch & we've been talking about Cuba. And art & literature & sex—all day. And feeling calm & warm and strongly friendly. I am so happy with my life I wish it could go on this way forever. With love & friends & work & guests/sisters (& brothers) and time to meditate & reflect.

I want to write a different kind of book. Will I?

Welcome back, Zora. Welcome all the citizens of all our Eatonvilles. You've survived!

Modern Language Association, a scholarly organization that seeks to strengthen the study and teaching of languages and literatures.

*   *   *

I am more optimistic this year than ever before. Even the threat of a 3rd world war doesn't kill off the optimism. I think there is amazing stuff in the universe. That maybe human beings are working toward some inevitable perfection. Who knows?

In the meantime—

I am thankful for my life.
For the world
For love
& friends
& child
& work

I stand midway my life. But only if I live until I'm seventy.

PART THREE

BE NOBODY'S DARLING

THE 1980s

Jan. 14, 1980

Mama is very sick. And I've been dreaming about her. Last night I dreamed I was in a huge house (the house of life) with many rooms. In each room something interesting was going on. In one eating & drinking. In another study & learning, & teaching. I moved through them all flirting mildly with all the sensitive looking men. Outside, a wedding was going on & I stood on the second floor balcony watching it. Then I moved to a room that had benches & sat beside a man (somewhat older than the others, but sensitive and with a wonderful face, gentle, strong) who almost immediately said to the people around him: It's time to help Polly leave. And he rose, stepped past me, and walked over to a black skinned woman dressed in African style (though not African colors) in a dark dress & headwrap. She looked pregnant rather than fat. And he lifted her from her seat & he & several others dragged her carefully into the center of an adjoining room. I followed, not knowing what was going on. Then all her children, like small puppies, were placed on & around her, & they began to pat her body very lightly all over and as they patted they said, over & over: "Bye Mother," "Bye Mother," "Bye Mother." And the mother struggled under their hands to let her spirit go free. I could see the spirit struggling, like an unborn child, all underneath her skin, trying to get out of her body.

Behind the children there were rows of her women friends, and at her feet, her husband. They were all speaking soft encouraging words to her. They were all smiling. Even, once in a while, someone gave a gentle laugh. I understood that they were trying to help "Polly's" spirit escape, & rise. And that they understood this "freeing of the spirit" to be a joyous occasion.

So there I sat, in a corner, moved to tears by their love & understanding & method of meeting death, and yet trying to smile so that I would not be the one heavy heart dragging on Polly's spirit and keeping it on earth.

I told Rebecca about this dream & she told me hers of last night: Curtis[1] (recently very ill with diabetes) and Mama (ill now with, we think, pneu-

---

1 One of AW's brothers.

monia) died at the same time, met in the air, joined hands, laughing, & rose on up to heaven.

If my mother does die, it seems to me, she has prepared us, or is trying to prepare us, in the most loving way.

Jan. 21, 1980

Last night Robert & I went for a walk. And we saw the moon set! I'd never seen this, neither had he. It sets, just like the sun. And tonight it is higher in the sky & waxing. I was so moved to see it set. Watching it together in awe & joy is a symbol of our relationship. And I've been thinking of the Persian proverb: "Don't look for the moon in the pond, look for the moon in the sky." "Don't look for God in the Scriptures, look for God in Life itself." In yourself.

Anyhow. We're struggling with monogamy—whether to have it. Robert wants it. I'm not sure. There's no one else I'd like to sleep with—perhaps Bertina, but that's unlikely. I just don't know. I feel sexiest when I'm free.

I did our huge laundry today & accepted a reading date at Stanford for next month. Finances are looking up. And the new stories will go off to Wendy by the week-end.

Feb. 3, 1980

In a week I'll be 36 years old. I've just returned from Georgia & Mama. Mama has just had an operation to open a clogged artery. And is recovering nicely, according to Ruth. I've risen at 9; (Rebecca is overnight at Heidi's) (Robert & Casey at his place) and written two important letters. One to Kalamu ya Salaam[1] telling him I hate interviews and do not want to be interviewed about "what it is like to be a black woman(!)" Yawn . . . and that I will send him a story or poem in the normal course of my writing life. The other letter went to Mickey Friedman—The Examiner, Jan. 28, 1980.[2] I told her it was impossible for me to speak of "so-called oppressed people"

---

1 Poet Kalamu ya Salaam was editor of the *Black Collegian* magazine from 1970 to 1983.

2 The letter was in response to Mickey Friedman's article in the *San Francisco Examiner*, "The voices of black Southern women," January 28, 1980.

since my/their oppression is real, with nothing "so-called" about it. One problem with interviews is that I am not entirely coherent—and suffer for this because I'm <u>aware</u> that my mind fogs over—but also interviewers stick words in my mouth.

I regretted having said that <u>Meridian</u> is "about" Black men & white women. What a reduction! But in regretting this statement, something else became clear: it is—on this level—more about <u>black men & black women</u>. Setting each other free. Letting each other go, even if we are going to a white person.

———

The high point of my Eatonton visit was giving Mama a bath. I'd been so afraid I wouldn't know what to do, how to do it, etc. That I'd be embarrassed. That she'd be. But we weren't, especially. She said: You wash down as far as possible. Then you wash up as far as possible. Then you wash possible.

While I was with Mama I read to her. The stories from <u>I Love Myself</u> made her laugh. And "In Search of Our Mothers' Gardens" made her smile. A big, wide, gold-teeth shining smile. I came home with a cold, fatigue, a period & nosebleed but it was worth it. I had been afraid to see her because I was trying to prepare myself for her death—put distance between us. But she is totally captivating—I love her as much & with the same passion as when I was a child. So strange, & wonderful. She's nearly seventy. Her braids are gray. Her skin is wrinkled & she moves with her walker like a tortoise— & she's <u>cute</u>. . . . She is illuminated by that radiant spirit within.

However, she is a colorist—and that's unfortunate. It is winter & I'm paler than usual. She said "You look better lighter." I replied "I look healthier black."

———

One day while meditating I felt I knew that God exists. That I knew what God <u>is</u>. And that I <u>believe</u> in God! This was astonishing. It caused me to laugh & cry. I felt like a very funny joke had been played on me. My God, believing in God! How quaint, old fashioned and cowardly! But God is the spirit of Good in the universe & the spirit of Good in ourselves. God is the inner voice that is always right. God is the universe striving to perfect itself. The devil is the evil in the world & it is gaining on us.

Today I saw a sign that said: There is no future. I thought, no future for us, perhaps, but something will survive the holocaust, & the earth will endure the millions of years necessary to become pure again. This consoles me. A little.

3-3-80

Many perfect days with Robert. And I mean "perfect." Today, for instance, Monday, we spent mostly together. He stayed over last night. We loved this morning after almost a week's abstinence. He left me dozing.

———

He is a real friend to me: loving, kind, thoughtful & generous. He gave me an amethyst crystal. For protection. It is my birthstone, a stone for the highly evolved spiritually, or in my case the high & evolving. We went out to the beach to purify it & to let the moon wash it. Casey marched ahead of us with the flashlight.

———

I've never been so happy living anywhere! Or am I always happy where I live? I love the apartment, my big bed, the rocking chairs & shutters. I like that it is mine. That it is <u>ours</u>; all the people in the square "own" it with me. So it is "mine" but also "not mine." Like God. In me but also out of me.

    Robert gets cuter to me too.

    I must learn to cook with a WOK!

3-18-80

Mel's birthday. He is 37. Younger than Robert, which always surprises me. I recall that on that first visit home my mother saw "the old man" in him. She thought he was forty <u>then</u>. But it was tiredness. He was a workaholic even then—only I thought it attractive. I wasn't about to waste time on some Colored Person who'd spend Monday morning in bed with me & Tuesday letting me massage his scalp! How we change. Life does not require workaholism. To work all the time is to miss life itself. You miss the sky changes, the grass colors, the little wildflowers. You miss a day like yesterday, when R. & I made love in the sun in my study, ignoring his cold.

———

But I really opened this journal to record something that Jesus said in the Gnostic gospels long ago & that I wondered about. He said: Learn how to suffer and you will not suffer. And I think I understood this a little last night. I had been suffering with pain in my heart & left arm. The stress of this age is incredible! And I seem to register it all. Anyway, coming back from the airport I suddenly thought: Well, if I must suffer, I must & I will. I'll stop fighting it as something fearful, frightening, alien to me. I will accept suffering as a condition of my life. Immediately my body relaxed, and I felt much better. Perhaps this improvement isn't lasting. But I am pleased to have experienced this & hope to continue in this mode.

Today is clear and cold. I can see the St. Bruno Mountains clearly. But spring is also here. My daffodils have bloomed. And a couple of tulips. I feel my novel stirring within me. Hesitantly. Almost sleepily. Or is it fearing that I will shut it off again to teach, or to go cross country reading?

4/18/80

Back almost a week from my spring reading tour in the East. Also a week at my mother's house in Georgia. 3 weeks away in all. Too long. Of my mother's environment I can bear about 3 days before beginning to feel very closed in. Eatonton itself is ugly & decaying, though its countryside—especially Bell's Chapel Road—is lovely.

The town gave me a welcome home with a proclamation (my own week!) and key to the city. My high school classmates gave me flowers (daisies) & pen & paper. And Miss Reynolds introduced me from the perspective of one who knew me before I was born. There was a weird chicken salad & wonderful songs sung for me. Reminiscences. Miss Cook, my Home Ec teacher, remembered I'd made an extraordinary scrapbook out of paper bags. (No money for paper.) Ruth came—none of my other immediate family. Some aunts & uncles & cousins from Macon.

Undated 1980¹

Mama, why are you so sad?

Because I can't write the book I need to write.

Why can't you write the book you need to write?

Because it would be painful.

Why?

Because of the things I would have to talk about.

What things?

Oh, sex and color and class & how hard it is to love people & even to know what you're doing. If I write, I may hurt you.

Why?

Because you are my child & everybody would pity you for having a mother who says crazy things. Even crazy things about you.

Like what?

Never mind.

Like what?

Like the time you told me that you feel funny around people who are darker than me. I understand what you meant, but I was hurt. You would have felt funny around my father & my grandfather & my grandmothers, both of them. In the summers I become darker. Do you feel funny around me?

No. I think you look pretty darker. More healthy. Anyway, I am getting darker too. I can tell you want me darker. You like me better that way.

Sometimes I feel bad about that, but I can't help it. I want you to be brown, with me. When you are pale, I feel you are being stolen away.

---

1   This undated entry begins on the inside front cover of a dark blue spiral-bound notebook and ends on the inside back cover. The seventy-page notebook, which bears a price sticker declaring its value at 99 cents, contains several pages of expository writing about "Shug Perry," written in the third person, in standard English. Celie's story is also captured in this notebook in this straightforward, expository way. Then, just past halfway in the notebook, the very first page of *The Color Purple*, as we know it, appears.

But that's crazy.

See, I told you.

Undated 1980[1]

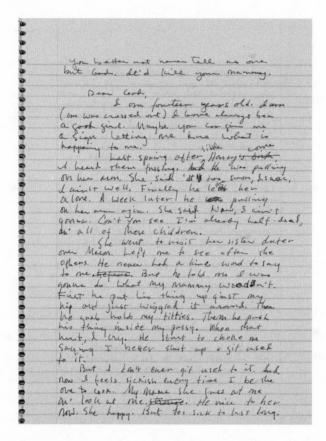

What do we want? My God, what do black women writers want?

We want freedom. Freedom to be ourselves. To write the unwritable. To say the unsayable. To think the unthinkable. To dare to engage the world in a conversation it has not had before.

—

---

1 This is a portion of the first page of *The Color Purple*, written in green ink, which appears in the middle of the aforementioned blue spiral-bound notebook, circa 1980. The first draft of the rest of the novel, handwritten in various colors, fills up the remainder of this journal and several additional notebooks.

Women's writing is going to be like women. Women are different from men. Women talk more & more easily, they tell more "secrets"—they reveal themselves periodically in order to grow, to choose, to move into a fresh decision. In this sense their writing is as it were influenced by the rhythms of the womb—& what's wrong with that? So is the ocean & growing corn.

Undated

Dear Diane K. Miller,

I am in the country working on a novel. This explains why my comments must be brief, and why they are not typed. My typewriter is in the city. Since you ask for a "critique" within a week—it must be in this form.

Basically, I am very inspired by all the <u>details</u> of the various periods in Hurston's life Bambara has been able to reconstruct; the first sections especially of the script are richly visual.[1] And it is a great joy to see the spirit of Hurston & the times shine throughout B's work on her. However, because the typing is so erratic, I found it difficult at times to decipher sentence sense. For the next draft, Ms. Bambara must be provided an expert typist and, perhaps, proofreader. Folk language is so pithy that to omit a single "and" or "but" causes incomprehensibility.

My primary concern is with the ending. It is impossible for me to believe, after all her struggle to achieve wisdom, Hurston saw her quest as mainly a literary one. For a person of Hurston's sensibility, the literary quest is really a manifestation of or "mask" for the spiritual. Personally, I think Hurston knew that one day her literary gift would be well received, and that she would be remembered along with Hughes & Wright. When your gift to a

---

1   This letter is in response to a script drafted by Toni Cade Bambara, an acclaimed Black novelist and short story writer, for a biographical film about Zora Neale Hurston.

people is themselves, they're bound to have to accept it sooner or later.

The spiritual quest, the seeking of wisdom or even knowledge, never does end—and who can say this understanding itself was not Zora's real goal, and that she reached it? Certainly each of her struggles seemed designed to contribute to her spiritual development and to deepen her powers of personal insight. Seen from this perspective, her critics served a positive function, a function completely hidden from her at first, but one which, eventually, she would have understood.

In other words, she was collecting herself (her folklore) for her own use, first. Because the foremost requirement of wisdom is self-knowledge. Though it is true that we are trying to place Hurston (as a part of ourselves) in a form, or literary tradition, that we can use to help us become more self-knowledgeable & eventually (we pray) more wise, this was not, in my opinion, a limitation she would have imposed on herself.

In all her searches Hurston was seeking more fundamental connections than literary ones, which seems clear everywhere in the rest of the script, what with her meager clothing and her black cat bone. Not to mention her persistent attention to non-literary sources of truth and inspiration.

July 9, 1980
Meadowhouse, Boonville, California[1]
The story "1955"[2] pleased me very much & reminded me that fiction, good fiction, brings with it a joy for the writer, a kind of free happiness. It is all

---

1   AW was working on her new novel at a rented country house in Boonville, California, in Mendocino County.

2   In AW's short story "Nineteen Fifty-five," Gracie Mae Still, the first-person narrator, is a blues singer with similarities to Big Mama Thornton, the first person to record "Hound Dog" (the song that made Elvis Presley famous). In the story, Traynor, a young white man, buys a song from Gracie Mae, records it, and becomes a big star—but has trouble finding

creative. It is all voices speaking through one's pen. I read the story in Santa Cruz at UC & the audience loved it. I did too. Rather I loved Gracie Mae's spirit. And I wonder where did she come from? I was lying on the bed near sleep and she began speaking. As naturally & intimately as an aunt. And I realize this is, to me, the best kind of writing—the writing which seems to be simply the writing down of a story overheard.

In any case. Thanks largely to Roberto's persistence, we found this quite charming house in the country, in the Anderson Valley, twenty-odd miles from Ukiah. Twirly roads coming through the spectacular mountains, but then the gorgeous valley of which I have a long unobstructed view. The house is on the very edge of the meadow/valley underneath a tall hill, near an apple orchard (this is apple growing country) & there is a white horse out cropping through the tall grass. Willis[1] loves it here & already is eating stuff she catches that isn't, apparently, very good for her (her bowel movements are nearly blocked by hair & fur! Ugh!). There is an apple tree just before my window—12 windows in the living room—and birds & <u>deer</u>. We have begun a garden. I have bought cabbage & brussels sprouts & tomatoes, etc. etc.

Rebecca is now in camp in New York—Timberlake—& I miss her. I have been spending every morning sewing curtains. They are uneven, but somehow just right. Last night we looked at the sky full of stars (so many! I had forgotten how many!) & Robert explained the Milky Way & the existence of other galaxies. We are very small, I thought.

Today I realized I must begin the work I came here to do. That the lingering anxiety I feel is fear that now that I have everything I want—as I told Robert—life is finished. But, he said, work is always before us. And so it is. And that's the fear.

---

happiness. The short story was first published in the March 1981 issue of *Ms.* magazine as "1955, or, You Can't Keep a Good Woman Down." It would later be the opening story in AW's 1981 short story collection, *You Can't Keep a Good Woman Down.*

1   Willis is Rebecca and Alice's cat.

August 5, nearly a month since we moved in. And I just ate a bowl of turnips from the garden. It occurred to me that when I thin the plants, those trimmed should be eaten, rather than thrown away. I was right. They're delicious! Strong & flavorful, unlike turnips in the city & these are only 3 inches tall!

I slept poorly last night. Missed Robert who returned to S.F. & to work. But also felt vulnerable in the house because of the flimsy doors. But nothing happened. Willis woke me enough to be let out. I drifted. Should not have watched "Intimate Strangers"—about wife battering. It is amazing to me that women trust men. This is surely one of the best examples of self-deception, since men are transparently untrustworthy, in general.

In particular? I realize I trust Robert in ways I've never trusted anyone. As I've come to know him, really know <u>him</u> as distinct from my fantasies or expectations. His is an ethical nature, though degraded to a degree by pain & compromise. It is a remarkably vulnerable nature as well. But at the same time, one capable of, even eager for, certain kinds of risks. But no, that's wrong. Not "eager for," merely aware that risks are inevitable.

I told him I am ready to resume my relationship with Pam. He seemed surprised & then pleased, as we talked of ways this continuation might help our collective relationship. Perhaps it will help me with Casey.

Suddenly I notice the birds are back: During the heat wave we've kept the windows covered. I fear they will start flying into the glass again, killing themselves. But perhaps they'll stay in the garden, eating my cabbage.

As long as they don't puncture my one ripening tomato!

And so, what to do about the coming year?

I think I should spend every available moment reading & writing. The winter course at Stanford? Precisely the one I taught at Berkeley perhaps, so as not to have to think about structure. But this is probably impossible for me. Twice would be boring to me. And what of Brandeis in the Fall of '81? A year from now? Too soon! everything whispers. Make it the Fall of '83. This is good advice.

Sept. 14, 1980

Rebecca returned safe & sound and gorgeous from camp.

We've been to the country twice since she's arrived & she loves it. I certainly still do. . . .

. . . I never heard my mother yell or scream at a single one of the white children she kept. She never used with them her "real" tone of voice, never showed her real anger. Never spoke to them the way she spoke to me. If she had yelled & screamed at them perhaps I could have accepted them as my equals—as children, but she was always forbearing, "long suffering"—but then, she worked for them.

When you are a maid you act a role.

But as a child, I mistook the acting for my mother's genuine behavior. I thought she was more loving & patient with her charges, not because their parents paid her $17(!) a week, but because they were white, and she did say she thought white children "naturally better & smarter," didn't she?

Why did my mother say this to me, when my teachers were frequently telling her how good and smart I was?

Why was I never affirmed by my mother?

But I was affirmed. Rarely in words—I needed words.

She gave me a sewing machine. A suitcase. Freedom. She never, ever, doubted my word. Freedom she gave me to lie in bed & read. Sit on the porch & dream.

How much can I blame her for finally giving in & saying yes, whitefolks, your house is bigger, food better, car larger, children better & smarter— They war on us on every front. Poor mom. Maybe you gave me so much freedom so I'd never have to be beaten the way you were.

Oct. 13, 1980

The house in Brooklyn is a wonderful investment. And sometimes I even think of spending a year there. Why not? I think. It is a charming little house and the garden has a few possibilities. Without the big bed the back parlor could be really wonderful, with a nice cheerful fire in the fireplace.

Robert said tonight: What more is there? That I have a townhouse in New York, a flat in San Francisco and a country house in Mendocino County. And a car. And I make a living from my work. And my work has value to me and others.

I am lucky & blessed. And thankful.

And must keep trying to dislodge the roots of my racialism. I think for instance that what attracts and repels me in Robert is a similarity to the things that are in me that I either find exciting or that I wish to repudiate.

I had the feeling that telling him I no longer love him was necessary and that indeed I no longer love the Robert of illusion, the Robert who attracted me because he and his family represented a kind of prize, a kind of advancement (based on color) or exception.

Now I know I hate the opportunism of the mulatto caste, hate their attempts at passing. Hate their assimilationist tendencies. In fact, hate all these things which I find within myself and I'm not even a mulatto. But Rebecca is! That brings it too close for comfort.

Robert repaid the $250 he owed me with <u>gold</u> coins from his collection.

There is a feeling between us that is quite extraordinary. It is the feeling of constant awareness and revelation. The feeling of <u>learning</u>.

And so, I lie here in my big bed alone, knowing that some form of relationship with Robert will continue. Not ruling out love or trust because anything is possible.

Oct. 22, 1980
I work, I love, I mother, I dream.

Dec. 2, 1980
Mama's birthday. She's 68. Born in 1912. I called her and we chatted for a few minutes. She had lots of guests for Thanksgiving. And Ruth and Linda over the weekend. Her voice sounds <u>free</u>. No worry in it. No hatred of anyone or anything.

Dec. 10, 1980
Preparing to do a reading at Claremont College. Did one last week at UC Davis—300-500 people, a packed house. Strange. And a standing ovation

after "1955," which was preceded by the sado-masochism piece. Worn out still from the East coast trip. But nearly done in completely by John Lennon's death.[1] I hadn't realized how much I loved him—<u>loved</u> the Beatles. How much "their" music (so beautifully influenced by "our" music) was a part of my life. God, how thankful I am for having lived through the Sixties—I respect so many of my contemporaries!

March 19, 1981

In bed with a cold and a hacking cough <u>and</u> my period! God help me. Willis asleep at my feet, cramps starting. Rebecca in school. Robert in the air on a flight to N.Y. for ten days. I am to do a benefit for the women's building tomorrow night and keep flashing on myself coughing and sneezing as I plow through the stories I am going to read.

Have been reading Katherine Mansfield[2]—short stories—and have no trouble understanding why Woolf considered her her only rival. Woolf understood that a great white woman writer is great indeed—though her male contemporaries refused to let themselves believe this. And that if a great white woman writer wrote equally well about the lives of rich and poor (and Woolf herself could only write—in fiction—about the well-to-do) then she was bound to be doing the best work in the western world . . . since there were no black working class women writing at the time.

This is not arrogance. Just the belief that novelists who stick to color and class—when they live in a multi-colored, multi-class society—lack courage and sufficient curiosity to justify long interest.

In any event. I am trying to get well, and will go on, helped, perhaps by Contac, which should keep me from sneezing, at least.

---

1 On Monday, December 8, 1980, John Lennon was shot by Mark David Chapman in the archway of the Dakota building, his residence overlooking Central Park in New York City. Having sustained four gunshot wounds, he was pronounced dead on arrival at Roosevelt Hospital. The killer remained at the crime scene and began reading J. D. Salinger's *The Catcher in the Rye* until police arrived and arrested him.

2 Katherine Mansfield was a modernist writer from New Zealand. In 1911, her first published collection of short stories, *In a German Pension*, was well received.

Last week-end in the country. Robert, for the first time, rapturous over its beauty. He has been different this whole week after his divorce.

He was afraid, I think, (and he said) that Pam would refuse to sign at the last minute. But she did. And he seems to be blooming, just this week. Talking. Smiling more. And saying "isn't it <u>beautiful!</u>" at the Boonville landscape. And being intent on helping C.[1] plant tiny violas in a corner of the garden.

Meanwhile, there are deer tracks in the garden on the hill and we must consider a fence.

Good news to report re: Casey. We're becoming friends. One day he asked me to show him how to "piece." (I am making a quilt.) And I did. And he loves sewing. And we sit and sew! Together! I am so happy about this. And our friendship makes Robert very happy. But that, though nice, is secondary. I thought I was polluting my soul being exclusionary. Casey and I gathered horse manure and straw from the pasture in front of our house. Then he found a bag of steer manure in the grass. And dolomite. Some early gardeners abandoned it. I wonder why? We put everything on the compost pile. And I can finally see progress there. I turned up some of the bottom soil and will do this even more thoroughly next weekend. We will have leaves and straw, horse manure, dolomite and perhaps some well-rotted wood dust from the old lumbering sites in the field.

I like Anderson Valley more and more. And have met people I like. Jan Wax and Chris and Sue Sellars and Janet. I've bought lovely pottery from Jan and Sue. And the Boonville house is beginning to look all handcrafted. What with bamboo rug beaters and a god's eye, and woolen rugs and Guatemalan cloths.

I have not disappointed myself about the novel, either.

As you recall, I arranged to have 3 months, unbroken, in which to write. . . . Did I dare try to work on the novel? Since life in the city is not as idyllic and uncomplicated as it was when I wrote last summer in Boonville? Since I must share my brain with thoughts of Rebecca's fights at school and

---

1   Casey, Robert's young son with Pam—who Robert has finally, officially divorced.

what to cook for dinner? Eventually, I plunged in—let what will, happen. And I've been very pleased. Not that the writing is perfect. Nor does it have that "completion of a dream" quality always, that I love. But it is adequate, even good, and I still enjoy the unfolding of my characters' personalities and the drama of their lives.

May 5, 1981

Before I meditate and while finishing my tea, what does my life look like this pale sunny San Francisco morning?

Times are very trying for poor people. For blacks, Indians, gays, lesbians, for everyone, in fact, except rich whites who are in power. I no longer watch television, except for some shows, like M*A*S*H. I can't bear to read the newspapers. And I lapsed in taking my vitamins. My eyes hurt. There is a blister on my eyeball.

My anxiety over the publication of the book[1] is lessening. And perhaps the tiredness comes from that. Now I can feel anxious because no one seems to have heard of it yet—though it was officially published only last Wednesday. I must remind myself (apparently) that they're good stories and what is more, <u>necessary</u> stories.

And I'm not really working well. If I could work, nothing would bother me. Of this I am certain.

May 12th

For the last few days it's been hard to keep up with the people in the novel. They are all trying to express themselves at once, and Celie has become <u>quite</u> an interesting person! And the men are growing! Slowly, reluctantly, but they're moving. Robert has helped me a lot to be able to affirm certain tendernesses in men.

Fatherness and gentleness. What I require in a man.

I am very happy with the book. I intend to call it:

---

1   The short story collection *You Can't Keep a Good Woman Down* was officially published on April 29, 1981.

The Color Purple.
        Or
Purple
I think the first.

Great Spirit bless us. All. Teach me the way to be like you. Show me
    how to do it.
                —S. WONDER

June 24, 1981
I've finished the novel!
    Rebecca is off to camp and her father's for 2 yrs!

The womanist writer is the story herself as well as the person telling it.

Aug. 13, 1981
Tillie[1] has read The Color Purple and has had almost nothing to say. I'm
sure she doesn't like it. She read it on the bus and gave it back to me in great
disorder, fifty pages missing. But no matter who dislikes the book, I like it.
And it is a true book. And just think—my first happy ending!

Nov. 2
For a while (August–September, part of October) I thought I might buy a
house and 24 acres of land in Mendocino. And it is a good buy. 110,000 or
perhaps 105,000. I was prepared to pay, from savings and advance: 25,000
at close of escrow, 15,000 on March 15th, 15,000 on Nov. 15th, for a total of
55,000 and up to 500 a month for however long it took to pay off the bal-

---

1   Tillie Olsen, born in 1913, was a white feminist author of fiction and nonfiction whose
writings spoke to the struggles of women and working-class families. Olsen's nonfiction
book *Silences*, published in 1978, explored authors' silent periods, including writer's blocks,
unpublished work, and the challenges that working-class writers, especially women, often
face in finding time to focus on their art. A San Francisco resident, Olsen had welcomed AW
warmly when she first moved to the Bay Area.

ance. I offered 90,000. The place haunts me a little still. Though in order to afford it I would have to raise my offer at least 10,000. Or 15,000. Which I could do if I got a 15,000 advance for the essays.[1] The main thing is I know I want to own a house <u>with land</u> in Mendocino. In the Anderson Valley.

Rick's house is perfect in many ways. There's the land. Then there's the house with lots to be done on it to make it ours.

But buying it would wipe out my savings. How could I do it?

As of next July:

20,000 CDS	900.00 Brooklyn house
<u>25,000</u> CDs and Savings	<u>-561.00</u>
45,000	329.00
<u>15,000</u> (advance on essays?)	<u>-264.10</u>
60,000	64.90 (taxes)
<u>15,000</u> (Brandeis?)	
75,000	

105,000
<u>-75,000</u>
30,000

Mentioned to Robert that I've been thinking of how pleasant it might be to live in the country. He said he'd been thinking we might start a business. Publishing? Something mail-order, in any case. Perhaps we could set up a 5 year plan.

To secure a house and land in the next 2–3 years, finances and the economy permitting (things look shaky to us both just now). I could accept a couple more in-residence jobs. After Brandeis the one in East Washington, perhaps. For Mendocino land, I'm tempted to sell the house in Brooklyn, but that would be a mistake, I think. Since it pays for itself and for my car-

---

1 This book of essays, written between 1966 and 1982, would be published in 1983 as *In Search of Our Mothers' Gardens: Womanist Prose.*

rying charges here. And Park Slope is such an excellent location the value of the house is sure to increase.

An invitation in the mail to read at the U. of Kentucky.

Readings look like this:

Howard University	2400
Reed	300
U of Chi	2650
U of K	2000 + exp.
New School	100 + exp.
Nassau	800
	8,250
	700 San Jose
	100 Oakland Museum
	9,050

Nov. 5—

Yesterday I went to visit Robert and Casey. Casey is home with a cold. My visit gave Robert the opportunity to go out for a bit to buy juice and things for supper. While he was out I read mostly, then opened up his picture album. Then I saw a picture envelope behind the album and I opened that. It contained copies of pictures Jan and I made at the women's music festival. The two of us nude to the waist and a former student entirely nude. Robert had made "copies" of our pictures for his own "use." I took the pictures home with me.

Last night, after he'd cooked and served a delicious beef stroganoff and broccoli, I asked him about the copies, while taking out the negative and destroying it. He said I had known about the copies. I had not. He said he never said there were no copies (he picked the pictures up from the Kodak place). He did. I reminded him that when he returned to the car after picking up the pictures, he'd made a big point of showing me how the seal was unbroken.

So then he sulked quietly for a while. Eventually I told him I felt he'd exploited my trust. That he'd deceived and lied to me. And that he'd invaded the privacy of me and my student and my friend.

He said he was sorry. But went on to explain that—if we were to be honest with each other, as I said I thought necessary—he had to admit to his inability to stop objectifying women. In short, he said, in our relationship he is not a pornographer but otherwise he is. I asked if he thought taking a feminist sponsored tour of the pornography district would help him. He said he already takes the tour, but as a customer rather than a critic. We discussed pornography as an addiction—which I think it is. And how it feeds and often creates in men sexual compulsion, which Robert has. I asked him to show me some of his new magazines. He was very reluctant but eventually complied. The first one was an Asian woman and an Indian man. He said: Well at least now my books are Third World. Then he showed me books full of very homely, very sad and physically odd looking black women. Then one of a plastic white couple.

I asked to see the books out of curiosity and also because he said something about me "sharing his fantasies." Rather he wondered if I ever could. He said to me there is no such thing as erotica, that because I'm concerned about who produces it and where the big money goes, it is all pornography to me. Yes. I looked at the scars on the Indian "lover's" back and wondered how he got them. I looked at the "oriental" woman (on the cover she's sucking his cock) and wondered if she were Vietnamese and whether she spoke English and whether this was the only job she could find. I can't separate the pictures from the real people. I asked Robert how he would like to see my face on the cover of a magazine wrapped around some guy's cock. He said: But you wouldn't do that! I guess he thinks I would starve to death or watch Rebecca starve to death rather than do this sort of "work." But I'm not so sure. I can imagine one day being in just the position I imagine my Asian (Vietnamese, Cambodian, boat person?) sister might be in. And, in the magazine, is in.

In any case, I kept trying to make connections for Robert between slavery and pornography. Between sexism and racism. But to no avail. This morning I woke up nauseous. And really unable to look at him. I wanted only to get up and out of the apartment, into the air. Coming home, I thought of Fanny Kemble,[1] married to a slave owner until she couldn't stand it any more. And I thought: that's the way I feel. And I wondered if revulsion would overcome love, as it apparently did in her case.

Yesterday Wendy[2] came by with muffins and raspberries and get well wishes. I thought of what her response would be to all this. I thought of why feminists are sometimes lesbians. Surely more would be lesbians if they dared, faced with men's addiction to exploiting women. The ones they claim to "love" and the ones they don't know.

And I thought of Faith.[3] Undrugged. Uncompulsive. Uncommitted to the exploitation of anyone. Beautiful. Bright. Spirited. And off in the wilds of Jamaica—a hotbed of sexism—alone. Struggling to learn enough about Jamaican health care to offer helpful insight.

Men and women are fundamentally different sexually, I think.

All day I've been sick. Through shopping, arranging flowers (Gloria[4] is coming for the weekend: how nice it would be to speak of this to her but I know I won't. I had intended to be so happy!) A nap this afternoon helped somewhat. But I still feel hollow and my throat is scratchy. Tonight I plan to see a film on Egyptian women _and_ go to pottery class.

My dilemma seems to be I'm being forced to choose.

Then I thought of Nana and other women-identified women (womanists) and the humoring look they get on their faces while discussing men. It is

---

1   Despite her moral opposition to slavery, white British actress and writer Fanny Kemble was, for a time, married to a Georgia slaveholder. Her battles with her husband over the harsh treatment of enslaved people eventually led to their divorce in 1849. During the Civil War, she published a book, _Journal of a Residence on a Georgian Plantation in 1838–1839_, that condemned the evils she'd witnessed on her husband's plantation, drawn from her detailed diary of her days in Georgia.

2   AW's friend Wendy Cadden, a white lesbian photographer and graphic artist.

3   AW's friend Faith Mitchell, a medical anthropologist who was conducting research on social and health policy issues in the Caribbean.

4   Iconic feminist Gloria Steinem, AW's friend and one of the founders of _Ms._ magazine.

clear they've long since stopped taking them seriously at all. But to humor me, their sister still trying to make it work, they rummage through their brains for anything complimentary they can find.

To give up men altogether. Is that the choice? The fear? I feel I am too dual natured to manage giving up anyone. I could be very casual, I suppose. But no longer romantic—running in search of the lost "beautiful" brother.

Besides, as I've said before, women are much more interesting to me than men, just routinely. Some men are wonderful but the great majority— well, turn on television for five minutes and scan the whole world. They're talking heads, cocks and guns.

Nov. 6, This morning I washed & set my hair, fearfully, because there is the danger of prolonging my cold. And I do feel chilly. I've turned up the heat, wrapped my head. Dressed warmly.

Last night Robert came by before I left for the film (on cliteradectomy and other abuse of children in Egypt). He apologized and said he wants very much to change. To become someone I respect and he respects. I said I'd help in any way I could and gave him Andrea Dworkin's book Our Blood.[1] I couldn't find her book on pornography. Let me look for it now. . . . Found it. It was hiding on the book shelf.

Amazing. A real creepy looking guy just came in to use the toilet. (He's helping Russell fix the leak in the fireplace chimney). When I see men now my first thought is the damage they're likely to do. Will this creep come back, I wonder, try to break in? But in this neighborhood he'd be mugged by a local before he got here.

---

1   Andrea Dworkin was a radical feminist and writer, perhaps best known for her criticism of pornography in her book *Pornography: Men Possessing Women*, first published in 1979. The subtitle for *Our Blood*, published in 1976, is *Prophecies and Discourses on Sexual Politics*.

25,000 (Letter from Brandeis saying this figure is possible for next year.)
10,000 (I don't see how Harcourt could offer less than this for the essays.)
 7,000 (So far, projected readings)
 <u>3,600</u> (Ms.)
$45,600

So: I should cease brooding over this and plan my classes at Brandeis. Also make arrangements for Willis while I'm away.

It might be nice to study:

Paule Marshall, Jean Rhys, Zora Neale Hurston & Virginia Woolf, and Agnes Smedley.

1. Frida Kahlo
2. Bessie Smith
3. Agnes Smedley

1. The womanist writer: Identifying womanism and its absence in the work of Paule Marshall, Jean Rhys, Zora Neale and Agnes Smedley—and its deep presence. A creative writing class.
2. The Inner Life: Visions & the Spirit, a seminar
   Twice a week, each, for 1 ½ hours
   Monday/Wednesday
   Tuesday/Thursday

Another call from Robert—He says, so sincerely, "I love you, Alice. Remember that I do love you, and nothing is more important to me than our relationship. I want to be a love you can respect. That I can respect." Later he said (after I told him again how broken is my trust): "I hate myself for doing this." He asked if we could talk. I said yes. That what has changed for me is not my willingness to talk but my trust, belief in him. I told him about something I'd thought about all day: about Ruth and the six years of weekend beatings she endured from Hood before she finally left him. How, coming out of <u>my</u> family, it was hard to trust any man, but I had tried. And I mentioned how hard I struggled to rid myself of the racism that prevented me from seeing Pam and Casey as simply human beings.

(Talking to men is hard because where feminist women routinely make race/sex analogies, men seem stuck.)

He said he'd been reading Dworkin's book and admitted feeling threatened. He realizes he will have to give up some male behavior he doesn't even like or respect, but which means he is "a male in good standing among males." But individual men will have to join the women, become identified as women lovers, just as whites will have to & have had to "join" people of color. I will never join either whites or men. I am fortunate, and I realize this, that I am already what I would join were I not it. If I were a man or a white person, I hope I would have the courage to join women (and children) and people of color.

I feel I have already—in my choice of lifestyle and housing—joined (although again, I am already it) the working class.

As the time approached for Gloria's arrival—and after reading her long letter, glowing, about <u>The Color Purple</u>—I decided to change into something more beautiful and colorful in which to greet her. I chose my embroidered Guatemalan skirt and a red paisley scarf to match my red socks—and a black sweater with many holes. I like the sweater and its holes. I think she will.

Nov. 7.

Gloria is wonderful! And I could easily fall in love with her. I guess that's something that happens to her all the time. She's so sweet and smells so good!

She arrived yesterday. Last night Wendy and Grace and I went to hear her speak at the Civic Center in Marin. Along with Holly Near (yeah!), Jessica Mitford[1] (um?), a comedienne (?), and all moderated by Belva Davis[2]

---

1   Holly Near, a respected white feminist singer/songwriter and social justice activist, and Jessica Mitford, an English-born author and journalist.

2   A Black radio and television journalist in Northern California.

(super smooth). We had fun. Were interviewed by roving tv people. Then went to someone's fine newish house in the Kentfield Hills.

Gloria and Holly were my favorites. Both so open and thoughtful. Hugging them both I realized some awful racial restraint is gone when confronted by women like them. And I'm so glad. Holly and Gloria both spoke of racism as easily as sexism, which is always heartening. Gloria also said I help her keep going by my work—to that audience of two thousand. There was a smattering of (appalse): I meant to write applause. Does writing it this new funny way sound like my brain is going?

It was a marvelous, funny evening. I wished <u>briefly</u> that Robert could truly share what women are doing. Just for the fun and outrageousness of it. When we went to put our coats away I took the opportunity to kiss and hug Wendy—who kissed and hugged back. There was another very dykey looking woman at the reception: a musician and Holly Near's lover. So brash. Dressed in boyish clothing. Very strong and confident—wearing a tie she made out of someone's floral decoration. Orange and white ribbon.

She said when Wendy introduced us: I hear you spotted me as a dyke. I had said this to Wendy but didn't think she'd tell! But the woman said: I don't mind. She smiled. And I liked her.

Later I thought: Jesus! I like everybody: Men, women, gays, lesbians, straights. All colors and stuff. But I really like, apparently, a certain kind of Jewishness. Mel, Gloria and Wendy have that (whatever it is) in common. They are dedicated, determined and very warm folk who also know how to laugh. You know you can have fun with them and also get a lot of work done. Maybe even more than you'd get done if you were not having fun.

—

Yesterday, Sunday, Gloria and I slept late. She says Rebecca's bed is comfortable and commented on all the rainbows. We had a breakfast of bacon and scrambled omelette and then went for the Land's End walk. Talking all along. Then came back and did the interview. I rambled on about all kinds of things: the accident, my "dream" of paying an eye to the bus driver to get out of Eatonton.

The visit was a joy, basically, though I cursed my nervousness and leaden tongue which improved by the end.

Gloria is beautiful. With marvelous eyes. Brown like mocha/java coffee.

She seems so "integrated" and relaxed and "into" life. As long as I've known her she's been the same age.

Robert returned and invited me out to eat. His retreat went well, although Ethnic Studies is in danger of being cut unless someone really takes charge of it. He may.

After Wendy and Gloria he seemed dull, leaden, cold and cloddish. No light. <u>Dumb</u>, as creatures are dumb. Locked up in himself.

He talked of trying to change—nutrition may be the key, he thinks. I hope only the best for him, but my mind kept drifting back to Wendy and Gloria. I couldn't imagine them doing the things R. does.

When we came home we listened to music and he took my feet in his lap and massaged them. Soon I was too tired to sit up any longer and he went home.

The interview is for a <u>Ms.</u> cover story. And I am to make tapes of my work for Stevie Wonder to hear. I decided I would rather have a quote[1] from him than from anyone: from him, Richard Pryor, Cicely Tyson, Bernice Reagon, not one literary establishment.

What will it be like? This new exposure? Whether it happens or not I know I'll be content. That's the main thing.

Nov. 12, 1981

Robert and I had dinner at which he cried—because when he reached over to stroke my hand I continued stroking the rim of my plate. No feeling. He was going to Pittsburgh later to read. (It feels tedious writing this. Boring.) Anyway, he asked me to forgive him. I forgave him. Held him and stroked his hair. We were back at my place by then and I had left him in the car and was watching <u>Cosmos</u>. I told him I think of him negatively. The images of him, all negative, derogatory. And no trust.

---

1   Gloria Steinem had come to interview AW for a cover story for *Ms.* magazine, to mark the forthcoming publication of *The Color Purple*. Alice is considering here who to ask for quotes—also known as blurbs or endorsements—for the new novel.

. . . Most of the women I <u>really</u> admire are womenloving women. Gloria's statement about just not talking to men about anything important to her (because they can't/don't understand it), but being committed to them anyway, doesn't sound good. I think we can both love and respect our lovers. Can share ourselves totally. I hate the thought of having Robert for sex and protection—but not for true sharing.

A week-end of rain and lovely clouds in the country. Robert and I. And I was happy almost the whole time. Singing, whistling. Energetic. Worked on my quilt.

We slept together, held each other, but that's all. I explained my feeling of sexual deadness—that it is as his friend only that I am staying in his life. We both cried a lot (at least I <u>think</u> he cried). And I felt sad for us. But here's the astonishing thing: I also felt free! That's why I was singing so much and feeling so good. I feel <u>free</u> of Robert. If he disapproves of me—what I wear to bed, if my clothes are too loose, whatever—I know it won't matter. He is not someone I am interested in holding the way he wants to be held. I am also not constantly <u>aware</u> of him and inhibited by him.

The push for land in the country: yet our place there is adequate for our use now. We will have been up only once this month. Still, the thought of my own space—where I can walk and invite my own thoughts. I know a country place that is truly mine will be good for my work.

Funny. I need to be in harmony to do my best work.

November 17, 1981 Rebecca is 12! I am sending her flowers with the following jingle:

To Rebecca—
In celebration of
our happiest day
A birthday for three.
You, your father, and me.
   love,
     Mom

But I took out the notebook to praise the day itself. After a week nearly of rainstorms, it is brilliantly clear and bright. And I slept soundly last night. No memory of dreams. The half joint I smoked with Wendy?

She and I spent the afternoon and part of the evening together. . . . Dinner at a new very good restaurant. (I <u>love</u> this city where people know how to cook!) Really a good evening with lots of talk and some laughter. . . .

Then Robert came over to watch television and have a glass of wine. He asked if we could have a trial period of one month for him to try and "clean up his act." How terminology trips us, I thought. But I feel better letting him try than saying it's too late, nothing you do will change how I feel. This is partly how I feel. I don't see how I can forget. On the other hand, not to support someone who is sincerely trying to change is damaging to one's own spirit. (I am learning all of this it seems from reading Thurman Fleet's <u>Rays of the Dawn</u>: such a mysterious book.[1] So full of wisdom everyone should have a copy beside their bed—as I do—and yet I don't even know who published it. It is the kind of book that the reader must be ready for— once I loaned it to Robert and he soon gave it back, unchanged.)

So we talked and he read aloud from an Afro-Am Studies newsletter from L.A. and I cut up one of my old beautiful dresses to add to my quilt. It was a remarkably domestic scene—and very comfortable! When he was ready to leave he held out his arms to me as he usually does, and we embraced.

Through all of this I've felt, when not numb (earlier) and angry, very happy, as if my spirit finally understands that my happiness is within me, just as my "God" is, or my sexuality. Everything I need is within. I put my face in my hand and cup my forehead and wonder about the Spirit that lives behind my eyes.

Dec. 1,

Tomorrow Mama will be 69. Or is it 70? I've sent flowers. I used to fear she'd die before me, and I thought I couldn't bear it. Now I realize I can bear her passing because, dying, she would still be part of the soul within me.

---

1 *Rays of the Dawn: Laws of the Body, Mind, Soul* was self-published by Thurman Fleet's Concept-Therapy Institute in 1976.

There is also a feeling that I would be freed in some way. To be more myself. But what I try to remember is that the struggle to be free must mean becoming free <u>among</u> others, not <u>over</u> others: the dead, the weak, the forgotten.

Dec. 9,

Robert and I are seeing a lot of each other. Went to see <u>Rich and Famous</u> last night. I'd rather they had no black people at all in their movies than have them as backdrop. . . . I feel pity for Robert. He knows he has broken our happiness in breaking my trust in him. He is sorry and tries very hard to make me feel optimistic about our future together. I can't. I feel as though I will always think negatively of him. Without respect.

It does seem such a waste. All we've been through—as he said this morning—to end here. But nothing <u>ends</u>. It merely changes its form.

Dec. 19, 1981

I gave Robert back the keys to my apartment. But requested he give me back all the pictures of me that were in any sense provocative. He did. We are friendly.[1]

Once I let my numbness thaw, the writing I'd put off for weeks began to come. Perhaps writer's block is simply unresolved emotion in one's private life. Of course, being machinelike, some writers probably have learned to ignore their block and write anyway—that could account for so many bad books.

The writer Ding Ling[2] is to be here Monday night, a gathering at my apartment planned by Tillie.

---

1   There is a gap in the journals that raises questions about AW's apparent reconciliation with Robert. After their one-month "trial period," she gives him back the keys to her apartment, as she records on December 19, 1981, and he apparently attends the gathering at her home in January 1982 for Chinese author Ding Ling. Though a big chunk of journal entries is missing—spanning January to August 1982—it appears that she and Robert continued to struggle along.
2   Ding Ling was the pen name of Jiang Bingzhi (born in 1904), one of the most celebrated Chinese authors of the twentieth century. She was best known for writing fiction that centered the experiences of independent Chinese women, as well as for openly criticizing the Communist Party, particularly on women's rights issues.

Jan. 12, 1982

So much has happened! Ding Ling was here. Walking slowly, looking slowly all around her with interested, wise eyes. Short and round. Lovely eyes. She reminded me of Mama. How Mama would have been a great writer. She rested in the big chair in my bedroom. Her husband and the interpreter on the floor. I served them tea. Then she came out to us: Tillie, Jack, Susan G, Kim C, Wendy, Robert, several others.

Hugs when Ding Ling left.

But the big news is we found the land!

20 acres of very hilly but beautiful Mendocino land. . . . A handmade yurt which will do nicely for my studio. Two structures that can be used as cabins until we build our house. We plan to build our house way up on the knoll with a sweeping view of lower hills, ponds, trees and grapes— vineyards way in the distance.

Sellers are two 60ish lesbian women. Very nice. Decent. One a potter. One a postmistress in Navarro.

A meadow with old fencing at the foot. It slopes, as does everything. Creek below, old trees, then a knoll, on which sit the cabins.

Then, higher up, the yurt and the spot for our house, then, higher still, the wellsite.

We will be able to see the sky in all its glory. The sun! Moon!

Jan. 13, 1982

Belvie[1] and I had a great time at the gym. Then dinner at a fine cheap Vietnamese restaurant. I feel easy with her. She reminds me of the good side of Mamie.

I am sleepy, though it is only 10 o'clock. I shall lie here and dream of the land.

---

1   Belvie Rooks, a Black writer and social justice activist, was a new friend who'd first met AW in the late 1970s.

Undated, 1982[1]

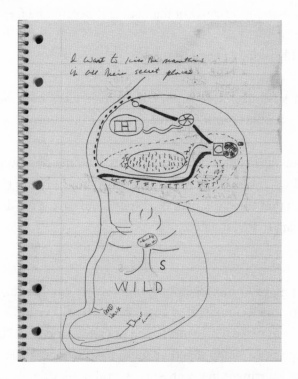

I want to kiss the mountains
in all their secret places

S

WILD

Aug. 15, 1982

This is so wonderful. Wild Trees. When I am here, I am home.

What can I say about Robert? The past year has been <u>so</u> hard on us. He has felt his work overshadowed by mine. His funds are low. And we had a senseless falling out because he wanted <u>The Black Scholar</u> at "The Litera-ture Table" (as he put it) at the book party.[2] I said No: My party is not to be

---

1 This is a drawing AW made of her plans for a country retreat on the land she would soon purchase in Mendocino County, California. The plans identify three structures—Harkle House, in the center, and below, Pond House and Guest House. She named the property Wild Trees, as the drawing shows.

2 The book party was for *The Color Purple*, published by Harcourt Brace Jovanovich on June 28, 1982. The novel received instant critical acclaim: *Kirkus Reviews* called it "a lovely, painful book," while the *New York Times* hailed it as "a striking and consummately well-written novel."

used by The Scholar, or you. He was irritable for a long time. Throughout his vacation, actually, because of that, but also because he feels this is "my place," not his.

But it really is ours. I want to share.

Someone says Ishmael Reed says I have labeled black men rapists. Could this be the sum of his profit from reading <u>The Color Purple</u>? Astonishing![1]

Lately, in thinking about this charge I ask myself: Am I <u>Newsweek</u>, am I <u>The Daily News</u>? Or am I a black woman who also must endure the charge by white society that the black man is a rapist? And isn't it my duty as writer & human being to investigate?

6 Sept. 82

Tomorrow I go to Cambridge.[2] Last night as we cozily snuggled in bed, Robert & I planned our visits to each other. He will visit me in 3 weeks. I will come here twice. Once at the end of Oct. & once for Thanksgiving. We have been very happy together these past few weeks. He and Casey are using the apartment in my absence & I think they'll enjoy it. Thinking we'll be together in 3 weeks makes being away less punishing. I do so love my apartment, Wild Trees, California. And when Robert & I are really together, life is a kind of daily bliss. Whatever happens in Cambridge (& Waltham, etc.), I here report my gratitude for existence, for my friends, for Robert's love & tenderness, for all that has made my life one of happiness & peace.

---

1   Novelist and critic Ishmael Reed harshly criticized the novel's depictions of Mr. _____ and other male characters, charging AW with portraying Black men as violent, sexist stereotypes.

2   AW had accepted a semester-long teaching position at Brandeis University near Boston. She stayed at Wild Trees, her place in Mendocino County, when she was back home in Northern California.

Oct. 31, 1982

Home on a flying week-end. Arrived Thursday night, exhausted, depressed, pre-period. Really upset by a couple of hate letters that arrived at Brandeis, and an article that said "Blinded in One Eye" in large type, advertising a reading I am to give at Clara University on Wednesday. Too tired & depressed to make love. Behind me: a week of teaching, interviews, hate mail, weird students, a strained, too short reading from Purple at Brandeis. But next night we made up for everything. But only because I was able to share all my psychological & physical burdens with Robert, who counseled & consoled me. . . . I felt better immediately after I told Robert what bothered me. This never fails to amaze me.

And now it is Halloween, a clear sparkling day full of people ambling about in shorts & the bay full of boats. We took a spin along the ocean.

Casey on the door trick or treat decorating. Robert & I in the study. My overall feeling is better, much, than when I came. And reading over this notebook, the past year, is interesting. How quickly & thoroughly I forget (now) the bad things. This must be growth.

Dec. 22, 1982

Thanks to the Great Spirit

I am home again. Home again for good!

And what I have learned decisively is I need never again be away. The 3 months away were incredibly hard. The homesickness was almost unbearable. There were periods when I felt like crying. And I missed Robert severely. But, on the "good" side: Rebecca & I had a wonderful time together.[1] Visits nearly every week-end (8 or 9 in all), with much running around together, shopping, partying, giggling & snuggling. And I was glad to have time alone with her to work on our relationship. Such a fine one it is, too.

---

1 Rebecca, now twelve, was living in New York with her father, Mel, her stepmother, Judy, and their young children.

Or seems so. She is maturing into a thoughtful, often serious person who loves to laugh and explore. . . .

Some good things—other than the time with Rebecca—in Boston. The Zinns, whom I love as much or more than ever. Fanny Howe & her children. Mary Helen. But a closer look at the Cambridge/Harvard scene made me joyful not to be there. Too much competition, acting & fear. People don't seem quite real. Which is frightening, since I'm sure they <u>are</u> real. Being at Harvard one must give the illusion of constant creativity & constant rest.

And now, what do I want. Better weather, for one thing. But no. I love all weather, if I am warm & cozy, and I am.

While in Cambridge I put the Brooklyn house up for sale. Asking 190,000, would accept 175,000. This because I'd like to build a house & have Mama visit for months at a time, if she'd like & is able. Eatonton is so limiting in terms of what she can do. There's little that stimulates her. Out here she gets more exercise, sees more things of interest. Says <u>she feels no pain</u>!

—

Now the rainy season is upon us. I long for sunny days in the garden, preparing the soil for summer & fall crops. But perhaps I should work on my quilt, rest & rest & rest.

Jan. 25, 1983
I spent a lovely week in Mendocino with Belvie. Pulling straw, composting, making pies in the new stove. I am all of myself there in a way I am not anywhere else.

Very grateful to the Universe for its many beauties & blessings.

Many calls & letters to speak or read. I'm doing one a month, on the theory that I'll soon fill up again & be able to work/play. Write a novel.

Feb. 1, 1983

The month of my birth, 39 years ago. My mom, lying ill. I wonder how she felt then? Heavy, restless.

A wonderful day with Belvie. Hours listening to tapes at the Howard Thurman Trust. Then lunch at an international restaurant in N. Beach. Then a swim downtown (Mason & Sutter) then beans & rice at home & a facial & hairdo & so on & so forth. Fun & harmony. Friendship & Spiritship.

Feb. 18, 1983

Finally, the day of my reading at College of Marin. I hope it goes well. I have no real desire to read. One reading a month I can tell will be more than enough. I feel a drowsiness that seems connected to the weather which is unsettled, winter trying to become spring. Had a kind of fight with Tillie.[1] She thought my MLK day speech was not "useful." She believes that technology has the answer to everything. But beyond running water & electricity for cooking & lights, I'm not terribly impressed by it. There is a point at which technology must stop—& after t.v. & record players is fine with me.

Of course she doesn't agree.

She sent back the copy of the speech I gave her covered with outraged comments. She thinks it is "arrogant" to view the earth as anthropomorphic. I think it is arrogant not to. What to do with a relationship that doesn't strike me as healthy? I feel her resentment in much that she says. She keeps repeating she "doesn't know me." And this apparently bothers her.

Oh well. As I see it perseverance is likely to bring only limited success because she is not a person one can talk to. She doesn't listen. At all.

Robert & I happy, thanks to the Great Spirit—I am still <u>thrilled</u> to be home & with him. Whenever anyone mentions the possibility of my being away—even for a prize (TCP was nominated for The Book Circle Critics

---

1 Tillie Olsen, a white writer whose work explored the struggles of women and working-class people, had been a longtime friend and mentor of sorts to AW—though their relationship was sometimes strained.

Award)[1] I bristle. I can't imagine wanting to leave home for any reason. Though I will have to go to Minnesota & later to Wisconsin.

March 19, 1983

Back from Minnesota. Two events, very large, capacity crowds & actually a third event, gratis, to the YWCA in honor of Black History Week or in honor of Black Women Writers. Nice people who brought their children. The other events, at the College of St. Catherine, largely white, though as always, a surprisingly diverse number of blacks looking & sounding proud & happy & bearing gifts: poems, books, etc. Presents from all colors, in fact.

. . . I read the essay "Everything Is a Human Being."[2] And the audience really seemed moved. Later a Native American woman came up & thanked me & we held hands & felt so close! She said: You know, I was sitting back there thinking, Suppose I were standing before these people saying those things! But then I thought: Wow, a black American woman is saying those things! We laughed.

We are going to be together yet—all the peoples of the world.

But home. To rest & rain & reading. And a clearing out of the books (200 of them) I feel I'll never read again. And a clearing out of the clothes I felt I'd never wear again. And a modest restocking (beginning) of books & clothes. The biography of Frida Kahlo, the Autobiography of Gandhi, the biography of Tolstoi. Which it now occurs to me I may actually have read. And, borrowed from Sue, a book by Blavatsky. And recommended by Wendy Daughters of Copper Woman. And the planting of 100 trees. Helped by Rob & Sue. 10 black locusts interspersed with 10 Siberian Pea Shrub, tapering off with 2 4-wing Saltbrush on one side of the road. Then: 8 Rus-

---

1   *The Color Purple* was nominated for the 1982 National Book Critics Circle Award in fiction. It lost to Stanley Elkin's novel *George Mills*.

2   AW wrote this essay to celebrate the birth of Martin Luther King Jr. and delivered it as a keynote address at the University of California, Davis, on January 15, 1983. The same piece that Tillie Olsen objected to, as recorded in the previous entry, this essay explores AW's passionate relationship with the earth and personifies trees, snakes, and the earth itself.

sian olive trees, 10 Shagbark hickories, 10 red oaks, numbers of Alderberry, chestnuts, black walnuts, etc.

Monday I go to Georgia to help with Mama. I'm trying to psyche myself up for the week. It's difficult, though. I shall take many good books, some smoke, & perhaps some pages from this journal to continue on.

3-31-83
Home from Georgia since Sunday, four <u>long</u> days ago. I arrived in Atlanta still apprehensive, rented a car, drove out to Ruth's house & picked Mama up. Then down to Eatonton for 5 days. Mama extremely weak, fell on the ground while trying to get in the car. Once in her own house, however, much stronger. Able to go to the bathroom by herself about 1/3 of the time. I almost enjoyed the week, though my poor crazy family is in the worst shape it's been in for a long time.

But I felt closer to everyone, eventually . . . because there is just something very humanly appealing about people in struggle—& they all are. In struggle & trying hard to be their best selves.

April 21, Thurs.
A week or so ago Winnie Kelly called to tell me <u>The Color Purple</u> had won <u>The American Book Award</u>.[1] This was very nice to hear; and then, this week—on Monday morning as I was answering letters and paying bills— a woman on KDLA called and said I'd won a Pulitzer. I thought she was joking. She said she wasn't. The media descended. And now I am worn out.

---

1   In 1980 the "National Book Awards"—first presented in 1936—were canceled and replaced by the "American Book Awards," sponsored by the Association of American Publishers. The awards were revamped for 1984 and were renamed "National" in 1987. The National Book Foundation became responsible for the National Book Awards in 1989 and officially recognizes a continuous NBA history from 1949/1950, so the award that AW won in 1983 is now known as the National Book Award—one of the most prestigious literary awards in the country. The awards were presented at a private celebration at the New York Public Library on April 28, 1983.

Fortunately, my friends at <u>Ms.</u> sent over a machine that takes telephone messages. Though now I find I dislike listening to it. For a few days my quiet mornings disappeared, & I realized anew how much I miss them. Need them. How much my serenity depends on quiet & non-talking. Perhaps <u>that's</u> what these prizes can mean (people keep asking & I don't know yet). That I will be free <u>not</u> to talk.

Robert has been <u>wonderful.</u> Supportive, loving, patient, fatherly/motherly/loverly. Shopping, cooking, straightening up. One night I just had to take him in my arms & have our way with him! He had the insight: "detach yourself from addictions & lust & good things will come to you." I was very happy to hear it.

And now I am going to Milwaukee for the weekend to address, or be feted by, the Deltas. Which seems utterly appropriate, somehow.

Meanwhile, I have had wonderful telegrams etc. from June & Toni Cade Bambara & Paule & a huge 3 ft high bouquet from Bill Jovanovich.[1] He says if I need money, someone to cry or laugh with "call on him." The ABA & Pulitzer moved them to print 20,000 copies of the essays rather than 10,000. Such caution! Astonishing.

<u>But</u> I am happy. Shug & Celie are happy. Everybody seems pretty thrilled & we've been calling it "The People's Pulitzer."

April 1983[2]

Hello, This is a very tired Alice Walker. If you are calling to congratulate me thank you. If you are calling for an interview I am all talked out.

If you need to talk to me about something else, please leave your name & number.

---

1   William Jovanovich was the director of Harcourt Brace Jovanovich, AW's publisher. June and Paule refer to two of AW's longtime Black women writer friends, June Jordan and Paule Marshall.

2   This undated entry was written after AW learned she'd won the Pulitzer Prize for *The Color Purple*. She was overwhelmed with interview requests from the media, hence this answering machine greeting.

April 1983

I accept this award for my novel,[1] in the name of the folk, like my parents, who have never written or read a novel; the folk of this country, robbed of education, health & happiness, & forced to labor for the benefit of the oppressor classes, and the folk all over the world who are doing the same thing, & who are struggling to end their exploitation at this time. I accept it in the name of our Native American, Black, & White radical & feminist folk ancestors whose words & deeds never fail to reassure us that no matter how poor we may be, the earth belongs to us. We must use all our anger & all our love to protect it from those who threaten it & whose every destructive arrogant act is subsidized by oppressed people's blood.

Together we can dream & build an America & a world where everybody writes & everybody reads & everybody paints & everybody makes music & nobody is afraid.

I understand that as one of those fortunate few of my class not only to escape illiteracy but to actually read & write novels, it is my duty to encourage you to believe that this is true.

I wish to thank my friend Mel Leventhal for his years of every kind of support. And I thank our daughter Rebecca Leventhal for all she has taught me of wonder, patience, encouragement & joy.

I thank my friends Joanne Edgar & Gloria Steinem[2] for their dauntless belief in my work, & I thank my companion Robert Allen for his delight in sharing adventures with me. I thank my mother for having faith enough to prepare me for a life that is totally different—except for gardening—than her own.

—

We are all children
Of wilderness
Eden

---

1 This is a draft of AW's acceptance speech after *The Color Purple* won the American Book Award, which in 1987 was renamed the National Book Award.
2 The founding editors of *Ms.* magazine.

Extravagant, colorful

&

Unkempt

Odd as Adam

Original

As Eve.

30 April 83

Robert & I have returned from New York & the ABAs ceremony. All in all a pleasant, not-too-much-of-a-strain time. I thanked my "family members" who were present (Joanne Edgar, Rebecca, Miriam (Mel's mother! He was "tied up" at the last minute), Gloria & Robert). Then I accepted the award in the name of The Folk. Them that reads & them that don't. I just hope I did my own folk justice. Such life! Such lives! And such optimistic wisdom expressed so directly! I really feel they did all this, somehow. That I really <u>am</u> a medium.

Then, after the ceremony, I or we were whisked off in a humongous "limo" to the Russian Tea room for dinner, where Mel caught up with us. He looks old & sick. I felt so sorry for him. His eyes are very guarded and he talked of being "on call" for the governor who needed legal advice re: a 2 million dollar case. Why can't I feel interested or impressed by legal matters of his! I truly wanted to but I started to doze almost & "click" I saw again the boredom of the marriage. The lawyer Mel is not like the Poet Mel that the lawyer Mel has killed off.

Many, many letters of happiness about the awards. Almost all of them expressing the feeling that they've won something too. Only a few people are negative. One, Loyle Hairston,[1] who thinks the prizes were given to me because of my negative portrayals of black men. I felt this was unjust and undeserved & wrote to tell him so.

But mainly people seem delighted. <u>Lots</u> of women & some men.

---

1   A Black male author and literary critic.

I know that if I'd made Celie enjoy the rape there would have been no complaints from most men. Or even most women, so brainwashed & divorced from their feelings have they become. But thank goodness they're waking up! And I'm going to be right here saying Good Morning!

5-11-83

Today I have a tremor in my eye from tension, after several days of energetic (swimming, walking, yoga) happiness that included singing. What is wrong: Well, a very dishonest letter from Loyle Hairston in which he denies having characterized my novel as being something white folks would give prizes to because it doesn't say anything against white folks. Why am I bothered by this? As with <u>Meridian</u> I expected more of him. I certainly expected fairness. But when women write about women men don't understand—or they refuse to. They <u>hate</u> not being center stage & will make themselves central if only by telling you they've been maligned—as Loyle did. But really, I don't know this man beyond the fact that he wrote a favorable review of <u>3rd Life</u> & at a book party for Rosa seemed nice enough.[1] At least was <u>present</u>, helping her sell books.

A more complicated problem is Tillie Olsen,[2] who, when I offered her $1,000 to help pay her way to China, keeps sending me reminders of all she has done for me. Yesterday she sent back $500 with a lot of souvenir Indian junk (stickers, etc., postcards) she'd picked up in the desert in Arizona. Also a Xerox of her letter to the Guggenheim people in support of my application!

I will try never to take anything else from her. Perhaps that is the les-

---

1   AW, Loyle Hairston, and novelist Rosa Guy were all contributors—in the late 1970s and early 1980s—to *Freedomways: A Quarterly Review of the Freedom Movement*, which described itself as "a scholarly magazine written in a popular style," founded in 1961.

2   AW had met Tillie Olsen in the mid-1970s. Admirers of each other's work, the two women had corresponded for several years, and when AW moved to the Bay Area, Olsen welcomed her warmly. She also wrote a letter supporting AW's Guggenheim application and was generally encouraging of the younger writer. Now, however, Olsen—born in 1912, the same year as AW's mother—seemed threatened by the younger writer's literary achievements.

son. That the uneasiness I've felt all along about her "gifts" was in anticipation of her feeling the need to remind me. And my resentment of being
reminded. She seems petty & pitiful to me, but she also gets under my skin
most uncomfortably. Also she reminds me of Muriel.[1] This same need to
be acclaimed mentor, originator of all thoughts. I don't like her very much.
That is the truth. Yet I keep sending her notes that are all signed "love." The
tremor in my eye has stopped.

A third problem which is merely a matter of $ came up yesterday too.

Whether to spend 2,800 for a foundation under the main cabin rather than
the $1000 I'd planned for. But this really is just money, I think. Though I have
to admit a certain uneasiness re: the steadily mounting costs at Wild Trees
while nothing much seems to be happening—on the other hand, assuming all
goes well, I'll have the <u>foundation</u> in the country that I need & by this time
next year can be in & comfy with running water, electricity, a new room.

Eye tremor returns.

So. Perhaps I <u>am</u> worried about money.

Alice, don't be. If you run out of money you can stop whatever it is.
There's money coming in. <u>You'll be fine</u>. And count your blessings!

You've written a bestseller about people you <u>adore</u>. There are now 50,000
copies in print. It is selling, & has been selling, like the proverbial hot cakes.

You have won an American Book Award <u>&</u> a Pulitzer Prize—which you
didn't even know they had for fiction.

You have a healthy & funny daughter who makes your face light up even
when you're talking about her to strangers in Milwaukee! You don't "have
her," she has herself which you <u>really</u> like. You also like & admire her honesty & cheerfulness. Not to mention her cute little shape!

---

1   Poet Muriel Rukeyser, AW's former teacher at Sarah Lawrence. Ultimately, AW believed
both Olsen and Rukeyser wanted to be mother figures for her and became angry when she
denied them that role. In an interview with her biographer, Evelyn C. White, AW said: "The
older white women who'd helped me seemed, finally, angered to find themselves in competition with my 'humble' mother and furious that I never forgot to put her first. I also think
they found it difficult to learn about my mother's success as a human being since she'd been
denied the various privileges they'd enjoyed. Such as just being white."

You have friends who delight & cheer you on—Gloria, Robert, Belvie, Jan & more!

You have readers who write ecstatic letters to you & send flowers, buttons & poems.

You're going to Le Mans in a week for an honorary degree. You'll see Mary Helen, Howie, Roz, Rebecca & who knows who all!

You're going to China in 3 weeks!

You've made the decision to do one public thing a month & are trying & sometimes succeeding in keeping some (& sane).

Perhaps the tension is coming from all these "good" things. But relax. What matters to you is the same as always: peace of mind, a place in the country near trees, a place in the city near Robert. Good health. Days in which to do nothing. Sufficient political work to justify being alive!

Today, for instance. Look how golden it is! So free & open.

13 May 83

(The name of it is "The Godmother Syndrome.")

Yesterday Tillie rang the bell & said she wanted to "drop something off." I met her on the staircase just outside my neighbor's doors. We had it out, as nearly as that is possible for us. I said if what she was dropping off came from her I couldn't accept it. Because what she gives, she keeps. And to me that is not giving at all. Why did she remind me of all she'd taught me re: China? Why did she send me yet another Xerox of her letter to the Guggenheim folk? Why did she have to tell me Alice Childress put flowers on A. Smedley's grave because of <u>her</u> direction, etc. etc. She said, as I expected, that I've misunderstood her. That it was "demeaning" for her even to try to discuss it. We must have been a sight, me above her at times, slightly, on the stairs, my neighbors coming home with kids in tow, etc.

At one point, feeling the futility of it all, I put out my hand, thinking touch might do what words could not. But she recoiled. Left, really, in a huff.

She said "you confuse me with Muriel." I said: "You behave like Muriel. Maybe it's cultural."

* * *

But really it is The Godmother Syndrome. Matronizing behavior where one expects equality & friendship.

And, so far, my eye hasn't quivered since. I slept all night & whatever happens I have tried to express my true being in the matter.

May 26, 83
Back from being given an honorary doctorate at U. Mass. Fun seeing Mary Helen & going to see the splendid "Say Amen, Somebody," & really fun paling around with Rebecca.

So tired. Everybody wants me to say or do something. All I can think is how pleasant it will be during the summer when I can go days, maybe even many days, without saying more than . . .

. . . And now, China!

I underline it & add the exclamation point, but what I really feel is And now . . . China. Wondering if I can hold up for 21 days. Already thinking of being on the beach in Hawaii & not talking.

Visit to China[1]
1983
The translator is so attractive!

June 6th
After visiting Agnes Smedley's grave.[2] A meeting at the Minority (National) Institute over Beijing. A beautiful warm day—the time with Agnes very emotion filled.

———

1 AW visited China in June 1983 along with several other American writers, including Tillie Olsen, with whom she'd recently had a conflict, and the acclaimed Black woman novelist Paule Marshall. The Chinese translation of *The Color Purple* was warmly received.

2 Agnes Smedley (1892–1950) was an American journalist and author, best known for her semi-autobiographical novel *Daughter of Earth*, as well as for her sympathetic chronicling of the Communist forces in the Chinese Civil War. "As my heart and spirit have found no rest

We must be sure to have some pictures taken together. That's what I'd like.

I am particularly interested in writing an essay on the joys of being a woman of color writer.

Wild Trees
July 13, 1983

The trip to China was exhausting. In fact, more about that later. Today I am lying across the bed in the new room at Wild Trees, enjoying the breezes coming through the window. The room, though small, is a perfect addition to the place. Gives us space to stretch out a bit. And it is always cool.

Invited to co-mistress an awards ceremony for outstanding Bay Area women—with Gloria. Not the slightest interest, except I would see Gloria & fulfill a "duty" (vaguely felt) to women. I've tried to psych myself up to do it (in September), but the minute I think about it my neck tightens. I think I'll say no.

Now, writing by lamplight, I look out over the valley & see the moon, bright above the trees. So much has happened to me this year. The Pulitzer Prize, the American Book Award, a N.Y. Times #1 Bestseller. China. Wild Trees beginning to feel comfortable. I feel extremely blessed. Still deeply tired though. So many invitations coming in for me to speak. But if I speak I don't write. And I write because I don't relish speaking. Each time someone reminds me I'm to "speak" on South Africa on the 20th of August I tense. But I shall read and ponder and do my best.

---

in any other land on earth except China," she wrote, "I wish my ashes to lie with the Chinese Revolutionary dead." She was buried in Beijing.

August 7, 1983

Word from Pocket is the 250,000 copies of Purple are in print & they expect to sell those & more! Meanwhile, the hard cover continues to sell. $36,000 is due me in October. From HBJ.

Work on the cabin/land is coming along. What we have now is your basic country retreat. Soon to have water & lights & already a mostly finished toilet . . .

Now to have a hot tub, a bench by the pond. A redone pond. And time to be here.

Aug. 19, 1983

At the P.O. in Boonville the postmistress shows me <u>Purple</u> in the Book-of-the-Month Club Catalog. . . . Apparently I and the book are much in the media & I am thankful not to be aware of it.

I dislike seeing a picture of myself wherever I go here in the Valley. It spoils the feeling of anonymity that I like. Though since I'm the only black woman living here anonymity isn't possible. Everyone seems to know not just me, but everything that happens on the land.

Now supposedly the wiring will be hooked up on Monday. Hard to believe. And yes, I am tired of trenches & workmen and the feeling of intrusion inevitable in a reconstruction such as I'm having done.

My sister Ruth called last night. . . . We discussed Mama, who worries, apparently, that they're all going to starve. I felt awful to think of her worry which I'm sure Ruth causes, by <u>her</u> worrying. Ruth says Mama can now go to the toilet alone, eat by herself & sometimes even wash herself. This is progress! I sent her $22 in cash so that she'll have a little cash of her own. So that she can have a "Pepsi a day." Poor darling. To have such a small want, & not have it satisfied.

I must send Ruth Gloria's article too, about <u>her</u> mother.[1] I think she'd enjoy it. I think it is the best thing by Gloria I've ever read.

---

1   In her 1983 book *Outrageous Acts and Everyday Rebellions*, Gloria Steinem published an essay about her mother, called "Ruth's Song (Because She Could Not Sing It)." A journalist like her

Soon Rebecca will be returning.[1] Her friends, the Mettinglys, are helping us find someone to act as "guardian" so that she can go to a school outside her district.

At the hardware store in town I bought snapdragon yellow paint for painting the privy. The walls will be yellow, to capture the sun & cheerfulness, & the seat will be marine blue. The door will be oriental red. I realize this sounds like a British telephone booth or perhaps a mailbox—except for the yellow.

Now I shall make a soup for lunch & perhaps put the finishing touches on my speech—or begin on the privy.

But, meditate, I must!

Meditation was wonderful—45 min.

Aug. 20, 1983

And great for peaceful dreams! Last night I had the most extraordinary beautiful & exquisite dream about myself and Langston Hughes. We were lovers. And he loved everything about me, even my shoes, which we were looking at for some reason. We loved working together. Talking. Laughing. He is so wonderful. We were at Margaret Walker's house when he arrived but she soon vanished. (It was as if she were the spirit connection). And for an endless warm time we kissed & hugged & said "I love you. I love you." It was one of the most enjoyable & fulfilling dreams I've ever had. We didn't "make love" we just loved. Deeply.

So much so that this morning upon awakening & coming into the big room & facing the rainy day, it all came back to me & I began to cry because it was only a dream. But I felt Langston's presence saying that for us, the dream is real. That that can be our space, our place for being together, in

---

daughter, Ruth suffered from mental illness, and young Gloria took care of her from an early age. She writes: "She was just a fact of life when I was growing up; someone to be worried about and cared for; an invalid who lay in bed with eyes closed and lips moving in occasional response to voices only she could hear; a woman to whom I brought an endless stream of toast and coffee, bologna sandwiches and dime pies, in a child's version of what meals should be."

1   Rebecca had been living with her father in New York.

love & happy. He asked me if I hadn't found it good & happy & full. And I had to admit I had. He seemed to be, I would guess, in his thirties. Quite handsome & so sweet.

Langston, wherever you are, you make me very happy and I love you.

Perhaps this means I should do the collected poems. If I did, I could be with you more!

Aug. 21

Last night my dream was of John Lennon. I was trying to pass him a copy of The Color Purple. The only remaining memory is of him sitting in a nicely decorated corner, in a hotel, dressed in a soft camel colored suit.

Aug. 23

Last night I dreamed of Howie (Zinn) & we were bicycling & happy as we always are together. Unfortunately that's all I recall. Later I dreamed of land and houses & thinking of buying. No doubt this dream was programmed by my thoughts of buying my neighbors' land next door. If they would sell for $90,000, I might put 45,000 down, (the 36,000 from HBJ & 10,000 CD) & pay them $450 a month. Then I could rent out their main house for 250 a month & refurbish the "studio." Demolish the "pump" house. Eventually have the power & phone lines undergrounded.

What an amazing day this is! So much more alive (I am) than yesterday this time. And I need, crave, fruit! Perhaps I should dress, go to the park for water, stop off at the Philo Café for breakfast & a paper (ugh—Robert says the news is as bad as ever).

Aug. 23, 1983

The water is flowing! And we have electricity! There was an impromptu gathering of our Valley friends. We made a pilgrimage up to the pump and toasted Don (& Manuel) with rain wine.

Robert took many pictures of our little procession & of our christening of the pump and of each other. In a word, it was lovely. Good vibes, good people.

Sept. 25, 1983

Early morning. 4:30 a.m. I've been waking up every morning at this strange hour. Tonight I woke thinking of the arrangement I've made to hire Brenda[1] to live with Mama & see after her in Mama's house. She needs 1100 a month. The after taxes equivalent of her pharmacist's salary. At first I panicked—but then I thought: even without help from Bobby and Jimmy, I could provide the salary for at least 6 months. And I should do this, & make it firm with Brenda, tomorrow. Though it seems a lot it is little to ask if it means Mama will be happier.

What possible better use could I make of whatever money I have? Plus, my affairs are in manageable financial order, basically.

The house in the country. The Brooklyn house. The apartment. Better to "invest" in my mom's happiness & comfort than in another house. So. If necessary, I can always do another reading somewhere. I will call Brenda in the morning.

I spent most of yesterday throwing stuff out, straightening up my study—& it is beginning to look wonderful again—like a place where a person can work. I'm keeping most of the letters from The Color Purple lovers. Some are quite beautiful.

I must read Tolstoy's <u>The Kingdom of God Is Within You.</u>

—

A woman wrote (the second one) to tell me of the "flaw" in <u>The Color Purple</u>: that the woman on the street "slaving" for the mayor's wife could not be Sofia. She goes on for a long time, listing the ages of children, time spent in Africa, etc.

I want to write to her & perhaps I will, that <u>Of Course</u> it isn't Sofia. Since that's chronologically impossible. That the reader's question should then be: Who is it? And then to wonder if it is possible that there was another

---

1 Brenda Walker, a cousin in Georgia.

woman, before Sofia, who suffered her fate.[1] Then the reader might wonder (without knowing its name) about the "contract labor" system in the South. The system much in use in the South after reconstruction when black people were "free" but white folks still needed their work done. The era of kidnapping that lasted, probably, through the 30s. A white person would ask a black person to work for him. If the black person refused it was considered assault. The person was arrested. The white person then simply applied to the jailer or prison official to have access to the prisoner as a laborer. He & the official signed a contract. Which is why it was called "contract labor."

This is what happened to Sofia. What is unique about her case, however, is that she actually did "assault" the mayor. Her resistance wasn't simply the white man's interpretation of a black person's no.

But there are other possibilities as well. Because Nettie describes the mayor's maid in standard "contract labor" terms, her description fits Sofia. Reading this description many years afterwards, Celie naturally assumes the woman Nettie saw was Sofia. And begins to write to Nettie about Sofia.

A third possibility is simply to accept the "impossibility of the woman being Sofia" as a puzzle. Since it is highly unlikely that if one came across a batch of letters spanning 30 years there would be no puzzles in them.

Perhaps it would have been helpful to point out more clearly to the reader that the mayor & his wife had picked up workers off the street before. That what happened to Sofia was not unique to her. That it was, in fact, part of a system in which black people, long after slavery was abolished by the Civil War, could be enslaved legally.

This is why Sofia refers to herself as a slave, but her son insists she is a captive.

Note: As late as 1968 I collected a story from a black man who was the victim of this system. Because he wouldn't go to work for local whites he was arrested for 5 years. He was arrested in May & not brought for trial until

---

1 In the novel, the fiercely independent Sofia refuses to submit to men (including her husband Harpo) or white people. After defying the town's white mayor, she is sentenced to twelve years in prison, but the sentence is later commuted to twelve years' labor as the mayor's maid.

October. During that period it is very likely that he was forced to work for the very whites he had refused. After that he was sent to prison.

A reading last night which I had dreaded but which turned out fine. Not quite a packed house—possibly because of a sudden downpour. Black people <u>dressed up</u>. Meanwhile, I showed up in very casual poncho & slacks.

It looks like I have a deal with Peter Guber & Jon Peters.[1] And if it flies, I'll have to become accustomed to having $, at least for a while. Basically the offer is this: 400,000 (350,000 as purchase price, 50,000 to be creative consultant), plus 3% of the gross at breakeven point of picture; plus, possibly, additional $75,000 if more option time is needed—which I doubt, 18 months being fairly long. <u>And</u> 10% of soundtrack royalties. What in the world all this means I can't really imagine. Then there's about 100,000 from Pocket and 35,000 from Harcourt. Who would have thought? That's half a million dollars!

Robert & I really fine. Amazing. For a long time now. I stopped inviting him to the country, where he becomes morose. Too bad. Wild Trees is spectacular! My garden riotously happy. Cosmos, morning glories everywhere. Tomatoes. Collards & turnips. This week-end Belvie, Wendy & I will plant trees. Poplars. Perhaps some fruit as well.

Oct. 30, 1983
Rebecca & I a cozy pair. This morning she was on the sofa in my study & fell asleep on my breast. It was so like the old days (!) when she was a baby. And she is like she was, more like herself. That is: cheerful & loving, affectionate, smart & funny.

And yesterday Brother Guber sent me a bottle of champagne & a reassuring note. But what bouts of anxiety I feel about the movie! I keep in mind Peter's words about hiring the <u>best</u> people in all categories.

Serious thoughts about buying the Harkleroad's property.[2] $50,000 cash in 6 months. $25,000 six months later. Or three.

---

1 These respected movie producers had made an offer to purchase the film rights to *The Color Purple*.
2 This property was in Mendocino County, adjacent to her "Wild Trees" home.

Robert & I discussed founding a press. Wild Trees Press. That we could set up on the land & run from Mendocino.

Dec. 17, 1983

Last night my sister Ruth called. She said Mama is back in the hospital, she fell down—one of her legs isn't functioning—& she can't open her mouth. This bit about opening, being unable to open her mouth (& "bit" reminds me of horses' "bits" designed to keep their mouths open for the reins) nags at me. Could she be feeling unconsciously that she has said too much? God I hope not. Brenda[1] is feeling very bad & thinking we will blame her for Mama's breakdown. But of course she shouldn't—I called but she was asleep.

And today, what is happening with me? A photographer from The New York <u>Times</u>, a gentle & sensitive woman named Sara Krulwich, is here photographing me for a cover story in the NY Times Magazine. Robert is on the deck grading student papers. The sun is coming out. A fire is going in the stove & click click click the camera is going. Meanwhile, my mother may be dying.

The last time I talked with her she said she'd been exercising & that she was sore. I told her she sounded stronger & that exercise is good for her. She said "Well, maybe it's good for other folks, but maybe it's not for me."

Jan. 7, <u>1984</u>

So I made several offers on the land but all were refused. Then we decided we didn't really want it. There's a chance we'll get nice neighbors & in any case we'll probably start our house this summer. Tomorrow, I will appear on the cover of the Sunday <u>Times</u> magazine. A rather chipmunky picture—& from my clothing, I could appear on the world's worst-dressed list. The article on me by David Bradley strange, over all.[2] <u>No</u> consciousness of women's struggles— where has he been?! But also very moving in places . . . of course one reads these things as if they're about someone else; someone else one used to know

---

1   Cousin Brenda had been taking care of AW's mother in Georgia.

2   Author and journalist David Bradley's cover story on AW appeared in the *New York Times Magazine* on January 8, 1984, under the headline "Novelist Alice Walker Telling the Black Woman's Story."

rather well. And liked. And worried over. There's one serious misquote that is so nonsensical I'm amazed they printed it. And he says my eye is artificial. Well.

I suppose I must take de bitter wid de sweet. And the sweet is that Robert & I & Rebecca & I and Casey & I & all of us together are at our best. A reconstituted family, going strong.

No matter in what anger I have written about the black man, I have never once let go of his hand. Though he has kicked me in the shins many times.

The more I think of Bradley's article the more dreadfully dishonest, self-serving & condescending it seems. And I have <u>no</u> memory of having had lunch with him, much less "flirting!"[1] The I Ching says I never should have let him in, that doing so without already having developed mutual trust was wrong. And Brother Ching is right.

And here I am at the end of this notebook started in 1976, nearly 8 years ago!

---

1 In the *New York Times* piece, Bradley writes this of his first meeting with AW, several years before interviewing her for the article: "Alice Walker in person was as many faceted as Alice Walker in print. She was a scholar of impressive range, from African literature to Oscar Lewis, the noted anthropologist. She was an earthy Southern 'gal'—as opposed to lady. Her speech was salted with down-home expressions, but peppered with rarified literary allusions. She was an uncompromising feminist, capable of hard-nosed, clear-eyed analysis; she was also given to artless touching and innocent flirtation. She had a sneaky laugh that started as a chuckle and exploded like a bomb. Her eyes sparkled—I did not know then, and surely could not tell, that one of them had been blinded in a childhood accident."

There have been rough times, but, overall, I feel, continue to feel, blessed. In fact, when I consider the possibilities, & the realities of many other lives, I feel this intensely.

Next month I will be forty. In some ways, I feel my early life's work is done, & done completely. The books that I have done already carry forward the thoughts that I feel the ancestors were trying to help me pass on. In every generation someone(s) (or two/or 3) are chosen for this work. Ernest Gaines is one such. Margaret Walker. Langston & Zora. Toomer. "One plum was left for me. One seed becomes an everlasting singing tree!"[1] or words to that effect.

Great Spirit I thank you for the length of my days & the fullness of my work. If you wanted me to move on, come home, or whatever is next, I would try to bear it joyfully. Though I am quite joyful here. I love Rebecca & Robert & Casey (Casey makes great fires & loves to be hugged). We are a family. This seemed an impossible dream so often, in this very book. And yet it is real.

Langston was right: The dream _is_ real. And if we work at it hard enough, in the dream we will always have a place.

Thank you again. I love you. I love your trees, your sun, your stars & moon & light. Your darkness. Your plums & watermelons & water meadows. And all your creatures & their fur & eyes & feathers & scales.

Jan. 26, 1984[2]

The new year, the year prophesied, has begun. Today is sunny, bright. Gorgeous in the best SF style. I've had many happy days already, but several not so happy ones. I still feel betrayed by David Bradley's article in the Times. For such a well done piece I hope the Times paid him 30 pieces of gold. I thought I was over any real pain regarding my eye, but apparently not. Just when I felt comfortable discussing its blindness he writes in the Times that it is artificial. And implies that this (& the way it happened) accounts for my "dis-

---

1   This line is paraphrased from Jean Toomer's poem "Song of the Son."
2   AW drew a purple heart around 1984.

torted" vision. I see falsely because I have a false eye. The rest of the piece is as dishonest. None of the discussion of my "politics" which was the Trojan horse that got him inside my door. Of my essays he made hash. Of <u>Meridian</u>. But I have received many wonderful letters and writings of support. Everyone, except for one or two people I don't trust anyway, seems to have seen through it. Mary Helen[1] says someone said they put the wrong picture on the cover. It should have been Bradley, since the piece was about him.[2]

So. Down from that. And my mother's third or fourth stroke—and she rambles hurtfully at times about Brenda's lesbianism. Ruth says she called her a "hermaphrodite" & said she shouldn't be around "normal" people. This is amusing though: because if she is around my family she isn't around "normal" people. And do "normal" people exist? What would be normal to Minnie Lou? Only the Jehovah's Witnesses, no doubt.

Robert disappointed me, again. While we were in the country he paid for 300 worth of trees for me. When we came home I gave him 5,000 as his "consulting" fee & asked if he'd take the tree money owed out of that. He said of course. Next day however he changed his mind. Wanted the tree $ as well, in another check for $300.00. SUCH pettiness, stinginess, cheapness & short-sightedness made me cry in frustration. So I wrote him the second check. Then, next day, he told me that while he was in Colorado last year where his old high school girlfriend teaches they'd "had a relationship, sexual, but based on friendship," which he saw as an improvement for him. This was a blow—but following the tree business I felt such <u>pity</u> for him. Especially because he said, when asked why he waited so long to tell me: Mary Helen (Washington) is coming (to teach for a semester at Mills) & she knows A., they're friends & perhaps she knows. I want to tell you myself, rather than let you hear it from her.

But Mary Helen wouldn't tell me, I said. She wouldn't want to hurt my feelings. But I shudder to think of her opinion of you.

---

1 AW's longtime friend, literary scholar Mary Helen Washington.
2 Indeed, Bradley writes the article in first person, and he goes on for several pages before AW's voice is heard; that is, before he ever quotes from the interview conducted with her for the story.

This interpretation hadn't occurred to him, I don't think.

For several days I felt unclean, because of his duplicity. Was she herpes-free? for instance. And all that goes with infidelity. Now I just feel sad for Robert. We've had some very nice times together since he told me. And he's been more loving than ever. But, as I told him, I can't trust him. He wouldn't even give me a fraction of the money I gave him. And he only told me about an affair because he feared someone else might. But he has many good points—and I try to appreciate those.

Undated, January 1984[1]

I regret that D. Bradley finds me less likeable after discovering I also have good-sized feet of clay. It may help him to know that my blind eye, which he also perceived as artificial, is flesh & blood.

On a less technical note: I cannot imagine having said "white feminism is not a tradition that teaches white women . . . they are capable," unless my brain & tongue echoed the exhaustion Bradley sound-stamped in my voice & features. The opposite is true. Where the womanist tradition differs (from the white feminist) is that it assumes out of historical knowledge that black women can do almost anything—because usually they have already done it. When Sojourner Truth said "nobody ever lifted me into carriages and over ditches . . . and ain't I a woman?" and continued to talk about working like a man & eating like one she was voicing this tradition loud & clear.

I don't choose womanism because it is "better" than feminism since womanism means black feminist, but because it is mine.

Undated

Quincy Jones[2] asked me to write the script for the movie. I said yes. But then, having mentioned it to Wendy, I had to think about whether it is

---

1   This is a draft of AW's response to David Bradley's cover story on her in the *New York Times Magazine*. A longer response was published in the magazine's February 12, 1984, issue.

2   Legendary musician and producer Quincy Jones was part of the team working to pro-

right to do it for free. I think not. So I should just write him a note to that effect.

Undated[1]

The story really begins circa 1903 with the lynching—by envious whites—of Celie's father, a striving & beginning to be prosperous entrepreneur/farmer in a small Georgia town. Celie's mother becomes mentally unstable but is wooed & married by a man more interested in her trim (small, neat, white) Victorian house, fields & property than he is in her or her two daughters, Celie & Nettie. When Celie is 14 this stepfather, whom she believes is her father, begins to rape her, causing the birth of two children whom he gives away to an old friend who has become a missionary. Celie's mother dies angry at Celie &, because she's been warned by her stepfather not to tell anyone (but God) who fathered her children, she dutifully writes letters to God.

Later, when her younger sister Nettie runs away from home she runs to the home Celie has made with Mr. ___, a mean-spirited, often brutal man, who being denied Nettie by her stepfather, married Celie because he needed someone to look after his children; his first wife, Annie Julia, having been murdered by her lover. Because Nettie spurns his attentions he turns her out & Celie sends her to the same missionaries, Corrine & Samuel, who have unwittingly adopted her children, Olivia and Adam. With them Nettie goes as a missionary to Africa, where she remains, writing letters but never hearing from Celie for 30 years.

Beaten down for many years by her life of drudgery & abuse with Mr. ____ and his obnoxious children, Celie's spirit begins to rally when Shug Avery, a blues singer & lover of Mr. ___'s is brought home by him, ill, for Celie to nurse. Celie & Shug fall in love, & Celie leaves Mr. ____ to accompany Shug to Memphis where Shug makes a grand living singing the blues

---

duce a film adaptation of *The Color Purple*. The reference to Wendy here is to her literary agent, Wendy Weil.

1   AW is beginning to imagine *The Color Purple* as a movie, as these notes summarize the plot and outline the major characters.

(earlier she made her living as a domestic) & where Celie begins a happy independent life designing pants.

The last straw for Celie in her life with Mr. _____ was the knowledge, provided by Shug, that Mr. _____ had hidden all the letters Nettie had written her over the years. In these letters, which she finally receives, Nettie's life unfolds: She & Celie's children & Samuel & Corrine live among the Olinka in a small village of thatched huts (some round, some square) in West Africa. They all teach & Samuel preaches. Corrine gradually recognizes the resemblance between her adopted children & Nettie & (with help from a tropical fever) agonizes herself to death. After her death, Samuel & Nettie marry. During this personal drama, the Olinka's village is destroyed by an English rubber company & they are forced onto an arid reservation. Adam marries Tashi, an Olinka young woman. Nettie, Samuel, Olivia & Adam & Tashi return to America.

Meanwhile, Shug has left Celie to have a fling with a cute boy of 19 who plays blues flute. They travel to the Southwest & meet Shug's grown children, one of whom works on an Indian reservation that is a mirror image of the one the Olinka occupy in Africa. Celie, whose father has died & left her real father's property to her, including a large, beautiful house, forgives & becomes friends, for the first time, with Mr. _____, whom she now calls Albert. Though missing Shug, she is content, with her friendships & her designing/sewing. Naturally, at that point, Shug comes back.

With Shug & Albert by her side, Celie needs only one thing to make her life complete. Her sister Nettie. One day, as they are all sitting companionably on the front porch, Nettie, Adam, Olivia, Samuel & Tashi (after Celie has received a telegraph saying their ship was sunk by German mines off Gibraltar) arrive.

Celie

In rural & small town culture of the turn of the century through the forties, at least, the voluptuous, the portly, the stout, female form was admired. And even a very _fat_ female was admired if she was as well good-natured and "light on her feet" i.e. a good dancer. Skinniness, boniness, (though not slenderness, which was admired if it was also strong) was considered, in a woman, to be almost a deformity.

Being skinny is Celie's major fault. Since when one is a woman & very skinny (with tiny breasts) one's form was not considered womanly. Hence Mr. ____'s frequent reminder to Celie that "you shape(d) funny." Today we would say Celie has a model's figure. Her other "ugliness" consists of a furtive, beaten down manner, & unkempt hair & clothing (she had no one to teach her to care for herself). As she begins to create herself through her writing, her love of Shug & Nettie, she begins to take on an outer beauty that approximates her extraordinary loveliness of spirit.

Shug Avery

Shug Avery is modeled after one of my aunts who worked as a domestic most of her life. I could never believe this because when she came south to visit us—swathed in rhinestones (diamonds) and furs (hand-me-downs from her missus) you couldn't imagine her cleaning her own house, not to mention anybody else's.

Shug has the requisite "stout" (see photos of any of the early blues singers: Bessie & Mamie Smith, Ma Rainey, etc.) shape to qualify as "womanly." The exact opposite of Celie's. In addition she knows how to dress, carry herself & doesn't fumble verbally like Celie. She's gorgeous and knows it, with only happy thoughts about her very black skin since during this period the black & lighter skinned black women had about the same chance with black men. It was the stage shows & movies produced by whites that encouraged the colorist sexism later exhibited by blacks. Shug looks like Pearl Bailey[1] & acts like one imagines P. Bailey would act in an all black setting. Assertive, funny, unselfconscious & relaxed.

---

1   Pearl Bailey was a voluptuous, dark-skinned African American singer and actress who began her career singing and dancing in Black nightclubs in the 1930s. She made her Broadway debut in *St. Louis Woman* in 1946 and remained active as an actor and singer until her death in 1990 at age seventy-two.

Albert

Albert is a small, bitter, weak man at first. A man whose father has made the most important decisions in his life. Though married twice, with at least one longtime lover and two "sets" of children, he knows almost nothing about children or women. He's the kind of person who really thinks of women as a separate species whose feelings are not as important as a man's. What saves him from total failure as a human being is his irrational but sincere love of Shug Avery. It is because he loves Shug & <u>she</u> loves Celie that he can begin to see something in Celie (& other women) to appreciate. He is still following someone else's lead but, unlike his father, Shug & Celie lead him to the source of love itself, i.e. wonder over the universe. Existence itself. The man who comes to treasure the beauty & fragility of sea shells without having ever seen the sea is very different from the man who raped his child bride while her head was bandaged.

Squeak/Mary Agnes

The most important thing externally about Mary Agnes is her color. She is white-looking (like the early singer/actress Fredi Washington[1]) with gray or green eyes and light hair. She represents many light skinned black women who find themselves pursued by black and white men because of their color & because as "mulattos" they were stereotyped in books & the media as wanton and easy (to the white man) & "beautiful like white women" to the black. Many white looking black women were lost to themselves because neither society permitted them to be themselves. Squeak finds herself through struggle with Harpo & Sofia & their children—& most of all, through singing, without which, she would have gone under.

---

1   Fredi Washington, a Black dramatic actress and civil rights activist, was best known for her role in the 1934 film version of *Imitation of Life*, in which she plays Peola, a young light-skinned Black woman who attempts to pass as white.

Harpo

Harpo, like his father before him, & largely <u>because</u> of his father, thinks of women as a subservient race. Yet it is precisely Sofia's non-subservient nature that he fell for. He is a very slender young man when they marry, but by story's end is quite portly. Since his father remains small & slender Harpo begins to look like the father & his father like the son. And this mirrors their inner growth, for Harpo matures & begins to become a real human being before his father does.

Nettie

Nettie is neither skinny nor stout, but medium. She is brown, not black skinned (Corrine is several shades lighter, as befits her bourgeois Atlanta status) and she wears her hair unstraightened in a neat Victorian style, parted in the middle & twisted up at the back of her head. She wears long missionary skirts & white blouses with bowties. Lace up shoes & a short jacket. Hers is a plain, straight beauty that radiates kindness. Unlike Shug & finally Celie, it would be hard to imagine Nettie really angry. Though she was angry enough at Albert to fight him off. She & Shug will eventually become friends, but at first she will be taken aback by Shug's occasional swearing.

Samuel

Samuel is a large, black, kind & gentle man with a priestly look that belies the ease with which he gets on with women. Sexually & as friends. He is a "touching" person & a natural comforter. With Samuel women feel no need to appear other than themselves because they sense he loves them (& likes them) as they are. Though Nettie claims she never thought of him "as a man" before he cried in her arms, he is the kind of man women have fantasies about because the woman he is with generally seems so content. He is a vulnerable man, capable of tears, capable of being wrong. Capable of admitting failure. In this he is a success as a human being, as well as a success with women who desire a man who is human like themselves.

Sofia

Sofia is a bright-skin, stout, spunky woman with "big legs," & plenty of hair, perhaps the ideal of early 20th century country beauty in America. One of the first womanists, she can work & fight her own battles like a man, enjoys men, sex, her children & her home. The kind of strong hardworking woman who, once out of her overalls & into her lipstick & dress, makes a man blink in disbelief not once but many times. Women also like her (though Celie doesn't at first) for her directness, humor, generosity & ready loyalty.

—

About the music: If the movie starts (as it might) during Celie's happy baby life, before her father's death, the late 1890s, 1900, the music would be ragtime. Perhaps just a tinkle, to let us know there was something upbeat, before the fall. Almost anything by Scott Joplin, je pense.

For the rest, the songs made from the book & Celie's life (which would illustrate how blues are made) & then the traditional jook woman's blues—by the woman on "Mean Mothers" & Bessie Smith.[1] Some of the early songs (in the film) could be typical "female as victim" songs, but they must develop into songs of self-possession & independence. The kind of songs Mde. C.J. Walker hummed to herself. And Shug Avery began to sing after she gave up men as the center of the universe, in favor of herself.

———

1   There's a wonderful song* of Bessie's I'll find about how you treat a no-good man:
You make him
Stay at home
Wash & iron
Let the neighbors think
He's lost his mind
(In Bessie's mouth iron & mind rhyme)
    [AW's note to herself.]
*   The following lines are paraphrased from Bessie Smith's song "Safety Mama."

What is important to me is that the suppressed independent women's music—music as sassy & free as the jazz the male musicians accompanying them played—be reintroduced to the world. We need it.

It might look like this:

1895 – 1903 fading ragtime
1903 – 1914 Celie's period of silence
1914 – 1925 Songs from The Color Purple
1925 – 1940s Popular songs from Bessie, "Mean Mothers"†[1] of
    the period, instrumentalists of the period. Including for the
    Harlem section (1920s) whoever would have been playing: Duke
    Ellington, maybe. Just a riff. (& in the churches, collecting $ for
    Africa "Lift Every Voice and Sing!") In Africa, traditional West
    African women's music. Not drum.

——

Most womens can do a heap more to pleasure themselves than a man can. If you don't believe me, ask one that don't give a shit what men think. Shug didn't give a shit. Many a time I heard her say—cause she was talking to me—I got more cock in my finger than you got in your pants.

Feb. 21, 1984
Last night Quincy Jones & Steven Spielberg (looking rather like some kind of bird, perhaps a parrot—he says he broke his toe against his parrot's cage: two fingers were broken last night, in a cast from falling downstairs) arrived. Quincy first, in an enormous limousine that had difficulty turning into my lane. Quincy beautifully dressed and hair done just so. And Steven,

---

† Two of my favorites from Vol. I are "There Ain't Much Good in the Best of Men Now Days" (Shug) & "Keep Your Nose Out of Mama's Business" (the liberated Squeak/Mary Agnes) [AW's note to herself.]
1 *Mean Mothers/Independent Women's Blues, Vol. 1*, a collection of classic Black women's blues of the 1920s–1950s, compiled by Rosetta Reitz and released on her Rosetta Records label.

who arrived later, casually & in (partly) someone else's clothes. Quincy had talked so positively about him I was almost dreading his appearance—but then, after a moment of near I don't know what, uneasiness, he came in & sat down & started right in showing how closely he has read the book. And making really intelligent comments. Amazing. And Quincy beamed.

Robert & Rebecca & Casey were with me. Rebecca amused & Casey looking for something to munch. Robert quite charming too. Well. We went to Ernie's for dinner, where Quincy & Steven & I got slightly tipsy and energetic in our thoughts of a movie about Celie & Shug & Nettie. And after three hours they brought me back to my humble abode & rode off into the night in their enormous limo en route to the Warner Brothers jet & then home to L.A. & to bed. Q claimed not to have slept the night before because leaving L.A. at nine in the morning was so early.

Anyway.

It is agreed that Steven & I will work together on the screenplay. I will write it & confer. Write & confer. I feel some panic. I want so much for this to be good. Something to lift spirits & encourage people.

March 15, 1984

Yesterday was Quincy's birthday. I called to sing happy birthday to him. He calls me very often, on the flimsiest excuses. But he was somewhere neither office or home and sounded false. So I made it brief.

So much has happened.

This is my third week in the country writing the screenplay. The first week went remarkably well. And the second. But now I feel stuck. I've been lying in bed reading and feeling less energetic than usual. Probably because of the sweet cookies & custard I had last night & yesterday.

Robert. I still don't trust him. Often don't even like him. But the habit of him is very strong & he's very tenacious. . . . There is a lot of sadness, but not so bad. We go to yoga together. To movies. I feel I am doing things with someone I know. But there is no joy for me. No excitement. . . .

I'm stuck in the screenplay. But at least I've brought it to the place where Celie & Shug leave home. Now I must show Celie & Shug in Memphis

& then the death of Celie's stepfather, then Shug's infatuation with the 19 year old, & Celie's return home & Albert's friendship, & then Shug's return & Nettie's—and it seems hard to do in 50 pages. But thank the U I have 2 1/2 more months to do a draft.

Meanwhile, Whoopi Goldberg[1] is auditioning for the role of Celie & I go to L.A. to see her on Friday. In this too I feel myself moving away from Robert.

I am also buying the property next door! 40,000 down & 70 over 15 yrs. at 10%. It finally just made good sense to buy it—as a guard of my privacy. As free space, but also as a place friends & visitors can stay. The main house has a bath, too. And a hot tub.

Curtis[2] has been indicted on the charge of conspiracy to deal in narcotics. On the same day I heard this, from Ruth, I learned I'd won the Townsend Prize[3] which is I know not what from the Atlanta magazine in Ga. Also, on the same day I learned of having won the Lyndhurst Prize,[4] out of Tennessee—it carries with it (or is) 25,000 a year for 3 years. This has a certain unreality.

Mar. 31

The evening with Whoopi went extremely well. Quincy sent a jet for us & Steven's building is beautiful. Whoopi was <u>wonderful</u>. And I've been typing the screenplay. Trying to get my taxes completed. The land in the country nailed down, & my garden started. I <u>love</u> that there will be lots of

---

1 Whoopi Goldberg—born Caryn Elaine Johnson in 1955—was a young comedian and actress who had caught theater producers' attention in 1983 with a one-woman show composed of different character monologues. Titled *Whoopi Goldberg*, the show ran on Broadway from October 1984 to March 1985.

2 One of AW's brothers.

3 The Townsend Prize was created in 1981 and is presented biennially to a Georgia writer who has published an outstanding work of fiction during the preceding two years.

4 The Lyndhurst Prize, presented by the Lyndhurst Foundation in Chattanooga, is a monetary award to individuals who have made significant contributions to the arts, particularly literature.

space to do all kinds of outdoor things & no one will see me! This is the way it often was when I was a child. I remember a garden I started out of sight of the house, down the hill. I tried to grow beans & corn in sand. Everything came up, but soon died. But at WTs[1] I just bought huge <u>mounds</u> of composted manure. And feel so good having it. I've been double digging a nice long bed for carrots & lettuce. Yum. And I'll plant mustard & turnip greens, & tomatoes and perhaps some kind of beans. Okra would be nice. Onions. Peppers. And I'm continuing to plant trees. Very slow on this. Waiting for the Harkleroads to leave before I plant poplars in front of their house.

So. June Jordan[2] was here last night. Thin. High strung. With a young friend/lover. I felt awkward trying to talk with her with the friend present. But we went for Chinese food & that was good. It was good to see her too.

Rebecca has started an aerobics class & loves it. Her little cheeks are bright pink & her eyes sparkle. I'm so glad she's getting exercise.

To be honest, I feel the sadness & the <u>ache</u> of being without an intimate companion. Even now I think I would take Robert back if I could. But I distrust him so deeply. And the worst of it is, I don't think he knows <u>himself</u> what he is doing or is really about. So it would be like throwing in my lot with someone I could expect to keep attempting to hurt & sabotage me, but who would always put the blame for his behavior on his childhood. As if all childhoods aren't to blame for many of our troubles.—& so what? We're grown now.

But this is, I think, a good time to see less of him. I'm very busy with the screenplay. And my garden. And Rebecca's here. And perhaps I should try—very gently—to live for awhile without hugs & snuggles—which I love so much. An electric blanket is not a substitute for arms.

---

1 Wild Trees, AW's property in rural Mendocino County.
2 AW's old friend, the acclaimed poet.

Well, old friend. I'm thankful I have you.

Now don't <u>you</u> get sad!

—

Robert called to say there's a group that wants to ban <u>The Color Purple</u>. Banning The Color Purple would be like banning the color blue—you'd miss it. Whereas—why don't they ban nuclear power?

June 18, 1984

I finished the draft of the screenplay a couple of weeks ago. Got it back from the typist yesterday & sent it off to L.A. today. There is nothing like relief! And I've told my agent to tell Warner Brothers that I'm not signing the chain-resembling contract they're offering. I am too happy thinking of nothing but the colors I will/am using to paint my little round house.

Fame exhausts me, more than anything else it does. I am still tired from being "recognized" by the Pulitzer Prize. But I am slowly getting back my strength & in the country, at Wild Trees, I am very, very happy. The days are long and golden—they seem almost endless. And the full moons are astonishings. (What a sentence!) There is hay stacked neatly in the neighbors' fields, and everywhere we look there's beauty.

June 27, 1984

Irregardless![1] I've just finished reading the collection of stories by California Cooper Wild Trees Press will publish. Yes. It appears there will <u>be</u> a WTs Press.[2] With Robert as partner & business manager. We had a quite beautiful party to celebrate the Press & the summer solstice on the 23rd. From 2 – midnight. About 70 people—50 adults, 20 children. Overall it was a wonderful party. With swimming, walking, music making, a couple of magicians, and then <u>dancing</u>!

August 17 or 16th

The summer is going quickly! Already the leaves are turning & apples are ripe. This season I've feasted on berries & peaches & wonderful greens & vegetables. Slowly I feel strength & equilibrium returning. And the best news is Joan[3] who comes in to work several times a week. She's an excellent cook and having her here means I can eat more healthfully. She's got me eating iron foods—rhubarbs and beets!

Quincy sent mauve roses & a moving note. I love him already. Whatever happens or doesn't. Love is the way to feel.

August 27, 84

10:30

At home in bed. SF. Several hours clearing my study of incredible debris— books, papers, galleys; things people have sent. I want to be able to work at my desk again. I haven't been able to for over a year. All my time is spent responding to correspondence. The first day back in the city & a

---

1 AW was aware, of course, that "irregardless" is considered nonstandard—a misuse of the word "regardless." But, like other educated speakers who use the word, she uses it to add emphasis—and to pay homage to the innovative wordplay of the African American vernacular. Zora Neale Hurston celebrated this innovation—calling it "the will to adorn"—in her classic essay, "Characteristics of Negro Expression."

2 The first book to be published by Wild Trees Press was a collection of short stories by J. California Cooper, called *A Piece of Mine*.

3 A new friend and household assistant.

long, tiring lunch with the HBJ publicist. . . . We showed her the poster, or what will be the poster & now HBJ wants to buy 1,000, which will pay for a large part of the run.[1] So we're glad of that. I still feel a bit nervous about the poster—the hair, a little. But on the whole it is a striking, warm poster with a good message. Without hope there can be no justice, without justice, no hope.

Robert & I had some good talks in the country & some good lovemaking—the best we had since he told me of his affair with A. And when we're alone together we fall into a kind of routine of domestic harmony. But it doesn't really last.

Undated

Rebecca—

Two serious things—

1. See telegram. I don't want to desert you on your birthday, but I must have told these folks I'd come in November—not on the 17th, though. That's new. What should we do? Also that night I have 3 tickets for Cicely.[2]
2. We may never get a good dependable cleaning service. So I propose (until we can find somebody) that we clean a little each day ourselves. I started in the bathrooms today. You could do the areas (tubs) I missed. Also floors. And take out the garbage. Your room smells, too.

---

1 HBJ refers to Harcourt Brace Jovanovich, Alice Walker's longtime publisher. The poster in question is a color photograph, taken by Robert Allen, of AW in her garden, kneeling, holding some pink flowers and smiling as she looks at the camera. Her hair is braided, and she is wearing blue jeans and a purple shirt; she has an orange flower behind her left ear. The upper right corner is overlaid with text: "I am the woman / offering two flowers / whose roots / are twin / Justice and Hope / Let us begin. /—from Horses Make a Landscape / Look More Beautiful / by Alice Walker."
2 The great actress Cicely Tyson was to perform in Los Angeles, possibly for a touring version of *The Corn Is Green*, in which she'd starred on Broadway the previous fall.

I've gone over to the office to put in some hours. We got a great (C's book) review[1] in Publisher's Weekly, <u>very important</u>. It's what librarians read. And folks "in the trade," i.e., bookstores. Harcourt also paid us for the posters they bought. $4,000! So—on to the warehouse where there are thousands of boxes to fold!

I love you,
Mom

—

Mommy![2]

I bought you these flowers today on my way home from work. I've been thinking of you <u>all</u> <u>day</u>!

Don't worry about the L.A. thing on my bday. If you're up to it—GO! I won't be doing anything. You know. That's great about the reviews and the posters! I'll clean the tubs. If not tonight, tomorrow. (I have a short schoolday).

I love you ☺
R

Undated

The Color Purple hit the 1 million mark in sales today! The publicist & publisher sent a small bouquet of flowers. It means about 150,000 dollars more, according to Robert. I expect I'll buy a really gorgeous house—perhaps with Robert—in the city in Noe Valley, which we both like. I enjoy investing in houses & if we get 2 flats we can always rent one out. That might work very

---

1   The first book released by AW's Wild Trees Press was J. California Cooper's debut short story collection, *A Piece of Mine*, officially published in December 1984.

2   This note is in Rebecca's fourteen-year-old handwriting.

well. I am probably going to have to think of selling this flat. I love it but it really is too noisy either to write in or meditate. I saw a little brown house that's just the thing in Noe Valley. If only it were for sale?

In my emotional life I feel I am stagnating. It is as if my love for Robert never reaches a level in me that pushes me forward. I feel so sorry for him, basically. To have done so much harm to what was such a live & vibrant love/emotion. My love feels now domesticated, whereas before it was wild. But I can see us being companions for a while longer, even a long time longer.

When I tally these things up it is now just an exercise. A feeling of distanced amazement:

American Book Award
Pulitzer Prize
1,000,000 sold in paper
70,000 in hard cover
1 year NYTs bestseller list
1 plus years Publisher's Weekly
& SF Chronicle list between #1 (mostly) & #3
Movie sale 400,000 (including consulting)
Foreign translations:
  1. French
  2. Swedish
  3. Chinese
  4. Japanese
  5. German
  6. Italian
  7. Danish
  8. Turkish
  9. Hebrew
  10. Hungarian?
  11. Finnish
  12.
—A best seller in England. Ditto for In Search

Nothing is missing from this success except my capacity any longer to <u>feel</u> it. Though I <u>do</u> feel it, as a kind of cushion, a way or a means of getting me out of the rat race (of whatever sort); slowly I'm beginning to feel secure about money. That is <u>having</u> money. And it's nice that Robert has money. And God knows he earns it. The Press is off the ground in a good way, thanks to him.

Undated

Dear Quincy,

I hardly know what else to say about Shug Avery. It is like trying to explain a poem. If you could, you wouldn't have written the poem. However, one thing occurred to me, finally, & it is that size is irrelevant, essentially. That Diana Ross could be Shug if she really wanted to. I saw & loved her in Lady Sings the Blues & what I loved was <u>her</u> love of Billie that was manifested so clearly in her hard work. She would be a different Shug and it would be hard to see someone so slight standing up to so much, but, slight folks have done so.

Shug is a free person. This is her rarity. She has decided to give herself & her love where she pleases—she has understood that society, not having been arranged for her benefit, is not owed any of her loyalty. But this doesn't mean she was born with this attitude or that she isn't vulnerable. She is in fact, like the rest of us, shaped by her experience. Her time of greatest vulnerability would have been as a teenager, dealing with a cold, critical mother and then with Albert, a passionate but sexually irresponsible & cowardly lover. This period of vulnerability continued into her sojourn in the North (working as a domestic & then singing) and culminated in her complete physical & emotional breakdown.

When Shug is brought home by Albert to be nursed by Celie, she is prepared for death. This liberates her. Snatched out of the jaws of physical death by Celie, Shug's spirit changes entirely. She becomes free. In a sense it is her lack of attachment (to things, man, money) that causes them to become plentifully available to her. Death is a lack of attachment. But Shug lives, with this same lack, because she loves—though, again, without attachment. It is only after running off with Germaine that she begins to feel her attachment to Celie & it is a surprise to her. She is free of everything except the ability & need to love.

I mentioned Diana Ross because I know you have been considering her (& to my mind she'd make a much better Squeak) but there are other women who would be absolutely right in terms of having in a sense "lived the role." Too bad Esther Phillips is dead. But Tina Turner isn't. I <u>know</u> <u>The Color Purple</u> must make her think of Ike. Or it could be someone unknown.

I hope this is useful, & that you still have the notes I sent you on all the characters some months ago. I have a copy if you need it.

Robert & I spent an idyllic four days at Wild Trees. We had a traditional Thanksgiving dinner of red beans & rice (with Louisiana sausage!) & turnip greens from the garden. And he cooked his classic Deep South & Dish Sweet Potato Pie. Then we spent most of the day planting a bushel of daffodils, my astrological flower—which, to my joy, I read in <u>Western Gardening</u> gophers <u>don't</u> (the bulbs) eat! So I planted dozens in gopher holes.

Rebecca spent the holidays in Georgia visiting relatives & my mom. Going to dances in Eatonton & having to beat the Negritos off with a stick, I hear.

Now I've nursed the fire to life & will soon drive to Boonville in search of peach trees. The deer ate the one I had.

Love,
Alice

Undated

Dear Robert,

As we enter into this newest phase in our relationship I find I have anxieties too. I want to go ahead with our plan, of course, but I feel some things should be made clear so that I don't feel trapped.

First of all, can we agree that it is understood that we are entering into a business relationship that will be conducted as such? That your decision to work full time for the Press, and to help me with: correspondence, vendors, paperwork, bookkeeping, consulting, travel, speaking engagements etc. is in no way a proposal of marriage, common or otherwise. And that my decision to repay you for your services & to provide you with a house in the country is no more than should be expected from an employer? I would like it understood between us that we are not talking about a permanent union of any kind. That I agree to pay you between 25,000 (minimum) & 40,000 (maximum & the figure to which I will aspire) per year for from 1–3 years. At the close of each year we will decide whether we wish to continue & how, & at the end of three years we should do this seriously. With the understanding that I do not have to continue a salary to you if I do not wish to.

I want to be very clear about this since I cannot foresee what financial, emotional or other changes might occur in my life. Just as you cannot. I would like us to remain flexible & free.

If you agree with these terms, please sign this letter & return a copy to me for my files.

Sincerely,
Alice

Feb. 8, 1985

In one day—less—I'll be 41! I feel just the same as always. Only happier. This morning Robert went back to the city, after a few days in the country with me (nursing a cold) and I was glad for the time together <u>and</u> for the time alone. I love my solitude at WTs. I had a big bowl of oatmeal & nuts & fruits & then started cleaning house. . . . When I sweep I am instantly joined to Celie (Rachel) and to Mama. So sweeping here in the country is deeply satisfying. Then I went up to the studio and planted snapdragon seeds and lots of mustard greens & turnips. I also dragged out the futon & took a nap in the sun. How lovely to live in a place where I can <u>plant</u> on my birthday →

which I intend to do tomorrow. But I also want to plant something on the new moon. Just to see if what the old timers say about more rapid growth is really true.

Feb. 18, 1985

My birthday was lovely. I woke alone at Wild Trees and had a slow somewhat early morning, then went up to the studio to clean; then Rebecca [and a friend] arrived & soon Robert & Casey & we went out to dinner at a restaurant in Mendocino. It felt very "family."

The event at the Oakland Museum officially launching The Press had many warm & high moments. Belvie[1] did a wonderful job, pulling it all together. California[2] unfortunately read the least appropriate story for our sponsors/audience (The Deltas). But Will Sand Young saved the day for me by singing the most beautiful song to me! And there were hugs aplenty from lots of folks—all persuasions!

Feb. 20, 1985

Finally spoke up about my feeling that Robert/The Press is squeezing me out of my space & my resentment about it. After renovating the Press house I offered it to Robert to live in. He eventually complained that it was too small for all "his stuff"—a lot of which is mine loaned to him—and the Press. I let that pass. Then he observed that the location of the Press house is gloomy & damp & that he intends to spend his days at the studio. I took the hint & offered to make the studio the Press house, effectively cutting my private workspace to zero since Robert is still sharing the house. Today as soon as I got up two phone calls from people who want something about the Press. Then the realization that Robert has moved his computer into

---

1 AW's good friend Belvie Rooks was the publicist for Wild Trees Press, and Robert was the general manager. Belvie had left *Mother Jones* magazine, where she was director of national affairs, to become the new press's director of marketing and publicity.

2 J. California Cooper, author of *A Piece of Mine*, the first book Wild Trees Press published. Will Sand Young was a Bay Area singer.

the studio. I felt all my struggle to find a place to work had come, almost, to nil. So I said so. . . .

But there's an uneasiness. And. For instance, I feel <u>he</u> should furnish his house & that I've given him too much furniture already. Yet when he complains about not having a table & chair (& no money to get them) I have to struggle to keep from offering him mine, here. Yet his house in Oakland has <u>two</u> tables, one of them mine, & four chairs, all of them mine. He has my rug, my pictures & I bought his sofa! I hate feeling responsible for furnishing his house. And the money. I've paid him 4000 already plus an advance of 2000 for his taxes. This is better than Mills has ever done.

So I kvetch & complain! And wonder how much of this sudden sensitiveness & indignation is pre-period blues.

March 15, 1985
The day after Quincy's birthday. I thought about him all yesterday and called but he was out/busy. I sent flowers "I love your life." & signed Mme. Katherine. I hope he's well, but sense an overwhelming busyness/tiredness connected to the producing of the movie. . . . I realized I'm afraid of seeing him again. Afraid I'll feel even more attracted, yes, but also that he will disappoint me & be just another ambitious Hollywood ego, albeit with some of the most thoughtful impulses known to woman.

May 1985

My soul forsaken
until you come
My heart so heavy
bowed down in shame
But now you here . . .
don't go no where
I b'lieve my life
be turnin' round.

This song begins in Celie's hum, to Shug, Shug takes it, jazzes it up, names it "Celie's Blues" but sings it to Albert (where its meaning still applies) then, at the end, Albert "sings" this song to Celie (via jukebox). It applies to all three of them and makes a circle of their love.

June 10

On the set Monday:[1]

Unlike last week, which was sweltering, today is cooling off to an alarming degree. I want to go home. I'm feeling tired—and I've invited the actors to dinner in a Chinese restaurant near the hotel. If only I'd brought my coat!

The experience of a set is strange. Today I feel less center stage, just as my horoscope predicted. I don't understand the ways of film. Talking to Rod Temperton[2] made me realize this. He said When you see the "dailies" you don't see anything. Everything is constructed in the editing. This pressed my cynical button. Why waste my tears—as I did the other day—on the dailies if they're not necessarily what's going to be seen? But then, my less tired self says: Whatever is constructed will be constructed from the dailies. So cheer up.

WTs

June 17, 1985

As I was coming down the hill from the studio just now it occurred to me that Sofia in the movie will work in Harpo's, not in Celie's store. Also Harpo has been made into a "man" in the heavy duty sense of owning something & lording over it. I don't mind this, it's just that Celie's industry is not made

---

1   The film adaptation of *The Color Purple* was being shot partly on set in Burbank, California, and partly on location in Monroe, North Carolina (near Charlotte). AW served as a consultant on the movie, which starred Whoopi Goldberg as Celie, Margaret Avery as Shug, Oprah Winfrey as Sofia, and Danny Glover as Mister. For Goldberg and Winfrey, the film marked their mainstream acting debuts.

2   An award-winning composer and musician, Temperton was cowriting *The Color Purple* soundtrack and score with Quincy Jones.

anything of. I think as the script stands now there's one scene of her & some women sewing on the porch. This change is obviously because men are in charge & they cannot apparently break the stereotype that the man provides & the woman is subsidiary. This is very different from the first version of the script which followed the book more closely. The emphasis on the jook joint reflects also the way the music has been expanded.

I went back down on Monday. And asked Robert to come down on Tuesday. He was good enough to bring warmer things for me & Rebecca & also some suggestions for the script I'd given Menno[1] but which he'd forgotten to take.

When I'm on the set I'm so into communicating support to the actors & enjoying the characters coming to life that I'm sure a lot of things (changes in meanings, etc.) slip right by me. And I notice that the few things I suggested, other than language, have not appeared in this new script, which in my opinion falls apart ridiculously near the end where there are odds & ends of people long cut suddenly appearing.

I'm impressed by Steven's dedication to getting just the scene he wants—no matter how many times it must be shot. In the heat, the heavy oil based smoke, he seems perfectly relaxed and happy. Rebecca called to tell me Steven & Amy's baby was born while Celie was in labor. Another in the long line of oddities, synchronicities. Oprah = Harpo, etc. Margaret Avery/Shug Avery, Steven Spielberg/Whoopi Goldberg.

I feel the assistance of the Universe on this movie; I feel reassured by this when I see the changes wrought to the script.

Aug. 16, 1985
On location in North Carolina
The 58th day of shooting.
I feel remarkably little need to write anything, but I won't let that stop me. Robert and I arrived here in #157 at the Holiday Inn in Monroe two nights ago. It is our third visit to the Southern set. The air conditioner is noisy, so is

---

1   Menno Meyjes, the screenwriter for the film adaptation of *The Color Purple*. Director Steven Spielberg had decided not to use AW's script.

the street (highway), so are the cars in the parking lot coming & going. It is hot & muggy. Food terrible. The good news is that the film is going well. That is to say the performances have been excellent & both acting & directing has often seemed to me inspired. Rebecca is convinced that Steven doesn't listen to me—& we talk <u>very</u> little—& I agree with her. He doesn't listen to anyone. But suddenly, days later, you notice he's changed the thing that bothered you or he's managed to put your idea somewhere in the scene. It might not look <u>exactly</u> like your suggestion anymore but there's still enough of it to recognize. The end of the movie—which we saw last night—is really the cinematic expression of the alternate title of my script "Watch For Me in the Sunset." She's disillusioned by his absorption & apparent callousness; arrogance. But, as with Whoopi, all is forgiven once you see what is on the screen. Almost all.

Whoopi is <u>incredible</u> as Celie, and Margaret[1] is wonderful, I think, as Shug. And is, in many ways, the most vulnerable & brave of the actors. Since she is aware that there are those who thought Tina Turner more appropriate. Not me. Margaret has an immense sweetness (which is, after all, how Shug got her name) and an innate, frustrated dignity. And she tries so hard & unfailingly to do the scenes right. I like the vulnerability that's in her eyes. She has beautiful eyes; it's what you notice first and last. And in the scenes where nothing else could hold you, her eyes do. They're real eyes that show experience as plainly as her face does—not marbles that show nothing no matter what they've seen.

Anyway, after dailies she came up and kissed me & wanted to talk about a movie premiere benefit in L.A. for Kwanzaa?

My daughter amazes me with her beauty and competence.[2] Everyone congratulates me. It is the purest joy to hear her loud, ringing voice piercing through the set (over hill & pond) "Rolling!" "That's a cut!" "Hold that vehicle!" Etc. Etc. And to see her striding in her yellow Reeboks, dreadlocks flying with bullhorn (which she rarely needs to use—her natural voice is louder, I tease her) & walkie-talkie on her hip. I like her tallness, her direct-

---

1 Actress Margaret Avery, who played the role of Shug in the film.
2 Rebecca, fifteen, is working on set as a production assistant for the film.

ness, her characteristic cheerful & no-shit attitude. I know she would not like to get along without me, but she could. She is already herself.

Meanwhile, the trip home was good because I saw a very patient ophthalmologist (with a nice stutter) who convinced me I'm not going blind just because my eyes are dry! And sure enough the drops he gave me seem to do the trick. Rebecca commented on the largeness of my eyes. I realized they've seemed smaller because of the dryness & consequent squinting.

6:45 a.m. Sept. 7, 1985
In two days it will be Daddy's birthday. He would have been 76, I think.

Deep insomnia. Pre-period, I suppose. But an interesting dream, before I woke up. I was more or less driving a large black plastic (in the sense of very flexible, like a cartoon) car—very fast on a somewhat crowded freeway— The car was full of people, all kinds & colors and I was zipping in & out of traffic like a pro, and as if I could actually see where I was going, which I could not. Fortunately I realized what the chances were of not having an accident & careened off to the side of the road where I knew I would either switch drivers or conjure up a smaller, less plastic & speedy car.

Perhaps this reflects my feelings about the film, now that it's done—the shooting, that is. My recent, & last, trip to the set, Africa, U.S.A., was very strange. I hadn't planned to go at all. In fact, I'd just bought and planted hordes of petunias, a kind of flowering sage, & three wonderful purple butterfly bushes to celebrate being home for good after North Carolina. Then—because I had an appointment—I went down to the city. At some point Quincy's secretary, Madeline, called to tell me I would be receiving some of the music for the film shortly. Since I am to write the liner notes. While we were talking Quincy arrived & we started talking about the African music, & I realized I should be there when it was played, especially since he has hired the best kalimba player in the world to play. Then I remembered Steven had asked that I be present when Akosua[1] (Nettie) did her voice-overs. And there was also my daughter down there working hard & no doubt needing a hug.

---

1 Akosua Busia, an actress of Ghanaian descent, played the role of Nettie.

So off I went.

Of all the scenes I felt least happy with the African ones. The location of the village is wrong, the scarification ceremony is wrong (not to mention how every person's scar has a different design whereas if they're from the same tribe the scar would be the same) & there's no way you could have a rubber plantation on this dry, barren land. So anyway I arrived on the set & almost immediately got into an intense, sad conversation with an expatriate Liberian physician who is one of the extras. (One good thing is there are lots of Africans in this movie—in fact, when Nettie returns to Celie, Carl Anderson (Samuel) is the only non-African in the bunch: Susan (Tashi) is from Kenya, Akosua (Nettie) is from Ghana, "Adam" & "Olivia" are from Zambia. Anyway, this man, beautifully dressed in rather Nigerian looking robes, sat beside me on the hot dry grass & told me, among other things, that Firestone rubber[1] owns 168,000 acres of rubber plantations in Liberia for which they paid 1 cent per acre, in perpetuity.

He talked about the lack of health care among the workers. The high incidence of blindness because of the fumes given off when ammonia is added to the latex (?) to change its character. He talked of having devised an eye wash solution & of teaching the workers how to use it. He was very sad. He spoke without emotion and almost as if drugged, as he told me about the coup in Liberia in which five of his friends, cabinet ministers, were killed.

I asked about the African-American settlers who'd "returned" to Africa after the Civil War & settled in Liberia. He said there was little distinctive trace of them. That though they had been mostly, how do you say, "high yellow," they were by now quite dark. It was an amusing thought: that the people who "returned" to Africa for the most part had never been.

I hang out a lot with the mothers & the children, my natural allies. I'm

---

1 Firestone Natural Rubber Company, LLC, has operated a rubber plantation in Liberia since 1926. Considered to be the largest contiguous rubber plantation in the world, the plantation has been the subject of various media reports in recent years concerning its operations, including a *Frontline*/ProPublica investigative documentary titled *Firestone and the Warlord*. In response to these reports, Firestone has denied all allegations of wrongdoing and insists that it is a benefit to the Liberian economy and adheres to local labor laws.

so impressed by the motherlove & pride. They come and stand for hours as their children go through scenes. I was especially moved by everyone's response to the sudden cold weather, for which no one was dressed—this being sunny, hot, Africa & all.[1] Between takes the mothers, shivering themselves, rushed up & laid their own light sweaters & jackets across their children's shoulders. Whenever they could, they'd point out their children to me & tell me how happy they were that their child was in the movie. One little boy, the absolute most cold looking & most stoic, came up to tell me quite seriously that he'd read the book & thought it very good. He looked about 6. In fact, I worried that the children would have negative thoughts plus nightmares from the scarification ceremony scene. But just as I was at my most worried one of the "African elders" in a lovely Sierra Leonian robe and a Cameroonian hat came up & gave me a book about the peoples of Kenya. I opened it almost instantly to a page describing female "circumcision," i.e., sexual torture & mutilation. The author, Joy Abramson, tells of having witnessed such a mutilation ("circumcision" is definitely a misnomer & an offensive euphemism) done by a group of women to a small 12 year old girl. The child was held down by several women, on the ground, in the cold, while the "surgeon" rubbed her genitals with dried chicken dung, "washed" her dull knife in "greenish filthy" water, and proceeded to cut off the child's clitoris, after which the child was forced to jump up & down three times to see how much or whether she'd bleed. If not, the "surgeon" got a goat, as payment for her "services." If so, only eggs. Ms. Abramson kept her eye on the child, last seen slumped exhausted & stunned on the ground, & on the severed clitoris. This she noticed was placed between the toes of another woman whose task it was to kick it away, out into the bush.

I flipped back to the front of the book hoping this event had taken place decades ago. Alas, the book was published in 1968. The rationale for cliteradectomy: no one would marry a woman whose clitoris was intact. A woman without sex drive is, I suppose, thought to be more docile. I turn page after page, every woman's face—violated & hurt—breaks my heart.

---

1   The African scenes in the film were being shot in Burbank, California.

So let them have nightmares, I thought, let them have negative thoughts. Anything to help them know in their souls that children should not be hurt, period.

I thought of the Kenyan exiles I met in London & about the atrocities committed by so many African leaders against their people. These atrocities have their foundation, I believe, in the "cultural" and "traditional" atrocities inflicted on women and children & particularly on children who are women.

Undated, Fall 1985

London: I am giving readings at The Lewisham Theatre, The Poetry Center of London & The Africa Center. We are also trying to sell our first Wild Trees Press book to English publishers. Mid-week there is an urgent call from Steven which it takes two days to answer, given the transatlantic difference in time & the nasty hoarding of the single lobby telephone by our receptionist: Alice, he says, how is it that Nettie knows Albert's name? he asks. Everyone knows his name, I reply. Even Celie. She doesn't write it on her letters out of fear. That's what I thought, he says. But we were wishing you were here because some folks felt differently. Anyhow, we shot it that way.

What are you doing in London?

Readings.

Sept. 22, 1985

A bright, sunny morning in Robert's new apartment. Casey sprawled on the couch.

—

Two "moments to remember" on the set: The day, well into shooting in North Carolina, when Whoopi told me she'd never read the script.

The day Steven referred to "Gone With the Wind" as "the greatest movie ever made" & said his favorite character was Prissy.

Oct. 31, 1985

> Whoever you are
> Whatever you are
> Start with that
> Whether salt of
> The earth
> Or only white
> Sugar.

—

There is impatience now when I write. I'd rather muse my thoughts than write them.

All in all, while my energy seems to be returning, with the help of massages, colonics & gym/yoga, my self seems suspended. I am in limbo.

Undated, Early December 1985

I have mixed feelings about the film.[1] I've only seen it once, in such a state of tension I left the theatre with a crushing headache. I'm afraid I saw more of what is not there than what is there, and have been mourning the characters & events that were lost in the editing or never attempted from the book. There were scenes I didn't like, but many that I loved. But in order to know what I truly feel about The Color Purple film I'll have to see it again, perhaps many times, when I am able to be more open to what it is rather than grieving over what it is not.

Dec. 6, 1985

I am being besieged by reporters—L.A. Times, N.Y. Times, the Chronicle, etc.—who want to interview me about the film. Which I have by now seen. I've managed to cancel or avoid most of them. Now the publicist at Pocket

---

1   The film *The Color Purple* was officially released on December 18, 1985. AW wrote this entry, and the one that follows, after seeing the movie once, at a prescreening.

wants a statement to hand out. One basic way I feel about the film—after one viewing—is terrible. It looks slick, sanitized & apolitical to me. Some of the words coming out of Shug & Celie's mouths are ludicrous. The film looks like a cartoon. There are anachronisms: Shug's father driving horse & buggy in the 30s, for instance. In short, on first viewing, I noticed only the flaws. Plus, I went into mourning for the characters who appeared much better actors in dailies than in the finished product; in the finished product they seem miniaturized when not actually chopped to bits. Samuel almost doesn't appear. Harpo lacks fullness—the fullness I <u>saw</u> in dailies. Oprah is wonderful but too aged, regardless of how hard a time she had. And who straightened her hair? The big house is just that. Everyone is too well dressed. And Shug's song to Celie seems to be coming from a much smaller woman.

These are all my negative thoughts. I sat there tense as a bow & my head has been aching ever since.

The things I like: Not the Oliver Twist or the carved heart in the tree which is so cutesy as to be alienating, but the parting scene, between Celie & Nettie, which is good, though not the best of the efforts shot, and the scene where Nettie defends herself against Mister. Nettie, in fact, is quite wonderful. The kissing scene between Celie & Shug. The whole section where Shug & Celie find the letters & begin to read them. Especially the scene where Celie smells the dried flower petal. Shug in the juke joint, first song. Second song sounds strained & too small for Shug's body, so the effect is a distancing from the emotions of C & S. The scenes in the church are all fine, although the last one is hokey & I resent the imposition of Shug's father between her & "God." The music is wonderful. Although Nettie in Africa is teaching reading & writing, not music.

The ending is moving.

The BBC was just here for 2 days. The director, a white male named Nigel (after I had agreed to do it because of a black woman named Samira whom I thought would direct) told the story of 2 reclusive artists he'd filmed & how horrified they were at the results. They said, when they saw what he had done: "Well, I suppose it turned out as well as it could have done." Perhaps that is how I feel. But I feel disappointed too that it didn't turn out better.

But it didn't turn out better because—? I <u>saw</u> how hard everyone worked. How earnestly they tried to do it right. I helped as much as I could. All this week I've wanted to weep. I fear I have failed the ancestors.

But no. I did my best & the ancestors themselves are far from perfect. We try everything in an effort to express ourselves. They did this. <u>I</u> do this. I do so hope it's true that there are no mistakes, only lessons. This one could be big.

Jan. 11, 1986

A beautiful cold day in the country. I am recovering, I hope, from the worst flu I've ever had: chills & fever, aching joints, painful muscles, headache. I slept relatively well last night, for which I am grateful. I've been agitated (and very angry) because Mamie[1] has written Mama and Curtis & finally me saying she is the origin of the title of the book, <u>The Color Purple</u>, and in my letter she talks about "blockage" & not being able to read my work, apparently because she feels I ripped her off via use of the title. In the others' letters she outright accuses me of plagiarism. At first I sat down & tried to write her my usual patient letter, calmly explaining myself. But then I decided that this method obviously doesn't help her & that she should be told she needs psychiatric help. So I wrote a briefer letter & sent it, suggesting this. But it is still an outrageous & amazing thing to come up now, nearly 5 years after the book was published & such an utter contrivance on her part.

But what hurt was how hurt I was by her charge. I felt all the pain I used to feel as a child when she could & did make us all feel so wrong & backward and foolish. It hurt to realize the family still has the power to wound. That people like Mamie still <u>want</u> to wound.

And in my weakened state I couldn't laugh it off as I am sometimes able to do. So I talked it over as best I could with Robert. He was wonderful. He had encouraged me to send her flowers for Christmas. I had talked myself

---

1   Mamie is AW's oldest sister; Curtis is one of their brothers.

into sending her $2000 for her "museum."[1] And I'm OK about that: good is good no matter what else is happening. Besides, today I've meditated, long & well. My little house is clean & comfy. The sun is more or less shining. I am getting better. Purple is #1 on The NY Times list & The L.A. Times & The Philadelphia Enquirer. It has reached the 3,000,000 mark in print. Rebecca is beautiful, smart, sweet & in love. I love Robert and Quincy. We're renting a lovely house in Bali for February. I am blessed. The Universe loves me. Why fear?

Jan. 22, 1986

This notebook certainly reveals the chaos of the last year. I trust this one will be somewhat calmer and <u>orderly</u>. A lot has happened; in my stars and elsewhere. Just before Christmas I went shopping for Christmas presents at Women Crafts West, a store owned by a beautiful gray-haired, young faced, black sister named Pell. I bought lots of lovely women made things: for Quincy, Peggy, their daughters, myself. And, just before leaving the store I caught sight of the real reason I was shopping there. On a shelf, down low, behind glass, there was something I knew instantly I had to have—a magic wand! It is over a foot long with a handle made of black walnut & with almost a two inch crystal on the end. I bought it with great joy and recognition. Then I felt ready to see the film a second time at the premiere in New York. For which Robert looked (& was) spectacular! Dressed in a tux that only a laid back Mendocino philosopher & lover would wear, with a cummerbund & headband and a fish as his bowtie. Well. I was myself resplendent in a black silk dress covered with sequins & gold leaves. A sister named Deborah Matthews, who does it for love & a living, dressed me. It was wonderful. I felt very Shuggish & quite protected by the wand.

There were all kinds of people there: Everyone from the movie, my sister Ruth & Betty, a <u>lot</u> of black women writers—yeah! Toni Morrison &

---

1 In 1980, Mamie founded the Lee-Stelzer Heritage Museum in Atlanta, which sometimes served as a food pantry.

Toni Cade Bambara, Sonia Sanchez; there were Ruby Dee & Ossie & Bill Cosby & Camille—& best of absolute all, my friend Carole Darden from Sarah Lawrence. Looking lovely, smelling sweet. Big smiles. I was so happy she was with us & that we could send her home in the limo. Which again tickled me. They are like prehistoric cars & in New York you truly feel you are lumbering along on the road to extinction.

I loved the film. So did Ruth, who had also had deep reservations about it. I was finally able to see it, & to let go of the scenes that were not there. It is far more conventional than the novel, especially in terms of religion vs. spirituality & Shug & Celie's relationship & even Celie & Mister's relationship & Harpo & Sofia's too, but I still felt a lot of the soul of the people—& that was lovely. It is just the opposite of reading a book—I mean, seeing a movie with lots of people—which helped tremendously. Reading a book is a solitary pleasure. You don't want someone guffawing in your ear. But watching a movie is better with lots of people—unless of course it's a dreadful film. Which I'm happy to say Purple is not.

I think my magic wand helped & afterward Gloria & Mort came up & we hugged & she was very happy. I felt so much for her. For of everyone she's been the most supportive, a real champion of me & Purple. She said, knowing how worried I had been: "You don't have to worry, anymore. It's beautiful." Quincy had been saying this all along, of course, but somehow it wasn't quite the same. Yet I do trust both of them because of what I feel is a deep, abiding, innate decency. And both of them are models of love.

Robert, Rebecca, Carole & I got to sit with the Reading is Fundamental folks which was a bit of a struggle. Long involved questions over the table that I declined to answer. My greatest joy was that I sincerely loved the film. It had bothered me greatly that I would have to say publicly that I thought it was terrible. I had lost sleep trying to think of new & painless ways of phrasing it on the Good Morning America show—which, incidentally, I'd never seen. It went well, I thought, next day, and I talked about Mama & how excited she was thinking of the Eatonton première coming up in a month & of how, bedridden though she is, she wants to come to see the movie in a gown & slippers with heels.

—

Dear Danny,[1]

I have been thinking a lot about you, as actor and spirit, and hoping
you are well. In a few days the Academy Awards nominations will
be announced, and I wonder if you will be among those nominated
for an Academy Award. It isn't that you need the award. You don't.
You have, in your acting, reached the level of healer & whether you
get an award or not, this capacity to heal through your work will
probably always be yours; unless, of course, you spend the rest of
your life playing evil detectives and drug profiteers. Which I don't
think you will. On the other hand, for a genuine healer, there is
even healing power in the portrayal of evil.

Let me tell you a story: When I was a little girl I had a very
traumatic experience that meant I could not live with my family
for a while. I was sent to live with my grandparents for a number
of months. Stories about my grandfather, always told with furtive
admiration, indicated a rather autocratic, wild, renegade outlaw.
A man who gambled & drank whiskey and carried a pistol. It was
even said he shot someone in the behind (this was told so that it
sounded amusing: it was never said that he shot someone in the
back!). There were many stories—that even my barely teenage
brothers and sisters knew—about how energetically PaPa beat our
grandmother, his wife. About how he used to chase her all over
the farm, shooting off his gun. Chillingly, these stories were told
as if this behavior was amusing, & even the children mimicked my
grandmother's fear, laughing at how she pleaded for her life or ran

---

1   An undated draft of a letter to Danny Glover, who played the role of Mister. The nominees for the 58th Academy Awards were announced on February 5, 1986. Though Danny
Glover was not among the nominees, *The Color Purple* was nominated for eleven awards,
including Best Picture, Best Actress (Whoopi Goldberg as Celie), Best Supporting Actress
(Margaret Avery as Shug and Oprah Winfrey as Sofia), and Best Adapted Screenplay. When
winners were announced at the awards ceremony on March 24, 1986, *The Color Purple* became one of the most nominated films in Oscar history without a single win.

off through the corn. He also, <u>always</u>, all his life, absolutely loved someone else.

But they were getting old, when I lived with them. The autocratic order still prevailed: he called her "woman," she called him "<u>Mr.</u> Walker," but he no longer beat her. By then, I don't think he had to. His word was law.

But in fact, he rarely talked anyway. Rachel, my grandmother, did 4/5ths of the work—mostly housecleaning, cooking, seeing after chickens & pigs, tending the garden, although he liked working in the garden, too—and I remember long hours of the two of us, my grandfather and I, sitting quietly on their front porch, or counting the cars that came by. Each of us would choose a color and the one whose color drove by most frequently won the "game."

He was inscrutable, was Henry Clay, & never was violent and never raised his voice the whole time I lived with them. And yet, the effects of his violence I could see plainly in Rachel's slavish behavior.

Now, Danny, from playing the role of <u>Mr.</u>, some of this you already know. But what you might not know—because I wasn't conscious of it for a very long time—is even though I understood on some child's level that he had been, & still was, in many ways "a devil," <u>I adored my grandfather.</u>

And over the years in my life & in my work, I've struggled with this conflict: how to love a dictator & a torturer. It wasn't until I saw the movie many times that I fully realized I had been longing & needing to be able to love my grandfather even as he was when he did the worst things. And the last of the conflict was washed away by your acting. You helped me relive my grandfather's early life, to see him objectively (There he was!), and to take his psyche completely into mine.

I will tell you where it happened: When he runs out of the house, & down the walk, gets on his horse, with his little hopeful bouquet of straggly flowers—that he didn't even

BE NOBODY'S DARLING **255**

plant!—& goes off into the sunset, still trying to court a woman he was too weak to marry & by whom he has three children! And the song "Oh Careless Love" strikes in me the grandfather gene & makes me know that part of the reason I love him so is—he is like me! With us love is absolute/eternal love. We cannot stop loving because of other people's marriage vows, or our own. When that love is thwarted, we turn mean or morose. And I realize too, that he sensed I was like him, that he must have all along, & that was why we could sit together contentedly for hours without talking!

Danny, I thank you so much for this healing. For your hard work, which just amazed me, & humbled me. Especially when I saw you carrying on, quite heroically, with five (?) children cavorting about the set. My concentration would have been ruined; but somehow you managed to incorporate the tension and distraction into the scenes you played—& they were actually deeper, because of that.

Isn't life astonishing!? It is always managing to "hit a straight lick with a crooked stick," which is one of the ways I think about the entire movie experience, which I sense also had very deep meanings and connections for you.

I'm so glad.

With love & thanks, Danny,

from

your granddaughter & sister,

Alice

March 1, 1986

A strange, blessed, & in some ways anxious week. We all returned safely from Bali, where we had a wonderful time, over all. I love much of the art—though it is repetitious, like life—and the spirituality and warmth/openness of the people. While there I didn't think about Quincy very much. Robert & I discussed my love for him & talked about the possibility of a "foursome" developing between us and Q & P.[1] I have very mixed feelings about this. At the same time I understand the fact that any relationship at all will be complicated. I've really suffered since I returned because although there were presents from Quincy—champagne & crystal glasses for my birthday & the tape from 60 Minutes—the cards seemed cool to me. And I've been back a week & he hasn't called. Though I've left numerous (2) messages on his service—which I'm beginning to hate.

I go along pretty well & then my longing for him swoops down upon me & I miss him terribly.

March 5

He has called twice since I wrote the above.

I'm drawn to him so strongly. At the same time, my love for Robert only deepens. I can't imagine life without Robert as easily as I once could. We are like, and are, really good friends who also love each other's bodies and touch. And after 10 years! I think perhaps I am simply ready for another experience of love & the Universe has magnanimously offered the possibility of Q. On the other hand, Q is so busy, so distracted, so not physically available, that perhaps we are attempting to come together in the wrong century. I feel that way sometimes. Why is it taking so long? I ask. How can he not fly here to hold me? When I have flown there we've held each other but always before an audience of at least a dozen.

April 15, 1986

A very good morning of work. Two brief essays about Bali & Rebecca's smoking[2] which I typed & put away. They're not finished, but nearly so. In the country & the city I now have typewriters and am in the middle of

---

1 Here, "Q & P" refers to Quincy and his wife at the time, actress Peggy Lipton. Though AW is still with Robert, she and Quincy Jones have developed a strong connection, and they are trying to figure out a way to pursue a romance without being dishonest with their partners—and perhaps including them.

2 This essay, "My Daughter Smokes," was eventually published in 1988 in *Living by the Word: Selected Writings, 1973–1987.*

journal transcribing. The red journal is interesting. The blue one makes me yawn. It is hard to believe the amount of energy I put into Robert's conflicts. But great to see what good times we managed to have through it all. Or <u>around</u> it all. Have decided pretty much <u>not</u> to pursue buying the house,[1] though it seems ideal. Facing a park, lots of light, a classic Victorian—even a landmark. But I've felt strained and stressed and disgusted with myself for being greedy. I have the place in the country where I am truly happy. The apartment here is, for the most part, very comfortable. The dogs don't seem to bark as much or maybe I've gotten used to them. . . . Rebecca found the house & loves it; that makes it harder to give up.

But it's good for the soul to give up coveted things. I've been stressed but not in a way that didn't teach me anything.

Anyway, if the house sells in Brooklyn—on time—this would still be too shaky for me.

Let me put it in the hands of the Universe. If it is for me it will be mine. If not it won't.

May 6, 1986

Just talked to Joanne[2] & asked about my request that they raise my fee per "column" to 3,000. She says they can't. That's (1,500) as high as they can go. Etc. Everyone's being paid this. If only people understood how little writers are paid! I explained that since half my income goes for taxes, half of 1500 is only 750. The amount I received as an advance for my first novel!

Oh well. If I wasn't feeling the pinch of buying a house I'm sure payment size wouldn't matter. After all I've sold <u>Ms.</u> pieces for years for very small fees. One wonders though how successful the magazine has to be before they can pay writers above starvation wages.

* * *

---

1   Now that Rebecca has returned from New York to live with Alice, AW is considering giving up her city apartment and buying a house in the San Francisco Bay Area so they can spend more time in the city, in addition to their time at Wild Trees in the Mendocino countryside.
2   Joanne Edgar was one of the founding editors of *Ms.* magazine.

I've just completed a draft of "In the Closet of the Soul"[1] and dedicated it to a woman I met when I read at Davis. My mind wanders. Thinking about money, which I rarely did last year, a great relief. For the first time in my life I felt financially secure, unstrained. So much so it was difficult for me to gear myself to the stress of trying to buy the Steiner St. house.[2] But that seems to be going well, and a year from now I will no doubt be happy with the decision & consider it financially astute. When I'm here, though, a house in the city seems superfluous. But when I'm in the city the apartment seems more & more cluttered, noisy. Rebecca tells me there's yet another dog on the side of the apartment my study is on, and last week we watched two men, our newest neighbors, peeing into the shrubbery in front of their gate. But it's as if, now that I'm planning to move, I notice these things. The violence in the projects a block away. Most recently an Asian woman was mugged & her husband started shooting at "anything black" as a young resident—his hair Jheri curled to death—said when Belvie asked. Then yesterday there was a massive fight when Rebecca drove through. I feel bad to be leaving the neighborhood. The one we're going to isn't that much better & is also close to the projects. But it is a bit better, and the park seems quiet and well kept.

It will be as if Rebecca & I are completing the circle—from the beautiful old Victorian on Midwood Street (then Garfield, 1st street, Geary Blvd, Galilee Ln) to the beautiful old Victorian on Steiner. We both love roomy old houses. With our scant furniture this place will seem roomy indeed.

Robert & I went to Belvie's housewarming on Sunday and I think it was one of the best parties I've ever been to. Her house overlooks the river & the ocean. We went up river in the canoe. Then ate seaweed off the rocks at the beach. The radioactive cloud drifting our way from Russia was mentioned only briefly: people were in a worshipful mood & stared out to sea quietly or

---

1   This essay—about AW's reaction to the criticism of the Mr.____ character (sometimes written as "Mister") in *The Color Purple*, both the novel and the film—would be published in 1988 in *Living by the Word: Selected Writings, 1973–1987*.

2   AW has decided to move forward on purchasing the house in San Francisco.

took out the canoe or laid in the sun. Then we went & had a delicious dinner & listened to music & played some. Donna showed me how to play the berimbau, an Angolan/Brazilian instrument of great resonance & beauty.

June 16, 1986

Wouldn't you know I've bought the house; I'm to be handed the keys on Thursday. The Universe gave some clear signals. Asked Mel for possible help if I needed it—15,000 or so. He said of course, then later reneged. Nothing new. I felt so sad for him. Each time I think: it isn't possible that he doesn't mean to help us ever, at all. But—and now Rebecca says he and his mother are reneging on their promises to help pay her college expenses. Well, so what? We'll make it. For instance, the day after Mel backed out (after I had pursued the buying of the house based on his "of course!") I received 18,000 in the mail from the paperback of The Third Life of Grange Copeland. Then 10,000 unexpected dollars from Harcourt. And, finally, in L.A. at an awards ceremony for Quincy, I was told by Wendy my agent that 25,000 would be coming from WBs.[1]

So, two more nights at the apartment, which I think Rebecca & I will miss. It's the place I think we'll remember as our first real home. Totally reflective of us.

Mel was here for the weekend. Pale and quiet. Very mellow, I thought. Reading lots of old books on the movement. He wants to write a book, Rebecca says. It was good to see him, & very good for Rebecca. Although she found so much fault! It is hard for me to believe we were ever married. I felt very happy about me & Robert. Robert is brown & beautiful. And flexible. And the most kissable person imaginable. We kiss sometimes for half an hour. Just kissing & drifting. While Mel was here I thought about the life R & I have built. It could only be built by people who put their relationship first. Not their work. And it is beautiful. The hills, the houses, the trees, the ponds.

---

1   WBs is Warner Brothers, producers of the film adaptation of *The Color Purple*.

July 5, 1986

Finished the Bob Marley essay[1]—I think. Perhaps it needs a paragraph about the subject matter of his songs—why they're so important & moving to me especially.

My tenants in the Brooklyn house had not left as of the first & seem to be stalling in the hope that I will pay them to leave. Only one of them has a lease. I've been <u>very</u> angry with them; with thoughts of doing them bodily harm. But then, because they didn't seem or feel right, I repressed these angry fantasies only to have them turn on me. So that for a couple of days I had self-attack & self-mutilation fantasies that scared the shit out of me! Then the other day we went over to Belvie's & I picked up a book she has on Ayurvedic healing—Never repress emotions, says this teaching. Let your anger express itself fully to your consciousness. Watch it—with detachment. So I did that. I stopped trying to halt the mental slaughter of me & my tenants but really sharpened my weapons—Result: Far fewer self-attack fantasies & even far fewer homicidal ones. There is a good supply of anger left but it doesn't seem to dominate.

The collection of essays is coming along nicely.

1. Everything Is a Human Being
2. On My Father
3. Longing to Die of Old Age
4. China Piece
5. Sometimes a Name Is an Ancestor Saying Hi
6. Not Only Will Your Teachers Appear . . .
7. Journey to Nine Miles
8. In the Closet of the Soul | Letter to Mpinga
9. My Daughter Smokes
10. The People Do Not Despair
11. Trying to See My Sister

---

1   This essay, "Journey to Nine Miles," would be published in 1988 in *Living by the Word: Selected Writings, 1973–1987*.

Undated

The bad news is that most of us will always have to struggle.

The good news is that struggle makes us beautiful.

My father's birthday   **Sept. 9, 1986**

I don't know how old he would have been. I am 42. Which amazes me. In eight years I'll be 50. As Rebecca pointed out last night. I am Miss Domesticity these days. Learning to cook primarily vegetarian fare. Loving being at home. Last night Robert & I went out to pick up a writing table & chair for my bedroom. A Mexican peasant set—and now I write in front of the window in my bedroom overlooking the park. Today is sunny & clear, there are many children in the park. Rebecca slept with me last night, & I had a wonderful dream which I don't remember. She had a bumpy re-entry into school & was angry with me for not being here when she returned the first day. I had wanted to be. We waited for her at the computer place & called the house, but she was out.

She talked about her hurt and anger over being left behind so many times when she was younger. Of her hurt when her father listened to his new wife and forbade her coming into the bedroom to snuggle. She says many bad things happened to her and she didn't tell us because we praise her for how well she manages. We sat & talked and cried. There's so much truth in what she says. She's very honest and yet hating hurting me. I encouraged her to be herself, irregardless, as that is what I want for her more than anything—even more than loyalty to me. (She said she'd felt disloyal liking Spike Lee's movie "She's Gotta Have It," when I obviously found so much lacking in it. I told her that this will happen more & more, her individuation. And that we should both expect it.) She wants to be her own person, yet all my arguments & comments & ways make so much sense! This was exactly my dilemma with my mother. I loved her desperately. And, as with Rebecca, I doubted her love because it too had a certain elusive, preoccupied air about it.

Rebecca asked me whether I doubted her love. I said no. I don't doubt it—no matter what she does or says. The bond between us is eternal. I have every faith in it. I think she's feeling very much our impending separation when she goes off to college. In many ways, this is our last year together, probably. She wants me home more. I want to be home more. I love spending time & nights with her.

Sept. 13, 1986

The house continues to be supportive. I've been writing well here. . . . Yesterday I typed half of what I'd written into Rebecca's computer & was so pleased with myself! Then I unplugged the computer! All gone. It was depressing, but I accept it as a lesson. I like the computer. This is so amazing. But it is simple, fairly easy, so far, to operate, and doesn't strain my back or eyes as much as typewriting.

Sept. 23, 1986

Just back from the city & the Sweet Honey concert; it was a wonderful success.[1] Sold out. A wildly receptive audience; my singing went well. I enjoyed myself. Bernice regal and great and intimidating as usual. She literally frightens me & frightens most people, I think. Her manner is so imperial. She is like few people I've ever met, an exceedingly strong will, fierce determination and forceful character. And she is supremely gifted with a magnificent voice that carries centuries of black history & souls wrapped in its folds and a spiritual & political understanding that makes listening to her an amazing event. I loved all the singers, so beautiful in their robes and hair! And gentle, strong & womanly throughout.

With my fee of 7,500, plus the approx. 4,000 profit after expenses, we should be able to send Winnie 12-13,000. Plus a copy of the tape & Maxine's divestment bill.

Maxine (Waters)[2] was her usual funny, feisty self. Angela Davis funny, giggly, dressed in a very hot silver suit, her dreadlocks coppery. Her friend Nikky[3] came with her & looks like her twin, only younger.

---

1 This was a benefit performance with the acclaimed a cappella group Sweet Honey in the Rock, cofounded by Bernice Johnson Reagon, to aid Winnie Mandela's work against apartheid in South Africa.

2 A longtime congresswoman from California, Maxine Waters was then serving as a member of the California State Assembly.

3 The poet Nikky Finney.

But the event floored me.

—

Dear Rosemary and Joanne,[1]

You tell me that my letter informing the editors of <u>Ms.</u> that I am leaving the magazine upset you. I regret this. At the same time, I am glad. For if you are upset enough perhaps there will be some changes in the magazine & particularly in the way it presents itself to the world, which is of importance to me.

Though you say you do not remember it, Joanne, I remember speaking about <u>Ms.</u> covers more than once to <u>Ms.</u> editors. The time that is particularly vivid was shortly after I came to work there, in the offices on Lexington Street. We were in the conference room and I was prodded to speak what was on my mind. I say "prodded" because being in that room reminded me very much of how it had felt being a board of trustees member at my old alma mater, Sarah Lawrence. I would arrive for those meetings by subway and train & would then walk up the hill to the college (having flown to NY from Mississippi) and I would be passed on the way by the limousines of the other members, the president of CBS & so on. I would sit across the table from white men talking about raising millions of dollars for the school, and knowing that such talk led inevitably to destruction of something, I was immediately concerned about the protection of the campus' trees. Sure enough, to build the expensive building that soon loomed out of the projected millions, the trees—the last large ones on campus— must be murdered. But when I spoke up for the trees, it was as if I'd provided the meeting with comic relief. These <u>Ms.</u> meetings were like that, for me; whenever I spoke there was a curiously

---

1   Rosemary Bray was an editor at <u>Ms.</u> magazine in the 1980s. Joanne Edgar was one of its founding editors and wrote the cover story, "Wonder Woman for President," in the inaugural issue in July 1972; she was an editor at the magazine for seventeen years.

respectful silence punctuated by even more respectful chuckles. Then the business of the magazine continued. This is true of the day I brought up the question of the cover, and the white women all too frequently on it. One editor said: Of course we agree with you. There <u>should</u> be more people of color on the cover. But if we put black faces on the cover, we lose money. (More or less.) Did the cover of Cicely Tyson (a recent cover with a black face on it) lose the magazine money? I asked. I don't remember the answer, but since I thought it one of the magazine's most beautiful covers, I could only feel sorry for anyone too racist to buy it. And of course I wondered: Who in the racist world are you selling to?

Another editor said, in effect, that her idea for the cover was that it should be an "idea" cover. This, I think she assumed, did away with the question of color. However, all the "idea" covers I saw were expressed by white models: recently for instance: The "idea" of "Remaking Love" is expressed by a white woman and a rather snakelike white man who appears about to kiss her; the "idea" of stylishness is expressed by one stylish white woman sitting on a chair; & of course the "idea" of young and old women having babies is expressed by two (one older, one younger) white women heavily <u>encinta</u>.

I stopped attending conference meetings because it became clear that what racial color there was to be in the magazine <u>I</u> would basically provide or represent. God forbid that I should make a suggestion for an issue & not have at hand the black person best suited to fulfill it. Even as I was telling you, Joanne, I was leaving, you asked for the name of someone who could take my place! Throughout the major part of my tenure at <u>Ms.</u> I separated myself from the other editors (first as the only person in a large office, then in a tiny one) because to me it was less stressful to work there if the reality of my position agreed with the appearance. And the reality was that, though concerned about color representation in the magazine & on its cover, my larger concern was with the level of <u>consciousness</u> itself. Why was I the only person horribly oppressed by Ms.' insistently white covers? The reality was, I was alone.

Now you will say No. That is not so. We were with you! We listened to you! Or, why didn't you tell some more about how you felt?

But I say, why is it necessary for me to tell you, more than once, how I feel when your response to how I feel inevitably takes us to the land of magazine sales and your oft remarked comment that black faces, faces like my own, don't sell magazines? Though, curiously, you also never fail to point out that Ms. has more non-white readers than any other (white) women's magazine. Isn't there a contradiction here, I wonder. Or, when I tell you how insulting and oppressive is your cover that shows two white women pregnant, you say: but if we showed a black pregnant woman on the cover it would play into a lot of negative stereotypes. So make her happy & smiling, I say. Pregnancy in black women is not necessarily pathological, after all. Then you tell me about Bill Moyers and Patrick Moynihan[1] and that they have been saying bad things about black teen-age pregnancy. (I don't watch t.v. so I miss a lot of distressive white men). And this astonishes me. That Ms., a feminist magazine, would fail to put a pregnant black woman on its cover because of anything two white

---

1   In 1965, Daniel Patrick Moynihan, an American sociologist serving as assistant secretary of labor under President Lyndon B. Johnson, wrote "The Negro Family: The Case for National Action," which became widely known as the Moynihan Report. A product of his time, Moynihan believed that fathers must be the breadwinners in American families, and he criticized "illegitimacy" (the word generally used at the time to identify out-of-wedlock pregnancy) in Black families. Sparking fierce debate for "blaming the victim," among other offenses, the Moynihan Report became one of the most controversial documents of the twentieth century. Moynihan, however, experienced much success, becoming a senator from New York and publishing more books advancing his perspective. In January 1986, television journalist Bill Moyers aired a documentary on CBS focusing on the breakdown of the Black family, as discussed in Moynihan's latest book, *Family and Nation*. The documentary lamented statistics indicating that a majority of Black families had no man as its head.

men said. Terrible. Not to mention the fact that the grandfathers & great grandfathers of these recent authorities on black teen-age pregnancy undoubtedly impregnated many a black teen-ager themselves. Why don't Moyers and Moynihan do stories about that? And about how some of these teen-age black women and men they study, are, quite possibly, their own relatives and kin, descendants of white men who bought, sold and impregnated them?

I feel nothing but sympathy for Marilyn Monroe, and disgust for all those men who still try to fuck her even though she's dead. However, I think it is wrong for her to be on the cover twice and Winnie Mandela (Am I wrong? I hope so!) hasn't been on once. I think it is wrong for Marilyn Monroe to have been on twice and Tina Turner (Am I wrong? I hope so!) not once. Nor do I agree that for a black person to be on the cover she or he must be excruciatingly famous, or dead, or even "Black." Black, brown, yellow and red people make & "remake" love, they are stylish, they get pregnant & sometimes feel great about it, Goddess knows.

What is your vision? Is it of a white middle-class feminist world with three famous people a year in it? To me, that is what your magazine covers say. If it is your vision, you can perpetuate its life. It isn't mine; and I can't.

December 13, 1986

Nearly the end of the year and I've written little in my journals. Finally my record of ups & downs with Robert bored me: besides, I began to see that the bond between us remains no matter what temporary problem we have. It was also the year of "the movie" with tons of letters, the experience of making the movie, the various premieres. I told Robert tonight as we sat in the theatre about to see The Golden Child—which I liked a lot—that it all seems unreal, as if it didn't happen. Or perhaps it all happened, but to someone else. To my sister Ruth, for instance, who seems to have enjoyed every bit of it all <u>thoroughly</u>.

I am thankful to have been able to return to my former way of life—

except that thanks to Purple & the sale of my Brooklyn house, I'm in a larger, more beautiful house in San Francisco, and I was able to pay off the mortgage in the country. It is truly wonderful living in a house you like, one that is beautiful. One that perhaps sooner rather than later will be yours. I honestly don't expect to move from here.

Just had a long talk with Quincy. He sounds lighter than I've ever heard him. More himself, more free. I still worry about him down there in Hollywood, but he seems to thrive. His daughters are with him & his son is coming. All this is very good.

My novel(!) is coming along. Good people, interesting sinners. Sin is a great teacher and when there is real love there isn't any sin. Actually I'm enjoying a new freedom in the writing of this book. I let myself go with the voices of the people even when they take me to foreign countries & don't speak much English.

I think learning Spanish is like learning to quilt, for me. Its real function is to further the novel. Ditto the cooking, and that is what I must get back into for this last push on the first draft. Odd to think in terms of drafts. Purple didn't really require drafts. Grange & Meridian did though. I think I will call the novel something that came to me in a dream:

The Temple of My Familiar
& Other Memories

or just

The Temple of My Familiar
by
Me

"Recuerda?"[1] will appear on the first page & will also perhaps be the name of Mary Anne's boat.

---

1   The English translation for this Spanish word is: Remember.

* * *

Learned last night that both Ding Ling[1] and Bessie Head[2] are dead. I can't believe it. I've felt dull and depressed & sat in the bathroom crying. Ding Ling was 82 and I can honestly say I fell in love with her. She went <u>straight</u> to my heart & I know she loved me. I feel anger that Bessie had such a brutal life and was so shattered. I feel as if SA[3] murdered her. Still, she managed to witness for the people of Botswana & they will always exist because, in a sense, she rescued them and their history in her writing. I discovered these deaths in <u>Ms.</u>, the magazine I resigned from after all these years because it suddenly seemed unbearable that Marilyn Monroe & then two pregnant white women appeared on the cover. But I already miss the "home" that the magazine has been for me. And I love Gloria, who was just here.

I am weary. I will have some grapes and—to bed!

Feb. 14, 1987

So. I am 43. Who can believe it! My wonderful eyes, so loyal and beautiful, are with me still. Through them I am permitted to see, to witness, the goodness, the amazingness, of the Universe. I am more & more astonished at what I see. Yesterday, when I walked to the studio to pick greens for supper, there were three fat deer in the meadow looking up at me. I said hello. The orange tree is <u>loaded</u> with oranges. The apple trees are almost too tall to prune. Daffodils are all over. And the little studio itself: so sweet with its new windows and doors. Oh! And the pond filled from the rain, and water

---

1 Ding Ling was one of the most celebrated Chinese authors of the 20th century. She was best known for writing fiction that centered the experiences of independent Chinese women, and she and AW had befriended each other in the early 1980s.

2 Bessie Head, though born in South Africa, was considered Botswana's most influential writer. In 1977 she published the first collection of short stories (*The Collector of Treasures*) to be published by a Black South African woman. The Botswana government granted Head citizenship in 1979, which allowed her to travel overseas. An outspoken critic of apartheid, she wrote novels, short stories, and autobiographical works. She died of hepatitis in 1986; she was 49.

3 South Africa.

is flowing everywhere. That is the sound one hears, the rushing water. And the water from our well tastes clean and cold & fresh!

Everything looks miraculous to me. The scarf that I have on my head— made by magicians of weaving in Guatemala—and the orange peels littering the table. Oranges are orange, but by what process of love? For love makes all of it. The energy of love makes all that is good and beautiful and it is the energy of love blocked that causes disaster.

In my family only my mother seems to see the miracles in life that I do. Only she is always praying and appreciating. Everyone else is complaining. Why is this?

Charlayne Hunter just left. After an interview for MacNeil Lehrer.[1] All I'm really thinking about as these camera/sound people work on this shot of me "writing" is whether I'll look really fat in this sweater! Such trivia. The interview was interesting, even fun. Charlayne is funny; such an effervescent Gibson girl, Southern belle, but tough minded type. With really elegant clothes. By comparison I feel dowdy. So odd. That one even thinks of clothes.

She thinks I've dropped out of sight. But really it's just that now I do only what I like to do—& I don't like being "visible" in the style of American celebrities. On the other hand, it's true that my energy level has been low for the past couple of years—I've had remarkably little. But now, for some reason, I feel I have more—is it the folic acid? The chelated iron, or the period of withdrawal & relative rest? In any event, I'm coming back to life: enjoying seeing some people, going to plays, playing the occasional game of grump with Robert & Casey. This has been a wonderful time to spend with my child. A very necessary time to have had with Robert.

I don't know about other people, but it seems sensible to me to stay

---

1   The *MacNeil/Lehrer NewsHour*, created in 1975 as the *MacNeil/Lehrer Report*, aired on PBS stations nationwide. Charlayne Hunter-Gault, a civil rights activist and award-winning Black journalist who'd also grown up in Georgia, was a national correspondent for the *NewsHour*. She'd earned her journalism degree at the University of Georgia in 1963 after desegregating the university with fellow trailblazer and classmate Hamilton Holmes.

close to one's loved ones especially when one is "successful." What can I now afford that I couldn't before? Attention to detail in my life & behavior with Robert, Rebecca & Casey. And what is the "profit" of this? It is that we're closer than we've ever been. That Rebecca feels really loved and at the center of my life, which earlier she was not able to feel.

August 26, 1987

Yesterday Robert & I took Rebecca to the airport and put her on a plane to New York, en route to Yale. For the past several weeks we have been distracting ourselves from the inevitable parting by frenziedly helping a young refugee family from El Salvador. A young 23 year old mother, Reina, & her two small children, Sandra, 5, and Denise, 8 months. They are living in the guest room & this is quite an experience. It interferes with writing of course but I get to kiss the baby a lot. I really love babies—and so does Rebecca & so does Robert! We're all comically attached to Denise. She's round, heavy, fat & beautiful. Or, as I tell her: pesado, gordo, y bella! She has 2 teeth.

Anyway, I was so tired—from trying (& succeeding) to enroll Sandra in a school & line up a school for Reina & an apartment—for, I faced it, I can't work with 2 children playing next door—I was numb. We drove to the airport in a daze. Rebecca had more stuff than I was aware she owned. But no matter. We convinced the airlines to take it all. But then, when it was time to put her on the plane, we both cried & we all hugged & kissed. Robert has been such a wonderful friend to us and a super para-parent to her. I had looked forward to this day of her independence, but it was hard to let her go. We sat & waited nearly an hour for the plane to leave. It didn't, so we went to get algo de comer.[1] It finally left. We went home & I went to bed suffering fatigue, loss & an incredible migraine.

She called when she arrived in New York & I felt better. Planes are so frightening these days. But then today she called again, in tears & miserable. It's her father & his family—within hours they've called her a yuppie & a snob. Plus, it's hot & dirty & she wonders why anybody lives there. We

---

1 Something to eat.

tried to think of ways to pass the next day & a half. I suggested meditation, politeness, & that thank God she has Frida (Kahlo)! She's been reading the biography & loves Frida. I love Frida; I'd like to write about her. I don't think her biographer does her justice & Goddess knows the Leduc film[1] misses the point. The best thing so far really is Ester's[2] painting of Frida, "If This is Death, I Like It."

It is hard for me to know they criticize her—her dreadlocks, in particular. She's so beautiful. But they're too oblivious to see it.

Anyway. She's so like me. She's changing her name legally to Walker & that causes Mel & his mother to accuse her of anti-Semitism. Meanwhile they've declined any meaningful support beyond a monthly allowance, which I asked Mel to give her because he had to make a gesture of at least symbolic support.

But, try as I might, I can only be but so sad. My beautiful, great-hearted daughter is off to Yale. My children's book[3] is being printed; my book of essays[4] is within a hair's breadth of being put to bed at the printer. My mother is spending a blissful few months in the country; Robert is happy & planning a new book about men, may they see light!, and soon Reina & the children will be on their way. I'm putting Sandra in the private school two doors down. Reina will enroll in English language classes. I will give her 1000 a month for her support for one year. I love doing this. It makes me feel that everyone can do something & that the planet can be a paradise & let's start where we are. Meanwhile, I've said no in my heart to any more appeals for money from my brothers who stupify me with their frequent requests & no thanks when I respond.

---

1   Paul Leduc's 1983 film *Frida Still Life*.

2   Artist Ester Hernandez.

3   *To Hell With Dying* would be published in August 1988, with illustrations by Catherine Deeter.

4   *Living by the Word* would be published in June 1988.

Sept. 26, 1987

I am an African woman; naturally I insist on all the freedoms.

Oct. 1, 1987

Who can believe it is October? The long golden days, the orange pumpkins, the honeysweet pears and succulent tomatoes. I've been picking beans & greens and tomatoes & eggplant and soon my very own corn! Last week we (Robert & I) went swimming in the river—wonderful, cold, stimulating, after a brisk—through the redwoods—walk.

How beautiful Robert is, to look at, to be with. Impossible not to hug and kiss him really, even if I am having my cyclical hard time with sex. Men are so beastly, I get turned off just reading the newspaper. But Robert is growing & shining and is such a good friend. Even so, I don't think I'll give up my single bed (the big wooden double one that feels single when he's in it too.)

As I was withdrawing my body from Robert I offered him my novel[1]— part one. He was dazed, and this pleased me. I feel so good about the people who've come so far. I've discovered something: I'm not really good at creating characters who are like me. They bore me. It is the wildly imagined souls that are really like me archetypically, that are my delight.

I am taking it relatively easy. Saying no to almost everything. There's so much to be done, but I've faced the fact that I can't do it all. I've chosen a few things. Reina & the children, a few benefits, one or two major readings & trips. There are several months that are free. I found myself longing for the quiet rainy days of fall when the house in the city really comes into its own. Days of waking warm & centered and moving from meditation to prayer (writing).

The country is beautiful as ever. I putter & mutter there endlessly. It is even more enchanting: with the circular garden still in bloom, the serpent path, the swings, the ponds.

Let me thank you, Universe. I've felt distant from you & don't want to be. Ola.

---

1 *The Temple of My Familiar*, still in progress.

Oct 15, 1987

A few days after an odd trip East to see Howie & Roz[1] & Rebecca & Steven & Mama & Ruth. Robert & I flew to Boston and spent the first night with the Zinns. They are still beautiful, aging—for the first time Roz seemed older. Her hair is graying & she has cataracts, the imminent removal of which we discussed at dinner. Roast leg of lamb, which I declined. We talked about animals, the cruelty of their lives, or rather human cruelty towards them. I ate some leftover shrimp that were good. I seem to have come to rest on an occasional fish, shrimp, abalone or chicken dinner. 10% of my diet. I've tried formulating a philosophy—perhaps it is this: that since everything is alive and nothing wants to die, yet I must eat to live & so must everything else, the right course is to eat as little as possible of everything, except those seeds, fruits, vegetables that literally fall into your hand. I felt very good the 3 months of my strict vegetarianism, perhaps better than I've ever felt. A clear conscience energizes the body! But I am at this stage too lazy to keep it up. When I'm really hungry & there's a piece of chicken about it's hard not to eat it. Even given my bonding as a mother with mother hens.

———

Mama is about the same, though more shrunken. She says she's not in pain, just "drawed up." She was happy to see us & I'm afraid we brought chocolates, which no one in my family ever needs.

We ate. We played softball with Ruth's grandson Kyle. . . . More relatives & friends began to arrive. Aunts & uncles & cousins and even my old boyfriend Porter and his son, Brandon.

We went by to see the graves of the ancestors. The church. Our old house.

But eventually we made it home! San Francisco gray, beautiful, quiet & hilly. My house spacious and modest & comfortable & all the white petunias blooming in the boxes on the deck.

I will help Ruth winterize the old house so that she & Mama can stay there through the winter next year if they want to.

1　Historian, activist, author, and AW's former professor Howard Zinn and his wife, Roslyn.

Oct. 16 –

I almost failed to write the most important thing. My growing awareness of The Goddess (on a cosmic scale one could think of it as the little woman behind the man!) and my own lesbianism. I almost feel this is a case of everyone knowing I'm a lesbian but me. Still, it is a new idea to bat about in my psyche. I realized that the only way I can relate sexually to most men is to think of violence, & this destroys me. But when I think of The Goddess & of loving other women, making love to them in particular, there is no need for violence, since I don't associate violence or pain (physical pain) with women.

Chris, a lovely man, gave me some remarkable marijuana & also made me a little pipe (with clay, I think, from the pond) to smoke it in. It helped me to see that, in relating sexually to men, I lock my true sexuality behind walls. I have interior walls. This, I think, is what many men and women do.

On the whole I am happy about this. In fact, I felt really gay all day yesterday, and true.

So then I walked up to the studio & called the house for my messages—One from Quincy & my heart leapt into my throat. I love this man, lesbian or no. His voice moves my very vitals (smile): Am I hopelessly caught between men & women, then? Oi vey!

Or am I hoping Q, a man, will save me? In any event, he didn't recognize my voice on the answering machine. Thought I was Rebecca. Says he came by the house when he was in SF last month, got good vibes. Will, maybe, call from New York. Whenever I hear from him I'm thrown into turmoil & don't like it! Turmoil, that is.

Well. It is in the hands of The Goddess. As is everything.

Nov. 7, 1987

I love Robert, but being with him makes me feel terribly cut off from lesbian women, whom I respect and admire. They, of course, & with reason, are suspicious of women with men. I'm a little (sometimes a lot) suspicious of them myself. But the solution isn't to throw Robert out—and besides I don't seem able to, he's so in my heart whenever I try to throw him out I find myself falling through the air.

* * *

I went with Angela and some friends[1] of hers, Byllye & Mary, to a women's club to dance, Halloween night. It was lovely being with Angela, and she and I won second prize in the costume contest as "Siamese Twins," because although we weren't dressed very creatively—I had my dreads divided in four sections and sticking out from my head & she had on some weird glasses that looked like two forks, and were very hard to see out of, we were nonetheless joined at the hip because we were both too shy to be out in the costume competition alone. It was fun, very free and innocent. There were two Tina Turners, a couple of Morticias and three women dressed as Three Blind Mice who won first place.

But finally I have to admit it seemed sterile to me. Not the women themselves, but the awful, meaningless disco music, and the smoky atmosphere. Only the costume competition was meaningful and personalized. I met many women who seemed sweet and interesting—and deserving of better music.

Angela & Toni Morrison came to dinner Monday night. Toni's hair is quite gray, and very beautiful and <u>soft</u>. When they were leaving & we were discussing hair, I touched it. "Angela, feel Toni's hair, how soft it is!" And the evening was like that. I'd made soup and vegetables and there was bread & butter & fruit and wine. Toni talked about the critics of her book— actually she talked about <u>our</u> critics, since some of those who don't like her work don't like mine. Apparently there's a horrible review in <u>The New Republic</u> & reprinted in <u>The Village Voice</u> by Stanley Crouch.[2] Someone handed it to her just before she went on a television or radio show. She says she's called "Aunt Medea" and that there's a funny/weird caricature of her.

---

1 The political activist Angela Davis and her friend Byllye Avery, who'd founded the National Black Women's Health Project in 1984.

2 Called "Literary Conjure Woman," the 3,700-word piece was published in the *New Republic* on Oct. 19, 1987. In it, Black critic and contrarian Stanley Crouch focused on Toni Morrison's most recent novel, *Beloved*, dismissing it as "trite" and "sentimental."

She talked about being able to erect barriers, psychological ones, to protect herself. She feels she has a power to protect herself from crazy people and from dogs. She says she mentally choked a dog someone was holding & it shat in their hands.

I think Toni does have a brilliant, dark power, that she is more comfortable studying evil than I. I can study confusion, which most times only looks like evil, & I'd have a hard time even mentally choking a dog.

She was also very kind in her remarks about Ishmael Reed, saying she could never take him seriously. She seems to have known him for a long time and recently had dinner with him. She explained that when Ishmael was a little boy, around 5, his mother took him to meet his father, "a successful businessman" who threw them out of his office. This was Ishmael's first meeting with his father. I said this story explains I's hatred of black women writers: we keep taking him to meet his father.

We talked of whether Tar Baby would be made into a movie; she thought not, but later when Quincy called about Warner's decision to offer me my 3%, he said plans for it were indeed moving along. Euzhan Palcy's husband is to direct, not Euzhan! This is not good news. He said Toni would be hearing soon.

Anyway, he also commented on the fact that Toni and I were having dinner together. "Anyone would expect you to be enemies," he said. But why would "anyone" expect that? Even when I've felt bad about something Toni allegedly said or did against me—for instance keeping Bob Gottlieb from taking me on at Knopf when I was trying to leave Harcourt—I've always also felt that if I did my work things would be okay.

I explained my absence at her big (City Arts & Lectures) reading. That I was in Boston doing a welfare women's benefit. And I congratulated her on the success of Beloved, which I pronounced Be-Love-Ed. I said I had it but hadn't read it yet because I was working on something and knew when I did read it "it would blow me away."

She has been offered a substantial position at Princeton.

I feel glad for her success. It isn't my kind of success. There doesn't seem much laying up for days with her lover in it, but perhaps there is. I hope so. I know I couldn't stand Princeton for a day.

Dec. 1, 1987

A slow, rainy, draggy morning in the country, and now the news that James Baldwin has died.[1] Last night, of stomach cancer. He was 63. I'm rarely sad to hear that people have died; I am sadder to hear they are sick. The dead have escaped, I feel, some part of me feels, and I see them rising, laughing & free, astonished by their good luck, above the earth.

Baldwin was my spiritual brother, uncle and father. I remember how I felt when, in the early Sixties, I got off the bus one summer in Boston and his book Another Country filled a whole rack. It was the first time I realized it was possible to be a black writer of note. A "success" in the American fashion. One's books on racks in the Greyhound Bus Station. Besides, I loved the book; I especially appreciated Ida and her black fingers and her snake-eyed ring. She was a woman I could recognize, relate to. When I first slept with Mel, I sometimes thought we were like Ida & Vivaldo.

Now he is free of suffering. The pain the world caused him because he was black, a man, gay, all of this, one hopes, is no more. His anger is stilled. And over all there is his absorption now, one feels, into the universal love.

Do I regret never having seen his body? Yes. But I know his spirit has been with me from the beginning.

He was one of the lucky ones: he left an example of courage, commitment to the struggle of all human beings to be free, and a love so pervasive—in all his words and work—that perhaps one did not seek to be in his physical presence because one always felt his gifts had already been given, even without knowing one specifically, and also received.

Goodbye James, and welcome to the Universe to which death is a door. You have done well. Here there are tears, I am sure, but also singing & celebration.

---

1   Early on December 1, 1987, the great writer died of stomach cancer in Saint-Paul de Vence, France.

Dec. 17, 1987

Just had a highly upsetting conversation with the assistant to the dean of students at Yale. Rebecca has been trying to move off campus. Her reasons: unsafe, unsanitary, too small a space.

—Here I had to stop yesterday because of intense pain in my wrist caused by my foolish effort to paint a large wall with a tiny brush. I've almost incapacitated myself, in the enthusiasm over having found the right color for the inside of my house—a deep earth coral, created by mixing a soft orange/rose with white & brown. Beautiful! Instantly things are warmer & there is more of a feeling of emotion, life, in the atmosphere. White walls are really beginning to bother me.

Anyway, a month ago it was trouble with my left arm, at the shoulder. A couple of weeks of excruciating pain. The lesson is: don't overdo! Listen to my body! Which speaks up so clearly. Each time, just before I damaged myself I heard in my mind: Alice, don't do any more. I said ok, prepared to stop, but then decided to finish just that one little spot over there and that corner and . . . pain!

Dec. 18, 1987

So two days spent dealing with Rebecca's dean(s). I'm calling them The Witches of East New Haven. So this morning Betty Tractenberg called & offered R. use of a study room somewhere on campus. And said she'd have first crack at any single that comes available. I told R. And also said the choice is hers. She cannot stay there on her terms; she must stay on theirs. Or she can leave. They will not permit her to move into the space she found off campus. I also let her know how weary I am of trying to solve her problems from 3000 miles away. But, enough.

I went ahead & planted daffodils and tulips & will plant more today.

Thursday,
Feb. 26, 1988
11:15 a.m.

I just, an hour ago, finished the novel <u>The Temple of My Familiar</u>. I got out of bed, washed up & dressed, strolled through the garden on my way up to the studio where I will continue to transpose chapters on the Mac. On the way up the hill, my eye caught something out in the field that appeared to be a tan plastic laundry or cleaners bag. I took a step towards it to pick it up.

What do you suppose it was? It was a large, tawny colored cat, lying there calmly in the middle of the field. I looked at it and said hello. It simply moved its head, looked back at me & said nothing.

I felt I had ended the novel right. From Suwelo's dream, which was my own several years ago—two men, a middle aged one & an old one talking at the older one's bedside—to Mr. Hal's next work of vision, being able to see cats.

Undated
Written in Italy

Did I relate anywhere that HBJ agreed to buy the novel[1] for 2.5 <u>million</u> dollars. This means in actual money only 1.6 million. But still. I've been in a daze. Can't quite grasp/believe it. I probably would have settled for a 5th of that. But—to get 400,000 a year; to spend, for 4 years . . . It seems very amazing to me.

So I've paid off Ruth's house & finished paying for the renovation of the old house. Given Mamie a check to cover expenses after her hospital stay.

May 9th – Belvedere, Castelfranco di Sopra, Italy

We've been here two days. It seems longer. The countryside is beautiful but the air is awful. Full of such pollution you can't see the sun. But there are lovely red poppies, cascades of white & yellow wildflowers and thousands of lavender irises. We went for a walk in the woods, over the terraces & through olive groves, and Robert asked me questions about writing a screenplay. He's writing one on Nancy & Henry.[2] "His version" of their experience, as he says. A typical male attitude. The way they present them-

---

1   *The Temple of My Familiar.*

2   Henry Crowder, a self-taught Black jazz musician, and his muse, Nancy Cunard, a white avant-garde poet, shipping heiress, and publisher of the 1934 anthology *Negro*, which was inspired by and dedicated to Crowder.

selves is more interesting to me. I doubt that Nancy was very "hot" and Henry was probably as stiff as he was gay. Anyhow. I felt a sharp sadness and grief as I remembered my struggle to write the screenplay for <u>Purple</u>. I still blame Robert for undermining my efforts. But most of the time I deliberately don't think about it. There seems nothing I can do. It was a marvelous opportunity, for which I was not sufficiently prepared. But now I see more clearly what motivated his undermining. He wanted to write a screenplay himself. And had in fact written one with St. Clair that went nowhere. It would have been hard to see me write one. I guess. So he tells me of his affair with A. . . . & needs me to give him another chance. And so on.

Meanwhile, I still think of Bubba[1] every single day. Belvie told me of a conversation they had and he said he loved me but was afraid of the "physical." Afraid he would "mess up." She tried to encourage him. I am so afraid. Afraid of rejection. Afraid to be hurt. Afraid. Afraid. All I know is that I want & need him in my life.

The 24th of June, 1988

Yesterday I finished TMF for the second time! Incorporating all the "bits" I wrote in Italy—an otherwise rather unproductive trip. . . .

Anyway, the novel is now completed to my satisfaction. If it confuses John[2] that's just too bad. I am unable to work with him face to face on this book. He feels alien to the spirit of it. And last time, on LB the W[3] he said to me: Anais[4] never balked at my suggestions, or something to that effect. Implying that: Who are you to do so? I calmly listened to his every suggestion & worked with him quite compliantly. But he'd destroyed our already fragile bond. I <u>loathed</u> being so condescended to in my own house!

---

1   Quincy Jones.
2   Her editor at Harcourt Brace Jovanovich, John Ferrone.
3   "LB the W" is *Living by the Word*.
4   Anaïs Nin, the famous writer.

Sept. 5, 1988

Today I completed the second round of editing.[1] An humbling, learning experience. As I told Robert, being edited by John makes me wonder that I have the nerve to write. On the other hand, I can see why editors edit instead of write. They're so picky they'd never give themselves permission to flow. . . . My eyes are very tired—the injured one floating out, the other tight, sore. My fingers are sore also. But I sit here in my studio and look out over treetops and the vineyards and the valley, and I know I'm in the most beautiful place on earth. Even the vultures are beautiful here, and so graceful.

I have felt the depression of finishing a long work. I miss the characters in Temple; it is such an odd feeling when I realize I've truly finished something and there's nothing left for my people to do. I've felt so empty, so full, so fearful, so trusting—as I've struggled to manifest this story. Finally it was trust that brought it through. I will just live, and trust the Universe, and let my skills and self be used for the highest good.

Sept. 18, 1988
Sunday

Two days ago, on Friday, I made the final payment on my house! 720 Steiner Street is now "home." The final payment was the largest check I've ever written—223,000 plus. After setting $ aside for taxes I'm still left with 200,000. And a million more dollars to come. I'm calmly elated at all this. I now own—or am legal caretaker of my spaces in the city and the country. I figure if I had to, I could rent out this house & live in Mendocino or rent out one or all of the houses in Mendocino. But the plan of which I think is to buy another dwelling, as an investment: 2 flats. Rent them out. Let the rent pay the mortgage, etc.

Robert and I enjoyed a highly passionate not to say torrid couple of nights—I give up. This must be love or some kind of high powered infatuation. After 10 years I still love his smell, the touch of his fingers & other parts!

---

1   This refers to her work with Harcourt editor John Ferrone on *The Temple of My Familiar*.

We're experts at hanging out. And Berkeley is a great place to do it in. We sit in cafes over the paper, we shop in wonderful little shops. We find beautiful foods. And we come here after dinner in one of a dozen restaurants we frequent & we watch movies or videos, & we go to bed and kiss & kiss & kiss.

I encouraged Roberto to get a second job so I don't feel like a primary employer. He became a staff member of the Oakland Men's Project, which makes him happy & me proud! Their motto is: "Men's Work: Stopping Male Violence."

Sept. 21, 1988
"Alice and the too expensive coat."

Two days ago I bought a beautiful coat—if you like Southwestern symbols of snakes, Mexican peasant hats (sombreros), chili peppers and little beads with (presumably) tiny replicas of Chicano people hanging down—it seemed a good idea at the time. I bought it at Obiko's, whose clothing by artists I really like, as I like Sandra Sakata, the proprietor herself—also Kinondo, her assistant. However, each night I've awakened filled with remorse. The coat is the most expensive item of clothing I've ever bought: 4,500.00, and this seems—in these times of homeless people, floods in Bangladesh and devastation in Jamaica—an outrageous sum to pay for a coat. So I've been finding all kinds of things wrong with it—and with me. This is the first time I've felt so badly about something I've bought. I feel guilty. Partly too I feel unsure about the coat. It is so different from anything I've ever worn.

I lie in bed thinking: I should have bought the shorter, cheaper, sweater version. Only $1700! Or, I should have had the wherewithal to resist the temptation of the coat. I've felt extremely foolish over this. Will I ever have the nerve to wear something like this?

Oct. 5, 1988
P.S. Several days after return from New Mexico:

Finally, while still in New Mexico I couldn't stand it any longer. My conscience was beating me to death. I decided to call Obiko & tell them I was returning the coat the minute I returned to SF. Which I did. I felt better immediately.

Nov. 29, 1988

I am back from a terrific visit to New York. Staying at Gloria's, hanging out with Rebecca. Eating. Shopping. Reading—Everything great, much to my delight.

Last night, rather, early this morning, I had an invaluable dream about me & my father. It was very real, very good—and it was a <u>political</u> conversation, between equals. I don't remember all of it, but I woke up just as we were discussing white oppression of people of color & the way they try to destroy our faith in our own beauty.

Dec. 2, 1988

Late at night. My eyes are closing. Quincy called & we had a long, two-hour conversation. He received the large shell I sent him & my little "make peace" note. We both apologized for any hurt, etc. His life, as usual, unbelievable in its complexity. Wives, children, his mother . . .—oy vey. <u>But</u> it's crystal clear there's <u>nothing</u> romantic between us. He's wonderful but belongs to a definite world that gives me a headache just to think about.

Dec. 20, 1988

Tomorrow is the Winter Solstice! The sun will begin its journey back to us. Hallelujah!

Spent the weekend Fri–Mon. in Georgia. First there was the homecoming celebration and the pleasure (& exhaustion) of relating to family & friends in Eatonton. A real pleasure to be able to <u>read</u> to the folk—poems and two chapters from <u>The Color Purple</u>. And to meet the young people the Foundation supports.[1] It all went well even though the 1200 seat au-

---

1 With AW's financial support, Ruth Walker has started The Color Purple Foundation, which offers scholarships to students in Putnam County and their hometown of Eatonton, Georgia.

ditorium was only partly filled. I guess there were about 300–400 people. Mainly, I thought, relatives.

But we had 3 suites at the Terrace Inn in Milledgeville, and Gloria came & was lovely, as ever, and Rebecca flew down from New York—on her way to Miami and Antigua.

I spent wonderful moments with various nieces, nephews and cousins. Fred's son Mike is lovely. We must all work hard to keep his gentleness from receding. I felt all the children loved me. The little ones kept clutching me about the knees. And I really <u>looked</u> at them & saw their preciousness.

A birthday party for Mama. Lots of cake. She wasting . . . and wasting.

Jan 2, 1989

I've spent the past six days rereading <u>Temple</u>. It's gorgeous. And I can't wait to give it to people. But the eye strain! Because each sentence has to be scrutinized & there's always the fear something will be wrong. Not much is. And between us, John & I will fix it.

Jan. 24, 1989

In Casa Patricio, which overlooks Las Banderas Bay in Puerto Vallarta. Hardly a wink of sleep all night. Incredibly raucous musica from la ciudad. And muchos perros ladridos. I woke poor Roberto up to keep me company, and the two of us lay tossing and turning until dawn.

The house is a mansion compared to most of the houses around it. Huge. Three bedrooms that look out over the ocean. And built on 4 levels. There is a modest swimming pool. It makes me think of the house we are planning on the hill at WTs.

Feb 1,

We came home early by two days. We were stopped again by the army's roadblock & the sight of all those machine guns in the hands of all those young men removed any interest in returning to the interior beaches. We spent the last two days lying in bed working on our teleplay, which we drafted, and which looks very good. We had an interesting, frustrating adventure returning. Somehow we got on the wrong plane, then, as soon as we'd stopped the right plane from running off without us, & settled, reclined, into our seats, we were informed that, because of "security reasons," we had to go back to the plane we'd originally boarded. So that meant being separated from our luggage and stopping in beautiful L.A. before coming to SF. We were both pretty tired by the end of our journey, & thankful to be home.

My beloved spent the night, and next day we, more accurately he, typed the script on the computer, after we devised a couple more scenes.

We were very happy—to have created something else together.

And his book[1] is getting great reviews—in PW & Kirkus. Although there is a sleazeball out there trying to steal the story. Robert very upset. But calmer after talking to our lawyer Mike.

I've spent the past two-three days catching up with the deluge of mail that awaited my return.

Quincy asked if I'd write a requiem for Ray Charles and a play from The Color Purple. It would be an opportunity to put back many of the things left out of the movie.

Mar. 21, 1989
Spring!
An exceedingly quiet, mauve gray day in the city, after a wonderful day yesterday with Roberto. We worked & puttered about the house until 2:00 and then went to Oakland for a walk half way around the lake. Just being out in the warm sun was heavenly. I was knocked out by it, though, and took a nap at Robert's apartment afterward. Very quiet & colorful & cozy there, I must say!

Then home—after an early dinner & grocery shopping in Rockridge,

---

1   Robert Allen's book, *The Port Chicago Mutiny: The Story of the Largest Mass Mutiny Trial in U.S. Naval History*, was published in early 1989 to strong reviews in *Publishers Weekly* and *Kirkus Reviews*.

which I like very much—and the last half of <u>The Women of Brewster Place</u>,[1] which was beautiful & moving. I must send a telegram to Oprah.

And how are you? My trusty confidant? I write less and less in you. And even now I'm aware that just from writing half a page, my fingers hurt. Is it early arthritis? Anyway, I find I have little to say, though much has happened. Dreadful (or, as Rebecca says dread<u>less</u>) reviews of <u>Temple</u> in PW & Kirkus.[2] Then a really splendid one in Library Journal. Also quite a nice quote from Isabel Allende.

I've been exhausted by the speakings & fundraisings recently, and realize it is time for me to conserve energy for the long haul of the publicity trail, in May. And for the D.C. demonstration on the 9th. And for the readings in New Jersey & Pennsylvania.

July 12, 1989
9:15 p.m. Though there's still a little light outside. Just scared a raccoon out of the studio, then walked down the hill feeling sorry for myself. This is so unusual I thought I'd better confront myself honestly in this journal—in which I haven't written in donkey's years.

Today I felt restless, trapped. Yet yesterday I felt all this beauty around me was the most complete luminous gift anyone could have.

---

1   *The Women of Brewster Place* was a television miniseries produced by Oprah Winfrey and adapted from the National Book Award–winning novel of the same name that launched the career of Gloria Naylor. The TV adaptation—starring Winfrey, Jackee Harry, Lonette McKee, Paula Kelly, Olivia Cole, and Lynn Whitfield, among others—aired on ABC on March 19 and 20, 1989.

2   AW's novel *The Temple of My Familiar* was published on April 1, 1989, to mixed reviews. "Though it has its own strengths," *Publishers Weekly* lamented, "the book never achieves the narrative power of *The Color Purple*." *Library Journal* disagreed, writing of the novel's large cast of characters: "Out of the telling of their stories emerges a glorious and iridescent fabric, a strand connecting all their lives and former lives and seeming to pull all of existence into its folds. Walker's characters are magnetic, even with their all-too-human flaws and stumblings; they seem to contain the world, and to do it justice. Highly recommended."

My eyes are <u>very</u> tired. Haven't recovered from the interviews and flash bulbs of the book tour. And I am eating, eating, like a crazy woman. I don't need all this rest. That's the crux of it, I think. And besides, it's too cold to have much faith in planting a late garden & the pond is chilly! I should start researching my next novel. That's what novelists <u>do</u>! They don't lie around for 5–7 years between novels.

Undated
The Temple of My Familiar is not a novel of research, but rather of silence, waiting, meditation and dream.

Sept. 13, 1989
Have been feeling the stress of so much travel, & interviews (one for the San Diego Union this morning!) & am slowly building for the time I will go nowhere, but will sit on my porch in the country & let the world come to me.

Really tired, tonight.

I finally admitted to myself how hurt and frustrated I am by some of the more vicious reviews. I find the unfairness particularly hard to bear. Mostly white male critics who obviously don't understand that my metaphysics includes them even though theirs has never included me.

Tonight Rebecca, Robert, Casey & I went out to dinner—the food was inedible (!) practically unheard of in SF. And I came home & made scrambled eggs.

And so I close this notebook. Robert & I are together. Tired, but solid. Rebecca is home for a while working on her film & going on walks with me. In the country I'm building a huge house. Well, 3 bedrooms. In this house I'm creating a sanctuary for Robert & me to frolic in. Another window will be cut and the room all white. Rebecca's floor is being re-painted.

It should all look swell—& then, this summer, the rest of the house will be painted. Cool white & grayish blue.

What must I do, for health and happiness <u>& creativity</u>?

1. Maintain the calendar I have. Delete perhaps <u>but never add</u>.
2. Get back to work.
3. Remember the goddess and Mother Earth.

Thursday, Oct 19th, after the big quake.[1]

I was in the basement taking Rebecca's last load of clothes from the dryer when I felt the earth move. It didn't occur to me that it was an earthquake until I heard the house groan & the ceiling started to shake. I rushed to the garage door, which failed to open because the power went off. I then ran up the stairs & outside. Michael was just coming out of his house, with his tiny dog. And we ran into each other's arms. Later we had tea & listened to the news in his car.

Some fallen plates, but mostly it's the breaking of a single Indian pot that I most regret. A very simple brown clay one with the most subtle shape & patina imaginable! I bought it 10 years ago at the Grand Canyon.

We're all glad to be alive. And last night Robert & Casey spent the night, and as I lay in bed next to a softly breathing Roberto I surprised myself thinking how happy I am.

Oct. 23

Many thoughts of things to write but I've resisted, for fear it isn't quite "ready." But how reassuring it feels to know that within 3 days of having peace & rest and solitude, plus meditation, my imaginary planet asserts itself.

---

1 On October 17, 1989, a deadly earthquake struck the San Francisco area at 5:04 p.m. and lasted for fifteen seconds. The Loma Prieta earthquake, named for a peak near its epicenter (near Santa Cruz), measured 7.1 on the Richter scale, and its aftermath was witnessed on live television by millions of baseball fans watching the third game of the World Series, held at Candlestick Park in San Francisco. The quake hit moments before the start of the game, and sportscasters were soon reporting on the resulting pandemonium in the stadium. The earthquake killed sixty-three people and injured more than three thousand others.

Nov. 7, 1989

Election day; and soon I shall go down the hill to hear what's become of Dave Dinkins, next mayor, perhaps, of New York.

It's been a slow day for me. After a wonderful evening alone with the radio & news & blues and an appreciation of the new local station WZYX, 90.7 on my dial! So many things shock my system: I'm sure that's behind my lethargy. First, the earthquake, which I experienced directly but not, apparently, to the same extent that viewers experienced it on t.v. Everyone seems to think all of the Bay Area's devastated, when it isn't. There's something positive about the earth moving from time to time. It is alive, after all. But the other shock, yesterday, was learning there is a vineyard going up on the ridge across from the new house. I felt immediately a sense of futility. That there will always be encroachment; that there's no escaping. But eventually I pulled myself up and walked up the hill to view the destruction. They've pushed over some of the oak trees, but fortunately they can't come down the side of the hill because it's too steep. Also, it is all far enough away so that when the grapes are in their foliage should add spots of color to the landscape, so I felt better. And then, Anne in Wendy's office called. And she said she'd wired over 135,000 to my account. This was also a great shock. I don't know where it's from, possibly Pocket, and it struck me again—the feeling of having a lot. Too much? The only salvation is to continue giving it away. Though I must save some, too. A bonus for Roberto is in order, I think, and Rebecca's 5,000 for her film.

And today I think I've given to just about everyone. Including 10,000 of a 25,000 grant to KPFA. And I get to name their new 3rd world department for Ida B. Wells. But 5,000 to Children's Defense Fund, 5,000 to the Women's Foundation, 5,000—a fairly long list.

I've felt badly because I've told a wonderful person & so-so journalist that one of her questions to me about "how the success of black women writers was 'allowed' to happen" was silly. But all her questions were silly. She spoke as if black women writers only write about "the black situation" which, after all, is itself becoming more & more everybody's.

I am weary of silly, stupid questions! She also seemed to imply that to the publishing companies black writers are charity cases. Meanwhile Pocket has made millions off of me alone & I still question their accounting. Annoying.

Dec. 17, 1989

I can hardly believe I've lived through the last book reading/signing of the year! Last night at Marcus Books in Oakland. A packed bookstore, overwhelmingly black which is so unusual. With lots of children & elders. I signed books until my arm rebelled. And kept on.

Tonight, flipping the channels at the Press House, Robert was flipping, trying to find <u>anything</u> worth watching: There was Quincy, dancing on his music video. So beautiful & funny and what can I say? I started to grin, just out of pure happiness at seeing him, & love. It amazes me. My love is like a playful animal that leaps up with bright eyes whether I want it to or not. And I welcome it, actually. It no longer hurts. Just kind of shimmers— & seeing Q is almost like seeing a sunset I almost missed.

Robert & I are marveling (I am) about the way this year has gone. So much travel, hard work (because public) and so much togetherness & love. We haven't seriously quarreled once. There was the time I told him he should take his vitamins with food!

Boston was fun. We saw Gloria & Rebecca & Bill & Gay & their children & Roz & Howie & Marilyn & Charlie & Mary Helen! But oh, how can people stand such cold weather? And Derrick & Jewel. And Tufts. An overflow, turn away crowd.

And now I have a month and a week! To do as I like, with no more travel! It feels like paradise.

Dec. 29, 1989

<u>Well</u>, by now I've actually heard Q's new album[1] & I'm practically on the floor! It is so amazingly alive and him and there are songs that I feel are

---

1 Quincy Jones's 1989 album, *Back on the Block*, featured legendary musicians and singers from three generations, including Ella Fitzgerald, Sarah Vaughan, Miles Davis, Dizzy Gillespie, Ray Charles, Chaka Khan, Luther Vandross, Bobby McFerrin, and a then-twelve-year-old Tevin Campbell. The album won seven Grammy Awards, including Album of the Year.

addressed to me. I've faced the truth that I love the man. And I'm so afraid. For the past several days I've been in a terrible state—that horrible euphoria lovers feel when everything is against the love & the heart obviously doesn't give a shit. What's the cure? Maybe tons of ice cream or chocolates. Or <u>work</u>. But how many more novels can I write?

PART FOUR

YOU CAN'T KEEP A GOOD WOMAN DOWN

THE 1990s

Jan. 8, 1990

Already into the new decade. I went out today and bought a really beautiful 1990 black SAAB convertible. It nearly killed me. I traded in the red SAAB and the difference between the two cars was 23,400. So much money. I could only bear spending it by thinking how much I deserve it! And it was fabulous, speeding back across the bridge in the rain, Q on the stereo, and my four hour purgatory at the car dealership behind me.

I've been very blue. But reading this journal I see why. Whether my love for Q is "real" or not, it is a definite passion and has thrown me into disequilibrium. Since Q is, as the Twelve Step people say, "unavailable" I must contain myself. And so I've turned my thoughts to new cars & gardening. But it's the wrong season for gardening & the car is wonderful but can't hug.

Anyhow, I'm worn out by <u>passion</u> & there are worse things to be worn out by, I say to myself philosophically.

Spent a great evening in bed with Georgia O'Keeffe—the new biography.[1] It helps to see that artists <u>always</u> have complicated emotions & lives & that they knock themselves out with <u>feeling</u>—& Georgia lived to be 95!

The trip to see Catherine (Deeter)[2] very good. Though sleepless & strange, too. The book is going to be beautiful & everyone's in it!

Forgot to record my & Rebecca's encounter with Henri Norris[3] after five years of estrangement! We went to hear Patti LaBelle who was as if in

---

1 *Georgia O'Keeffe: A Life*, by Roxana Robinson, was published in October 1989.

2 Catherine Deeter was the illustrator for AW's first children's book, *To Hell With Dying*, and was now working on paintings for a second children's book, *Finding the Green Stone*, which would be published in 1991. When AW writes that "everyone's in it," she's referring to herself and Robert, Gloria, and other family and friends who inspired characters in *Finding the Green Stone*.

3 Henri Norris was a Black woman attorney and a former assistant to AW, whom she'd hired to help manage the demands brought on by the Pulitzer Prize. They'd parted company, not so amicably, in 1984.

drag & I couldn't understand a <u>word</u>. James Ingram much more intelligible & sweet & to my taste. Henri invited us & it was nice to be with her, but a strain, too, since what her real agenda is I know not. I feel intuitively that she still thinks I need pulling out of the closet & by her sweet self. But that is more than ever not the case.

Then she & Rebecca went out to a sex & love addiction meeting & R came home & grilled me about her miserable childhood & my neglect of her and her feeling of being abandoned and so forth & so on. I was devastated. And angry. And tired. The childhood she remembers—with tons of people called in to take care of her—is not the one that happened.

The discussion brought up much unpleasantness. . . . My addiction to Robert. His affair with A.; my effort to write the screenplay . . . my failure. . . . The debacle with Henri. My lost friendships. My feeling of not knowing how to <u>repair</u> a friendship that is broken. I was actually very glad that Henri made the effort—which must have been considerable. So there is more of why I am tired! So many emotions! So much pain to recall. So much sadness.

Jan 13,

Half the month is gone. I lie in bed, depressed. But alone & that is best. I've been unable to respond to Rebecca or Robert. Just—inert. Or, I drag myself along to kitchen or toilet.

My house is a wonderful refuge, and, at last it is raining. I sit up in bed in my old red robe—Rebecca no longer wants it—and I try to feel as vivid as it is. But I'm gray, pewter colored as the rain that streaks the windows or the tears that streak my face. So much sadness! Sometimes I feel so sad I think perhaps it is hormonal.

Jan 18

Today is better. After lots of much needed rain the sun is shining. Birds chirping. Sky blue. I've been working on the Zora festival piece.[1] I'd feared

---

1   AW was preparing a talk, to be delivered later in January 1990, for the first Zora Neale Hurston Festival of the Arts and Humanities in Eatonville, Florida, Hurston's hometown.

I had nothing more to say, and I don't, really. It is all now memorializing, institutionalizing, and that's never the fun that creation or discovery is.

My gloom is lifting a bit.

Yesterday Ruth told me that Mamie[1] had come down to Eatonton to stay a week; that she plans to "unveil" a portrait of Mama that apparently hangs over the television. That M. accuses me of being a "rotten" mother; and says that if I were what I'm supposed to be, I'd move Mama out of the projects. This hurt, even though the projects is Mama's community & she is happy there, & has never expressed any desire to leave.

It's Mamie who wants the big new house, to unveil her portrait in. . . . Anyway. She plans to write an "exposé" to tell the world her side of things. One of which is that Mama herself was a rotten mother.

And perhaps she was, to Mamie. It's hard to imagine Mama, at seventeen – nineteen, with two small children & six more on the way! We always forget that she was an unwed mother for at least a couple of years.

Casita Careyes, Mexico, Feb. 5, 1990

Robert reminded me that we've invited Mama out for a 3 month visit this summer & she & I can decide then on what is best to do.[2] I am ready, at <u>last</u>, to take care of her in my house—or will be, when the house is finished. I've gone through such incredible changes: thinking at times that it would be best if she took her leave from life. But now I feel I'll be happy to help her live as long as she can. I've felt traumatized by her illness, as if I am slightly sick & weakened, because she is. I wonder if this is typical. Have a feeling it probably is.

---

1   Ruth and Mamie are AW's older sisters. Alice is the youngest of eight.

2   AW's mother had suffered the first of several strokes nearly a decade earlier. Since then, Alice had been working with her siblings Bobby, Curtis, and Ruth to care for her, with Alice shouldering much of the financial responsibility. While the siblings had all offered her the option of leaving her small apartment in public housing, Minnie Lue had insisted on remaining in her community, among her friends and several children she helped raise.

Feb. 17, 1990

So much has happened: Nelson Mandela released on the 11th. A tall, trim, beautiful old man. With Winnie beside him looking, above all, <u>tender</u>, for him. It was a vision I shall never forget. As I have never forgotten meeting Dr. King, and the creases in his grey "shark skin" suit. It was almost too much to take in. To see this man who has been shut away from us for nearly 30 years. And to know he comes back into a world white racists have ruined.

Feb. 27, 1990

June sent me a fabulous piece she wrote about Nelson's release, in which she says, basically, that he has outlived South Africa's ability to kill him.[1]

There is still some lethargy in me. But I've consistently taken my hour long walks with Gina & her dog Mara. We walk to the conservatory in Golden Gate Park & back. And this has been wonderful for my stamina & for all the aches & pains that I was experiencing in my legs.

From my study window I see the plum tree in the backyard is in bloom. And the cherry tree in Michael's yard is coming into leaf. Spring in February. But cold, too.

March 6, 1990

I am feeling <u>much</u> better. Am very thankful for this.

Have decided to change editors. Hope this isn't a mistake. But—I realized I always dread working with John, even though he's good & I appreciate what he does. There's no joy. I hope Willa will be better for me.[2]

I also let go of Mamie. I just gave up.

March 31, 1990

I've decided to give Robert the Press House for his birthday. Hope this is right to do, in the interest of greater equality between us. He mentioned

---

1   South African anti-apartheid leader Nelson Mandela was released from prison on February 11, 1990. June Jordan's essay, "Mandela and the Kingdom Come," was published in the *Progressive* in April 1990.

2   Willa Perlman was to become her new editor at Harcourt.

in Mexico his fears of growing older with nothing set aside for security. I don't know—part of me marvels that he doesn't have more to show for his money, but I try not to think negatively. He says he's quitting marijuana, & perhaps that will improve his finances. I feel women generally speaking (& me in particular) are much more cagey with their coins & Robert often comments in wonder & perhaps envy that almost all the women we know have big houses. It is the nesting instinct, he says. Yes, I say, & the sense to buy the nest.

We had a nice spat in Careyes & I told him I don't want to be responsible for his pension plan (which we'd discussed) & so forth. He mentioned something about "community property." And that really annoyed me. I explained that that term had no relevance to our relationship. But thinking about it all later, I felt I would give him the house he's been using for the past 5 years & that I will sacrifice it in the interest of his stability & our friendship.

Besides, I am buying Casa Pacifica, a beautiful retreat cottage in Careyes.[1] It has 3 bedrooms, wonderful views, a pool, lovely garden, fruit trees, a hammock and four different colors of bougainvillea. A quiet road, cobblestoned. Many flowering trees, bougainvillea termite caves in trees alongside the road. Robert & I excited at the prospect of going to & exploring different parts of the country. Learning the language well enough to really speak.

The house comes furnished. Down to a pair of binoculars used to see the green flash at the end of the sunset. A white, two-story structure, with two bedrooms upstairs, & one bedroom, a living room & dining room below. A large Alberca (pool) just outside the living room. They asked 250,000 & I offered 240,000. They accepted & off we went to the lawyer's.

We are thinking of spending 6 months in Mendocino, May through November. Jan – March in Mexico. Dec. & April in the city. Something like that, anyhow. I look forward to growing watermelon, mango, cherimoya, peanuts, as well as collard greens in the garden.

* * *

---

1   This retreat home is in Jalisco, Mexico.

So:

The house in Mendocino should be ready by June 1, and will be spectacular. I know I'll only want to leave it to get out of the cold & rain of deep winter.

—

This year so far as difficult as last year was easy, in terms of my relationship with Roberto. He sees it as the natural ups & downs of life. I think he is probably correct. Because he is a wonderful person, my dearest friend.

April 13, 1990
Where has the time gone?!

The most interesting thing this week, aside from the truly fabulous lovemaking with old gorgeous Roberto who is always right prescient as a lover (!), was a meeting with Donna Vermeer & Lindsay Fontana who want to option Meridian. Donna dark, big dark eyes, very attractive. Lindsay blonde, big blue eyes. Strikes a more L.A. note to Donna's New York seriousness. Liked them both, though. This would be their first feature. I've sent them off to talk to Michael.[1] They suggest Euzhan Palcy[2] & if she said yes I'd be in heaven.

Then last night a meeting with Barbara Masekela (& Timbor?) (& Hari Dillon) of the ANC.[3] I am to be invited to South Africa soon. She wanted to be sure I knew it was ok to go when invited by the United Democratic Movement. I just hope they don't invite me before fall. Nothing is coming between me & my garden this summer.

So, The Goddess continues to shine on me. The paperback of Temple will be out in three weeks. My copy looks great. I sit here in bed looking out the

---

1   AW's attorney.

2   Acclaimed filmmaker Euzhan Palcy was noted for being the first Black woman director produced by a major Hollywood studio (MGM), for her 1989 film, *A Dry White Season*.

3   The ANC, or African National Congress, was the main opposition party in apartheid South Africa. It would soon become the ruling party of postapartheid South Africa, beginning with the election of Nelson Mandela as president in 1994.

window at the thick green leaves that now hide most of the house across the street. 1,300,000 copies of Temple will be published. Amazing. My other books are selling, and being read. Dr. Lui[1] has helped me get my energy back. Robert & I are lovers again.

May 22

Roberto & I drove up to the country for the day & night—and it was raining, raining, as if the earth loves us Californians after all. The trees dripped, the flowers bloomed. The waterfalls gushed. Heavenly. And we were wonderful together: friends and lovers.

June 20, 1990

I hadn't realized how completely oppressed I was by the thought of Mama's visit. Along with Mary Alice, Ruth and Kyle.[2] I knew it felt like a lot, especially since I've been struggling back & forth with my feelings for Robert, but I finally faced the fact that Mama probably didn't want to come, as she'd told us two years ago. And so I called Bobby & asked him to ask her again if this was something she really wanted to do. Or if she'd prefer to stay home & have me visit her. She does. She was coming because she thought it something we wanted her to do. She "wondered" why I would ask her to travel so far! I am inwardly relieved. Especially because the house isn't finished. How long, oh Goddess, how long? is my cry. The flooring people didn't make enough flooring. The tile people didn't make enough tile. So everything's held up while they fell more trees and dig out more clay. And every day is money—and I was beginning to worry until Wendy called to say The Color Purple (movie) had suddenly (from t.v.) netted us 99,000. And that HBJ is buying the poems, minus Doubleday's share, for 100,000. There will also be royalties in September. Pocket's 150,000. Anyway, I'm weary of thinking about money. Water is actually more precious & it is raining outside in the hollyhock bed, where the soil was hard as a rock.

---

1   A doctor of Chinese Medicine that AW was seeing.

2   Alice's sister Ruth, her grandson Kyle, and Mary Alice, caregiver for AW's mother, were scheduled to accompany AW's mother on the visit to California.

July 3

Watched three of Pratibha's films[1] last night: Disturbing, beautiful, enthralling, and like poetry. And though short, so powerful I couldn't bear to watch a fourth. I was filled completely by the worlds revealed in the first three.

It is the 4th of July. Mrs. Bush has invited me to do a literacy campaign event with her—I've said no. Better George should spend money on education, food & shelter for America's children than that I collude with his wife in the pretense that reading comes before eating.

Now to strike at least a <u>few</u> of the weeds from the garden!

July 18, 1990

Ruth, Kyle, Mary Alice[2] are here. And Rebecca is home from Africa! Today we went to the De Young to see the Amish quilts. Glorious! Then to dinner at the Silver Moon. Then to the beach. . . . Kyle quite energetic and jumping about alarmingly. But overall, a cute, bright little boy. Tomorrow I see Jane[3] again & look forward to exploring my insight that I resist a real relationship with Ruth (& perhaps with others) because as a child she never observed boundaries & I felt swallowed up in her or that she tried to live through me. This is perhaps the root of my feeling that nothing that I have must be my own. Which is to say I am always giving others credit for what I do. Or, I share partly because I have the feeling that nothing must be mine alone.

The credit given to me, I pass on to others. The compliments, too. I pass them on to Ruth, or to those women who remind me of Ruth. Even naming

---

1 Filmmaker Pratibha Parmar, a new friend, was born in Nairobi, Kenya, after her family moved there from India during the time of the British Empire. Parmar's family later migrated to London, where she grew up. Parmar's work reflects her strong identification with her working-class roots, and she uses her films to explore the intersections of class, race, and gender.

2 Alice's sister Ruth, her grandson Kyle, and Mary Alice—caregiver for AW's mother—had decided to visit AW in the Bay Area after all, even though her mother had canceled her trip.

3 AW's therapist.

the main character of The Third Life of Grange Copeland "Ruth" exemplifies this. It is a way to memorialize & praise my sister, yes, but it also shows how I have felt merged with her.

July 29, 1990

Another insight regarding Ruth & Mama's "generosity" to me. I now believe they felt guilty for leaving me with my father & brothers & that Ruth gave me pocket money, fixed my hair & made dresses for me to assuage her guilt, not out of love for me. And that Mama, after freeing herself from the horrible environment of our shack, felt guilty also. And that fueled her intense desire to move us to a decent house—which she always said was for me. So if she was leaving me alone in order to provide a better place for me, how could I complain?

I grew used to thinking of houses as Rewards! And that is one reason I have 3 now[1]—plus all the little beautiful "shacks" that remind me of the beauty my mother was able to provide out of ugliness. My love of my mother is completely bound to her expressiveness as an artist and a lover of nature—as I've said somewhere before.

Anyway: Robert & I separated while Ruth, Kyle & Mary Alice were here. It was like a leaf leaving a tree. (I've often joked about Robert being my "tree"!) I've felt constrained, trapped by his presence—the heaviness of it—and weary of being the sun that lights him. He of course was concerned that 6 months was not long enough for him to get another job. (I asked that as of January 30 he not be my business manager.) I reminded him that when I fired Belvie he'd said six weeks was enough. Anyway, as with Belvie, I'm attempting to soften the blow by giving him 25,000 with which to put a down payment on a second condo.

Meanwhile, here I am, alone at last! In my cozy bed in the loft, in the country. The day is bright, breezy, warm. My vegetable garden is wonderful. I

---

1   At this point, AW owns three houses: the city house on Steiner Street in San Francisco; the Wild Trees country compound in Mendocino County, California; and the newly purchased home in Careyes, Mexico.

shall have greens for dinner & peaches & corn throughout the day. Reading at the pond & mooning about, generally!

August 3

My mind has been much occupied with Jane's question: Why the severe 3 year exhaustion/depression beginning in 1983? Which echoed my earlier depression . . . & what in 1983 resembled my childhood trauma.

What indeed. We discussed this: my feeling that Robert's revelation re: his affair devastated me. But I couldn't leave the relationship because I depended on him to protect me through the brouhaha of Purple's success. Likewise, after my brother shot me I lied to protect him/them[1] and also depended on Bobby to protect me from kids who harassed me. It was horrible. Swallowing my anger, not feeling able to break free. And yet I remember when I almost did break free from Robert how light & good I felt! But then I caved in when he said he was giving up drinking & changing himself.

August 15, 1990

So much is going on. Rebecca & I returned safely from a weeklong business/ pleasure trip that took us to Eatonton, New York City, Boston & New Haven. In Georgia we endured an interview for Diane Sawyer's Prime Time. A walk through & around the old haunts.

Talked to Bobby about putting Mama in the local nursing home. He favors the idea. Then Rebecca & I visited the nursing home. Not great, but a possibility. An option.

Then on to NYC & Gloria's sheltering beautiful house. Then next day to New Haven & an apartment for Rebecca. One bedroom. A nice view. Across the street from campus. Then back to Gloria's & a hellacious day of shopping/museum going. Then finally home. Then to the country. The house <u>still</u> not done.

---

1   When they were children, one of AW's brothers shot her in the eye with a BB gun. She lied to her parents about what happened to protect him.

Meanwhile, I've been able to speak to Ruth about the possibility of putting Mama in a nursing home, but not about how I don't plan to put Kyle through college. I keep putting that off. And now I'm too tired & must sleep.

Thank you, Great Spirit of the Universe, for the beauty that is ever in my life.

August 17, 1990

Dear Ruth,

The problem for me in "adopting" Kyle along with Keon & Chauncey is that I feel I was manipulated into doing it. I resent this. It occurred to me that the only reason Kyle knew anything about the arrangement for the Hunt boys was because you told him—and the way he felt was a result of how you explained things to him. In turn, in telling me his reaction: that he felt left out, etc., you made me feel sorry for him and somehow responsible for his bad feelings. I am not responsible for them.

A more reasonable explanation for my "adoption" of the 2 boys, in my mind, was the one I gave you. That without help they are likely not to make it and that if they don't have assistance Kyle is likely, eventually, to lose them as friends, as they fall behind him in school & in other ways, as very poor children frequently do.

I wish you had stuck to your original explanation to Kyle, which is true, does not leave him out, and shows, in fact, that he is "first." That is to say, in buying your house for you I was thinking of Kyle, too. And in supporting your foundation, and in paying you a salary, for helping with Mama, insufficient though it may be.

I have thought long on this and have decided to un-adopt Kyle, after all. I've done the best that I can already for the two of you. And I was glad to do it. But my gifts are at an end, now.

Copied this letter and am mailing it to Ruth. Immediately my mind dropped the whole mess of entangled feelings I've had about just what my responsibilities <u>are</u> to Ruth & Kyle. And, interestingly, for the first time in a couple of months I feel like I can probably soon stop seeing Jane. What is the principle help I've needed so far? To start setting boundaries. Not to let myself be manipulated into more responsibility than I want. I'm also going to set a limit to my giving of funds—200. Even after my final check (for Temple) comes from Pocket/HBJ. These are all matters that have occupied my talks with Jane, far more than I thought they would.

August 20, 1990

A <u>very</u> odd & oddly typical exchange with Quincy via his secretary. I had asked him to accept an award for me from P.E.N. in L.A. on the 23 of September. I shouldn't have done it. But I chose him over Whoopi, whom I understand even less than I understand Q. Anyway, he said he would if he could. We had a nice, empty of meaning, chat. Exactly like those we've had over the past 5–7 years. Today his secretary called to say he can't accept the award. And I don't blame him at all. I just realize how unkind a use I was hoping to make of him. The award means absolutely nothing to me. I don't know a single one of the persons attempting to give it to me. P.E.N. is not my favorite organization. Why, then, did I bother this busy, kind, brilliant person? And set myself up to feel bad no matter what he did. For if he accepted, all it would mean would be some kind of public, external link between us, that would be false—and if he said no, which he did, I'd feel rejected.

It's the feeling of rejection that feels "familiar." And by "choosing" to relate to him, I'm setting myself up for a familiar feeling.

I think Quincy is Porter, my boyfriend throughout high school. Dark, handsome, sweet, who rejected me, I felt, before the operation on my eye removed most of the scar tissue. But then, when it was removed & I came back to school glowing—and pampered by Miss James, the teacher of French who drove me to school each day—he became my boyfriend. So perhaps I am still trying to affect the same experience with Quincy, who has sense enough to avoid it. Because there is in fact, no true passion between us—I don't think. Maybe some. But for a number of years, on my part, a kind of hysteria, feverishness, where he's concerned. But more "addictive" than truly loving. I seemed to "love" him because he was so distant. Which also seems to be a pattern: started, I'm beginning to think, during my early years with my mother, who was very distant at times & when I was growing up, physically distant, because she was someone's maid in another part of Eatonton.

I remember once trying to kiss my mother on the lips, and she said she didn't like to be kissed on the lips. So I never did. We didn't exactly cuddle either. I lay—when I <u>did</u> lie with her—with my head on one of her pillow-like arms. There was no cuddling, with her arms around me, as I do with Rebecca.

I believe now that my mother, faced with a child so obviously starved for affection, compromised by holding hands. We held hands because I was always reaching out for her hand, as I still reach out for the hand of Rebecca, or Robert or . . . it is second nature, or even first nature, to me.

When Q's secretary said he couldn't pick up/accept the award for me I felt a rush of humiliation, as if he'd done this, said no, to deliberately "put me down." But I say no all the time to other people, including to other people who have a crush on me. It's his <u>right</u> to say no, and <u>not</u> to feel responsible for my feelings.

But it is as if I want something from him that says he loves me. But every act of his proves he doesn't. So why can't I "get over it" as Rebecca says.

When Rebecca & I talked about it the other night, we agreed that he's an archetype for me. And that I've projected this inner idealized figure onto Q, or, that he resembles it so closely I think he's it. But really, all that Q is, or rather, all that I project onto him, is within me. I don't need to project it onto him. What he is in himself would no doubt be very inharmonious in my life.

Still, the feeling of humiliation, just a flash of it, was a telling signal, I feel. Why do I seem to will it into recurrence?

Anyway. Robert & I spent a pleasant day here at the house day before yesterday. He came to write checks & "business manage." He's rail thin & looks good. I told him about my work with Jane & my talk with Gloria in which I was able to "see" little Alice, abused and abandoned, in a "barn/house." She was slumped in a corner. In a kind of dark blue print sleeveless sack dress. I told her I was going to take her out of that desolate place. (Any one of the many horrible shacks we lived in.) She couldn't believe me. I said I'm taking you with me to a better place. I took her little hand in mine, and started up the slight hill toward the main road. (This is the house near Wards Chapel.) But a huge circular chain saw came whirling across the field and severed her from me, literally cutting off her hand. Next I devised a huge, thick sheet of metal between us and the chainsaw, and we made a mad dash for the road. But then the giant chainsaw started cutting into & breaking through the metal. It was at that point that I realized I could never get her out by holding her hand. I could only get her out safely by taking her into my heart.

And I saw her, very small, dark & frightened, in her blue dress, climbing into my heart. I don't know if she got all of the way in, but I know my heart is where she has to be.

Sept. 24, 1990

Incredible that the year is drawing to a close! At this rate I'll be fifty in two weeks, rather than four years!

The housewarming party given by me & Rebecca (with Joan's[1] immense & competent help) a delight. Much good food, dancing, hugs & smiles. I read a poem in praise of Charlie & the other builders. Arisika Razak[2] danced. Happy danced. Many guests—about 20-25 stayed overnight—& then we had coffee & cake & for lunch lasagna.

Oct. 24, 1990

A warm sunny day in the country. In the new house. Quiet. In bed. 10:00. After meditation thinking: the very best thing in life is meditation!

My work is not going & I try not to panic. You cannot serve two masters came into my head this morning, & I called Joan to cancel a speakout about

---

1   Joan Miura, AW's assistant.

2   Arisika Razak, a new friend, and a healer, ritualist, spiritual dancer, and educator.

nuclear testing. I had been feeling expansive—what with December & Jan. free. And suddenly I didn't, after saying I'd do it.

I've retreated to my land. My house. Sleep. Yesterday I slept, from one sunny spot on the floor to the next. The house is wonderfully open to the sun, yet solid & sheltering.

October 28, 1990

So much to think about: Lear's[1] invitation to cover Winnie's trial, Ayi Kwei's presence[2] in my life. And soon I shall be virtually out of debt!

When everything is paid for, as of the end of this year!!! I will be faced with the following expenses:

Rebecca's tuition, lodgings & etc.
20,000 a yr.
45,000 Mary & Joan's salaries
25,000 Mama's upkeep

These will be my largest expenses.
Added to these:

insurance
health, travel, clothing.
Gifts!

---

1   *Lear's* was a magazine focused on women over forty-five and published from 1988 until 1994. Its slogan was "For the Woman Who Wasn't Born Yesterday." Its editors had invited AW to cover the trial of South African anti-apartheid leader Winnie Mandela—an assignment AW declined. In 1991, Winnie Mandela was convicted of kidnapping and being an accessory to assault, but, on appeal, her six-year jail sentence was reduced to a fine and a two-year suspended sentence.

2   AW had begun to develop a friendship with Ayi Kwei Armah, the Ghanaian writer best known for his novels *The Beautyful Ones Are Not Yet Born* and *Two Thousand Seasons*.

Have promised 5,000 to <u>Spare Rib</u>, 500 to Sister Bernard from South Africa.

Now, to close this section, a final dream. Again about "flooding," "deep water" Robert & me. He dives into water well over his head in this dream, to rescue me, I feel, though I do not see myself. And so I feel I trust Robert, as I trust myself. And that he represents my self in this dream which is plunging into the unconscious to save my soul.

Dream Poem
Nov. 27, 1990

> And if indeed
> I fail
> let me know
> let me know
> let me know.

Dec. 6, 1990
There are people who know things they have not been taught. And that was the beginning—when this fact was recognized—of education. Other people trying to learn what they knew.
                —AW, INSIGHT

Feb. 20 or 21, 1991

> Creator/
> O Mother of All, be with me now
> & in every hour of my eternal transformation.
>
> ——
>
> Resistance is the secret of joy.
>
> ——
>
> Life goes on!

April 2, 1991

A few weeks ago I slept with Mercedes.[1] My first time making love to a woman. Surprised at how easy & natural it was, though what it means I know not. She & her grandson are now staying in my house in the city because she's been threatened by her landlady/roommate & is afraid to return to her room in the woman's house. This complication & involvement is too much too close too fast, and feels like the kind of crisis I get into with Ruth & Fred & Denise & Mama & other members of my family. I fear being taken for granted. Used. Hustled. And so I withdraw my emotions, even as I try to find or provide a solution to the problem(s).

Mercedes & I had a long talk over the phone last night. I was rather blunt about my fears. She was hurt. But, overall, I feel speaking the truth clears at least my internal air.

Mercedes is a beautiful brown woman who has a kind of Marley look & energy. Fiercely devoted to her 4 year old grandson.

11:00 pm, Sunday, April 21, 1991

Very tired. Safe return, with Robert, from 10 day Southern Exposure Tour for My Blue . . . no, HER BLUE Body![2]

June 9th – a Sunday.

O lucky day. Home alone at Wild Trees, in my house with its new wall almost done, & its name over the entrance. "Temple Jook House"[3]—where worship & sinning (being one's real self) are one.

I am inhabiting my body & my space in a new way. I still enjoy making love with Mercedes. But what I've really learned is how deeply embedded I am in

---

1 Mercedes is a new friend of AW's, a Black woman artist whose name has been changed in these pages to protect her privacy.

2 *Her Blue Body Everything We Know: Earthling Poems, 1965–1990 Complete*, a comprehensive collection of AW's poetry, was published in early 1991, and AW had just finished a tour to promote it.

3 "Temple Jook" was AW's name for the house at Wild Trees, her land in Mendocino County, California.

my relationship with Robert. After my first couple of nights with Mercedes I had a dream in which I felt the most horrible sense of loss, of grief. I think this was because I feared losing Robert if I expressed, physically, with a woman, my bisexuality. I think all the "potential" lovers I've chosen have been chosen not to compete with our relationship, which feels like "family" "unconditional love & support" "shared memories" "the comfort of home."

When I told Robert about Mercedes he was very scared too. But then I felt such an outpouring of love for him & expressed it, that I think he understood unequivocally my love for him & my delight in our relationship. We're friends. Sometimes our lovemaking is wonderful. Sometimes it's just ok. Occasionally it's a drag. He & Mercedes are both good lovers. What is different is the knowledge Mercedes has of my body, & the way lovemaking with her seems like a long, healing romp during which she—sort of by the way—has _many_ orgasms (a great shock to me, the cool, one orgasm a time, Aquarian) and my own delight in _her_ body. I love to touch her. Her knees, for instance, her stomach & breasts.

June[1] & I were talking yesterday about being bisexual. And about how the proof of it is not only in the mind or spirit but literally, in the body. You know you are bisexual if you respond sexually to women and men. Presumably lesbians respond most powerfully with other women. Or solely.

I find it hard to believe there _are_ heterosexuals & lesbians. It seems to me that if you have a female parent & a male parent you'd have to be both these things yourself, and capable of responding to both.

Fundamentally, I find it hard to respond to The Dominator's (man's) word about anything as if it is the truth.

This running away to something else is something I've examined during this last several months of therapy with Jane. I buy houses because I need places to run to. And now I realize I bought the house in Mexico to _send_ other people who might instead visit me!

Anyhow. Therapy sessions concluded for now. I'm committed to finish-

---

1 AW's longtime friend, the poet June Jordan.

ing my novel. Also I must write a preface to the 10th anniversary edition of <u>Purple</u>.

And what of the tour for <u>Blue Body</u>? <u>Exhausting</u>. But a real honor & <u>sweet-ness</u> to meet my readers, whom I like as people. The white the black & all other colors & kinds.

July 23

My life seems to be in transition. Just as my novel[1] is in mid-stream. Chang-ing Woman, that's me. Changing Again.

More about Mercedes:

She reminds me of my grandmother, Rachel. Sweet, patient, loyal. Childlike. All good qualities & yet I'm easily irritated by her combination of them.

August 9, 1991

Today I finished the first draft of <u>Possessing the Secret of Joy</u>. The name that has stuck.

Just started browsing through the dictionary: "Ruth" means "sorrow, pity, remorse." Ruthless = pitiless, etc.! "Sabbatical" which I'm on, means (from Sabbath, Saturday for Jews, Sundays for Christians) a period of rest, vacation.

Sat. 12:30 a.m.
Aug 19?

Drove down to the city[2] with Rebecca. We listened to Tracy Chapman, Ladysmith Black Mambazo & then Jean Bolen, who talked about God-desses within. R & I decided we're both heavily Aphrodite & I'm heavy on the Hestia. A pleasant ride—R driving—but tiring. Now she's down-

---

1   At this point, AW is writing the novel that would become *Possessing the Secret of Joy*.

2   From Wild Trees, her forty acres of land in Mendocino, to the city house on Steiner Street in San Francisco.

stairs talking to Jonah just back from Mexico & I've bathed and gotten into my warm summer in San Francisco flannel nightie that Gloria gave me.

Dreading seeing Mercedes & all her expectations. I've said I'll rent the backroom of her house for six months. A place for me to be when I'm there; but also a subsidy so she doesn't have to live with a roommate. The relationship is very tedious—& she drops entirely too many names: Angela Davis, Audre Lorde ad infinitum. Also drops too many hints about what else she needs. However, I don't love this woman.

Meanwhile I've finished a draft of my new novel: Possessing the Secret of Joy. My "duty" novel. I was wrecked by every page.

The challenge facing me is this: I am spending entirely too much money! I'm spending & spending & can't seem to stop. Surely a sign of some malady. Meanwhile, R & I bought some gorgeous Huichol art from Isobel. My painting depicts the behavior of insects during the last solar eclipse in Mexico.

A big earthquake today in the country—shook the house. The house rocked & rolled, very gracefully.

This morning the city is shrouded in fog. German tourists taking pictures of themselves in front of the house, finally becoming bold enough to come up for a snap in front of the door. Very loud. I rapped on the door & sent them scurrying down the steps. But they came back! So this time I shouted "Go Away!"

What a wonderful house this is: its view of the park is superb. But I don't think I can live here with the tourist buses pouring out ever more disrespectful tourists. Perhaps I can rent out the house, furnished, to visiting scholars or something & get a small spectacular city flat for myself. I realize the tourists have already chased me from the front of the house to the back, where my bed faces the city, not the park. Fortunately there is a sycamore tree and a palm in my view.

After finishing the draft of "Joy" I felt so tired. Almost ill. I sank into my bed and slept until 4:00 pm next day. It has taken me a long time to understand the energy drain that accompanies creative work.

*   *   *

A brief chat with Mel yesterday, whom Rebecca had called. He has thawed a bit with us. I think it is because this is Rebecca's last year at Yale & he has not been asked to help with tuition & now feels he never will. After much stress to her he bought her a car. It is his worst trait: offering things & then holding them back & making conditions. She was reduced to crying on their porch, alone, during the great process of being given the alleged gift. Gloria says somebody has called this (offering money & things but with conditions) the green penis.

I hate the manipulation I feel with Mercedes. My passion has already turned to pity. Pity is disagreeable in intimate relationships. And I feel bored.

Other than that, how does life look at 47, the year of perfect balance?

1. Rebecca is healthy and smart and has a caring heart. Her summer's work teaching writing & swimming led her to the decision to pursue art therapy. So, graduate school looms & she seems ready for it.
2. Robert is healthy . . . and seems finally ready at 49 to embrace his career as a writer. We still share lovely times together.
    I still enjoy cuddling with him. Sex is rather iffy.
3. My mother is still dying & is stable. My sister Ruth is flourishing. The rest of the family chugs along as usual: overeating, overdrinking, overdrugging.
4. My houses are beautiful and paid off. My finances good. But dwindling because I'm spending so much on eternal furnishings. After the party next Saturday & after Rebecca's departure, I'm going to sit down with Robert & assess things. I am tired of buying. I just want to <u>be.</u>
5. My orthodontic adventure continues. I feel my fangs being pulled in by my braces. In a year's time my smile should be much more comfortable & I intend to smile a lot. One year has passed—& I've surprised myself bearing it all with a certain fatalism. Of course what else can I do?

6. Gloria is cooler since I mentioned my relationship with Mercedes. Nor has she had a single question about her, which I find odd.

On the downside: my bones ache more than they used to. Especially my feet. And, close to my period, my hips and knees. Perhaps this is a symptom of the change. I should study it. A new phase of life could be beginning.

Rebecca said to me: you'll be writing for at least 30 more years! Until I'm 77. My mother is already, at 78, older than that.

Casa Careyes
Mexico
Nov. 30, 1991

Last night we were invited to share Thanksgiving dinner at one of the hotel restaurants right above the ocean. We participated in a pumpkin carving contest before dinner—they've merged Halloween with Thanksgiving—& I was surprised at how much fun it is to carve a pumpkin. Gloria, Robert & I carved one & then Rebecca carved the best of the lot, one that is like an Indian mask. We brought them away with us. The dinner was low key, but/and pleasant. The four of us are like family and so entertain ourselves in gatherings where we don't know many people. The director of Careyes is a Contessa, who knew Miles Davis & used to go shopping for clothes with him, among other things, and is like a cartoon of an aristocrat—unintentionally funny, often. Her first name is Bianca, which says most of it and I get the feeling she's spent a lot of her life trying to put color into that.

The gardener seems to be chopping up the ground out back. The day is hazy & overcast. Yesterday we went to a beach we'd never visited before, huge waves between big rocks, quite too strong for me, but not for Robert & Rebecca who seemed to enjoy being tumbled about.

Today there is no energy or optimism. Perhaps it will come when I rise from bed. Rebecca keeps telling me I've raised her "neglectfully." I keep thinking, perhaps, but raise you I did.

Last night I thought: maybe writers & other artists shouldn't attempt to raise children because our work, by its nature, causes us to be distracted.

Dec. 3, 1991

Back from Careyes.

We saw Adrienne Rich[1] on the street. I saw this woman standing alone outside The Hyatt Regency. I was attracted to her cane & followed the cane to her face. We embraced. I told her "I love you!" She is warm & alert & beautiful. Fine eyes & gentle smile.

Dec. 28, 1991

The manuscript is all done & is now at the copy editor, or soon. I added a chapter and a few lines to the original. . . . Anyway. The contracts should be arriving from HBJ, Pocket and Cape Vintage quite soon.

Dec. 31, 1991

Quincy sent lovely gifts: a video, Listen Up, a photo of himself with N. Mandela, and then, something really wonderful, a doll from S. Africa, one of two given him by the Mandelas. She's remarkable. I placed her on the table behind the couch & she refused to stand, so I thought she was congenitally unbalanced (ah, a member of my family! I thought); but no, she's fine. When I placed her on the bookcase (next to Beverly Buchanan's shack,[2] which she matches) she stood serene.

What about Quincy? In the movie he looks exhausted, confused, old & tired. He needs sun. He needs rain & the earth. He lives, obviously, in the studio & all his color goes into his music. I played Back on the Block yesterday as I was sweeping and nothing happened. My mind actually wandered. It is as if writing to him in Careyes was a last act of exorcism, of mourning.[3] And this morning I realized: Quincy has been my imaginary friend! For the Q I've been over the moon about isn't the tired, aging, rootless man whose children don't know him & whose voice is hollow. I manufactured

---

1 Adrienne Rich was an influential American poet, essayist, and feminist.

2 Beverly Buchanan was a Black southern artist whose work AW collected, particularly her wooden shack sculptures.

3 AW had written Quincy Jones a love letter in November, while in Careyes, Mexico.

the warmth I needed from <u>someone</u> instead of giving it to myself. Mercedes has a lot of this warmth, actually, and certainly the presence of person and the goodness. She's just poor, & like most poor people she has to depend on others for help. This I've held against her. It reminds me too much of myself, when I was trying to become and needed people who'd already scoped the escape hatch. Muriel, Jane, Charles, Howie. Etc.

After Robert's infidelity I coped by living an imaginary double life with Q. Escaping to him when the need arose.

But now I understand that where I was trying to escape to doesn't exist.

Men, to a very great extent, have lost their appeal. The erosion of trust is greater even than the loss of respect. And there's the endless male waste of planetary reserves and their arrogant creation of laws that control women & children.

Feb. 18, 1992

I believe today is Toni Morrison's birthday. Happy Birthday, Toni. There are so many of us Aquarians, all being creatively mad (like my sister Mamie) or madly creative.

At home in the country with Frida.[1] A long, slow, steady rain. The soil can hold no more water, & so there are slides, trees uprooted, etc. We are warm & dry, lying on the teal sofa in front of the fire. Last night I was chilled, oddly. Tonight I'll be sure to put on something warm.

Mercedes is still in Cuba. Last night, for the first time, I really missed her. Her warm, sweet smelling body (she got rid of the loud oils that used to nauseate me) and her heavy sleep. Waking in the morning to caresses and delightful dozing as contented as cats.

Gloria left a couple of days ago, still on tour.[2] I can't believe how much she does. Her book is #1, as it deserves to be. Women need to rethink why they fall for paper guys. I realize my attraction to Q was just what she is talking

---

1   AW's cat, named after Mexican artist Frida Kahlo.

2   Gloria Steinem was on tour to promote her new book *Revolution from Within: A Book of Self-Esteem*.

about. The "romance" of escape from an intolerable situation. One you don't at the time have the courage to change. Now, amazingly, my "attraction" to Q is still completely gone. As if it never existed. He still sends flowers, birthday & valentine's day greetings & sweet expressions but there is no rising resonance in me about them. It is so odd. And I think it is because of Mercedes. Her love is so real. So present. So unconditional. And so, in a way, humble, as love is. If she were here we'd lie on the sofa together, with Frida. The perfect "threesome." And she would remind me that her gift to me is 52 massages & I'm due over 45 more. And I'd say Yes! and feel her hands that are so used to caring for little babies, baby me. My body misses her. Between her touch & Robert's there is a chasm. By comparison his fingers seem peculiarly blind, his touch always missing the spot.

Thoughts of Mamie: That too seems to be over inside me. I feel sorry for her. . . . I sent her a check for $10,000 & though she promptly cashed it she is too far gone to write a note of thanks. She's someone I feel sad about. I feel her hatred of me & there's nothing I can do about it.

Feb. 19, 1992

I wish to co-produce & narrate a one hour documentary film about all aspects of genital mutilation. I wish it to be filmed on site in countries where the ritual of "female circumcision" is practiced. I wish to visit elders, matriarchs and young & older married couples and interview them about their experience—sexual & psychological. I wish to visit hospitals where these modern "surgeries" are done, in Third World countries as well as in Europe, England, & North America. I would like to assist in the filming of a clitoradectomy. I would like to show the resulting appearance of a woman who has been pharaonically circumcised and infibulated.

My point of view is that following publication in the U.S. & England of my novel Possessing the Secret of Joy there will be a rare window of opportunity to be candid and connected (the book will serve as the tool of connection) regarding this subject, which endangers women & children wherever they live, and also impacts negatively on people's lives & health around the world. The likelihood that genital mutilation hastens the spread of AIDS will also be explored in this film.

Without necessarily condemning anyone this film will present the facts about the horrors & hazards of a thousands year old practice, with the intent to encourage people to re-evaluate their "traditions" & to change those that are obviously detrimental.

I firmly believe education will make the most difference where stopping this particular violence is concerned, and a committed openness about discussing it. I feel strongly that, working with filmmaker Pratibha Parmar will be a strong asset for this particular film, because of her expertise and her background, and that together we will produce a film that serves the world.

AW

April 9, 1992

Dawn approaches. I feel the flow of cold air that precedes the sun. I'm awake because this is the night before my period begins. First, I had the obligatory migraine, just as much fun as usual, and now the sleeplessness.

I have broken off my relationship with Mercedes. She's wonderful in so many ways & one of the most beautiful women I've ever seen, and she's sweet—but I feel kind of dragged around by her. There's not a lot of "lift," to conversation, to thought. I have felt suffocated by her presence and jammed by the many crises she has. The most recent being that someone snatched her bag & made off with most of the film she shot on our trip.[1]

Anyway. What I'm feeling is a burst of creative energy now released because I'm not toiling over the "work" of Robert or Mercedes. I actually found myself thinking a new short story beginning, which hasn't happened in years? Well, months.

I feel:

1. Clear hearted & headed
2. Extremely blessed in my work & in the opportunity to work more, i.e., against genital mutilation.

---

1   Mercedes had traveled with AW to Australia and New Zealand.

3. Not as if I'm acting in the grip of premenstrual "craziness."
4. Balanced in my friendships
5. Reconnected with Belvie[1]
6. Having wonderful times with Deborah[2]
7. I called my brother Bobby today on the spur of the moment just to say "hi." I haven't felt this close to him in 41 years.
8. I've taken an interest in and responded to most of my family members. And instead of feeling like an onerous duty this feels good. I can be helpful without being swallowed up. Or having to be someone other than who I am. Good news!

I will propose to Mercedes that she & I talk only once or twice a week. She calls so much I have nothing to report & she herself is not much of a conversationalist on the phone. I think she wants the relationship primarily for the growth it provides her. Trips, events, etc. But I feel free. And am beginning to feel that future travel can perhaps be done alone.

April 10, 1992

Robert called to tell me how he likes/loves Daughters of the Dust.[3] It is an incredible experience, this film. And I told him it is peopled with Lissie & Hal's community. The photographer especially seemed to step right out of Temple.

Good talk with Rebecca who informed me she'd "made out all over the place" with a woman. I was happy to hear this. She was tired but happy to have discovered she is skilled. I laughed and assured her I am too.

* * *

---

1 AW's old friend Belvie, from whom she'd had a painful break, used to work as the publicist for Wild Trees Press.
2 Deborah is a friend AW had met around the time of the movie premiere of *The Color Purple*.
3 *Daughters of the Dust* is a 1991 independent film written and directed by Julie Dash. It was the first feature film directed by an African American woman distributed theatrically in the United States. Set in 1902, it tells the story of three generations of Gullah women on an island off the Georgia Coast, as various members of the Peazant family decide on whether to leave the island for a new beginning or stay and maintain their way of life.

I am happy. In a calm, pensive way.

Sleeping wonderfully. Feeling like a bird in the sky.

Undated

My finances never looked better. When I'm in SF I'll set aside a 100,000 CD for anti-genital mutilation work. My houses & various vehicles are paid off. Rebecca graduates from Yale next month! My dental work is nearly done. I've reconnected with Belvie, who is precious to me. I am a friend to Joan Miura. Deborah is my friend. Bertina. Robert is my friend. I've reconnected with Ruth—I admitted that she is as much my mother as she is my sister. But she was not "pure" like Mama, & this confused me, made me more critical of her. Also, I was hurt to see how much of Mama's "mothering" work she had done. Mom, exhausted by eight children, shunted the last 3 onto Ruth, who never really had a childhood. So, guilt. She was a blurred identity to me. Sometimes sister, a daughter, like me. Sometimes a mother. This is why my father's rages against her felt incestuous & strange to me as a child. My mother tried to protect Ruth—physically (when my father beat her) but she didn't protect her sufficiently from her own abuse, which was to use Ruth to raise her children. And to take on many wife-mother duties. Mercedes is Ruth. As well as the split off part of me that "distanced" from Ruth. Only to try to come back in this fashion, i.e. through a "love" relationship.

May 20, 1992

Bless all the people in my life. Deborah, my good friend who is so easy to be with. Bless Belvie who is my sister & makes me laugh. Bless Mercedes who is my lover & makes me feel. Bless Robert who is my brother & friend & who makes me compassionate. Bless Rebecca who is the icing on the cake! Bless Frida who is my familiar & who teaches me the value of rest. Bless the Earth in all its splendor. I am completely happy with it. Overjoyed, in fact. And a red peony is opening on my dresser.

June 16, 1992

I was awakened this morning by a call from Bobby McFerrin.[1] He's in New York narrating Peter & the Wolf. He has a beautiful voice—rich & lively. I've agreed to write a libretto for him, to be completed end of December. I'll aim to give Nov. & Dec. to the actual writing. Robert just called in the midst of this. Paule Marshall & Unita Blackwell[2] have received MacArthur Foundation grants. This is wonderful. They need the money, deserve the money, and furthermore know what to do with the money.

Mercedes. Poor Mercedes. After all this time she hadn't read my book. I couldn't believe it. She'd just tried to talk about the book with others based on what she'd heard me read or say in Australia & New Zealand. When I asked her if she'd read it she said she had, but couldn't recall a single thing about it. After I came back from the East Coast she gave me a letter saying she'd now really read it, etc. & that when I'd asked about it before, she'd been struck blank by sheer terror.

She's coming this afternoon and I feel——very little. But why should it be so hard to love someone who can't read or won't read, and who lies about it? Surely any way you look at it there's a tragedy here. But talk is so much a part of sharing for me & I love to swap ideas. I like for the other person to <u>have</u> ideas.

Great Beauty, which is the name I choose for "God,"[3] thank you for your blessings which are endless. Thank you for leaving me vision enough to see the wonders spread before me. As I move into this period of deep inter-

---

1   A widely acclaimed vocal artist and multiple Grammy Award winner, Bobby McFerrin narrated the American Ballet Theatre production of the classic ballet *Peter and the Wolf*.

2   Paule Marshall is an acclaimed Black woman novelist, and Unita Blackwell is a civil rights activist who was the first African American woman to be elected mayor of any city (Mayersville) in Mississippi. In 1992, they both received a prestigious MacArthur "Genius" Fellowship, a five-year grant to individuals who show exceptional creativity in their work and the prospect for still more in the future.

3   "Great Beauty" and "Great Spirit" are names that AW continues to use as terms of endearment for God.

action with others, I pray for strength with which to function in harmony with others & that I do not pine constantly for my beloved isolation— sometimes known as solitude. There seems now to be so many people in my life. Help me to be the blessing to them you are to me.

July 12
9:00

In bed at the Stouffer-Waverly Hotel outside Atlanta. I've cancelled everything in Atlanta except signings & one interview with a woman from HealthQuest magazine.[1] I've cancelled Chicago & can go <u>home</u> Tuesday morning by the first thing flying. I've been mobbed, saddened by people who want me to sign books for them even as I explain my arm is falling off! And at the University of Maryland there was a near stampede as I finally stopped signing after a couple of hundred books, leaving 300 or so people waving & shouting at me. I smiled and waved as I left & blew kisses.

HBJ has over scheduled me, with not nearly enough time to rest and what I most resent is the fact that when I'm tired I can't really be present for the people. I'm unable to give them my best thought, which they deserve & which I always want to give. The audiences, by the way, are almost always incredible. Responsive, massive, warm, gift-bearing, grateful.

I was met at the airport by a very lovely Southern gentleman in a very long car & taken down to Eatonton to see Mama. She poor thing is unconscious with an oxygen tube in her nose. I can't understand this tenacity of hers. I know she must hate being so helpless while everyone around her is letting go. Three funerals on Saturday. Ruth went to all of them.

The word from Wendy's office is that Whoopi Goldberg is interested in <u>Joy</u>.[2] She'd make an incredible Tashi. Rebecca says I should ask for a pro-

---

1 *HealthQuest* was the nation's first nationally circulated magazine focusing on African American health. It was cofounded in 1991 by Sara Lomax-Reese and Valerie Boyd, the editor of this volume.

2 *Possessing the Secret of Joy*, published in June 1992, tells the story of Tashi, a minor character from *The Color Purple* and *The Temple of My Familiar*. The novel explores Tashi's strug-

posal, outlining the approach she'd like to take. This is a good idea. It pays to raise children to help you think.

I shared the chair in D.C. with Dr. Toubia, who is Sudanese & a surgeon![1] A very impressive woman, very Arab in her bearing. She is forthright and clear headed, a great asset and resource on this issue because even though I can move people emotionally I sometimes forget to give them important details.

August 1, 1992

A warm lovely day in the country. Many hours of sorting correspondence for Joan. Yesterday I dealt with bills. Late in the afternoon I went for a swim & then lay in the sun. Yesterday also I wrote Bobby McFerrin & said No to the opera collaboration. A great relief. Esp. since I've recently consulted with Pratibha regarding our film[2] & it looks like I'll be going to Africa Spring of next year. Joy is doing great. #1 for two weeks, locally. Then #2. It's been on since it went into the stores. #4 on the Times. Overall I've felt heartened by the response. Some reviewers are myopic, narrow, unimaginative & rather slow, but some are right with it even though GM horrifies them. I continue to enjoy the story myself, & admire the characters. Once again I feel I've healed myself on many levels and I adore Pierre and admire Lisette. For Adam one feels sympathy, for Olivia, sadness, for Jung, compassion, for Raye & Mbati, joy. For Tashi, release into the Great Beauty, soul intact.

---

gles to recuperate emotionally and physically from female circumcision—or female genital mutilation—as she struggles to understand why women of her tradition (the fictional Olinka people) must undergo this torture. Apparently, Whoopi Goldberg, who played Celie in *The Color Purple* film, was interested in making a film adaptation of *Possessing the Secret of Joy*.

1   Dr. Nahid Toubia, a Sudanese physician, is an expert on female genital mutilation.

2   AW and filmmaker Pratibha Parmar were moving forward with their idea of making a film about female genital mutilation.

August 16

Robert & I hung out a bit at the rally for The Third Wave.[1] He told me he's seeing a woman named Roberta. Someone he met in grad school. I've mourned some but overall I'm happy for him.

And so to bed. Rebecca wherever you are in the great heartland of America, I am thinking of you & wishing you all that you wish for yourself. I am awed by what you are doing & in fact just crazily proud of you. I try to hide it, because I don't want my grin to attract thieves, but you're just the daughter I want!

Oct. 1—

Sleep like heaven & earth last night & this morning. Before going to bed I listened to Back on the Block—Robert brought over, before I left the city, the Newsweek photo of Quincy & Nastassja Kinski[2] announcing their coming baby. She looks like a teenager, at 31; he looks like a fat, balding letch at 59. This pattern of his—young white women, pregnancy before marriage, general messiness & distraction, is so clear even strangers can see it. Do I have a similar obvious pattern? And if so, what is it? What is my shadow, in matters of the heart?

This room, my kitchen, is perfect for writing. Mbele[3] is lying outside on a towel, enjoying the rain just off the verandah. I'm at the pine table in front of the beautiful windows & the fogged over view. With a cup of half-caffe, for which I had a taste, on waking. I look about me, with wonder & gratitude, always. Already the yard is "full" of the plants planted a couple of years ago. Everything has taken hold. The eucalyptus trees are tall; the sycamores dropping their yellowed leaves.

And I am procrastinating!

---

1   Rebecca was one of the founders of the Third Wave Direct Action Corporation in 1992. In 1997, it became the Third Wave Foundation, dedicated to supporting "groups and individuals working towards gender, racial, economic, and social justice."

2   The German actress/model and Quincy Jones had a daughter, Kenya, who was born on February 9 (AW's birthday) in 1993.

3   Mbele is AW's new dog.

Thursday Morning, 5:30, Brown's Hotel, London
Wide awake after a sound sleep following an exhausting but wonderful day spent with Efua & Ben and the refugee women's community in Tottenham. Efua[1] has asked me to be matron of Forward International & I've said yes. I've warned her I'm not much good at fundraising. We'll see. . . . Life is as usual amazing beyond anything.

Deborah[2] is a fine companion—helpful, alert, funny. Tonight she wore her suit and tie & looked lovely. The doorman addressed her as "sir."

More interviews, etc. tomorrow. I couldn't be more weary of them. But after Amsterdam it'll be over. I'll go home, spend a quiet November in California, an even quieter December in Mexico, and begin the New Year working on the various films. Meridian, Like the Pupil of An Eye[3] (Pratibha began filming today) and possibly Possessing the Secret of Joy. Then to Africa in March. Home for the entire summer!

Before leaving on this tour I had dinner with Tracy Chapman.[4] She arrived in jeans & boots, and carrying a coffee cake she baked herself. We ate pasta & salad & talked for 5 hours. I found her sweet, smart, beautiful and very intelligent. She told me about her ranch & her dogs & horse. I told her how much I admire her singing. She seemed balanced & happy. I certainly felt that way.

------

1   Efua Dorkenoo, a London resident of Ghanaian descent, was helping AW find contacts for the film she intended to make, with Pratibha Parmar, on female genital mutilation. Dorkenoo became a leader of the global movement to end the practice.

2   AW's friend Deborah Matthews accompanied her on this trip, an international tour for *Possessing the Secret of Joy*, which was published in June 1992.

3   This was the working title for the film on female genital mutilation; it would eventually be called *Warrior Marks*.

4   The singer and songwriter had released her first album, simply titled *Tracy Chapman*, in 1988. With the singles "Fast Car," "Talkin' Bout a Revolution," and "Baby Can I Hold You," the album won three Grammy Awards, including an honor for Chapman as Best New Artist. AW was a fan of Tracy Chapman's work, and vice versa, but this was their first in-person meeting.

Oct. 21 1992   6:00 a.m.

My book is # 2 on the bestseller list. Sarah Wherry, the publicist, has worked hard. She is brown, very light, with black curly hair. A sweet face & plump body. Because of her the tour's been bearable & even fun. So much has happened. I've met Efua Dorkenoo. Ben Graham, her husband. Aminata Diop. Linda Weil-Curiel. Hung out with Pratibha & Shaheen— who is lovely. And through it all, is Deborah. A friend I enjoy as I enjoyed my friends in grammar school. Funny. Alive. Brave. Thoughtful. Herself to the max. We have great talks & laying about times. There's always music.

One chat with Robert. One with Rebecca. My true family. Great Beauty you are good to me. I love you.

Undated

Retroactive Reconstruction:

Last night at Pratibha & Shaheen's[1] Aminata Diop[2] and her friend & lawyer Linda Weil-Curiel came to dinner. I don't know what I had expected—and actually I have a picture of both of them on a wall in my study—but they were <u>more</u> somehow. More real, more warm, more loving, more hurting, more strong. More sincere. I loved them almost at once. Aminata doesn't speak English. My French has lapsed & of course no one but she speaks Bambara. We talked of logistical things, over dinner. How tomorrow's shoot is being planned, what time we are to meet, etc.[3]

---

1   Filmmaker Pratibha Parmar and her partner, Shaheen Haq, were living in London.

2   Aminata Diop fled her home country of Mali for France in 1989 to escape a female genital mutilation procedure. She applied for asylum in October 1990 and is thought to be the first woman to cite FGM as a reason for seeking refugee status.

3   The women are shooting scenes in London for the documentary on female genital mutilation.

Nov. 2, 1992

Dear Family,

As you may have heard, as of January 1, 1993 there is a strong possibility that Mama will be placed in the local nursing home in Eatonton. After nearly thirteen years of home care,[1] I believe it is time to make this change. It is not simply a matter of money. Although Mama herself would be shocked if she knew her care costs approximately 40,000 a year, I have felt privileged to pay my share, and have enjoyed working with Bobby & Ruth over the years to give to Mama what she herself requested: years of remaining in her own house & in her own bed.

I had hoped some years ago to entice her to California to live in the country with me—and for that reason my house today has an unused wheelchair ramp!—but she did not wish to come, & told me so. Ruth has stressed as well that it is important for her always to be near her friends—cousin Cora Mae, Lucille & Ms. Reynolds, for instance. With this I agree.

The caretakers, all of whom deserve our undying gratitude, are definitely feeling the strain, mentally & physically. There is also the consideration of the health of those of us who have assumed responsibility for the major portion of her care. I am concerned that some health problem will suddenly strike one or all of us, leaving Mama in a vulnerable & unstable situation. I have had Lyme disease for the past decade; it is chronic, so far incurable, and unpredictable in its behavior. This in addition to my visual disability, which is not helped by age, or my chosen occupation.

In any event, I have discussed this at length with Ruth & Bobby who have agreed that this move can be a positive one. I've also discussed it with Mary Alice whom I've offered the job of attending

---

1   AW's mother was suffering from complications from several strokes.

Mama in the nursing home so that Mama has the security of seeing someone she knows & loves every day. I've discussed this as well with Ms. Gunthier, the director of the nursing home who understands perfectly the high quality of care we will demand for Mama. She has been instructed to be in direct contact with me, as well as with Ruth, so that we are aware at all times just what is going on. Mary Alice, as I've said, will also be there. She is to spend at least a few hours with Mama every day.

More than this I don't think can be done. It is as much as I'd wish Rebecca to do for me when my time comes.

Those of you who are concerned for Mama's care in this new arrangement can express this perhaps by visiting her more, calling to check on her at the nursing home, and in whatever ways you can think of. The furnishings from her apartment could be transferred to the Old House. On holidays & reunions Mama could be taken there where she'd once again be among her own things. It would help also if you could offer supportive, positive feedback. Though I think this is the best solution to the problem of long term care, and the best I feel I personally can conceive, it is an extremely difficult decision & step to make. I have to keep reminding myself that a nursing home is not, for instance, a concentration camp. And that in fact, as Mama grows even more frail & subject to infections, etc., it will actually be better for her to be where medical assistance is always close at hand.

Because you are also her children I know this decision will affect you, which is why I am taking the time to present what is going on as clearly as possible. I have received communication from Mamie & Curtis that they would like to assume some portion, financially, of Mama's care. This can now be in the form perhaps of nursing home expenses, beyond Mary Alice's salary.

I hope each & every one of you is well and happy. Rebecca and I are holding on, fighting the good fight—as I hope you are too—on many fronts. The evil in the world continues to astound, but so does the courage of the human spirit to express itself at ever higher levels of compassion & hope. This keeps us going, though exhaustion is a constant companion.

Sincerely,
Alice Walker

P.S. Please respect that this is a confidential matter, for family members only. At least until all issues are resolved.

November 9

At Temple Jook, in bed. The sun is making the fog rise up from "the lake"— everything moving slowly toward the ocean.

I feel myself ready to love & to love an equal. Someone who thinks as herself or himself. Someone who can pay his or her own way. Someone who has a life already. And is in love with it. And someone who loves him or herself.
So.
Many film irons in or about to be put into the fire. "Like the Pupil of An Eye."[1] "Meridian." "Possessing the Secret of Joy." I would love Danny to do "The Third Life of Grange Copeland." He'd be fabulous.
Deborah & Rhyan[2] were here for the weekend. A good visit for them. I was tired & preoccupied. Deborah expressed again her attraction to me. I maintained my feelings of sisterliness. The pendulum seems to be swinging back to men, incredibly. Odd. Interesting. Joan called to tell me Arthur Ashe[3] had written to invite me to something—& I realized I'd love to meet him.

---

1   AW and Pratibha Parmar had begun filming sections of "Like the Pupil of an Eye," the working title for the documentary that would eventually become *Warrior Marks*.
2   Rhyan was Deborah's adolescent daughter.
3   Tennis legend Arthur Ashe was the first African American male tennis player to win the singles title at Wimbledon, the U.S. Open, and the Australian Open. After retiring in 1980 due to heart surgery, Ashe used his profile as a legendary sportsman to promote human rights, education, and public health.

What would I like to do: 1. Write short stories in Careyes 2. Work with Lisa Jones or Nina Pierce on <u>Meridian</u>. 3. Work with Pratibha & Efua on our film. 4. Be lovers with an equal.

Nov. 18, 1992

Audre Lorde[1] died yesterday, Rebecca's birthday. Spike Lee's film of Malcolm's life[2] also opened. Belvie & I went to the premiere, in Oakland at The Grand Lake. A very good movie. Not very lively, but fabulous as a record of yet another trying time for us Colored. All over again I realize how much I love being black & brown & red. It is true we suffer so much but the other side of it is intense life. Joy. Ecstasy of being. Great welling swoops of pain. Sorrow. Grief. Love and Happiness. The fog is lifting, slowly drifting toward the sea. My neighbor brought a bag of figs while we were filming Tuesday. They're before me on the rough pine table, black & luscious. I adore them with my eyes before putting them in my mouth. We are both of the earth. The eater & the eaten. It is a perpetual feast. I will be relished and eaten by something one day. May I be thoroughly enjoyed!

Dec. 3.

Yesterday Mama was eighty. I sent flowers that, hopefully, will have a scent. Mama does not often open her eyes, but she can still smell!

The filming [of] Like the Pupil of An Eye: Genital Mutilation & the Sexual Blinding of Women went well. Pratibha enriched with the crew—all women: Black, Indian, Japanese & white. I invited Mercedes up for the shoot. We drove up in my new green Jeep, which I like very much, and have had our usual strange time. Thanksgiving which occurred last week was the most beautiful I've ever experienced. Deborah, Rhyan, Trajal, Stefan, Frida & Mbele were here. We cooked & walked & talked & shared music &

---

1 A self-described "black, lesbian, mother, warrior, poet," Audre Lorde dedicated both her life and her creative talent—as a noted writer of both poetry and prose—to addressing racism, sexism, classism, and homophobia. She died of breast cancer on November 17, 1992.
2 *Malcolm X*, Spike Lee's 1992 film, stars Denzel Washington as the iconic leader.

ritual. I finally experienced what it must be like to have a family in which one feels comfortable. Seeing all the people I'd invited I was tempted to hide in my room—but soon I realized I didn't have to. I could exist among them without fear. So I lay about on the couch reading. I had a sauna. I cooked greens. They did their thing. It was heavenly. Easy. Something so peaceful & happy none of us wanted to end it. They all stayed until late the next day. Robert arrived bearing flowers that, next to Deborah's, looked tired if not passed on. The quality of feeling changed. He became "the man." "The father." He was hungry, so I fixed him something to eat. I found myself trying to placate something critical I found in him, in his spirit & attitude. He is I'm afraid my grandfather, William Grant, Mama's father, whom she was always trying to please. All repressed anger & horn-iness. He stayed the night & in the morning came up & got into bed with me & Frida. We snuggled & drifted back to sleep. Where I, true to form, dreamed beautiful dreams.

Jane said, when I went for a 2 hour session with her, that perhaps a life with Robert is "not quite" what I need. I had told her I felt ready for commitment & why not with Robert? She's right, I think. It could almost be right, but there's that quality of deadness that is now so apparent to me. My easy boredom. My feeling that Robert is not generative.

Mercedes said the other night that she's responsible for my new ability to give of myself. She is the most interesting combination of sweetness & goodness, arrogance & ignorance. I just gaped at her.

Howsomever. She is definitely my shadow & I've decided to stop slam-ming the door in her face. Perhaps that is what my dream was telling me. To get up & face my shadow—which isn't even Mercedes but a family of wild, despondent children; and my fear that letting them in will take me right back to Eatonton, home of so much misery.

It is another gorgeous day in my valley. After stunning cloudbursts & gentle showers over the past two days, today is sunny, crisp, clean. The air is so fresh it is intoxicating.

Time to start work on my journals—always so easy to put off.

Re: Mercedes. She seems very much my sister Ruth. Not as intelligent or articulate, but with Ruth's interest in the physical. Her fascination with the body & its processes. It is such a mystery—how we continue to try to create harmony out of the chaos of family life. Are these things ever resolved? Is there ever peace? Just thinking about this takes me to the edge of sleep. The mind literally slumps before the enormity of the task.

December 15, 1992
Careyes

Rebecca has just emerged from the shower singing along with Tracy Chapman. "Deep in my heart" she sings, the only lines she knows perhaps or the lines that resonate. Angel[1] can't come on the day planned. R. is lonely for her, devouring the lengthy fax A. sent yesterday. I am enjoying a cup of "forbidden" coffee (left, the coffee, by someone who used the house over the past several months). I'm in fact, happy. R. & I had our usual tense couple of re-entry days. With her short hair & ready grin she reminded me of her father, with whom I'm still unfinished. Anger, mainly. Puzzlement. Disappointment. Pleased he won't be coming to Careyes in Angel's place. I am constrained by male energy in the home. Especially the heavy kind that just sits like a lump, reading the news.

I love hearing Tracy. I'd suggested playing her before but Rebecca nixed it. Said the friendship T. & I have developed makes her seem "different." She was used to her being "out there" somewhere.[2] Powerful & mysterious. Having spent two evenings together I think she is still powerful and mysterious & I wholeheartedly appreciate her aesthetic.

She lives on a large ranch, part of which is in the clouds. On clear days, from this point, you can see the ocean. Cozy, just right. I gave her a foot

---

1   Angel was twenty-three-year-old Rebecca's new love interest.

2   To clarify: Rebecca seemed to be missing the distance that allows a fan to be a devotee of an artist's work while the artist remains at arm's length, "out there," remote, "powerful and mysterious." But getting to know the artist as a friend—as AW was doing with Tracy Chapman—threatened to take away some of the mystery and, consequently, some of the fan's devotion. As Zora Neale Hurston wrote in her memoir *Dust Tracks on a Road*, "The one who makes the idols never worships them, however tenderly he might have molded the clay. You cannot have knowledge and worship at the same time. Mystery is the essence of divinity. Gods must keep their distances from men."

massage. When I told Rebecca this she almost wailed. It's ok, I said. I'll give you one! But she said: Mama, please leave something in the world for your daughter to do! How can I compete with that?[1]

Dec. 20, 1992

You'd never know the Christmas season is nigh. Tomorrow is the winter solstice! And that's what matters. The sun is coming back to the Northlands. Plenty of sun here that's never left. This morning is lovely and bright. I just heard Robert sneezing and coughing & realized it is the sound of men in a house that I find so jarring. Their heaviness. They are downstairs. I am waiting to go down because I've put hair coloring on my hair, the white spot at the front of my scalp that makes me look like I'm balding. Soon I'll stop this—I know it doesn't go with dreadlocks & meditation. I'm sensitive to it, however, as I am to my eye—on which I frequently put a brown contact lens, and until I'm ready to let go of these remnants of insecurity I'll hold on. It is the same with the houses. I think often that I have too many though I use all of them well. They make me feel secure in a world where housing is not promised.

The music is up—people are here for the holidays.

Life!

Now to wash my hair & go down to see my guests. Taking my Mahalia with me!

Dec. 22, 1992

Rebecca, Deborah, & Rhyan went off down the beach and R. & I sat under a palapa & waited for our fish. He was like a beige shadow. Silent. Empty. His eyes showing nothing but maybe fear when I looked into them. I let myself go into the sunset which was beautiful—and suddenly I was able to let myself feel something I've suppressed for years. I found my-

---

1 Again, Rebecca's response wasn't based on a desire to "compete" directly with AW for Tracy's attention. She was simply responding to the cooler-than-cool opportunities for joy and fulfillment that AW seemed to attract to herself—saying playfully, *Leave some cool stuff in the world for me to do too!*

self beginning mentally to write an ad for the personals columns: Father wanted. I wrote a lengthy list of possibilities. He could be gay, like Baldwin. He could be hetero, like Howard Zinn. He could be bi, like whoever. Like me. Black, though. Loving walks by the ocean, fried fish and good books & jokes & hugs. And how lovely to have someone with whom to share my problems & joys! So I sat there writing all this & fantasizing about what kind of man would answer such an ad, and wondering as well what kind of paper to run it in. I felt the tears welling up from some very deep place. Bottom of the shoulder blades? Because that's where the bitterest tears collect. And I started to weep, silently, as I acknowledged how deeply I miss and need and want a father. I am 48. I want a father. That is what I've wanted in the men I've chosen & I've gotten bits and pieces of "fatherliness." Especially from Mel. Perhaps this is why sex always seemed somewhat incestuous—especially with Robert who has seemed like my idea of a brother.

I've felt grateful for this insight. It came after a particularly vivid dream the night before Robert & Deborah & Rhyan arrived. I dreamed I had misplaced someone's child, a small boy, & that it was gone for three days. I didn't know how to tell its mother. And then on the third day I went into the dark dormitory where the child & I had been sleeping & there he was. Sitting up in bed healthy, chatty, & happy. He was fine, he said, and had spent the 3 days at summer camp. He was beautiful. Bright black eyes & mocha/coffee skin. I noticed & touched a few silver color hairs on his head. In my joy I picked up the phone & tried to dial his mother's number. I couldn't get through. Then a male telephone operator tried to help me (Robert's voice I thought) without success. And I thought in the dream: what do I need him for? He's doing no better than I am. So I kept trying to reach her by myself but didn't seem to have the right #. But I knew she'd be happy, as I was happy, when I did get through.

Now I think this little male child is my inner male child that left me when my brothers attacked me during childhood. He was banished, by me. And now he's back. A little old child. But in good spirits. I didn't lose him after all! Yeah!

Dec. 22, 1992
Casa Alicia, Careyes, Mexico
This unfinished notebook marks the end of this journal. It has been a year of major change, growth, knowing & not knowing. Of sadness. Loneliness. Joy. Love. Awakening. Great Beauty, I thank you. So many blessings in my life! Creating, like you!

Dec. 27, 1992
The 10 days with Rebecca settled into a warmly loving routine. Work, cuddles in the hammock, walks by the sea. It takes a week to "get the house back." Sweeping, cleaning out old papers & junk, debris from my guests, etc. My guests. I'm tired of having them. Too many. Too varied. And I am resentful that they (some of them) require so much help getting here. Anyway, this should easily be handled with a "no."

Anywho. The dog is out & barking. Robert just hung a light shade for me. He's packing. Taking his coffee, coffee maker and granola! Not once did we cuddle, though I felt like it once or twice. It's hard to end a relationship as lovers. It has taken a full year to do so.

But finally—Goodbye. Goodbye, my lover. No more romps on the Mendocino hillsides, or rolls in the bushes & trees. No more moonlit reveries, still lit by the afterglow. You grew. And now you've just come to the door to tell me you're on your way. I see a tall, pale, graying man, trying to look cheerful. We talk of a quiet day for me. Hope the neighbors don't play loud music all day & that Mbele doesn't bark at everything that moves. We smile at each other—& now you've driven off,[1] Mbele barking madly.

And now it is quiet. I hear music but so far it is faint.

Our hearts & lives have been so intertwined! For so many years! And now . . . you deserve a happy life of love & joy. I wish this for you.

*   *   *

---

1   Robert was not leaving Careyes just yet, but was going to stay elsewhere with his visiting girlfriend, Janet.

And now what:

Wilma Mankiller and Charlie Soap[1] are coming along with Janet. Gloria arrived last night & she, Robert, Angel & Rebecca & I had dinner at Playa Rosa. As always the food was delicious, though the music left much to be desired. Angel speaks Spanish & tried to improve the music. It remained what Gloria described as "Eurotrash" music. "Brazilian" music sung by recently settled white people. Horrible. Empty. Soulless.

We will all meet for dinner at 8:00. Next Sunday this time we will be flying home. It hardly seems possible. This long, sweet, complicated month here.

In one month I go to Africa—to Senegal & Gambia. I've asked Deborah to go as my assistant. She's agreed. We will also go to Burkina Faso to the annual film festival. This all has a certain unfamiliarity about it. Yet once reunited with Pratibha[2] & the crew a measure of "being in the flow & on the path" will, doubtless, return. Today I mourn the passing of something valuable that inevitably changed. Like the seasons.

Jan 1, [1993]

Next to my last day in Careyes. Last night we all gathered in Charlie & Wilma & Gloria's casita: me, Rebecca, Angel, Janet, Robert. Before the others arrived Gloria, Charlie, Wilma & I sat on the verandah talking of the difficult things 1992 brought. All three of the women suffered from public attacks in the media, Gloria perhaps the most. Wilma was hurt because the attackers were friends. I talked of fighting back. I gave Wilma a foot massage, which she seemed to enjoy. I certainly loved doing it. And realized that, yes, foot massage is definitely something I want always in my

---

1 Wilma Mankiller was a community organizer and the first woman elected to serve as chief of the Cherokee Nation. She married her longtime friend Charlie Soap, a full-blood Cherokee and fluent Cherokee speaker, in 1986.

2 AW was to meet director Pratibha Parmar and her crew in Africa to continue filming their documentary on female genital mutilation.

life. Giving & getting. . . . We watched fireworks, & hugged as the beautiful designs filled the air. We embraced. It felt good & right. I keep having the feeling of being with the people I'm meant to know. I love Charlie & Wilma & feel we've known each other always. Wilma's hand feels familiar in mine. Charlie looks <u>just</u> like Grandmother Rachel! He says as well that in Cherokee Alice = Celie!

He & Wilma wrote my Cherokee name: She Who Brings the Powerful Message. The Cherokee alphabet is beautiful.

Then I began to dance—I couldn't help it. It just took over my feet. Soon we all were dancing & we danced for a couple of hours, until I felt I had danced myself back into my body. This was the best gift for the first moments of 1993. I embraced Robert & Janet & wished them happy new year. I dressed all in white. So did Charlie. I felt like an initiate—so much new life beginning & so much dying of what no longer lives.

Great Beauty, I thank you for new friends & for old friends. I thank you for being with me even when I despair. I thank you for the promise of this moment, that it may well stretch to cover an entire year. 1993.

May I walk, think & act in beauty, according to what is natural & for the highest good of all.

Jan. 12

Tracy C. & I had a date for Sunday night. She arrived in her black Mercedes with phone & CD player, and off we went to see "The Crying Game" which I liked very much. Then to Zuni where I had potato & leek soup & she had polenta. I am attracted to her. I love her darkness. Her big black eyes. Her white teeth. Enchanting. And all this with her voice, so rich and compelling. She gave me a book on how to play the guitar, also a tape. And a dog book: How To Be Your Dog's Best Friend. Written by Monks. I gave her a Huichol painting I bought in Vallarta.

2-4-93

Early morning in London. I am in bed. The traffic outside is increasing. Another gray foggy day & how do Londoners stand it? Pratibha & Shaheen's[1] house is wonderful—I'm actually in Pratibha's room. Thoughts of Tracy ever present. I ripped out the letter I wrote her yesterday & will ask Sarah Wherry to mail it for me. I now realize I need a fax machine. Just for Tracy & me. Though there's something nice about the slowness of letters.

Deborah & her friend Mary arrived at the house promptly at eleven.[2] Tracy had just cooked breakfast & we were sitting down to eat. The dogs barked madly. Deborah looked quite crestfallen. She has told me several times of her attraction to me; I always maintain a loving sister-friend attitude. So I was surprised seeing Tracy with me hit her hard. Also the fact that we went to the airport in different cars. T wanted to drive me. Saying goodbye at the airport would've been harder if we hadn't practically exhausted our emotions during the past week. She looked exquisite in her white shirt, jeans, black vest & black boots. I love the look of her. So androgynous.

The plane was six hours late, so D. & I went back to my house & she confronted me, gently & with dignity, with her feelings. Saying she didn't know if she should come at all. She admires Tracy & loves me—still it would hurt & she's learned she must take care of herself. This I understood. I suggested coming for half the trip. Leaving with Pratibha. In the end she came, but there's still a bit of strain which I regret. Perhaps it will ease. I don't know.

A sad time with Mercedes, who also arrived a few days before while Tracy was there. Unlike Mercedes, Deborah can articulate her hurt and understand I am not trying to cause distress. I am in love & though this is a problem for Mercedes & Deborah it is a joy for me. I consider it a gift from the universe—at last the figure I've walked behind has turned around! And she

---

1 Filmmaker Pratibha Parmar and her partner Shaheen Haq were living in London, where they hosted AW during a brief stopover before heading to Africa to work on the film they were making on female genital mutilation.

2 Deborah was to travel with AW to London and Africa, to work as her assistant for the filming of *Warrior Marks*. In this entry, AW recounts the events leading up to her departure for London.

is a woman! And she is black! And she is a singer! Only the first fact, that she is a woman, kept me afraid of wanting this to happen before.

At the crack of dawn tomorrow we head into our African journey. Pratibha called last night & warned me about Banjul, which, though it is the capital of Gambia, has no paved streets. Senegal sounds quite predatory—everyone wanting money before they'll do anything. Horrible.

Last week I went to have an AIDS test. Up to now T & I've had safe sex. Wonderful but also frustrating. I'll go in for the results on my return.

And Robert? He & Janet very much a couple—& he seems happy. Thrown a bit I think by my relationship with Tracy. It does seem odd. I pursued her as if my unconscious rather than my conscious mind wanted & desired her.[1] A long flight through the dark to the dazzling light of her smile.

What happened?[2]

She came, through the storm, to the country, though I'd warned her of possible danger. Bearing flowers. We spent 2 days. Chaste. Close. Sisterly—but always with the strong undercurrent of my by now admitted-to-myself attraction. When I couldn't resist touching her I offered to massage her scalp. We danced. We cooked. We watched movies. On the last night I kissed her cheek as I said goodnight. I wanted so to hold her. Next day on the drive home, just when I had abandoned all hope she asked what I was doing for dinner. Nothing, I said, completely forgetting Mercedes & our plans to get together. So off we went to Zuni & then she went home. Later that night I smoked a joint & it helped me admit I was already missing her. I called & told her so. She said she would come to the "conversation" Jean Bolen & Isabel Allende & I were having the next night. I thought of nothing

---

1 AW pursued Tracy partly by having tiger lilies sent to her backstage when she was performing in San Francisco.

2 Please note, dear reader, that the previous journal mention of Tracy was dated January 12, recounting a pleasant dinner-and-a-movie date. In this subsequent entry, dated February 4, AW is recording what happened in the weeks between to lead to this new state of being in love with Tracy and engaged in a deeply satisfying romance.

else until, the next night, I saw her find a place in the audience. And I'm sure my face lit up. Somehow I got through the conversation & though both of us were about to be mobbed, we managed to leave, & get to my house, and as soon as I'd hung up our coats we turned to each other and kissed. A kiss that lasted two weeks. She did not go home that night. At a couple of points I went home with her. She & the dogs came back & stayed with me. I finally felt how love can feel when the beloved is someone you completely respect, feel proud of, and admire.

Feb. 6, Happy Birthday Bob Marley!

In bed in Banjul![1] Arrived yesterday & greatly surprised to find it so cool. Last night we had dinner with Pratibha & the crew at a nice Lebanese restaurant. I told P. about T. Like Shaheen she was very happy for me. We embraced, giggling like children. I have the photograph T took of us on the deck, right by my bed, and I quite literally feast my eyes on her. What a warm, expressive face she has, so filled with love.

There was a full moon! when we arrived. That was the most significant thing, after the unexpected coolness. Big & yellow & bright. Amazingly welcoming. We drove through the sprawling village of Serrekunda. Very basic, jammed with pedestrians and cars. The area is heavily Moslem. The women, most of them, mutilated as children. This exposure to so much mutilation has caused a mutilation tape to play at odd times in my head—and I see & almost feel the razor descending & slicing away not only labial lips but facial lips, and eyes & noses as well. These fantasies are extremely upsetting and remind me of a similar period when I had fantasies that involved self-blinding. I had to struggle to protect myself, my vision, my sight, by saying over & over: I have a right to say what I see. I have a right to see what I see. I need not punish myself or be punished for seeing.

*   *   *

---

1   Banjul is the capital city of the Gambia, a small West African country bordered by Senegal. AW and Pratibha Parmar were there to begin filming their documentary on female genital mutilation, *Warrior Marks*.

The hotel is pleasant. Right on the coast. Julius Coles[1] called the minute literally that I stepped into the lobby. He wants to be helpful, as does Ayi Kwei.[2] If only T were here! I miss her warmth & languor in the morning.

Feb. 8, 1993
Banjul, The Gambia

An amazing day yesterday. I woke at seven, dressed & rushed to join Pratibha, Deborah & crew for breakfast. After quite a long time we were packed up and started for the village of Dar Es Salaam.

We arrived at a house—but wait, our driver, Malign/<u>Mayline</u> (sounds like) was playing "Matters of the Heart" which was like a warm morning embrace from Tracy. He loves her music he said & wants to send her a present. I said I'd deliver it. Well then, at the house. A bare yard enclosed by a leaning fence. A long verandah & many dark rooms, one with a pile of sand in a corner, all with beds, except for a sitting room on the end near the street. A large group of children surrounded our vehicles almost immediately and what beautiful children they were! Dark browns & blacks, hair in all stages of kempt & unkempt. Large dark eyes filled with interest, curiosity, wonder. Within minutes they'd put on a show for us. Spontaneous music made with tin cans and sticks. The little girls doing clapping dances, the boys dancing in costume: masks & various draperies & brandishing sticks. Very joyous. The crew was enchanted. After a while Satufa—Sophia—arrived. She is my age, much heavier, wearing the sporty eyeglasses that look like space gear African women seem to like. After a few moments of introduction & chitchat I felt quite at home with her. ABC she explained, had just left last week & she had helped them. Now she wished we had arrived first. I assured her it didn't matter. She also indicated that our honorarium was a bit too modest. I said well, we are black women &

---

1 Julius Coles was AW's old college flame. They'd met when Alice was a student at Spelman and Julius was a student at Morehouse College, where he earned a BA in 1964. He would go on to spend more than four decades engaged in international development work in various African countries.

2 Ayi Kwei Armah, the Ghanaian writer, was AW's longtime friend and admirer.

our resources are not the same as those of ABC which is white & male. I refrained from offering more money.

I interviewed Mary, a large dark sister dressed in lavender & purple with a huge length of hair facsimile hanging down her back. Her daughter "little Mary" was being circumcised. Had been, actually. Was now in the bush & part of the ceremony we'd be filming. Why did she do this? I asked. Because it is tradition, she replied. Had it been done to her? Of course. Her mother had told her they were going to a place where there were many bananas. When they arrived she was captured by women she'd never seen before, circumcised, and kept secluded for two weeks. Was she frightened? Yes. Did she feel her mother had betrayed her? Well, at the time perhaps, but later she understood it was "tradition." Did she think Mary would feel betrayed, angry with her? Well, she intended to take her some sweets and soon she would forget all about what had happened to her. Had she herself forgotten? Yes. But if she could stop this "tradition" would she? Yes. Why? Because of the pain.

I missed Tracy so much. Every once in a while I'd mentally leave wherever I was for a kiss.

When we arrived at the bush I was in a state of dread. Sure enough, underneath a large tree there was loud singing & dancing. On a long mat sat the circumcised girls, "little Mary" at 4 years old the youngest among them. They sat as still as statues as the grownups danced around them. There is a barren women's club. These are The Dykes, says Deborah. Their role is to dress as clowns and men in order to amuse everyone. One of them kept shaking her near naked butt in the children's faces. I stood behind them for a while, then moved across so I could see their eyes. Silent, grave, stunned. What is going on? They were all asking. Why is everyone else so happy?

I had to stop writing yesterday because I couldn't bear it. The enormity of what they've lost will not be clear to these girls until much later in life. For most it will never be clear. I'd asked "Big Mary" about sexual pleasure. You know, I said, that the removal of sexual organs lessens sexual response & severely diminishes enjoyment. Well, she replied, she thought her sex life was perfectly satisfactory. Thank you very much! At least this group doesn't infibulate. The girls have been robbed of their full capacity of pleasure. Their bodies have been violated, and by the very elders who should be protecting them.

I've never seen such emphatic, noisy but overall coldblooded dancing as that performed by the women & a few of the men of the village. Eventually this part of the ceremony ended. Then there was the sacrifice, presided over by the circumciser, an elderly woman whose eyesight can't be 20-20. Dressed in a white & red dress & holding her stick of authority, a piece of wood that looked remarkably like a penis.

She pontificated at length about "the tradition" and how she was chosen by the village to perform circumcisions—gold was "poured" over her. Two bulls were killed. All the women before her had been circumcised. All those after her would be also. Soon a man came forward & snatched up the trembling white chicken that rested at the base of the tree. Putting his foot on it to hold it still, he took a knife & hacked off its head. Blood splattered. Some of it on little Mary's feet. Her feet, the smallest of all, wrecked me. I thought of the circumciser grabbing her and of her, her eyes taped shut, not even knowing what or who was grabbing her or what was sought. I finally started to cry, looking at those small feet.

Nobody else cried. They were laughing. The children were crying inside. I understood the message of the sacrifice: Next time, we cut off your head.

Later, interviewing the circumciser, I asked what she felt when the children cried & screamed. She didn't hear them, she said.

So. It was "tradition." Their mother had done it. Her mother. The elders and ancestors. Yes, of course they would do it to their own girls. I wanted to take them in my arms & fly away with them.

Deborah & I joined the procession back into the village. The circumciser in front with her bundle on her head, the two of us bringing up the rear. Much feigned merriment, clowning, energetic dancing. A little girl, five or so, suddenly took my hand. Just for an instant. And I knew she knew I had come for her sake. She was the "one African child" of my dreams.

3 AM, Feb. 9, 1993

Wide, wide, wide awake! I woke up thinking of Tracy. Remembering the curve of her leg when she's driving. The whiteness of her teeth when she smiles. The way she covers her face when she sleeps. The way I feel when she arrives & when she's driving away. How in the mornings I love to invite her into my arms.

My life is wonderful. Even witnessing all this pain I am glad to be in life. Today I am 49, forty-nine. Twenty years older than Tracy. This happiness so unexpected and yet prepared for, even prepared for carefully. To be in good health. To be in love. To be doing work that will mean greater happiness to many. To be doing the work of protecting our children. To be in Africa. To realize Africans are doing ok, basically, if they'd just stop hurting themselves. And that I love both Africa & Africans. That Africans have "time" & "space." Westerners no longer have that. Africans really should be able to be wise, not just clever or smart.

So. Happy Birthday, my little wondrous brown body that has its period & is trying to get through menopause—hence my insomnia! You have carried my spirit well. I honor you & love you & vow I will continue to care for you with all the love I have found waiting for myself in my heart.

Feb. 14, 1993
Valentine's Day
Popenguine, Senegal

At last I am in Popenguine, in Ayi Kwei's[1] welcoming house, and, actually, in Ayi Kwei's welcoming arms & bed. All love & affection. Friends. Deborah sleeping in the children's room which contains bunk beds, a desk & a blackboard. Julius (Coles) just walked up the drive and presented me with a bottle of wine which T & I will certainly enjoy. We arrived yesterday in Sindia, on our long bumpy & dusty ride, via bus, from Banjul. Ayi Kwei, brown & beautiful, met us and brought us via taxi to Popenguine. At the

---

1   AW's longtime friend Ayi Kwei Armah, a Ghanaian writer, lived in Popenguine, Senegal, a coastal town about 155 miles from Banjul, Gambia.

last moment Deborah wanted to come with me & so we arranged for that to happen. We were delighted to set eyes on each other again. Into his tender black arms I went, my grin stretching from ear to ear. After a walk on the beach & a simple & lovely dinner we discussed sleeping arrangements. He has only 2 rooms & a kitchen & I was to sleep in his bed which is next to his desk & worktable & computer. Should he share the room with Deborah? No. Should I? No. Because he dreamed of me in his bed. So I said fine. Sleep with me. His face lit up & sure enough after much bathing & brushing of teeth this small, slender, gorgeous, beautiful black black man with his warm smile & laughing/sad eyes came into bed. And into my cuddling arms. We talked for hours, even though I was very tired. His beautiful voice a low rumble in my ear. . . . We talked of many things—& I told him about T. Which surprised him. I knew I couldn't sleep in his bed without making it clear that she's my beloved and that my sexual life is with her although my love for him is constant. We talked some more, hugged some more. Kissed. But oddly never on the lips, and eventually, all talked & cuddled out, we drifted off to sleep.

Today Deborah & I went for a walk on the beach & fell asleep in the shade of large rocks. Delicious. And when we woke her stomach was better, I was more content, the wind & dust didn't bother me quite as much. For the wind is constantly blowing. The dust always in eyes & throat.

T & I are to share Julius' beach house for a few days, on our return from Burkina Faso. It's an odd little Moorish structure that should suit us just fine for a few nights. But it just occurred to me: where will he sleep when he comes on the weekend? I'll think about this later. It would probably be for only one night in any case.

T & I talked this morning. She called to wish me a happy Valentine's day. I've yearned for her so much I'm almost afraid to see her. And yet—I can hardly believe she's coming. By the time I get to Dakar, on Monday, I'll have just 3 more days. And in fact she arrives—Inshallah—on Thursday. We are to film on Goree Island Thursday & Friday & then leave for BF on Saturday.

3-20-93
<u>In Bed</u>
<u>The Journals of</u>
<u>Alice Walker</u>

And so I am in bed. In San Francisco. It is a bright sunny morning, birds chirping away and because it is Saturday there is quiet. The truth is I woke at dawn because Tracy is coming into town for grocery shopping today & I invited her to stop by & give me a 5 minute kiss. We were together non-stop for exactly a month & only separated day before yesterday. She went to her ranch. Of course I stopped writing in the journal the minute she arrived in Dakar. She came on the 18th of February, while I was filming on Goree Island. I hurried back to the Savana Hotel where I had a suite, to discover she'd taken the small room beside it. I freshened up & knocked on her door. She seemed heavier, more solid, her face more interestingly contoured. It was such a shock, after so much longing. We both sort of hung there, looking. Then not being able to look. Eventually & rather soon we were in each other's arms where we more or less stayed or wished to be staying the rest of the time. Next day we were back on Goree & Pratibha filmed us together. Tracy in her full beauty—& me so happy I was in a daze.

Soon it was time to leave. We arrived at my house & T stayed overnight & then we went to her house & stayed overnight & then came back to my house. Then went up to the country . . . & then back to the city, where I am in my bed on this lovely morning & she is coming soon & we will kiss.

April 4, 1993
After many glorious, nearly unbearably close & beautiful minutes, hours, days, weeks together, we had our first real fight, brought on by exhaustion. And I feel myself going to a deeper level of my psyche than I've ever done. Tracy is so present I must be also.

Monday, April 19, 93

What seems to be happening: fear of loving someone so much. Fear of loving someone who is so alert, wide awake.

Meanwhile I've started seeing Jean Shinoda Bolen.[1] I went last Thursday. Within the hour I talked about how tired I am of this fear of intimacy that I have. And of how I can't seem to control it. She said a number of really reassuring things: One, that the mechanism of internal retreat that I'm asking to disappear has protected me for many, many years, and is not to be discarded just because I want that now. That the body remembers & honors all its traumas & is still trying to protect me from trusting before it is wise. She says T & I are very new together & that what usually happens is that trust builds over time. Later I shared this with T who seemed to understand that this could be so.

I regret that entries about T & I are so skimpy. When things are going well & they mostly do, I don't think of writing. There is a very prosaic peace, and a very steady intense passion. She is so beautiful to me. Yesterday, just because her dark skin looks so ravishing in cobalt blue, I put on sheets of that color—& there she lay in a bed of cobalt blue, her dark eyes shining, her skin glowing, her beauty absolute. So absolute I sometimes feel my love is worship. We kiss & kiss & kiss some more, and somehow the distances have not destroyed any of our closeness while making us more conscious of its preciousness.

So much work not done. Or done in tiny fits and starts. T & I love being together. To my amazement I'm completely happy not only with her in my house but her & her dogs! This is certainly new for me. Robert sitting up in my house always made me feel uneasy, even when we were lovers. Still, I must work on my body—must join a club or something. My writing. Must write!

---

1 Jean Shinoda Bolen, M.D., is a psychiatrist, a Jungian analyst, and an author. Bolen's books, which explore archetypal psychology in the development of spirituality, include *Goddesses in Everywoman* and *Gods in Everyman*.

How Things Look Today, April 20, 1993

I have not seen Mercedes since returning from Africa, over a month ago. T & I are close. We snuggle, cuddle, talk about every & anything. She loves to read to me! We go to movies, on walks. Our happiness has been marred by my inexplicable & primitive moodiness & withdrawals. On this I am working, with Jean Bolen. T is moving to buy a house in the city, to be near me but also to have a base while she records (& practices) her new songs. She called earlier & said Jeanne Schneider (realtor) says she's found 6 prospects. They're to visit them on Thursday. I hope this won't be a day of disappointment for T. I like T's sister, Aneta. Wish she had a lover. Reminds me of Ruth. Very smart. Sweet. Loves T who definitely loves her too.

—

Cuba Journal

Havana[1]
May 4, 1993
7:06 p.m.
Rm. 409, Hotel Comodoro

I've just showered and washed my hair after a solitary swim at the little beach beneath my window. It is simple and a bit tattered, as is so much here. Yet the swim was tranquil, the water refreshing, the sun warm, the beach lounge chair afterward comfortable as I dried in the cooling sun & half-listened to the keening, moaning voices of African American women singers coming from the bar above the beach.

We arrived in Havana around ten this morning after gathering—our delegation—in Miami last night. We are nine people, male & female, including Gloria La Riva, Jalayne Miles, coordinators, Dennis Banks, Ramsey

---

1   AW traveled to Cuba with a delegation of other artists and activists in defiance of the U.S. blockade against Cuba. She spent two weeks in the country touring schools, hospitals, and child care centers and having meetings with Cuban officials and conversations with ordinary people.

Clark, Mitchiko, a neurologist and David Levinson, a doctor who lives in SF and takes care of indigent patients. Then there's Berta Joubert, a psychiatrist, and Diane Wong, an activist. There's Joe Friendly who is videotaping our journey.

—

In Miami I was met by Jalayne Miles & Gloria & Jae & then Dennis & Mitchiko, whom I like a lot. He's Japanese-American, slender, recently married to an Episcopalian Minister at St. John the Divine in New York City. He's warm, has a sense of humor & a nice laugh. Ramsey arrived later & I like him a lot too. He's such a classic looking Texas cowboy—in his skinny jeans & country boy haircut, but when he opens his mouth to the press there's a wonderful passion & power and commitment to justice. Hard to believe that he was once, under Johnson, Attorney General. He feels deeply familiar as well, and, at 66, I find him attractive & vital. Dennis has already turned into an elder, and I loved it that he brought along a drum he'd made himself—a shaman style drum—and at our press conference in Havana he beat on this drum, painted in the colors of the four directions, black, white, yellow & red and sang a "Journeying" song from his people's tradition—he's Anishinaabe. I met him long ago at Evergreen College in Oregon. I'm sure he doesn't remember it & we weren't introduced. He was young & joyful. His eyes sparkled. His long dark hair was in two thick braids tied with red ribbon. I think he must have been the first really healthy & in his own body Indian I'd ever seen. He was there lecturing about the American Indian Movement of which he was a founder. The next time I saw him was at his trial for murder (of an F.B.I. agent, along with Leonard Peltier, etc.) in Custer, South Dakota. There I had exerted my final energy to witness this major assault on his life & healed myself by doing so. He and I are extremely comfortable together & sat on the floor in the airport, on our luggage that is, & listened to the tribal songs he's recorded for Whitney Houston's producer, a guy named Narada[1] who lives in Marin & wants me

---

1   Narada Michael Walden, multiple Grammy Award–winning producer, musician, and recording artist.

to come to dinner with Dennis when I get back to SF. I said to Dennis, A guy named Narada. How could I resist!

Tonight we all gathered in my room to watch us on TV. Lots of Ramsey, some of me, a little of Dennis. I regretted especially that Dennis' song wasn't given a moment. It is so important that Cubans see an Indian, who brings the message always of survival & survival with dignity. Dennis had, at the press conference & at our briefing in Miami (in a house right at the bend of a river!) linked the U.S. government's policy of starving Native Americans into submission after 1866. What a difficult time this was for Indians & Africans! Because of course this was the very same time many black people were freed from slavery but starved into going back to their masters and working for no money. Out of this sharecropping, which so resembles slavery, came into existence.

An interesting gathering at the house by the bend in the river.

We each told something about our lives & why we are committed to standing in solidarity with the Cuban people during this horrendous crisis. I mentioned that my first political action, not related to Civil Rights, was to picket the White House during the Missile Crisis while JFK was president. How cold it was & how deep the snow & how Kennedy had sent out coffee & tea. This small gesture humanized Kennedy & telling about it to this day brings a smile. (Now I think it was probably some sensitive woman working in his office who did this!)

May 6, 1993

Tonight our delegation spent 3 hours with Fidel.[1] A tall, gray haired, big nosed, brown eyed man, rather thin since the last photographs I saw of him. At first he seemed petulant, cross. No, not at first. He greeted us in an anteroom of the

---

1 Fidel Castro, the communist revolutionary and politician who was president of Cuba from 1976 to 2008, met with AW and the diverse delegation of activists with whom she traveled. Looking back on this moment, AW notes: "When describing Fidel it is important to acknowledge he became a communist only after the U.S. invaded Cuba, was defeated at the Bay of Pigs, and subsequently cut off all imports of things like food and oil (even chicken feed!) that they needed. He was a revolutionary, anti-imperialist leader of the Cuban people who ousted a brutal dictator, Batista, and later became a communist by default."

revolutionary palace, very warmly. To me he said, holding my hand & brushing my cheek: I saw you on TV last night. He went around the room shaking hands & brushing cheeks. Then we followed him into a large hall of marble with large rocks & giant ferns. Green plants everywhere. Delicious drinks. A mojito, & orange juice. But perhaps this was <u>after</u> our long talk around the large, long table, where he had numerous questions for each of us and listened hard to our answers. He'd never heard of "female circumcision" and was appropriately shocked when, at his request, I graphically described it. He & Ramsey & Dennis & Nora (one of the doctors) also talked at length. To Nora about optic neuropathy; with Dennis about Indians, treaties & the reservation. With Ramsey about International Law. I presented him with many books & like a child he started flipping through them. I could see he was delighted. He said I'd brought him just what he wanted: The Color Purple in Spanish. I also brought tapes, which surprised & pleased him. I felt quite warm & at ease with him. Goddess, he loves to talk! On & on. So did one of his colleagues later.

Then we were fed some wonderful fried chicken snacks & some kind of seafood rolls & some cookies.

If at first he seemed petulant, worried, annoyed & even a bit demonic, by the time we left he was positively jolly. We all took pictures with him. I asked if I could hug him. He hugged me back & kissed the top of my head. Very sweet. As we were leaving he told me he'd always remember me. I told him he'd inspired me all my life & that I love him.

I felt our meeting, though shared with a dozen others, was complete. I feel I know him in a way I could not before meeting.

Yesterday, Cinco de Mayo was also amazing. We delivered $75,000 of medicine to the Red Cross. We did this at a hospital for children born with heart problems. When I was introduced there was a rousing standing ovation which surprised & moved me very much.

I'm glad I came, after all. Tomorrow I meet other writers. The ANC representative to Cuba & perhaps I'll see Nancy Morejon[1] at Casa in the afternoon. I hope so.

---

1   Acclaimed Cuban poet, critic, and essayist.

9 May 93
Varadero Beach, Cuba

Mothers' day. After a lovely time dancing with Miguel—a really beautiful Bolivian who lives & loves with Margot Pepper (friend of Tetteh Kofi, a buddy of Ayi Kwei's . . . small world indeed!)—in walked Assata[1] looking extraordinarily amazing. She had come to the hotel two days ago & we'd only had time for a brief encounter. She's beautiful, real, funny, and has made a good life for herself in Cuba. She sat on the beach while I had my daily short swim. She has long dreadlocks with small white shells on the ends.

A very interesting & enjoyable session at the Union of Artists & Writers. . . . The publishers of my book in Cuba were there & presented me with 3 copies of my book, Cuban edition. The editor wants to print Possessing the Secret of Joy as well. I was very pleased. They were only able to print 80,000 copies of The Color Purple & they sold them immediately. The Cubans love to read. It has amazed me that so many people have the book & bring it forth for me to sign. There was also a radio serialization of it that ran for a week. Everyone loved the movie. They like Steven Spielberg in Cuba & I wonder if Steven has ever been here. I think he'd love it.

May 18, 1993

I returned from Cuba on Tuesday, a week ago! I can't believe it has already been so long. On my last day we visited a hospital where children from Chernobyl are being treated. . . . The children—some bald, some with clumps of hair missing, some spotted from radiation burn/vitiligo—seemed in good spirits. Dennis encouraged them to sing for us, which they cheerfully did. Then he taught them the honor song he's been trying to teach me. It was the high point of our visit.

In the midi I went off with Assata Shakur to her house. Small, warm, colorful. Books & music everywhere. A real artist's house or rather a real

---

1   Black liberation activist Assata Shakur, who went into exile in Cuba after escaping in 1979 from a New Jersey prison, where she was being held on charges of killing a police officer.

intellectual's. . . . She's funny, smart & incredibly beautiful. Very Southern too. Warm & gracious. We talked a bit about being womanists, loving women <u>and</u> men. This was refreshing, to talk to another woman who loves the soul first & then the body.

Dinner later was given us by the hotel management & we'd begged for Cuban food! Beans & rice, por favor! It was delicious. Afterward we made the usual speeches but kept them short. There was a delightful small band & we danced.

I was dancing my way back to Tracy. And after Miami and a second class feeling first class trip back to SF, there she finally was, meeting me at the airport, with flowers. Black & bright & beautiful and beaming at me. The dogs were happy to see me as well, and as we sped away toward my house I felt I was already home. We made love for the next two days. Sleeping in each other's arms, eating in each other's laps. Where did I end & she begin? Then for the weekend: I went to watch her play soccer. She's a jock which amazes me. She has a very remarkable kick; I always knew her legs were strong. And I met her friend Maria & her son Tyler who cried when his mother went out to play & so I rocked him in my arms. He loved it. Me too.

At Temple Jook, with a chicken in the oven. I must get up now & put on the rice.

<u>Next day:</u> A fine <u>huge</u> solitary dinner last night, and deep sleep—after a couple of chats with Tracy—and a peaceful lying about in bed this morning until Wendy called & then Leigh.[1] The book[2] (with Pratibha) is going on nicely on their end.

---

1   Wendy Weil, AW's longtime literary agent, and her book editor, Leigh Haber, at Harcourt Brace.

2   AW and Pratibha Parmar had developed a book to accompany their film. Called *Warrior Marks: Female Genital Mutilation and the Sexual Blinding of Women*, it would be published in October 1993.

May 24, 1993

10:10 En route to Boston. T left, kissed everywhere I could reach, lying in my bed asleep, the dogs on pillows on the floor. She hurt her hand playing soccer and we put ice on it and were careful of it.

On Sunday we slept almost all day. She was sapped by soccer & by her injury & she'd been up late putting together the furniture for her studio. It is sweet hearing her sing new songs & accompanying herself on guitar. I <u>love</u> this. Sometimes the guitar is all she has on, or sometimes the guitar & a towel. I follow her about, admiring her beautiful back & waist & hips and wonderful strong arms. She likes to sing to me. Our song "Ouagadougou" she's retired for awhile. But I long to hear it. Perhaps when I return.

May 30

At Gloria's, where the light is always dim![1] But cozy & comfortable & happy. We've seen two movies & had two fine dinners since I arrived Friday, quite tired, from my reading in Boston & 2 days with the Zinns. I was comforted as always by the humor & warmth of Howie & Roz.

Her back was out a bit—cold from swimming too early in the bay—& I gave her a healing massage. She proclaimed it a miracle. The first massage she's ever had. I couldn't believe it. <u>She</u> massages him, however. She called to him & asked him to watch me so he could learn, but he didn't respond. While I was massaging her Tracy called. We're lovesick, homesick, longing for each other. I miss her so much and dream & daydream of her constantly. . . . I fantasize about her hands, larger than mine, & want them on me, so strong & gentle. . . . "I love you" are the most erotic words I know when she is making love to me—in fact, the only words that come to mind. When I am loving her, I whisper these words into her mouth, as I am breathing. She is amazing. A goddess & a jock. A child & a woman. A new being.

Love is always the same, yet each time it feels profoundly different. I

---

1 AW is in New York visiting with her longtime friend Gloria Steinem, after book events in Boston, where she spent time with her beloved former Spelman professor Howard Zinn and his wife Roz.

really do think Tracy is the first person that I love & also feel wholly proud of. Last night during a talk that had us both breathing heavily & laughing about "giving good phone" I told her she has my heart. She said "I'll take good care of it." I said "I know."

Today Gloria & I were planning a trip to the lower East Side to look at glasses. I got up, got dressed after washing my hair & discovered I was too pooped to go anywhere but back to bed. So that's where I went & listened to wonderful music from Africa—that strange land that one loves because it is home. I never hate Africa. Interesting. No matter how much I despair.

June 21, 1993
Summer Solstice! Longest Day of the Year!
Quite breezy, sunny. Beautiful! And I've had a perfect morning. I rose early feeling fine. My stiff neck (from sleeping in a draft) improved. Last night I walked—before sunset—to the Press House & back.[1] Frida set out with me but gave up when she saw how far I planned to go! It was a great walk, no one on the road. Besides, half of the road is my road! Anyhow. Must take my pedometer everywhere I walk. My goal is to work up to three miles a day. Came home, stripped, climbed into the Jacuzzi. Came inside, showered, got into bed. Later T called & we talked & laughed for a long time. This morning I woke with lots of energy & decided to bite the bullet & clean out my closet, which I did. It was such a pleasure. I had so much hideous stuff. I threw out about a third of everything I had there.

Then I danced for 30 minutes. Then lay in the sun. Then it was time to close up my beautiful house, say adios to my loyal cat & come home to the city.

In the morning I am expecting Gloria (Akasha) Hull who wants to interview me about spirituality.[2] Then at 3 a new rug is possibly coming. I should arrange the week with Jayne my new trainer.

---

1 Finished with her long-distance travels for the time being, AW is back at her country home in Mendocino and commuting back and forth to San Francisco.
2 A version of this interview would eventually be published in Akasha Gloria Hull's thoughtful and important 2001 book, *Soul Talk: The New Spirituality of African American Women*.

T & I talk several times a day. We'd be breathing into each other's noses if we could. She knocked herself out trying to make Neta's birthday[1] wonderful. Poor baby. I felt she was trying to make up for all the people she feels should be in her sister's life but aren't.

Work on our film book[2] is going well. I'm pleased with the interviews.

And so. I sent Rebecca [money]. No word on whether it was received though we've had some conciliatory talks. I still feel distant, as if she's remote from me. It almost feels the way it felt before I became a mother. Perhaps this is natural. It's hard to imagine her here, now. Sometimes I miss her very much. I miss her conversation. The freedom & fun of it.

T & I are planning a camping trip to the Grand Canyon which she's never seen. She'll love it I know.

July 1, 1993
It is after 8:00 in the evening, still light outside. I am in my bedroom in the city in the chair I so rarely sit in, admiring the simple beauty of everything: the mahogany sleigh bed, California "king" size, the plum colored sheets, the quilt, the golden Japanese fan that covers the humidifier, my reorganized CDs. Paintings & drawings.

As usual, amazing doings! Two nights ago there was a preview screening of "Warrior Marks" at the SF Art Institute.

The film is gorgeous. Strong. Powerful. Visually & emotionally sweeping. I am so happy with it. I hugged & hugged Pratibha. Even Ms. Chapman had to admit it's great. She & I and Neta went together, and after Prathiba & I hugged, she & I embraced.

I spent last weekend at her house & slept most of the time. I was so tired. Part of it is the push to finish "Warrior Marks" the book, and also my much increased physical activity, which means my joints & bones ache.

---

1 Tracy Chapman was close to her older sister, Aneta.

2 The book AW and Pratibha Parmar were working on, to accompany their documentary on female genital mutilation, *Warrior Marks*.

July 12, 1993

When T & I were last in the country, a few days ago, she was eating collard greens that I had cooked & poured some of the pot likker over her rice. It was so like my father's way that tears rose in my eyes. Trying to control myself I went to the bedroom & tried to either cry or stop crying. Soon I returned to the table. T. asked if I was ok. If I was <u>sure</u>? And my face "churned" up (an expression from childhood that fits the contortion of the crying face perfectly), and with huge tears flowing I said: <u>I Want A Father!</u> W A I L I N G! I cried & cried & she got up and held me. I said: <u>That's What I Want!</u> And in a while, still sobbing: <u>My Heart is Breaking!</u> And yet at the same time exactly I felt it was healing. I cried two whole buckets of tears and T moved me to the couch where all the pain of my parents' life washed over me & I wondered how much of this pain was my fault for having been born. T says it's not my fault & that even if I had not been born my parents might have been just as poor & oppressed & worked just as much. Not my daddy I said. For he, like me, was made for loafing & inviting his soul.

When I blew my nose it was like a river. So much water!

I connected this to a dream I had a few nights prior to the dam burst. I was visiting Quincy, eating French fries from a paper plate. He was as usual busy & distracted, but he & I were to go somewhere together, leaving his house. I looked out & it was <u>pouring</u> rain. I mean pouring. Flooding. Buckets. Quincy is the "father" I latched onto for 5 years. The rain represented the tears that came.

Now I must nap. Jayne my trainer came at 11, just after T and I made love. Now it is after 5 & I am <u>dragging</u>. Very happy though. And T has found a house she likes. Maybe.

So through buckets of tears, a downpour, I've left my father's house—with him! For after all was said and done I realized—not for the first time—that I deeply love him. Not the mean-spirited, misogynist, <u>sick</u> father who was always complaining, but the funny fat one who loved me. T amazingly— & not fat!—is very much like Daddy. Very dark, those same big dark eyes. Love of music. Life. Love of being on the road. Love of loving. I said to her this morning: My daddy would like you. And he would. I felt a pang of sadness that they'd never meet. Sorry that he'd never know that, through T, I've come back to him. It is true too, as T says, I <u>am</u> my father. Those parts of him that I miss so much are also in me.

August 5, 1993

Last night in the midst of talking of how much we miss each other T said "Maybe we should live together." She was nervous & half-joking suggesting such a thing. But I am ready to try it. Away from her I pine & pine, and can accurately call myself lovesick. I haven't felt good since the last time I kissed her. We know we love each other. We know we can live in the same house, in harmony with her dogs. Other practical matters frighten us, though. We talked about her moving in with me on Steiner. Me moving in with her on the ranch. And us living together in the country in Mendocino. We've been acquainted for about nine months, in love for six, and we've actually managed to spend a good five of those six months together.

August 19th.

Leigh Haber[1] & I were just talking about getting someone to transcribe my journals. She is of course eager to see them. This isn't what I want at the moment, I don't think. However I just realized an interesting thing: for many years I've said I would begin publishing the journals at 50. And then, because of the film, I wasn't able to come up with a manuscript (transcription). But look! The journal I kept in London & Africa <u>is</u> being published in <u>Warrior Marks</u>, even <u>before</u> I'm fifty! The Universe hears every little wish, and gets right with the program!

This is how I know there can be world peace.

Today Tracy will look at houses with Jeanne.[2] Two "big" houses that I'm eager to hear about. She's serious about wanting us to live together and

---

1 AW's book editor.
2 Tracy's realtor.

so am I. Though I waver just a bit out of sheer wonder. Is it really possible to live with someone I pursued, wooed, won? Someone who sings & plays guitar & walks around naked doing both? Consciousness is changing in the world. More & more people understand we must be grateful for all that we have. We must appreciate our bodies and our souls and the earth.

Sept. 8, 1993

Tomorrow is Daddy's birthday. He'd be eighty four. It's been 10 days since I wrote in this journal. The barbeque at Tracy's was fun, though I was frumpily dressed in sweatpants & tee shirt. The weather changed suddenly from foggy to hot sun & I'd brought only warm things. Met Hazel, T's mother. I liked her. Which puzzled Tracy. I think Hazel's in shock that T's her daughter & is so hugely successful & famous.

Tracy made homemade ice cream & 2 peach pies. Everyone brought delicious food. Next day the film was shown & Pratibha & I spoke to the gathering, all piled into the downstairs bedroom & study. It's still beautiful, powerful.

Rebecca, Angel,[1] Tracy & I stayed in the country until Thursday. Eating wonderfully, sleeping late. Having a great time getting to know each other. Then we all came down to the city & they went on to New York. Rebecca & I much better. I like Angel. We all like Tracy & vice-versa.

Meanwhile Mama is finally in the nursing home—& seems to be improving! Suppose she gets better!

Sept. 10, 1993

My mother died last night. Sept. 9. My father's birthday.

---

1   Angel Williams, a Black woman, was Rebecca's romantic partner.

9-21-93

She had been in the nursing home less than a week. Now I am back from the funeral/ceremony and have spent an hour or so on the phone with my brothers who are (Bobby & Jimmy) going to help me with the funeral bill. I tried to ring Bill but no luck.

Rebecca & Angel met us, me & Tracy & Trajal,[1] in the Atlanta airport. We were met by Eddie, driving a long limo, and taken to the Ritz Carlton Hotel. A place with good beds, smoky rooms & dreadful food! This was Thursday. On Friday we went down to the plantation house for the wake, which was wonderful.

When we arrived everyone was eating. My brother Fred was there, Mamie, Ruth. Jimmy. I talked to Fred & Jimmy on the back porch. Introduced everyone to Tracy. Mamie took hold of her & even gave her a big kiss. All quite bizarre. Kept saying "She's mine." Anyhow, I went back into the air conditioned rooms where Ruth was. She was complaining as always. Nobody'd helped. She was in pain. Tired. Everything. I've heard all this before & was restless at once.

We waited & waited for Mama. Tracy & I decided to walk up the road a piece. I showed her Miss Reynolds' house. Cousin Lucille's house. When we started back to the old house we saw the hearse. We stood & watched it go past. Then stood—with Rebecca & Angel & Trajal & Miss Cook—as the undertakers (sons of Mr. Hurt) took off the doors to the room she (Mama) would be in. I picked up the trash from around the door & steps just as the man lifted the coffin & walked it the short distance between hearse & door.

They very gently brought her in, in her nice pine coffin, and surrounded her with flowers. So many. Two or three truckloads of flowers. At last they opened the coffin—& there she was. Still so beautiful, & with attitude! She seemed on the verge of speaking. Ruth & I went up to see her. And Rebecca & Tracy & Angel & Trajal. She was wearing a dress Ruth

---

1 Trajal was a longtime friend of Rebecca's, now part of the extended family.

had described simply as "green." But really it was more aquamarine & looked like Caribbean ocean water. She wore pearls, 3 strands intertwined, around her neck, and she had a corsage of pink flowers. A bouquet of them in her hands.

I reached under the netting and touched her hand. It still felt like her hand. I went to the head of the coffin and stroked her hair. Very soft & I thought darker than usual. Tracy, Rebecca, Trajal & I sat on the couch as people came & went. It was so beautiful. The many children, the soft spoken adults. The colorful flowers. There was such a feeling of realness, it was truly an experience of great fulfillment. I was happy.

At some point I asked everyone to leave & I introduced Tracy to Mama. Tracy told her she loves me & will try to take care of me. I told Mama I love Tracy & told her how compassionate, courageous, talented and kind Tracy is. I told her Tracy & I were together and in my heart asked her to bless us.

We went back to Atlanta & drove down the next day for the funeral. It was amazing. Surely the largest one ever had in Eatonton. The procession went on for miles. Every car we met pulled off the road & stopped. The police escorts took off their caps & placed them over their hearts. And Mama's little body rolled serenely along. Me, Ruth, Rebecca, Tracy & James Lee, a cousin, rode together just behind her.

The service was in the Kingdom Hall. A "nice" building, sterile & pastel, with "Blessed be Jehovah . . . Unify my heart to fear thy name" inscribed on the wall of the pulpit. It was a great shock to have a white JW[1] offer the opening prayer. A greater shock when people were asked to sing "All Things Made New," a completely boring unmelodic, tuneless tune, which to their credit the congregation didn't even try to mumble. Horrible. Then there came forward Bro. Hester, whom allegedly Mama wanted to preach her funeral. A complete disaster. Cold, no emotion, literally. No grammar, either. A proselytizing sermon whose only mercy was its brevity.

---

1   Jehovah's Witness.

Then my brother Jimmy came forward & talked about Mama. He was funny & warm. Human. He made people "see" & feel Mama. Remember her as she truly was. Full of the light of life. Appreciative, always.

Her told of her love of old things. How she'd give away the money she was given to buy a new dress—she'd decide her old one looked just fine.

He told about the time, while she was sick, she wanted ice cream. "If I don't get ice cream," she told Mary Alice, "I'm gon cry." This story made everyone smile. His reminiscences of Minnie Lou saved the day.

Rebecca, Tracy & I had walked in behind Mamie, pushing herself ahead of Ruth "because I'm her first born daughter," & Ruth, supported by two men as if she'd suddenly become too weak & "feminine" to stand on her own feet. I avoided letting the funeral home handlers handle me. Holding hands, Rebecca on one side & Tracy on the other, we stood in front of the coffin & wished Mama a safe journey to the abode of Willie Lee, Fannie Lou, Martin, Malcolm, Lorraine Hansberry, Ché. Etc.

I hadn't realized no one but baptized Jehovah's Witnesses are permitted to speak at their gatherings. Even Ruth couldn't speak because, though a member, she's not baptized. I thought this outrageous.

I had wanted to speak & Rebecca. But I was content with Jimmy's speaking—I also felt this was Mama's religion & although I detested it, it was what she chose for herself & for her last rites.

The service part of the funeral was very unfulfilling. Boring, dry, tuneless. I wished my cousin Carolyn had been able to preach over Mama. She'd have been perfect. These white male dominant rituals lack soul.

And so, back to Atlanta, & then on to SF. Throughout our time in Eatonton Tracy & I close and happy. Lying twined in each other's arms, marveling still that it's so good & we are so blessed. I enjoyed introducing her to my mother, my family. Everyone was fine.

—

Dear Angela–

I've given our 50th (can you believe it!?) birthday celebration[1] a lot
of thought; this is some of my thinking: That we rent Greens (the
restaurant) for our birthday dinner party. That we precede dinner
with a cruise (selected guests) around the Bay. We could watch the
sunset from beneath the Golden Gate bridge!

As you know, Greens is a beautiful big open space, with a lovely
view of the marina. I don't know if they ever rent it out, but I
could easily find out. I'd like this to be a real bash, and so I propose
inviting not only our friends but all those we've worked with over
the years as well as all those we admire enough to want to share
the evening. It should be a fund raiser. My half (after expenses)
would go to FORWARD International, the group out of London
that campaigns against genital mutilation, & your half could
perhaps go to the Black Women's Health Project (or whoever else
you wished.) Only our friends would be on the boat, though.

Tracy has offered to provide the music—she & her band! Maybe
you have to be fifty before the truly incredible things happen!

Anyhow. We could charge a lot for the tickets. But here I'm in
over my head. I would suggest Belvie Rooks as the person to be in
charge of this event. She'd do it all beautifully. We'd probably get
the black sister who catered Henri's birthday party to supply food.

It can be awesome!

I suggest doing it on Feb 6, Bob Marley's birthday, which falls on
Sunday.

Do let me know your thoughts.

My mother was serene & somewhat attitudinal in her
glowing knotty pine coffin, with photographs of her children &

---

1   AW and activist Angela Davis would both celebrate their 50th birthdays in early 1994,
Angela on January 26, Alice on February 9.

grandchildren tucked all around her. Her old spirit, resolute & irrepressible, shone bright. She seemed about to make a pithy, Sagittarius blunt comment to all who wandered up to view. It was an amazing, wonderful leave-taking. She was so respected in our community, it was as if the mother of the village had died. It was probably the largest funeral ever in our town & the people, relatives included, were on their best behavior & just as beautiful as they could be. Remarkable. Tracy & Rebecca & I were together, & I was able to introduce my mother & Tracy after all.

Love to you,

September 27, 1993

Coming to the close of this journal, which I bought last December in Mexico. My mother has died, after less than a week (?) in the nursing home. My relationship with Robert ended, finally. Painful, but what a relief! The way I see it now the relationship died in 1984 or thereabouts when he told me of his affair with A. So for the next <u>nine</u>, well, eight years, we were going through the motions. I was. He says he was always "performing" and so I guess he was just going through a different kind of motion. And I stood it as long as I could because otherwise I was alone. Then, Thank the Goddess, I just flat out got sick of him, the pretense, & of myself pretending feelings I hadn't felt in years. Threw myself at Mercedes, and what a distraction from my dilemma she turned out to be. But at least I learned one thing from Robert: don't let the distraction attach itself permanently. But how sticky she proved. And how hard to forget.

I went to hear Tracy in October, we met in November. . . . We dated in January. Fell in love in February. Now we've been breathing into each other's noses for 8 wonderful months, and I am happier than I've ever been, I think. I say I think because I've been plenty happy in this life of mine & never so much as when I'm in love.

And so, there are friendships that feel solid: with Angela, Deborah, Henri, Gloria, Belvie, Max, Joan . . . I wonder if I'll ever be friends with Robert?

My relationship to my brothers has improved, and mostly I like them, crazy as they are. I keep trying to understand what happened to them, & succeeding. I'm thinking of doing a documentary about them called "Brothers." I'm actually curious to know who they are.

I own three houses & feel I could let go of one or two. Houses no longer mean love to me. Love means love. I know I want to be with Tracy, wherever that is. Maybe in all our dwellings, maybe in one. I have money. Enough.

What do I want now? I want the film "Warrior Marks" & book to do well. And I want to stay home, with Tracy, doing the things we enjoy: cooking, eating, dancing, hugging, kissing, sleeping, making love, reading to each other, playing with the dogs, lying in the hammock. Talking. Laughing. I want to be with her. I don't need the travel. The audiences. The coming & going that destroys the "eternity" I once discovered in myself.

Great Beauty you have blessed me beyond my wildest dreams. I love you & Tracy as one. Thank you for your radiant shining self.

——

Not being true to yourself is the only death

San Francisco
Oct 8, 1993

Toni Morrison won the Nobel prize today.[1] . . . Everyone has been clamoring for a comment. So I jotted one down & gave it to Joan to disperse. It says something like this:

"No one writes more beautifully than Toni Morrison. She has consis-

---

1   The 1993 Nobel Prize in Literature was awarded to Toni Morrison in recognition of her body of work, particularly her novels, which were "characterized by visionary force and poetic import," as the Nobel Foundation said in its October 7, 1993, press release announcing the award. "My work requires me to think about how free I can be as an African-American woman writer in my genderized, sexualized, wholly racialized world," Morrison wrote in her 1992 book of essays *Playing in the Dark: Whiteness and the Literary Imagination.* "My project rises from delight," she added, "not disappointment."

tently explored issues of true complexity & terror & love in the lives of African Americans. Harsh criticism has not dissuaded her. Prizes have not trapped her.

"She is a writer well deserving of this honor."

Tracy & I were in bed when the call came—we spent most of last night "making up" after our stormy camping trip[1]—and when I got back into bed after listening to the message machine, I told her of my ambivalence. That there's no feminist consciousness (except in <u>Sula</u>, which I like a lot) in her work and that it is beautiful without moving you anywhere. She liked <u>Song of Solomon</u> very much, which I didn't. Anyway, she said "better Toni than some white man or woman who isn't half as good." And I agree. Anyway I sent flowers and a note to Toni. And I hope she <u>is</u> happy, as Tracy says she later heard over the radio.

———

Wendy just wired 157,000 to my account, my half of <u>Warrior Marks</u>, the book. I must invest or save this, otherwise I will slowly, or not so slowly, give it away. Ayi Kwei[2] wrote asking for a 10,000 loan to launch a publishing company out of his home in Popenguine. I've sent it. Also loaned Elizabeth Sunday the same amount for her line of children's "African" clothing. And so on. Frankly, I enjoy circling the creative energy of money in this way.

Deborah[3] & I had a great time shopping the other day. I bought black jeans, a black sweater, black slacks. Shoes. It was wonderful. Later we went to Khan Toke & had fried fish & rice & soup.

We leave for London on Thursday. . . . Apparently "Warrior Marks" will air on national television in Britain just before we arrive. Then on to Birmingham & Paris!

I turned down the wimpy BBC offer for <u>Possessing the Secret of Joy</u> & Joan says Pratibha may have found an independent producer.

---

1   Alice and Tracy had gone camping in Yosemite.

2   Respected Ghanaian writer Ayi Kwei Armah was AW's longtime friend.

3   Deborah was AW's friend and occasional travel assistant. Khan Toke Thai House is a restaurant in San Francisco.

I'm moving too fast. That's the major thing "wrong" with me. I keep dreaming of going really slow, just having chickens & the occasional book. I want a more settled home life. Predictable. Shared. Poor Tracy, she's trying to build and buy a house for us, but the going is rough. Everything on the market is either hovel or castle. And there's no way her house in the country can be built before next fall. I've been moved by her persistence in trying to find a place for us. Though how relieved I felt when I realized I don't want to leave my house; not the one on Steiner, where I am writing this, or Temple Jook.[1]

Finished, roughly, the transcription of volume one of my journals. The writing for the most part is that of a married woman & so not free. I was also young & inexperienced. There's a distance from myself that I feel keenly as I read. I was in reality learning how to live. Literally how to stay alive, to work, to love. With Mel's help I learned this. He was my Shug. One of them.

Oct. 13, 1993

Why do I keep trying to figure out what's wrong with me? The person I have most loved on earth (or in heaven) has died. I am feeling lost, bereft. Sad & sorrowful beyond measure. I thought it would be different. I wouldn't feel so lonely for her. I do feel lonely for her though. For her warmth and tenderness & generosity. Her absolute integrity as a woman & her kindness.

I went for a half hour walk on the marina. There was one brown seagull who adopted me, flying along beside me, then going on ahead only to stop & wait for me. It pulled me out of my gloom. For I was deep into it, feeling myself very quiet, too quiet inside. I met a woman on the path, a white woman my age with orange red hair & she was smiling to herself as I so often do: a smile signaling a delicious secret. A new lover perhaps. Joy, in any case. I recognized her happiness. It was mine a month ago.

Talked briefly with Henri[2] who says these feelings are normal, even

---

1 Temple Jook is the name AW uses for her house on the Wild Trees property in Mendocino.

2 Henri Norris, AW's old friend and onetime assistant.

the ones I'm having with my period. Emptiness. Lethargy. Absence of passion.

My brother Jimmy, who had Mama's money, has sent a blank check. I've taken 2,000. I'm so glad he sent it, as he'd promised. My brothers make me happy when they keep their word.

October 16, London, 6:45 a.m.

The premiere went well. Though the town hall, which seats 1,000 people, was too large & cavernous. 778 people came, a large audience that didn't seem as large because of the space. And the sound echoed a bit. Still the film is wonderful & the audience applauded strongly & long at the end. Then Pratibha, Efua & I went onstage to answer questions. Pervais, the director of the festival, was onstage with us. A sweet & good looking Pakistani-British man, who later took us to a terrific Indian restaurant.

I said to Pratibha after leaving the stage: one down, eight to go! Tues. we go to the opening in Paris.

It's Sunday. I believe the sun is shining—it has been since we arrived! Soon everyone will be up & packed and ready to get back to London by train. The ride here was fun. We had sunny seats & had tea & sandwiches. Tuna & cucumber. I was very grateful that it was edible.

And so where am I now? I slept well last night. I didn't wear my contact lens last night to the premiere. Felt fine about it. Showing my "Warrior Mark" that is. Wore my orange sweater & black Laize Adzer pants, the new shoes I bought & the vest with elephants that Deborah gave me.

I can see that I am aging. It's such an interesting sight. I begin to see a mature face & body. Well. I am forty-nine—perhaps I shall live as long as my mother. Perhaps not. In any event, I've lived over half of my life. I never thought I'd reach fifty. If I do, I will continue to increase my capacity to understand & to love, for it is in this area that I feel I <u>have</u> matured & in which I've found the most joy.

Asked Pratibha to write the screenplay to <u>Possessing</u> with me. I think she's a good writer & this collaboration should make it <u>fun</u>! I <u>like</u> fun. So does she.

I must get my book <u>The Same River Twice</u> completed while in Mexico.

The Same River Twice
A Meditation on
Making
A Movie
of
The Color Purple

10 Years Later

by

Alice Walker

Nov. 1, 1993, 3:27 a.m.[1]
In bed! The Lowell Hotel
NYC
My schedule looks full. I must eat well, exercise (the park is nearby) & take all my vitamins!

Pratibha's in the hotel. Gloria sent over a lovely throw with sun & moon on it. I feel blessed to have such friends.

Nov. 2.
A tense 5 minutes on the Today Show. Then a relaxed and lively half hour on WBLS, the black soul station that plays mellow music & that today was urging folks to vote. For Mayor Dinkins who looks like he may lose.[2]

I went for a lovely walk in Central Park. The leaves are red & gold & they've closed off a stretch just for walkers & carriages. I came upon the ice skating rink & was mesmerized by the skaters. I think I actually had

---

1 The tour for the film *Warrior Marks* took Alice and Pratibha to London, Paris, and, in this entry, New York.

2 New York City's first Black mayor, David Dinkins, lost his bid for reelection on November 2, 1993, by a slim 2 percent margin, to Rudolph Giuliani, who became the city's first Republican mayor in a generation.

a religious experience. They were a mosaic of the city, of the country. Of the world, really. Yellow & white & brown & black, all skating merrily along to quite good music. All young people, some of them just at puberty. I loved the gracefulness of their bodies, their nonchalant sloping steadiness. I was so moved! Above them & beyond the ring of trees there were the tall buildings of Central Park South & on one of them an American flag, roiling in the wind. I thought how much we need a new flag to represent the emerging America. But because it was presiding over this precious scene I felt close to it. Maybe because the song that was playing was "And You Were There . . ." & I mentally created a commercial for Love, with the skaters going peacefully around the rink, all colors, male & female, & the leaves turning, red & gold, and the tall buildings in the background . . . etc.

Didn't really want to come back to the hotel. <u>Loved</u> being out. My body was as happy as Ginger![1] But I came up & lit a fire & soon Rebecca arrived & she & I and Pratibha went to eat at an Indian restaurant Rebecca thought was great & I thought too spicy & overpriced.

Tomorrow I'd hoped to see Mike Rudell,[2] but that will have to be cancelled. I have something on CNN & a ribbon cutting ceremony & the opening!

Nov. 5, early morn.
In bed at The Mayflower.
The opening was terrific. Gloria & Bill & Bella Abzug were there. Rebecca & Trajal & Joanne Brasil & Charles. Mike Rudell. Sonia Sanchez. Wendy. We're all mesmerized by the film. Afterward there was a good question & answer period. I will write about it later though as I must rise very early tomorrow morning, fly back to NYC for the Charlie Rose Show, and then on to Atlanta.

---

1 One of Tracy's dogs.
2 AW's lawyer and old friend.

Wed. O'Hare, Chicago. En route to San Francisco.

Last night was wonderful. The people of Chicago packed the theatre—many couldn't get in. A warm, thoughtful, passionate audience who gave me many gifts. Including a coat woven by a young woman who was inspired by my description of the color Power Blue in The Temple of My Familiar. A beautiful dark haired white little sister whose face was like the humblest flower. I also received a notebook from a woman who told me it is from the last Islamic matrilineal society—in Sumatra. Someone else gave me pins—one says "African Amazon," the other "Sisterlove." Someone else gave me sunflowers. I also collected poems & hugs. The reception was in the Harold Washington Library, a new building built to look old. Spacious, elegant,— and we were greeted by 5 black women & a little boy playing shakeres. I spoke briefly, thanking everyone for their sweetness—which Pratibha & I felt the minute we landed in this otherwise cold & drab Midwestern city. My suite at The Ritz was sunny & comforting. The food very good. Chicken soup that actually seemed like the real thing.

Even though 600 people (according to the paper) came out in Atlanta, the energy was low. I felt the organizers were disorganized, not terribly happy to be working together, and tired. It was also in the middle of the afternoon, at Georgia Tech, a school I've never visited before. Still, the questions were good, and overall I thought people were thoughtful. The day after Tracy & Pratibha & I went to visit Mama. My old school. My old house(s). It was great being with them. Tracy drove. I took some leaves from the old house trees to put on my mother's grave.

I'm too tired to write coherently. We're all sitting here on the runway, very unhappy about the delay. Everyone wanting to be home. My biggest regret so far is that I was so wiped out by the time Tracy joined me in Atlanta. But she says she managed to have some good times with me even so. The night she arrived I was so tired I could hardly speak.

Nov. 23, 1993

At home in the country after the tour of '93!

Feeling a little stronger. The sun is shining. The valley serene. The tour exhausted me. After Chicago I came home for a day & a half, which I spent with Tracy. Very good. We went—she, 'Neta & I—bike riding near her ranch. It relaxed me wonderfully. I trudged off to Seattle & a wonderful crowd. There were 2 showings of the film. Bushed after a lovingly (by black women) prepared dinner of jerked chicken & peach cobbler. Then a day or so of rest & Belvie accompanied me to L.A. where the showing was fine & I saw Quincy after nearly 7? years! He looks good & was with his lover, Nastasia Kinski,[1] who seemed very sweet. It seems obvious that the love songs on Back on the Block were for her. I asked about their child, Kenya. They say she's big and fine. We hugged and it felt great. Also saw his daughter, Jolie.

Then back home. Then the final event at the Castro.

Just talked to Tracy. We're planning the Thanksgiving menu which sounds wonderful. Gumbo. Chicken. Greens. Rice. Sweet Potatoes. Etc.

Nov. 24

Thanksgiving Menu

Alice's Gumbo
Alice's Chicken (2)
Cornbread Dressing
Rice
Tracy's Green Beans w/ Mushrooms
Jackie's Cranberry Relish
Cornbread
Gravy
Pie
Drinks? – Wine, Ice Tea

---

1   Nastassja Kinski, the actress who was now Quincy's partner.

Nov. 30, 1993

Thanksgiving has come & gone. Rebecca & Angel, Jackie & Aneta, Tracy & I. Ginger, Tasha, Frida.[1] A full house. The house handled the day & the guests beautifully. In fact, six people can be perfectly comfortable here. Jackie slept on the sofa. Neta in Frida's room. Rebecca & Angel in the guest suite.

Jan. 19, 1994

Where to begin? Careyes was in many ways a disaster. I spent the 10 or so days there [addressing household maintenance issues] & putting Casa Careyes on the market. Not even reluctantly. It seemed clearly more than I can handle alone & I dislike having to think about "employees" while on vacation. There was no vacation. So the day after Christmas we packed up and came back to S.F. Things had gotten so bad we broke up! Fortunately, we didn't stay that way for long. Then the day after we arrived, Tracy came down with bronchitis. For the next 2 1/2 weeks she was very sick. During that period we were able to go out to Zuni for New Year's eve & brought in the new year with glasses of champagne & over 4 dozen oysters, which we all discovered we love! Even Neta, who'd never had any. It was a beautiful beginning for the year.

In my absence I was attacked in Newsweek by some African/Arab women—principally Nahid Toubia,[2] whom I nicknamed "the general" because of her military bearing. I've felt distressed by her comments. She thinks I'm doing the anti-FGM work because I am "a fading star trying to get back in the limelight." Which planet is she from? It hurts more to be criticized by black women—who you know must be just as tired & frustrated as you are—and even though the criticism reflects their desires more accurately than yours.

Then there was the letter from someone who said that in his culture there is a saying: "To tell the truth hurts the people." And that I've hurt Africa by

---

1 To recap the relationships: Angel is Rebecca's partner; Jackie is Tracy's best friend, and Aneta is Tracy's sister; Ginger and Tasha are Tracy's dogs; and Frida is Alice's cat.

2 Nahid Toubia is a Sudanese surgeon and activist for women's health rights; she specializes in research on female genital mutilation.

speaking out against FGM. This depressed me no end. Just the thought that somewhere there are people who think this way. I try to imagine such a society & it is a picture of hell. The beauty of truth is that it is reality. One breathes a sigh of relief to know what is, what one has to go on, to factor in, to survive.

Apparently there is much controversy & questioning of my "motives." It's all quite stressful & makes me wonder if anything substantive will occur to stop the mutilation of children. Adults like Toubia seem to want to own the issue rather than work to change it.

Jan. 25

Today was wonderful, and for curious reasons. Tracy left on Monday, yesterday? around noon. I went for a long walk, down to the end of the main road in one direction & then down across the field to the garden, where I planted bok choi & garlic.

This morning I meditated in bed with Frida at my knees. Went for another long walk. Had a nice dinner. Read. Made soup. Wrote Ayi Kwei . . . told him some of my troubles. His silence about my work disappoints me, but I'm glad I wrote the letter. I need practice on the new computer & I enjoyed working on it.

I caught some of Clinton's State of the Union message—very fine. Though he & Hillary look exhausted.[1]

And me? I'm rested, I think. Finally. Still a bit touchy, but, overall, I realize I'm probably the only person truly concerned about the attacks on me. Other people have their own problems.

Anyhow. Everyone I've invited is coming to my party.[2] Gloria, Wilma, Jean, Clarissa, Carole, Ruth, Aneta, Tracy, Joan, Angela, June,—moi—who else? Belvie.

I've missed my solitude so much! It is healing beyond words.

Great Spirit may I soon wake & walk & be in you. I miss your presence most of all. Your grace. Thank you for bringing me through the fire.

---

1   Bill Clinton had been inaugurated as president a year earlier, in January 1993.

2   AW was turning 50 on February 9 and was planning a private party to celebrate. The joint fundraising party she'd proposed with Angela Davis never came together due to scheduling conflicts.

Feb. 28, the last day of the month!

I can't believe the time has gone so quickly. At this rate I'll be a hundred before I know it.

My birthday gathering was delightful. The day before Ruth, Clarissa & Wilma arrived. I cooked chicken, greens & rice. Ice cream for dessert.

March 7, 1994

Meanwhile there's a major flap in the papers over the removal of 2 of my stories from the Calif. test for 10th graders. I hadn't a clue I was even on the test. Nor have these turkeys paid for the stories' use.

Anyway. "Roselily" is considered anti-religious by the Coalition for Traditional Values, or some such. And there's another group that presumably had "Am I Blue" pulled because it's "anti-meat eating." This is all so ignorant it's hard to focus on it. Yet it's tiring, too. So for two or three days—as Joan fended off the media: Today Show, Belva Davis, Connie Chung, Tom Brokaw, Hank Plant, Pacifica, etc.—I just stayed prone. In & out of the hot tub. Sunning on the deck. Reading trashy novels about middle class black bisexuals in the hammock.[1]

---

1 Likely E. Lynn Harris's first novel, *Invisible Life*, published in February 1994.

April 28, 1994

In South Africa black people are voting. Nothing over the past 342 years has swerved them from their goal of being free in their own land. I feel proud of them, and really like most of the world, awed by Nelson Mandela. 75 years old. Still sharp. Still a true lover of his people & respecter of himself. Still cute.

June 8, 1994

What a rollercoaster attempting to purchase a house with T has been! Three weeks ago we found the "perfect" house. Room for us, room for Joan/office, apartment for Aneta,[1] office/studio for T. We made an offer (1,000,000); very excited. Price was 1,195,000. The buyers countered. Testily. We countered. They countered. Aneta decided she didn't want to live there anyway. We canceled our bid. It was beautiful. Italianate Renaissance, 1903, on upper Ashbury. 900 in fact. I had practically moved in, & planned to rent out the house on Steiner. T very harsh in her negotiator mode. I would have paid the asking price & been in the house by now. But she maintained the house was not worth what the sellers were asking—in today's market. My thinking was: we love the house—I did anyway—and we have the money. But then with Aneta bailing out there was the question of tenants & would they leave gracefully, etc. All of this very stressful. I feel we've missed an opportunity to try something profoundly meaningful & different—& that the Universe offered us a gift that may not be offered again.

On the positive side: I don't have to move; though the camera toting tourists around my house drive me nuts. They're constantly taking pictures now of the gate I installed to keep them from perching themselves right in my door.

I drove up[2] mid-day. When I arrived I was tired but not really from driving. I seem to have a deep down fatigue & my feet and legs ache. I was shocked (again) to see how overweight I've become. I visited Alison LaVoy,

---

1 Joan is AW's assistant; Aneta is Tracy's sister.
2 To Wild Trees/Temple Jook, AW's country house in Mendocino.

my doctor, and told her of my odd aches & pains. She asked me to be tested for lupus and hyperthyroidism. I should hear something in 2 weeks.

Actually though I remember my slide downhill. I ate ice cream & cheese while Rebecca was here. She was always on the phone to Angel, and though we had a good visit together it was strained by her absentmindedness & her slovenliness. Not to mention her bad eating habits which I soon fell into!

T. accompanied me to L.A. to receive the Torch of Liberty Award from the ACLU. Not bad. Danny Glover presented the award & said nice things. I realized, not for the first time, that I don't care anymore about that whole side of life—the public side. At its best it's a nightmare—at least it was (the event) at a nice hotel & the food (room service) was good. The video they ran about me was poorly thought out. Imagine my surprise to have a white male voice talking about my life as if it knew about it.

Madness.

Anyhow. We came home & were happy to have endured the public & survived, one more time!

June 10

Nahid Toubia in <u>Newsweek</u> still feels genital mutilation is not my concern. She resents that I have "taken it on." She calls me an outsider. This is so depressing. Rebecca tells me G.W. says she "doesn't like Warrior Marks" but isn't going to say so publicly. To Rebecca's credit she told her, Good, because the other people who are speaking out against it are so reactionary.

T called yesterday and last night. I felt distant, cool. She goes on & on about her house. I'm past being charmed by her obsession. We talked briefly about her intention to send the dogs—<u>take</u> the dogs—to New Skete[1] for training. At least she realizes their bad behavior isn't cute.

And so, after being disappointed about the failed merger, I now feel,

---

1   An Eastern Orthodox monastery, located in Cambridge, New York, known for offering a comprehensive training program for all breeds of dogs.

truly, that it was for the best. I <u>like</u> having my own space. Living alone most of the time. Coming out of solitude into conviviality. There is also the matter of T's relative youth.[1] So much that fascinates her I absorbed 20 years ago. For instance <u>Living the Good Life</u>,[2] which she is reading, was given to me 10 or more years ago by Dan Wax.

—

One of the best days I've had for a while. And just to think, my calendar is empty! I can hardly believe it. I said to T: I want a year of not being "Alice Walker." Of not even having to think about the work people insist on sending me to do. I am sick of awards, of writing recommendations, of fundraising, of writing blurbs & forewords. Film reviews & comments too now & more & more entreaties from lesbian & gay groups with which so far (most are white, middle-class, extremely self-righteous & self-absorbed) I feel zero affinity.

Time to cheer up! I have more than enough money to support my year. I have a lover whom I love & who loves me. I have an abundance of friends—loving, courageous, strange, wonderful, full of themselves & the mysteries of the ALL. I have sore feet but will try to look after them. I will continue to exercise—since this <u>definitely</u> makes them better. I will improve my diet. Sugar must go. Those horrible sweeteners too. Olive oil cut to a minimum. Increase in walking. Swimming.

Great Spirit thank you for letting me see you. When I begin feeling gratitude I know I am healing.

---

1   At this point, Tracy was thirty; Alice was fifty.

2   *Living the Good Life: How to Live Sanely and Simply in a Troubled World*, by Helen and Scott Nearing, was first published in 1954 and reissued as a mass market paperback in 1973. It is the story of a couple who left city life in 1932 to move first to Vermont and then to a farm in Maine. The Nearings' food and living philosophies have served as models for many who seek a simpler way of life.

Monday 13

Last night I started reading The Dalai Lama. Not surprisingly I suppose—since I feel so Buddhist—he seems quite familiar to me. So sensible. So respectful of nature. He says he eats what's put before him & though he is vegetarian by nature he sometimes eats meat. He is honest about everything, though he declined to answer a personal question about shunya, emptiness. Of course this is something I'd like to hear about. Sometimes, like now, I feel so empty I can't imagine I've ever created anything or that I ever will. Each time there is a point at which I say: OK. I'll never do it. So what. I'll plant my garden & sweep my yard!

Still cold this morning. A smattering of rain.

I love the peace & quiet. The peace of mind.

Each time I vaguely think of turning on the white man's voice—radio or t.v.—I think Nah. What a joy to inhabit the world without its fake joviality, its treacherous (canned) laughter. Its relentless effort to make violence normal. Its hatred & fear of everyone & everything. Its sugary poison.

It is definitely raining. The view from my bed is of millions of trees. When I look at them I can feel them radiating endurance & serenity.

Aug. 23, 1994.

Tracy is auditioning musicians & she's found 2 she likes. I'm so happy for her. She called on her car phone sounding excited. She clearly cares for Roc, the drummer who is helping her set the band up. She's so unselfconscious when she sings. It's like breathing. I love it when she sings new songs to me over the phone.

The best new thing I've heard lately is Deepak Chopra. He's bringing Vedic knowledge to the West. He's wonderfully knowledgeable & upbeat.

Have been ringing Gloria daily. I was moved by the sweetness she is, on our trip to The Badlands. Tracy & I had to race to get our plane & didn't say a proper good-bye to her. I loved rambling through "The Door" & out into the landscape.[1] It is beautiful. Ravaged & beautiful & therefore extremely reassuring. Beauty abides.

Aug. 30, 1994

I completed the ms. for The Same River Twice[2] on the 26th, & yesterday gave it to Joan to copy. I'm sending a copy to Wendy & other copies to Gloria, Belvie, Rebecca, Robert & Tracy. Joan liked it very much, and I have her to thank for helping me dig deeper & aim truer at the subject.

Sept. 4

Few thoughts about my mother now, after writing about her in "River." I don't miss her as much as I thought I would. I appreciate her more, if possible. Whatever her flaws I remain in awe of her magnificent character.

Sept. 13.

Robert called yesterday to tell me he'd gotten the ms. of "River." And said "you caught me with my humanity showing!" And we had a good talk. I'd worried he'd be upset. He & Janet are getting "hitched" he says on June 11th. At the boathouse in Oakland. He's teaching at Berkeley, enjoying it; his book on Port Chicago's been bought by Turner Broadcasting. He's in a secure relationship. He sounds happy. I'm happy for him. We had some fabulous times together & were great, overall, as lovers. We learned & grew emotionally.

Meanwhile Tracy & I are trying to deal with the separations that seem a necessity of our life together now. She's auditioning musicians every day except the weekend. . . . I miss her severely at times & I know she misses me. Still it's wonderful to be able to come to Wild Trees for a few days. Renew friendships with people up here or just lie low.

---

1   Badlands National Park in South Dakota features an accessible trail that leads through a break in the Badlands Wall known as "the Door" and to a view of the Badlands. AW, Tracy, and Rebecca had joined Gloria Steinem and Wilma Mankiller, among others, to participate in a Pow Wow in South Dakota in mid-August.

2   AW's current working title for the book was The Same River Twice: A Meditation on Making a Movie of The Color Purple 10 Years Later.

Oct 20 – 1:30

Had dinner Sat. night with Angela & Belvie.[1] Angela as usual working on something re: women in prison. Getting ready for a class. She'd had some periodontal work done & had a swollen jaw. She had cut several inches off her locks & had 3 of them wrapped. She was sweet & easy to be with. I like her very much. I counseled her to dump the prison work temporarily & read romance novels.

Nov. 10, 1994

The Republicans & Christian Right swept the elections on Tuesday. Very distressing. Everyone: Rebecca, Tracy, Belvie, folks on KZYX sad. I called up the Native American broadcaster who sounded despairing & told him not to despair, that the Wasichus[2] had given us grief from the moment they arrived on the shores, but we are still here & we will persist in being us. Perhaps that is our only glory but it reflects Nature, our God.

Anyway, Scribner's offered 375,000 for <u>The Same River Twice</u>. We've made a counter offer of 500,000. Either way I'm apparently on my way into another adventure in publishing, Wendy[3] & I were saying: It might sell hugely. Or modestly. Scribner's is really buying my next novel, we agreed. Not this book. When we've reached an agreement on this book, I can begin the novel. I feel too much in limbo to start before.

Kate Medina, an editor from Random House, came to see me. She jokingly offered me the coat off her back—which I'd admired—to come to RH. We had a nice chat, but I like Leigh[4] better. I hope getting Scribner's to improve their offer doesn't do her in. (She later sent the most amazing orchid!) It lasted for a couple of months.

Great Spirit I thank you for the beauty all around me & that I am able to see and even occasionally to be it. Your rain is wonderful. Your sun superb.

---

1   Political activist Angela Davis and old friend Belvie Rooks, who AW once described as "the sister I always wanted."

2   Lakota Indian term for a white person—specifically a greedy white person.

3   Wendy Weil, AW's literary agent.

4   Leigh Haber, Alice's most recent editor at Harcourt, was moving to Scribner.

Your winds . . . everything you have created is cause for wonder. And that, underneath it all, is my permanent state.

Dec. 1! Unbelievable! Thursday. Very wet. Rain off & on.

I'm ready to begin my novel. I bought a new notebook & pasted a picture Angel took, of sunset over Careyes, on the cover. But like any commitment there is cause for patience. So even though I feel ready I won't begin until the story begins to write itself.

Dec. 14, 1994

Today is a wetter than can be believed Wednesday, and it is hard to believe indeed that the year is already coming to a close. I feel very happy, calm, centered. . . . Something seems to have shifted. Or perhaps I've just been combining the right minerals. I upped my dosage of calcium & magnesium & this stopped the aching in my hips immediately. And I've been taking cod liver oil.

Tracy called just before leaving her house to go to work. . . . I miss our great times together but overall I'm understanding of our situation. She's working so hard & there's so much driving back & forth! It saddens me to see her so tired. And oh, the music she's making for us in the world! So tonight she's coming to stay. . . . She & the dogs are like family. Even Frida seems to feel that.

Tracy has found—Goddess willing—a house! A big two story Victorian. There is to be an inspection tomorrow & she is to learn if the garage can be enlarged and a staircase installed connecting it to the basement. I hope this all works out. It seems to be the perfect house. Private, high off the street, roomy (Aneta will have an apartment) & peaceful.

Meanwhile I've agreed to loan Rebecca & Angel 50,000 to finance a coffee shop they want to open in Brooklyn: Kokobar. I can hardly imagine putting money into Brooklyn, but I love Rebecca & Angel & want to support them.

Now to meditate. Perhaps later to yoga!

Dec. 23, 1994
We are in Careyes.[1]

Rebecca & Angel arrived last night, Tracy & I the day before, on Winter Solstice.

Tracy said last night that it appears this house too is not to happen. She's afraid the tenants will give her grief. Not leave, etc. I feel so sorry for her. She seems so afflicted, as if everything must be hard & as if the universe can't be trusted to part whatever stormy seas that appear.

I doubt we are meant to make it together. She makes me anxious, self-conscious. I'm so used to flowing with life. With her I'm always backing up to explain myself. This is tiring to say the least. Anyway she's sound asleep upstairs. The house is wonderful—for sleep. Rest. Rebecca is also sound asleep. Angel & I are about to have tea.

What to do about the unease? Concentrate on having a good time. Concentrate on resting. Being in the sun. Swimming. Remember the guest is goddess! Be gentle. Smile. Don't get more upset over her ambivalence over owning a house in the city than she is.

Jan 1, 199[5].
Down below Rebecca, Angel, Tracy & Gloria are gathered. I've retreated to my bedroom. The day is breezy & overcast.

Last night we went to dinner at Playa Rosa. We made up a wonderful game using clichés. We eventually thought up hundreds or dozens. We had margaritas. I had one, very weak. Even so I'm suffering from it. At five of 12:00 we raced up the hill to Gloria's casita & brought in the new year there. I wish I could say I felt happy. I was, and have been, feeling very distant from Tracy who is too self-centered to notice most of the time. She & Angel lie about talking of computers & sports. But the long dinner game was fun. As was our drive down from Vallarta.

---

1 At AW's vacation home in Mexico.

Jan. 7, 1995

Incredibly I am home in SF, in bed. . . . Very happy to be home.

Tracy came by last night for dinner. We watched Marlon's last film "Black Is . . . Black Ain't."[1] It's wonderful if too long. We both contributed to its funding. bell hooks is very good in the film, so is Angela Davis, so is Essex Hemphill & Michelle Wallace. Michelle looks so hurt, I can't stand it. She's such a beautiful woman! As is Angela, who was recently photographed for Essence.

I finally became very weary of the way Tracy & I have been relating. She is obsessive about her dogs, her houses. She's doing so much now there's no time for us. When I see her she's tired, tight, no light or givingness. (Though on the material level she gave me tons of presents for Christmas: pottery, chilies, books, tapes.) As soon as we got to Casa Careyes she made love to me. I know she's stretched to the max—but the problem is, I want to be nurtured & her nurturing skills are limited. I want a companion with whom to share my life—almost daily. I want a home together with some-one. I'm ready to commit!

Tracy admits sadness. I told her we had come unbonded. And that I didn't see how, in our relationship, I could get what I need. She's committed to [her ranch]. I'm committed to Mendocino. I truly do love Mendocino. It feels like home, & is, in a very deep way.

I feel great. Very free. Relieved. Being alone doesn't frighten me. I enjoy it too much. And I now reach out easily & respond just as easily to friends.

---

1 *Black Is . . . Black Ain't* is an award-winning 1994 feature-length documentary by Marlon Riggs, exploring multiple, complex expressions of African American identity. Riggs, a tal-ented filmmaker, poet, and gay rights activist, had died in April 1994.

Jan. 20, 1995

Dear Tracy,

I am writing to apologize for being such a terrible host in Mexico.
However bad I was feeling, I wish I had possessed the will to be
more genuinely accommodating to you. My withdrawal felt awful:
it almost always does. I should have had the sense and energy
to go off by myself to the beach; that would have helped. Even
a walk up the road. But I was in the grip of a welter of painful &
conflicting feelings. And I'm so easily thrown off balance! When
Rebecca & Angel missed their flight my anxiety began. By the
time we reached the house I was fearful our time there would
be as difficult as all my other times. (Except for the time I was
there for a month—I always forget this—writing <u>Possessing</u>. . . .)
Then meeting two, three, four new people, having them
about the house, discovering the keys to the house (Rebecca's
responsibility) were lost, trying to figure out the new key set.
And the rest: Feeling so alone in dealing with the house, Estella,
Estella's children.[1]

I felt very unsupported. I was happy to see you & Angel connect
so well, but I felt much older, & excluded. Then on a day when I
was trying to regain balance Rebecca informed me that she & Angel
were separating. I found myself once again trying to be present
& helpful to them. Which was draining. I was also beginning to
see things about both Rebecca & Angel & their relationship that
disturbed me. I began to see how little I know the Rebecca who
lives with Angel.

Your comment about the amount of money I pay Estella was

---

1 Estella was the housekeeper and cook at AW's home in Careyes. A single parent, she'd
brought her daughters, nine and eleven, to work with her every day during AW and Co.'s
time there, and Alice found herself teaching the girls how to swim and taking on other such
child-care responsibilities during what was supposed to be a chosen-family vacation.

very wounding. In almost every instance, in every instance, in fact, in Mexico I've overpaid everyone. I have to stick more or less to the going rate so that I don't stick out as a fool—but I'm always approached for "loans" to build houses, pay for medicine, travel, children's needs. I've never said no. I am also extremely sensitive to the poverty of the people around me & am known there for my "regalo" giving. That is why Marcos[1] could ask me for a loan to build his house after a week, & why Rebecca said no. She knew I would never be able to. Because of my own poor background I have a hard time saying no to any poor person, & sometimes, as a consequence, I'm taken advantage of.

This may not make sense to you. But I wanted to express it anyway. Your judgment of me as someone who exploits others hurt me. It also made me realize how little you know me.

Anyway. These things—& more—notwithstanding: I am sorrier than you can imagine that those two weeks were wasted. It should have been a time of healing from all our separations. A time of rest & real relaxation. Instead it was tense & sad. I blame myself for not being able to rise above my internal conflict. But as I think back over it all I see many of the ways I might have gone rather than straight downhill.

First of all: Casa Careyes is beautiful & wonderful, but it was, as I said at dinner, a mistake for me to buy it. For all the reasons I mentioned. Basically it distracted me from my failing relationship with Robert—just as, years earlier, work on a magnificent ruin of a limestone in Brooklyn distracted me from a failed marriage to Rebecca's father.

I have a house complex. I really have believed that a beautiful place to live in itself meant happiness. Wrong. The happiness is made by the love shared by the people inside the house—no matter what kind of house it is. This is a simple but valuable

---

1   Marcos was the gardener for AW's home in Careyes.

lesson. It has made it possible for me finally to love people more than houses. . . .

When I see your obsession with getting a house(s) I see myself. I've watched you turn away from our relationship in the effort to build/buy a place for the relationship to be. Sadly, there is not to be the relationship we envisioned. But don't end up like me (not that this is how I intend to remain!) with two beautiful houses & no one to share them with. You are young. You will go on (as I will— though not so young) into other relationships. I urge you to make them more of a priority if you want them to last.

This is not to cast blame. I think you are wonderful, and I continue to love, admire & respect you. This is offered as a friend who has felt very low on your priority list for the past half year. After the houses, the dogs, Aneta, horseback riding, your work as a musician. All of these things important but, because of my anxiety over abandonment—from childhood & my mother—very hard on my self-esteem. . . .

. . . And so. I hope you are well & that you will get someone to help you. I worry you will exhaust yourself & fall ill. Take your vitamins, eat regularly. Keep warm. . . .

Love,
Alice

P.S. What I have left out, because I really didn't know how deeply I was affected, is my brother's diagnosis of leukemia. Bill is my favorite brother. The only one I feel I somewhat know & understand. The one whose love feels genuine. I knew that if Greg[1] was willing to call me in Mexico it was serious. And this too began to hang over me. These past days, speaking to Bill almost daily, I've

---

1   Bill's son, AW's nephew.

reconnected to some of my early memories about & feelings for him. I felt, when I spoke to Greg, that he has only the slimmest of slim chances. Because of his age & weight & general poor health. I've felt sad that I did not go sooner & tape his story—as he asked me to.

Jan. 26, 1995

In bed in Karla's room, upstairs in Gay & Bill's house.[1] I flew to Boston on Tuesday. A smooth, pleasant flight. I read half of <u>The Art of Raising a Puppy</u>, which Tracy let me borrow before I left. It's terrific; I've learned things about puppies I never dreamed. All of this in preparation for bringing Marley home on Bob's birthday, Feb. 6. Tracy & I went up to Sebastapol to meet Marley—& the breeder, Madeline Hill—last week. Marley, somewhere in the swimming pile of 10 puppies, was asleep, dreaming, snuggling for warmth. At 4 weeks she is deaf & blind, with only her sense of smell to guide her. And the need to be warm. The pups & their mother were in a clear enclosure in Madeline's garage. We met the father, an affectionate, curious, somewhat excited black lab. The mother is chocolate. The mother very appealing. The father a heavy licker.

Greg picked me up at the airport. We had our usual relaxed time on the way to Beth Israel. When we arrived my brother was surprised & pleased. And so I've spent the past two days massaging him. His legs, which are heavy with edema, his feet. His left arm. In fact, he is so water logged the second chemotherapy hasn't begun. But yesterday—after diuretic medicine & my massage (of which I am proud! Because he loves it, it relaxes him & puts him to sleep!)—he lost 14 pounds in one night! Lots of peeing. And today I bet he's lost another ten—and they are to begin the treatment this evening. He looks like Buddha. Very fat, very placid, very solid. He's losing his hair and yesterday when I massaged his head some of it came out in my hands.

---

1 AW is visiting her brother Bill and his wife, Gay, in Boston, where she's reconnecting with family, including Bill's children, Greg, Karla, and Kim, and spending gentle time with Bill as he faces his leukemia diagnosis.

There was a famous baseball star visiting him when I was there Tuesday evening. "Mo" somebody. Very nice guy. Lots of muscles. Thoughtful. Serious. I liked him a lot. He promised to bring Bill a Red Sox baseball cap. He's also sending a barber to cut his hair.

Also met one of Gay's nephews. Ronnie. Very handsome man. Dark brown, silvering hair. A lover of massage.

It's been fun meeting the people who love Bill. And the doctors & nurses are some of the warmest, most thorough I've ever seen. I especially like Dr. Robin Joyce—she explains everything. At length. She's funny & honest. Everyone touches Bill. He seems happy.

Bobby[1] flew up for a couple of days. Huge but really stylish. His hair in braids. Nice black jeans & black sweater. Beautiful buttery brown cowboy boots. I admired them so sincerely I think he might buy me a pair.

Jimmy told me, for an hour, all about his physical traumas. He looks bad. He's lost most of his hair. His skin is gray & slack. His body changed. Pot belly. Bony shoulders. A little old man already. I felt sorry for him & listened as best I could—given my exhaustion. My brothers are monologists basically. They rarely even seem curious about the lives of their listeners. And certainly not about my life. Although Bobby, who's going to Careyes in April, is very curious about Mexico. I hope he & Deborah will enjoy it. I must ask Rebecca to have Miguel replace the hammock.

I've loved being in the midst of family that seems to have love—& normal problems. And it's wonderful to be with Gay.[2] We've picked up where we left off. Talking nonstop. Going about. Today we're going for a walk & to the movies.

Bill told me about how Daddy organized the first school in our community. The Wards Chapel School. How he walked everywhere talking to parents. How the first school was burned down by whites. How he had to humble himself to get use of an abandoned shack for the school to be in until another school was built. He explained to the white people that with-

---

1   Bobby and Jimmy are two of Alice's other brothers, who also visited with Bill during Alice's time in Boston. Her siblings are: Fred, Mamie, Bill, Curtis, Bobby, Jimmy, and Ruth.
2   Gay is Bill's wife.

out knowing how to read black people could not properly care for white people's children. If the child needed medicine, an illiterate person might not be able to read the label on the medicine bottle.

He interviewed & hired the first teachers. Miss Lowery (described as snooty) & Miss Reynolds. Eventually East Putnam, the school I attended, was built. It was made from old army barracks my father & others finagled out of the government.

I love thinking of my father as an organizer.

How I wish I had known him then, when he & Mama were so in love & he was hopeful for the future. When I look at society now—how backward turning it is—I feel some of what they must have. Mama turned completely towards religion. Daddy became hopeless & bitter. Mama sublimated her disappointment & anger. Daddy grew more & more ill.

Tracy called last night. Her tour starts in a month. We talked for a long time. I love her so much. It's very hard to be separated. And yet I know I couldn't continue the way we were. However I realize I don't give her enough credit for her efforts. Considering everything she's doing, she has tried to spend time with me. It's just that it has rarely been of the quality we had before.

Anyway, I am content. Happy as can be to be near my brother as he goes through this difficult time. I love being of use.

Jan. 30, 1995

This morning I woke up missing my family, for the first time in thirty years! I wonder if I've repressed missing them before because I was unable to be with them anyhow. All those years at school, both at Spelman and Sarah Lawrence, I must have missed them. But I was too poor to travel to see them—except for Ruth, in her cramped apartment & her horrendous marriage—& they were too poor also. My brothers Bill & Jimmy had small children to support & worked long hours at boring, repetitive awful jobs.

Howie & Roz[1] came to the hospital the day before I left. Promptly at

---

1 Howard and Roslyn Zinn.

four. We spent an hour in the lobby talking. They're going to Italy, to Bologna, for three months. Howie will teach. Roz will paint. They look wonderful. Howie silverhaired & rangy. Roz thin, longhaired, wearing a beret. Very pretty. Both of them are in their seventies. We finally went in to see Bill.

They started talking to him about his work. He became quite animated describing it. How he'd driven to places like Vermont in the middle of winter to change tires—sometimes weighing 1000 lbs—& as tall as a door—on large transport trucks. He told of working in weather so cold—& he couldn't wear gloves because they made him clumsy—he couldn't close his hands. He told of a night one 1000 lb tire fell over, and how he managed to stand it up again. By putting boards under it until he was able to get his own body beneath it. He worked alone.

This glimpse into his working life moved me to tears. Each job took approximately 4 hours. The drive to & fro another 4.

Gay had told me that Bill was tired when he came home from work but never impatient or hostile to his family. She said he always came in the door looking happy to be home kissing her & hugging & kissing his daughters.

The Zinns left when Bill's nurse came in. I walked them to the elevator. They asked about Tracy. I told them she was well & making wonderful music.

Today I am back home. The plum tree outside my kitchen window is beginning to bloom.

Feb. 5

A painful talk last night with Tracy. She takes <u>no</u> responsibility for anything amiss in our relationship. I mentioned my sadness. Grief. She doesn't feel it, as much. It was a hard conversation in which I was not met, but rather kept at arm's length. Judged.

—

Tracy said last night: "I never thought it would end this way." Nor did I. But I've learned wonderful lessons. Love is what is important. Period. All the houses in the world can't make you happy if they're empty.

Now the sun is coming. Maybe. I'll rise, have my meditation & oatmeal & face the day!

—

And so, to bed. I survived one of the most painful days of my life. I did meditate. Did get up. While eating my blue bowl full of oatmeal I wandered out the door & down the hill. Daffodils are everywhere. The acacia is in bloom! The daphne bush. So green, too, everywhere. At the studio I swept & cleared the yard of twigs. At the guest house the sun caught me just as I opened the back door. I spread a blanket out in the pool of warmth it made & fell asleep. This settled me a bit.

—

Great Spirit, let me lean on you. I am weak today. I am sick. I am sad. Be with me, please, as I totter forward into my path & destiny.

Feb. 16, 1995

Dear Tracy,

I don't expect this letter to change anything but perhaps your understanding. I'm deeply sorry about what I said to you on the beach in Careyes, that I was no longer in love with you. Temporarily that felt true: I was in pain & not in love with anything. However it was not fundamentally true. I am still in love with you. In fact, I love you more than ever.

This is not a pleading letter, and, even though I am quite aware that I am suffering, having hurt & lost you, perhaps justifiably, I am also aware of beginning to feel better, to look forward to life.

In talking with Jean Bolen[1] I've come to realize there's no way you could read some of the weirdly conflicting signals I've been giving out. That you read my manuscript at your leisure, for instance, when obviously I wanted you to do it right away. Or, saying I'm out of love & then, later, wanting to make love.

I don't understand myself why I'm having such a struggle just now. One insight I had this week was that you are the first person

---

1   AW's therapist.

I've loved with the same depth & intensity I loved my mother. But that that brings along all the other intensities: fear of rejection, fear of abandonment, fear of criticism, fear of love being withheld if I am not "perfect."

I've missed you so much these past months. I tried hard to fill the time we were apart with other things, other people. Still you were not there. It raked up all my old feelings of being abandoned. When we <u>were</u> together. I couldn't switch back.

But enough.

When I told Jean B. what I'd said, how I'd regretted it, and furthermore, how untrue it is, she urged me to tell you my feelings before you go on the road.

I want you to know, as you go out there to face the madness, that you are deeply, deeply loved. Passionately, reverently. By someone who is totally awed by what you are accomplishing, and by the beauty & courage of your creativity. I am hurt because things went so wrong for us, but we are good people and I feel the universe loves us and will take care of us. Of you, as you go out into the hinterland. Each night I will pray for you.

Don't harden your heart. Forgive. Love.

All I feel for you is love, even when I'm angry or don't understand. I am imperfect. I withdraw when I should reach out. I am trying to learn.

I do have faith in you. And trust. I will try to be the best friend you've ever had. Or at least equal to Jackie![1]

My love always,
Alice

p.s. After writing your letter, I went back to sleep, peacefully. As if to confirm what I had written I dreamed we were about to catch a boat—a big ship—and it was overcrowded or late or otherwise not

---

1 Jackie was Tracy's longtime best friend.

available. But way over to my left I heard a fog horn & a huge gray ship appeared in a port I'd never thought was there. Another boat! I took your hand & we started towards it.

—

I wrote Tracy a letter as honest about my love and struggles as possible. It cleared my heart to a great extent. She called last night, said she'd read it. That it is beautiful & made her cry. She rarely cries. I don't know what will happen.

Feb 26, 1995

Marley Moo[1] well on her way to being trained. Loves the outdoors. Lies out on her little pallet on the deck. Pratibha here for the weekend: our usual relaxed, homey time.

Joan & I went to Tracy's mini-recital: she'd invited her friends, manager, accountant, etc. & friends of the band, to the studio to hear the new music. Which was wonderful. We arrived right from class (Joan) and therapy (moi). Tracy was singing a song I'd never heard before. Something about "falling in love with you again today, all over," very lovely. When we walked in she looked both shy & happy.

Later that night we talked on the phone. Very warm. But we still haven't been able to spend time together. Her work is all consuming. She's doing major creation. I understand it and don't feel resentful anymore. But proud of her.

March 13, 1995

So. Work:

I need to tidy up Same River Twice. Gloria has sent comments. She's always over intellectual, but I value her honesty & general willingness to be a sounding board. Leigh's letter didn't arrive, unless Joan got it.

Deborah & I are trying to sell Careyes.

I have (almost) a book of essays.

---

1   AW's black Lab puppy.

I have, as they say, the "idea" for my next book.

Not much writing energy though. I've been happiest playing with Marley & enjoying the last of my sabbatical.

Great Spirit, again I have to say I lie here bereft: weak & sad & pitiful. Longing for a love that is not good for me. A foolish woman who colors her hair & whose knee creaks.

4:00 a.m. March 25, Gloria's birthday.

Went, like a fool, to see Tracy last night. Performance at the Palace of Fine Arts. Not very good—entirely the fault of the weird space & sound techs. Tracy beautiful & funny. My mind drifted. Later, backstage, there were Jackie & Aneta. Tracy. Deborah & Rhyan & a friend of Rhyan's came with me.

Awful. Stiff. Phony.

I came home & went to bed, having taken some insomnia tablets. Even so, my heart woke me up, aching. I can't go on with this. I've taken all the blame for everything that went wrong. Clearly I'm being unfair to myself. Tracy & her sister & her dogs <u>are strange</u>. Anyhow, after feeling angry & hurt & very stupid for tearing the scab off my healing heart by going to the concert, I beat the pillow & then prayed. I remembered the eagle feather Charlie Soap gave me & I got it and laid it on my heart. I pray to be whole again. I pray to heal. Not to hurt any longer over this. I pray to let go; to have inner peace.

March 27, 1995

It is time to close this notebook. I do so gladly. It is a chronicle of 9 months of struggle with Tracy. A period in which I've felt the most sublime highs & the most <u>abysmal</u> lows. I've never loved anyone as much as I love Tracy. But I've found it hard to keep loving her as "a friend." She's been cruel to me. I have been to her, as well. I don't know why.

She gave her final concert last night; I didn't go. Apparently it went well. She & Aneta came by to see Marley & we sat for an hour or so, the 3 of us. It wasn't bad. My total focus is on letting go. I gave her the Huichol yarn painting I bought for her in December. . . . Marley & I go to Mendocino tomorrow or Tuesday. I can hardly wait. The city is hard. The country easy & peaceful. Even if it rains I'll manage. What I realized was that until I stop wanting to kiss & hug Tracy whenever I see her, I'll have to keep from seeing her. The stress of keeping my feelings repressed is unbearable.

Aneta talked more than usual. Seemed tired. Looks better, more pres-ent, than usual. I admire Tracy so much. She pulled off everything she set out to do & did it all brilliantly. She's smart, beautiful, funny. I'm glad she's in the world.

I've completed a final draft of the new material for SRT.[1] Joan is to FedEx it to Leigh tomorrow. I'm going on. Slowly, with: To My Young Husband. It's a different tone, this little book. It actually makes me think of Rilke's Letters To A Young Poet. I always liked the tone, the size, etc. of that book. It always seemed very pure.

So. I've just now corrected 2–3 glaring errors in my Hugging Fidel piece. But refrained from beating myself up over them.

Tracy & Aneta's visit was a strain. However, it was bearable. I didn't feel I had to care so much anymore. Or apologize any longer.

Evelyn White is to write a biography of me.[2] Bill is out of the hospital & says he feels great. Wilma & Charlie[3] want me to visit them.

Life goes on. Carrying me along. Great Spirit, accept my gratitude & love.

May 4th!
On Wednesday went to see Rebecca's therapist for 2 hours. Very helpful. Although I was shocked to hear Rebecca claim I left her with no food in the refrigerator. She says she was always at Kentucky Fried Chicken! No doubt by choice, said the therapist, and R. admitted that was true. I tried to get

---

1   "SRT" refers to the book in progress, *The Same River Twice*.

2   Evelyn C. White, a longtime San Francisco journalist, author, and editor of *The Black Women's Health Book*, was beginning work on a biography of AW.

3   Activist Wilma Mankiller, the first woman elected to serve as principal chief of the Cherokee Nation, and her husband Charlie Soap.

her to say what it was she wanted from me. "Three square meals a day," she said. She still wishes I were the mother Judy[1] is. At home all day, keeping house, baking cookies & chauffeuring children. Although I'd thought I'd done well as a mother, Rebecca's exposure to Judy has taught her otherwise. This hurts, but I can live with it.

We cried & struggled & at last we embraced & walked back through Central Park arm in arm.

On Thursday Anna Deavere[2] & I held our "Conversation" with Charlie Rose at the 92nd St. Y. Charlie's introduction was insensitive, too personal. Otherwise I felt the evening was good. Afterward I actually found myself in the hug of Skip Gates![3] Furthermore he smelled surprisingly good. Which I told him. He sniffed me back, under my locks, & said "you do too."

On Friday I went to Brooklyn to see where & how my children live. Angel's house very basic, working class Brooklyn. The dogs great. Rebecca's apartment impeccable & tasteful. Simple. Her.

Rebecca & I then took the shuttle to Boston & went to Bill & Gay's.[4] Where among other things, Brenda surprised us, and there was a huge bowl of fried chicken. . . . Bill looks wonderful.

Much too soon Rebecca had to leave. I tossed & turned all night missing her. (We had cuddled very sweetly the morning after sleeping together.)

Next morning I left. And came home. Deborah[5] was waiting (a surprise) at the airport.

---

1   Judy is Rebecca's stepmother, the woman Mel Leventhal married after the divorce from AW.

2   Anna Deavere Smith, celebrated playwright and actress, collects stories through recorded interviews with hundreds of people and then portrays the tellers on stage, in what the National Endowment for the Humanities aptly describes as "curated displays of American character organized around pressing questions of our time."

3   African American literary scholar and public intellectual Henry Louis Gates.

4   Bill, AW's brother, was still fighting leukemia, with the help of his wife, Gay. Brenda is AW's cousin.

5   Deborah Matthews was a longtime friend of Alice's who'd made several international trips with her and proved to be an especially valuable confidante during the turbulent times with Tracy.

Which brings me to the news re: 670 San Luis, Berkeley.

Deborah & I are acquiring a house together in Berkeley. Two stories, plus basement apartment stucco. A lot of beautiful old wood. Lots of work to be done. And it comes with a private park in which there is a large swimming pool & tennis court!

Is this my attempt to "fix" my life with another house? Tracy asked me this last night. I ask myself. I've asked Jean Bolen. What feels different is that I'm moving into this with someone I know & trust & enjoy. Deborah. A friend. She & Rhyan[1] & I will be family. It is a frank attempt on both our parts to be less lonely & alone.

June 5

I think of my two weeks on the road as a pilgrimage. Amazingly, I was able to visit and really be with all 7 of my siblings.[2]

—

Dear Tracy,

So much is ending, and beginning. Robert was married on Sunday, & he & Janet left yesterday for a five week tour beginning in upper Africa, & then via Crete & Santorini on through Italy & Wales. He & I talked over the phone before they left. A good, easy talk, full of his happiness & my happiness for him. He is a really good person & I feel we were meant to be brother & sister all along. He taught me a lot about love.

Did I tell you about the session I had with Rebecca & Mel? It was very good. Another transformation. I told Mel I thought he'd cut us off in exactly the way his father cut him out of his life when he was a little boy. Amazingly, he started to cry, & couldn't

---

1 Rhyan was Deborah's teenage daughter.

2 Starting with a visit to Atlanta to give the commencement address at Spelman College, AW had taken a trip to the East Coast and visited with Rebecca in Brooklyn, and with all of her seven siblings, from Atlanta to Eatonton to Boston.

speak. Later we had dinner in a restaurant & were able to really talk for the first time in many years. Today I received the first 2 of 50 letters I had asked for—from me to him—& which he'd always promised but never delivered. I'm always struck by my poor penmanship! He seemed surprised that I still care for him, & appreciate him. He thought I'd been unfaithful to him, & held this against me. I told him I only started seeing Robert intimately after he & I agreed to divorce. He seemed really stuck on my being unfaithful, though he was the one with a girlfriend—later his wife—on the side. Rebecca remembered noticing Judy long before Robert appeared!

I think it was healing for Rebecca to see her poor parents side by side talking to each other & to her. She grilled us quite relentlessly.

I still feel Mel & I need to weep some more together; but now I feel we will. I told Rebecca's therapist that when he cut me off I felt as though I'd lost my best friend. I had. We were a very insular little family. He was resented by my friends & family. I was resented by his. Etc. He was in many ways a "father" to me—plus, all those lawyerly skills withdrawn!

This isn't what I planned to write about. I was feeling so low & miserable that, when I began to feel better, I thought of you & of how you'd be taken care of if you got sick. I know there's Aneta, but I wanted to be sure to offer myself as nurse should the occasion, goddess forbid, arise. Tea & sympathy, soup, foot massage, etc. Please never hesitate to ask. Even if you're just feeling tired or need your head rubbed & locks separated.

I've now taken Estrace & Progesterone for 2 months. I think I'm better. My moods seem evened out. I realize I may also have something called Seasonal Affective Disorder (SAD) which means your hormones go nuts when you change climates. So weird. I'm grateful though that Dr. LaVoy seems to have a grip on things. It's a relief to think it possible not to feel crazy for half the month.

Love, Yawn, Good night. Alice.

June 13, 1995

I've talked about my "pilgrimage" so much that writing it seems redundant. However, after seeing Mamie & Curtis & being with Ruth at her house & in her car, we went down to the old house. The most important event there was going fishing with Bobby & Fred & eating fried catfish that Bobby cooked. A wonderful experience. I didn't catch anything but my brothers let me haul in the fish on their lines. Fred baited my hook. I felt very small & grown at the same time & I felt loved & loving.

My brothers are obviously doing the best they can & are as flawed as the rest of us. So what? They're also generous, sweet & crazy. My hand kept falling on my brother Fred's huge handgun that he carries in his pickup. So I finally faced my fear of "brothers with guns" & asked him to teach me to shoot it. He was delighted. So I spread my legs for balance & shot it, completely emptying the bullet chamber. It felt great. And some old fear disappeared.

At the Spelman commencement I made warm connections with Gloria Joseph, Audre Lorde's partner, & Alfre Woodard, & Johnnetta Cole,[1] who kissed me on the lips! in a crowded elevator. It was a very high event, spiritually speaking, but long & tedious.

July 4, 1995

Two nights ago, around 12:30 p.m. Tracy called to tell me she finished the album! It's been nearly a year of work. She started the process of looking for a studio & auditioning musicians last August. And before that she was writing songs & creating the music. <u>Such</u> a long haul. And not even over. Two more days for the record to be "mastered" & after <u>that</u>, another tour. She sounded fine.

A nice chat. I feel peaceful, centered, not needing anything, <u>home</u>. The best feeling in the world.

Great Spirit, maker of rain. Sunshiner. Fog-maker. You have blessed me with everything I need to be happy. I thank you & I love you.

---

1 Johnnetta Cole was the much-respected "sister president" of Spelman College.

July 9, 1995—Papa's birthday?

A night & morning of emotional clarity. Tracy's response to my series of letters, <u>after</u> I asked if she received them: "Well, if anyone ever doubted you were a writer. . . . " Such a paltry, pitiful response. Anyhow. Enough & more than enough. I've lived with Pema Chodron[1] these past weeks and she (& Tibetan Buddhism) has saved me.

Aug. 30, 1995

Two nights ago Tracy called on her way home from a meeting. I invited her over for soup. She came, looking glorious. I love the way she looks, walks, stands, sits, smells. She gave me many lessons on how to deal with Marley Moo[2] & I tried to be appreciative, although it felt a lot like the absentee father running in for ten minutes & trying to shape the struggling family up.

She showed me the photos she's had done for the album cover.[3] More open, more joyous—<u>present</u>—than on any other record. I'm so proud of her. I think she's amazing.

When she left I hugged her & told her I love you. She said she loves me too. We're sweet together, in whatever form, when we <u>are</u> together. Very alive. And alert. Very aware of every nuance of life—& very humble.

I can see so clearly how our lives have influenced each other. The cover of her album will look like an old fashioned seed packet. All photos of her are in fields, among growing things. There's even one of her lying in a cabbage patch! And I'm sure there will be a sunflower somewhere. I love all this, of course. And the sunflower is my favorite flower during this period of my life. I always have sunflowers in my house.

I, on the other hand, now have a black dog. Tracy has 3 black dogs. I have lost weight & find myself dressing more like her. She has become a com-

---

1   Pema Chödrön is an American Tibetan Buddhist nun and author and a leading exponent of teachings on meditation and how they apply to everyday life.

2   AW's black Labrador retriever.

3   Tracy Chapman's fourth album, *New Beginning*, would be released in November 1995 and prove successful, selling more than three million copies in the United States.

plete vegan. I am an incomplete one—having fish & chicken occasionally. When I talk to Marley & care for her, I sometimes hear Tracy's voice. She has taught me how to open to animals in a real way. How to respect & care for one. This is a very great gift.

The other thing we talked about was how, even though I didn't realize it, coming out as a bisexual has been frightening. And doubly so because Rebecca also came out. So in Mexico I was also feeling fear & feeling odd to be "out" among strangers in a very macho homophobic country.

September 5,

I wrote a new preface for Warrior Marks that I really like. The quality of my writing has improved with rest & reflection. And saying no to writing blurbs, etc. for other people. My work has life, engagement, passion (the suffering & the joy) in it. This pleases me.

Sept. 14, 1995

One day as I was sitting up in bed meditating, my assistant called with the following query. Announcements for this gathering of black gays & lesbians were going out,[1] she informed me, and the planners wanted to know how I wished to be described. One presenter was being described as an out lesbian. Another as an out heterosexual. Would I mind closing the gap, so to speak, and permit a description of myself as an out bi-sexual. Of course I am bi-sexual, if by that is meant I find both women and men sexually & spiritually attractive. And I have occasionally used the term. However, knowing I'd soon be coming to see you,[2] and being, as many of you know, picky about words, I decided that the word that I preferred to be "out" with you as was one that did not make me feel cut in half, as bi-sexual does, but instead makes me feel whole, even holy, a woman of all my spiritual & sexual parts. Rachel Bagby, the musician, has a chant

---

1   This is a draft of a talk that AW was to give at an upcoming Black gay and lesbian conference.

2   Here, "you" refers to the conference attendees she would be addressing.

that expresses beautifully the richness of this word I choose—& that I think fits someone who loves & is attracted to both women and men. The word is <u>full</u>. I am a <u>full</u> woman, she sings in her soulful black voice. And yes, I feel, so am I.

Like the word <u>womanist</u>, which I prefer to the term black feminist, it springs from the culture and from our own vernacular. He (or she) be full grown. You can <u>hear</u> this echoing down the ages in a way you can't hear "he or she be bi-sexual." So-&-So is a full soul, and of course a full human. She (or he) is someone who's free in him or herself.

Nothing is lacking, in other words. And for the full person, woman or man, there is the most reassuring sense that Mother Nature, being a full woman herself, has made sure that in times of drought or starvation there is always the possibility for a different adaptation, a new way for life, always the possibility of sea change.

Meditating further on this, I realized that it is the spirit in anyone that first attracts me to them, and that the spirit I most love is the courageous, thoughtful, rebellious & compassionate one. The spirit that not only <u>talks</u> about resistance and revolution, but the spirit that takes to the hills metaphorically or in reality to begin the assault. I love the spirit that hates war, but that fights, even so, for the well being of the weak and the poor. How anyone could <u>not</u> be turned on by Che Guevara or Frida Kahlo, for instance, is a mystery to me, if their personal, physical charm came anywhere near their magnetic rebel hearts & intellects.

The men I have loved and been turned on by have said NO to all forms of domination, racist, classist, sexist or otherwise, and the women have done the same. I loved and desired them in their moments of resistance & glory; I love & admire them now.

So this is my meditation on the question of naming. For it <u>is</u> important what we call ourselves. The word lesbian is growing on me as I find myself loving, desiring and admiring so many lesbians. In fact, the spirit of lesbians is often irresistible. I had resisted it because for me it symbolized an island and a separation I do not feel. I've always liked the sound of gay. I've thought the expression In the Life particularly fine. And very black. I hope that "Full" might be seen by others to be a useful, warm lipped word, too, that, while being said, with love, will draw attention, praises and perhaps the thought of kisses to the speaker's tender, sincere & generous mouth.

Sept. 21, 1995
Havana, Cuba
Hotel Copacabana
I took out this journal two days ago, when I was getting ready to come to Cuba. This time I am with a women's delegation sponsored by the U.S. & Cuba Medical Project. We've brought 5 million dollars' worth of antibiotics. However, today was so hot & the lemonade has so much sugar, I've had a terrible migraine all afternoon.

In short: we delivered the 5 million dollars' worth of antibiotics. We screened our film, we met with poets & filmmakers and writers. We listened to music. Visited a maternity hospital that was so impoverished it made me cry. Visited a polyclinic that was so simple & sweet it made me smile. Met with the radical faction of the Cuban Federation of Women. Marveled at how clean everyone is in spite of the fact there's almost no soap. Went swimming in the river. Discussed Colin Powell & viruses with Fidel Castro. Drank mojitos. Have a great bonding feeling with everyone on our United Nations looking delegation. Spent 3 days there. Two travelling. Was back before I knew it, full of energy & impressed as always by the spirit of Cuban people.

Yesterday was Thanksgiving: **Nov. 23, 1995**. Beverly (Guy-Sheftall), Joan & Belvie shared it with me & Moo & Frida. I had expected Angela but she didn't make it. Also Evelyn stayed home working on her work. It was pleasant. <u>Very</u> low-key. I made greens & cornbread & yams. B. brought flowers, Joan a rice & vegetable salad. Belvie made an incredible lemon pie. A feast. After dinner we made a big fire & listened to Clarissa tell folktales on "Theater of the Imagination."[1] A lot of fun.

---

1   *Theatre of the Imagination* is a twelve-part audio performance series in which Jungian analyst and acclaimed author Clarissa Pinkola Estes shares myths, tales, and poetry of loss, love, sacrifice, and survival.

While lying in the sun I thought about the dream I'd had in which missing Daddy came up. The pain of missing him swept over me, & I started to speak to myself in his tender voice. I rarely hear tenderness in his voice when I try to remember it. I was so moved that I wept—not much, but enough. I also began, I think, to write my next novel.

Meanwhile:

TSRT[1] got a glowing review in BookList. Joan brought up the beautifully typed ms. for the new book, Anything We Love Can Be Saved. Which I'm thinking should go back to its orig. title: Giving the Party. More resonance. Depth. Though the other is more hopeful. I have enough funds to make it to the end of the year—& more money due me. I'm reconsidering keeping my house. My God, I'm even reconsidering keeping my house in Mexico! This is because I've decided, I think, to turn Wild Trees into a Retreat for the Study of Womanist Practice, operable even in my lifetime, as opposed to when I die. The government shut down last week & the economy is changing. Also, with my views, & the fact that my books are frequently banned, maybe I should try to structure in an alternative source of income. I only know real estate. I don't "know" it. But anyhow, I seem to accumulate houses.

I want to do good in the world. I want to offer tired people lovely places to rest. And think & ruminate & commune. I have beautiful places all over. The universe gave them to me & I worked for them too. To share them seems right.

Institute for the Study of Womanist Practice, eventually, on Steiner. With the retreat, here.

Jan. 2, 1996

Amazed to be in the new year. 1995 was one of the hardest I've experienced. Almost the entire year devoted to varying intensities of heartache.

On New Year's Eve Rebecca & I had a nice pasta dinner in the country. . . . Near midnight we went out to the Jacuzzi & were there for about an hour. At the New Year we heard firecrackers going off in the valley. It felt

---

1 *The Same River Twice.*

incredibly right to be bringing in the New Year with her. In a big pool of warm water, under a bright moon, with fog slowly climbing the hill. It was very healing & felt like a rebirth.

Today is **Jan 10**—Someone called to tell me Scribner's has sent a bouquet of flowers. They're being delivered from Ft. Bragg. And arrived! Very beautiful. Leigh[1] called to tell me there's to be a small review, positive, factual, in the Times.[2] And to offer congratulations. It was a good day. Foggy brained. Or perhaps it is simply Winter Mind. Slow, sluggish, sleepy. Like everything else in nature. I've given up trying to flog it into activity.

Jan. 11

Meanwhile friends tell me I'm all over the place. Essence, Emerge, Parade?, The Chronicle—at the Berkeley Library they were able to seat 300 people—1000 showed up. The Smithsonian event had to be moved to larger digs. It sold out. Ditto City Arts.

I admitted to Joan that it pleases me to feel the support of the folks! And did I say the Essence piece by Evelyn is superb![3]

Jan. 27th near midnight.

Rebecca just left. I'm on tour. I've spoken/read to large audiences at Stanford, The Herbst, Pepperdine, The Smithsonian/Georgetown. And to smaller groups—still in the hundreds—at many bookstores. Last night at Borders in Philadelphia, tonight/afternoon at Barnes & Noble.

Before leaving SF I met Salman Rushdie at a gathering of writers at the

---

1   Leigh Haber, AW's book editor.

2   A short review of *The Same River Twice* ran in the *New York Times* on January 14, 1996. "Reading the book is like sifting through a drawer, but there are some surprises," the reviewer noted. A review in *Publishers Weekly* stated: "The book wonderfully illuminates Walker's 'born-again pagan' spirit and her boundless passion for the characters she creates and the audience she serves."

3   Journalist Evelyn C. White, who had begun researching a biography of AW, wrote a story called "Alice's Wonderland" that appeared in the February 1996 issue of *Essence*, a popular magazine for Black women readers.

Hayes St. Grill. I liked him, & was surprised that I did. He seems content, fit, his new book[1] is doing very well. We shared the cover of the SF Chronicle Review of Books.

Tomorrow I read & sign at St. Anne's in Brooklyn. Then at Kokobar.[2] Monday's free.

Feb. 1, 1996

Tomorrow is the last day of the tour! Though I have a couple of engagements in SF/Berkeley. But that will be home! I'm sitting in a pleasant sun drenched room in the Boston Harbor Hotel, looking out over the water. I slept fairly well last night; sleep has been hard to come by most nights. I think I'm relaxing. Yesterday was unexpectedly wonderful. To my surprise I was interviewed by Sara Lawrence Lightfoot.[3] On Say Brother. PBS.[4] It was by far the most intelligent interview on this trip. She was warm, wise, experienced, sharing of herself & respectful of me—I loved her! As I wrote in her copy of The Same River Twice: It was as if we'd just met. I hadn't warmed to her before. Now I feel I have a new friend.

Then, last night at The Brattle Theatre. A packed house. Tickets sold out in 7 minutes. According to the guy from Wadsworth Bill came! In a wheelchair, wearing a mask. A whole front row of Walkers! Family.

Then on to the Harvard Faculty Club & a dinner hosted by Skip Gates. Met Florence Ladd[5] in the coat room.

---

1   Elusive writer Salman Rushdie was on tour to promote his new novel, *The Moor's Last Sigh*. The novelist had gone into hiding in 1989 when Iran's spiritual leader, Ayatollah Ruhollah Khomeini, ordered Rushdie's execution after branding his novel *The Satanic Verses* blasphemous.

2   Kokobar was the Brooklyn Internet café and performance space that Rebecca and Angel founded and operated.

3   Sara Lawrence-Lightfoot, who received a 1984 MacArthur Genius Award, is a sociologist, longtime professor at Harvard, and author of numerous nonfiction books, including *I've Known Rivers: Lives of Loss and Liberation* (1995).

4   *Say Brother*, now known as *Basic Black*, is a long-running weekly public affairs television program by, for, and about African Americans, on WGBH, a PBS member television station in Boston.

5   Dr. Florence Ladd served as director of the Bunting Institute at Radcliffe College from

She was warm & sweet. We rebonded. Walked upstairs together. Sat in chairs next to each other saying "I love you." It was great. Skip walked over as we were saying this & glibly chimed in: I love you both. Howie had introduced me at the Brattle, very sweetly & funnily, vintage Howie.[1] Roz was there. I do believe she is one of the most beautiful women on earth. At dinner Howie was way across the table. I was next to Skip & Colin Powell's niece who seemed to have a razor sharp mind. Heart too, possibly. Skip & Florence said I should come to Harvard for a semester. I couldn't imagine it. There is a stuffiness & a feeling of being trapped, even in the faculty club.

Anyway. Boston was fine. Then on to Atlanta. Ice storm. But an interesting evening at the Shrine of the Black Madonna. Before that a very <u>damp</u> interview at the Atlanta Botanical Garden. A very pleasant dinner at the hotel with Ruth & Mamie. I massaged their feet. Fed them. It was the first meal with just the three of us in about 30 years. Mamie reminisced about a time when we gathered holly & made our own Xmas decorations. Ruth is silenced by Mamie & loses her bossy, commanding presence. Very interesting.

I dreamed this morning that I was completely reconnected with my family. We were embracing. Laughing. Crying. Together. Very bittersweet. But very real.

This is possible for many reasons but one is that I no longer try to give them everything they ask for. I give them what I can afford.

I am different. I am someone who can & does say no. Even to this family which I've often feared would engulf or devour me.

Can it be so simple? Maybe.

1989 to 1997. "Skip" Gates is Henry Louis Gates Jr., the literary critic, historian, and public intellectual who directs the Hutchins Center for African and African American Research at Harvard.

1   AW's old Spelman professor and friend Howard Zinn and his wife, Roslyn.

Careyes, Mexico   **Feb. 26, 1996**

Can it be true? That Rebecca & I both decided to "hug the monster" and come once again, together, to Careyes? I had forgotten how easy it is to get here. We took a 9:00 flight, got in just after noon, SF time. (Flight time is 3 hrs., 15 mins.). Marcos—a dancer who does gardening for us—was waiting for us. Our car was clean & shiny. The cracked windshield replaced. We stopped in an incredibly sparkling & laid back Vallarta to buy groceries—in a big new supermercado right on the road home. This store has everything: from freshly made rolls & tortillas to dishes & brooms. And also ready to eat food, both fast & cafeteria style. We bought about 100 dollars' worth of stuff. Pasta & tuna & shrimp & crackers & lots of fruit & vegetables. I bought something that looked like collard greens (a kind of spinach) which I cooked last night. Delicious!

We shopped for over an hour, then started home, Rebecca driving. The city is beautiful, now that the road is completed. No longer noisy, dusty & hot. Well, it was hot, but the palms are beginning to shade the road & there's bougainvillea everywhere.

We arrived at the gate and there was Estella[1] and her new husband who is a guard. We picked her up & arrived home, where everything looked wonderful. Clean, trimmed, brightened, buffed. An enchanting sight.

I went over to the new garden & discovered grapefruit on the tree.

We drove Marcos & Estella to the bus.

We had watermelon, then fresh baked bread, then sautéed spinach & tostados. Very delicious.

Today is blustery & bright. I've mostly lain about. I've a slight headache from the glare. But just enjoyed a slightly chilly swim. Rebecca let me listen to some Sufi music she loves. Very intense. I'm just letting myself relax. And so far I <u>am</u> relaxed. . . .

So I've found myself seeing this place once again as a haven, a refuge. Taken care of in our absence by gentle, honest people, and appearing, when we return to it, as a magical & simple world. Modest but abundantly sufficient.

---

1   Estella is the housekeeper and caretaker for AW's home in Careyes.

* * *

Rebecca is a sweet companion. Gracias a la madre de dias.

March 1, 1996 – Day 6!

It's hard to believe or to fathom how beautiful everything is. So many colors of bougainvillea. And the bird of paradise is by now a giant! The cup of gold is profuse. The little blue flower by the door is blooming just for us. As is the big tree by the front window.

Rebecca & I cuddle a lot. I've missed her & she, me. This feels so good. It is when our bond is ruptured that I feel profoundly out of sync with my world. She & I are still, at some very deep level, one, & will always be. When she falls asleep on my chest I feel her just as I did when she was an infant. Her movements in sleep are the same. Only she is larger.

And so, birds are singing. The pool is so clean it is vision-like. The sky is clear. The sun warm. Yesterday Rebecca gave me a haircut. So I am cooler & more pert & bouncy about the head.

Home again. March 6, 1996

I did not dream much or vividly, in Careyes. The place seemed like paradise—& we renamed it <u>Casa</u> <u>Paradise</u>. Itself vivid. The bougainvillea is more energetic than ever. And sure enough, there's a second purple one now climbing the trellis above the pool.

What we decided re: Careyes:

1. We are keeping it
2. We are going to improve it, paint it a wonderful earth color—it is white with mustard colored shutters now—& eventually construct a tower behind it with a thatched roof and cushions & a hammock. This will be meditation & extra guest space.
3. We give everyone—Estella, Marcos & Miguel[1]—raises. 50% raises to E. & M. And Miguel 20%. In addition, a bonus twice

---

1 The caretaking staff of the Careyes house.

a year. Miguel will also receive 15% of each rental. At my death they will each receive 10,000 also to Miguel's wife, Alicia, & their 3 children.

4. We've decided to rent out the house more aggressively. In that area hotel space is very expensive. Our $500 a week for 3 bedrooms, pool & car is a wonderful bargain. We've decided the family rate will be $200 & that we will still let our friends & some others use it for nothing.

3-9-96 Wild Trees

I've given my face back its eyes! After wearing & clinging to eyeglasses for forty years, I decided . . . to begin wearing <u>both</u> my contact lenses. In the past I've worn one, over the right, injured eye where there is still a trace of scar tissue. I'd felt too vulnerable without glasses to seriously consider using the contact I bought for the other, sighted eye. Anyway. What a revelation! Wearing the contact on my sighted eye gives me back peripheral vision, which I'd thought gone forever. Because my sight is improved, my eye is less easily tired, it feels stronger. Because it feels stronger & focuses better, my blind eye follows its movements more easily. Consequently, though my blind eye is larger & appears to be slightly crossed, the overall aspect is wonderful. My eyes look back at me balanced, dark, bright! I love this. It does feel like having my eye back. The zillion glasses I bought were attempts to regain clarity of sight. But none worked as well as contacts.

Perhaps this time lag—between me & the new—is something that has to occur. Maybe there's hope for me & the internet!

May 18, 11:50 Adam's Mark Hotel, Houston

I've read Pat Holt's intro to <u>Alice Walker Banned</u>[1] & like it very much. It will be published to coincide with banned books week, in September.

---

1 *Alice Walker Banned*, published in 1996, explores what various groups have found threatening in Walker's work and have sought to censor. *San Francisco Chronicle Book Review* editor Patricia Holt wrote the introduction to this collection, which includes some of the controversial pieces, as well as testimonies, letters, and essays about the California State Board of Education's attempts to censor Walker's work.

Perhaps I'll read from it at Lehigh on Sept. 11. Censorship as a Threat to Diversity.

Tracy is in France, still on tour, poor thing! She called from Lyon. Left a message. I feel distant, disconnected. But not unloving. Just filled to the brim with my own life.

And so, Great Spirit, you who give us the power to love & to dream, I thank you for restoring me to laughter & for sending such good company & good food.

Goodnight. I love the love I feel!

May 26, end of first day at 670 San Luis.[1]
A wonderful day! I woke at six o'clock, enchanted by the quiet and the stunning view. The green tile of the fireplace, the trees soughing in the wind. Yesterday was very hot, in the 90s. Deborah & I went sailing with Anthony Leighton & Sheila & Lillie & Greg & Jessica. Very nice to be blowing about the bay. Great lunch! Focaccia bread & olives & cheese & salad. Then back for a celebratory dinner with Joan & Belvie & Sue,[2] who had made sure all the furniture was basically in place before I arrived. Even contact paper in the drawers.

Today I tried to establish the kitchen, but was wiped out from sailing, the excitement/stress of the move, and I was pre-menstrual. (Period started today.) I didn't feel depressed at all, only a bit anxious coming to the house for the first time to live. It's magnificent. Peace, lovely. Spacious. Deborah is wonderful. A rare person. True, through & through.

Marley—snoring beside the fire after being a quiet sleeper since birth, has been her usual sweet affectionate funny self. She still reminds me of my grandmother. Wouldn't it be something if instead of recycling as humans

---

1 AW and her friend Deborah Matthews had just moved into a home together in Berkeley, along with Deborah's daughter, Rhyan. Deborah had overseen the house renovations during Alice's travels. AW planned to sell her house on Steiner Street in San Francisco.

2 AW's assistant Joan Miura, her longtime friend Belvie Rooks, and Sue Hoya Sellars, an artist and a Mendocino neighbor and friend, were helping out with the move.

we go into the other part of the animal world? And that Mu[1] is somehow Grandma Nettie?

Rebecca & I talked. She's having a hard time with Angel. They're breaking up. Painful. I feel for them.

From time to time I miss Tracy. But overall the move is right for me; I am content.

Oh Goddess of house selling please send someone to buy 720 Steiner.

June 19th (Thursday)

Yesterday, Wednesday, Tracy came. She is very thin. Still completely vegan—except for fish. She's still recovering from a bronchial infection which she'd treated with antibiotics, just as I did. I'd felt nervous before she came. But pretty soon it was ok. She admired the house—loved the blue color (her favorite color!) and said she was starving. I warmed some rice, toasted some sesame seeds, made a wonderful dipping sauce out of garlic olive oil, brewer's yeast and amino acids & sprinkled pumpkin seeds & sunflower seeds over the rice along with the sesame. I presented as well a salad. She ate every bite and enjoyed it.

She brought gifts: a great smelling soap she bought in Paris, a huge picture book about writers' houses, and 4 packets of seeds to plant. Two of lettuce & 2 of sunflowers (my favorite flower, which is on the cover of her CD!)

We rambled the world in our conversation. Marley trying desperately to get some play from us. Marley has always loved Tracy. In fact, Tracy helped me name her, and went with me to pick her out, even before I brought her home. At first T was cool towards her & critical. But by the time she left she'd become somewhat affectionate. I thanked T for helping me feel confident enough to have a dog. And I also thanked her for helping me reconnect with my family.

---

1   One of Alice's affectionate names for her dog Marley, aka Marley Moo, or simply Moo or Mu.

It was a good visit. Low-key, simple. We had the house to ourselves for most of it. I think she was amazed by the beauty of the house & the wonderful view from my bedroom. She talked about the family she's made for herself with the band, & the home she has made with her sister, Aneta.

On arrival we embraced. When she left we also embraced. She said she'd like us to get together again before she goes back on the road which is in July.

My heart is so calm I'm amazed. I keep poking it, thinking some corner of it must still harbor pain. But so far there's just an ok-ness. In general life is characterized by peace.

June 21, Wild Trees

Interestingly Joan called yesterday to say I've been invited to be at a gathering that includes the Dalai Lama. This feels right.

Rebecca back in NY. Tells me Tracy is going to shut them down.[1] Refused the 2000 payment they raised. Now the entire 60,000 is due or they're foreclosed. I don't understand this at all.

July 1, 1996

Dear Tracy,

It was a wonderful visit; I was so happy to see you! I have by now planted the seeds—all of them!—bathed with the soap (lovely!) and read most of Writers' Houses, which I am thoroughly enjoying. I hope you're plummy, your work & your recovery/rest going well.

My brother Bill is dying this weekend, after a year & a half of grace. I expect to go to his funeral in Boston this week. He really

---

1 Tracy had threatened legal action to close down Kokobar, the cybercafé in Fort Greene, Brooklyn, that Rebecca and Angel had opened in January 1996 with financial backing from several high-profile supporters, including filmmaker Spike Lee, Alice, and Tracy, who'd given them a $60,000 loan.

admired your grit—and would have enveloped you in his quite hefty arms, I know. He's suffering a lot, now, at the end, and his wife, my fiercely loyal & loving sister-in-law Gaynell, is so tired she can barely stand. I will go to hold her & the children.

I hope we can see each other again before you go back on the road. The phone system here is still peculiar—for instance, we still don't know how to retrieve messages, but I at least have a private # as well as the house one. Deborah tells me this rings in my office. I also check the machine at Steiner.

My work is going really well & the gardens here & at Wild Trees. Yesterday we planted a banana tree.

I'm thinking of eventually (after my house sells, please the Goddess!) getting a Land Rover. Most vehicles like it are too large for me, but I've noticed one on my street & it looks just my size. What do you think? Do you know anything about their performance?

Be well. Rest your voice, your chest.

Lots of love,
Alice

P.S. Ruth just called to tell me he died at 11:00 this morning. He was a wonderful spirit. An Aries—born March 23—stubborn. He'd told his daughter he'd be going today. And not a minute before!

July 8, 1996

Dearest Gay,[1]

You were so beautiful throughout Bill's ceremony. But you reached a zenith on the day of the funeral. Bill would have been so taken by you, & so proud.

---

1   AW wrote this letter to her sister-in-law, Gaynell, now Bill's widow, after returning home from the funeral in Boston.

It was all <u>so</u> sweetly & beautifully done. The children so admirable. Each one of them touched my heart. Just being together, being sincere, being ourselves, was healing balm.

Let me know when you want to visit.

I love you.
Alice

—

Authenticity is the only Praise

—

Casa Azul[1]
July 13, 1996

The most challenging news just now is that someone who is apparently very capable wants to make a musical of The Color Purple for the Broadway stage.

His name is Scott Sanders and he & Peter Guber arrived in Berkeley at the house for lunch on Thursday, the 11th. Pratibha, who's visiting, joined us. We were hoping Peter wanted to ask for the rights to <u>Possessing the Secret of Joy</u>. But no, they want TCP. Peter executive produced The Color Purple movie.

He looks exactly the same. Which is amazing. Anyhow. Warner Bros. owns theatrical rights. The visit was to find out if I'm interested. I have mixed feelings, which I expressed. I feel in some way stuck, in the public mind, with TCP. The color itself is beginning to be one that tires me. And I dearly love it! The American Way seems to be to use up everything to leach the life out of anything alive.

I worry that having a musical going on will distract me from the books I'm writing now. Will drain my focus. I worry about re-entering the river and knowing there are critics who really wish I'd drown.

---

1   Casa Azul is AW's name for the new house she shares with Deborah in Berkeley.

The upside is that, done right, it could be beautiful, thrilling. Life affirming. There would be wonderful roles for black actors—the music could be great.

Scott gave me a list of names of people who could tell me about him: I called them. He got good reviews from Shirley MacLaine, Rosie O'Donnell, & Bette Midler's assistant. I'm still waiting to hear from Whoopi Goldberg and Lily Tomlin.

Joan, Pratibha & Deborah are excited about the prospect. I've decided to go see some musicals.

The plan is to continue to get to know Scott, and to begin to study the nature of plays with music—which I think this would be, rather than an opera. I will plan to see Phantom of the Opera in SF, Les Miserables, if I can find it, and when I go to New York in September, Scott has asked to take me to see shows there.

August 6,

Yesterday Angela,[1] Fania & their niece & nephew Brittany and Reggie came for a swim. She'd tried to call me but I was talking to Jean Bolen. Gregg & Monica[2] were at the studio—picking up the easel for her; she's painting. I worked in the garden—planting beets & cleaning up. The garden never came together this summer. Still, I harvested berries, corn, broccoli and onions.

Angela told me there's a large article on Tracy in the Times. That her CD is now platinum plus. This is so affirming of her talent, her wisdom & most of all, her spirit. She's worked so hard. And she hasn't compromised. I feel immensely proud of her.

So last night I dreamed I was reading the paper and there was an announcement of her relationship with someone else—someone with a French or German name. It woke me up! And I thought: Yes, of course, having faced how much I love Tracy, of course I fear her attachment to

---

1   AW's friend Angela Davis, the social justice activist, and her sister Fania.

2   AW's nephew Gregg (Bill's son, sometimes referred to as Greg) and his wife, Monica, were visiting from Boston.

another. However, Alice, little child who was left too many times by those you loved, this is a reality of life. People you love leave you. And you don't forget it but you heal from it. You go on, as you're doing, continuing to create a handmade, heartmade life of other loves & friends & relatives and Mu!

So face it squarely: Tracy is gone. She is off into the life she dreamed. Let go, keep letting go, with love & grace. Friendship is possible. That is not a small thing.

August 12, 1996

A slow, quiet morning at The Lowell.[1] Then a 1:00 meeting with Kate Medina.[2] Shocked by her coolness, pertness, "You bet-ness." Whitebread to the core. However & hopefully a capable editor. Goddess I hope I haven't made a mistake. We discussed ideas for the book of essays. I've gone back to the original title. Anything We Love Can Be Saved.

Discussed the religion book as a little book with photographs.

She's "thrilled" about the novel rumors.

Oy vey!

I'm so glad Pratibha is coming to accompany me around NY. She arrives around 5:30. 3 more hours. Which means she's in the air now. After lunch I shall go out to the park.

Aug. 16. Today my house sale is due to close![3] I woke in the night quite excited. It's sunny & breezy but the air is filled with smoke. There've been fires all around. My eyes smart.

I've been feeling happy. Angela[4] comes by for swims. She comes by for dinner. I've helped nurse Sue through her illness (the flu). I'm able to speak

---

1   New York's Lowell Hotel, on the Upper East Side.

2   AW was leaving her previous publisher, Scribner, and moving to Random House, where Kate Medina was to become her new editor.

3   The sale of the house on Steiner Street in San Francisco.

4   Longtime friend and social justice activist Angela Davis was a new neighbor, having bought a place near AW's Wild Trees/Temple Jook home in Mendocino.

up clearly & directly to everyone. I work off & on throughout the day. I delight in knowing Tracy is well and happy & that her hard work & beautiful music is being properly appreciated. I just spoke to Monica & told her I miss them.

This is such a paradise I'm in. Thank you, Great Spirit. Beauty on top of Beauty!

August 17,

I just gave 2,000 to A. I. M. to go toward buying 2 buses that will travel the country trying to free Leonard Peltier.[1]

Joan, Deborah, Sue & I went to the benefit. Dennis[2] seems much older & is much heavier. We embraced warmly & he kissed me many times.

We went to 720 Steiner to say a final goodbye. Toward the end it was such a lovely house! It's beautiful & being left in absolutely pristine condition.

That chapter, in any case, is closed. . . . I am not over Tracy. Sometimes I feel I never will be. Being with her was special. Deeper than anything I'd experienced with another person. I still miss her, long for her, think about her. On the other hand I'm basically happy. Just miss her.

I love the communal life I've integrated myself into.

August 25,

I went to T's concert last night with my friend Diana and both of us had a marvelous time. Tracy was wonderful! Beautiful, poised, funny. I loved all the songs—and hearing her sing them in her amazing voice. The concert felt very full.

After the concert we went backstage. She was ill with food poisoning

---

1 Leonard Peltier, a leader of the American Indian Movement (AIM), is an imprisoned Native American activist considered by Amnesty International, among many others, to be a political prisoner. Despite inconclusive evidence, he was convicted in the deaths of two FBI agents in a 1975 shoot-out on the Pine Ridge Indian Reservation in South Dakota and sentenced to two consecutive life terms.

2 Native American activist Dennis Banks, a cofounder of AIM.

& was half an hour or so coming out. When she did, she came right over and we embraced warmly. I whispered to her that she had been wonderful, perfect, and that both Diana & I had almost keeled over from joy. I stroked her hair & her face—all my tenderness simply being there.

She had to circulate. But soon returned with invitations to an End of Tour party. We accepted & drove to another town—Lafayette, to a gathering at an inn. This was also quite sweet. Because of her delicate stomach she was eating plain bread. I had a couple of canapes & then a slice of her bread. While she circulated Diana & I talked about The Color Purple as a Broadway play. She's excited by the idea. Thinks I shouldn't worry about being overwhelmed. That I've already suffered & this time I could go for the fun. She's wonderful. Still a stone hippie after all these years—we've known each other since college. She came to the concert in Birkenstock-esque shoes, baggy pants, a shawl and carrying a backpack. We are very easy together. Anyway, soon T came over to get us & to invite us to circulate. We did. I continued my rather lengthy chat with Aneta, Tracy's sister, struck by how lovely she is. She's definitely blossoming. I embraced her & held her long enough for her to know I meant it.

—

The day of the concert was sweet as well. . . .

All day—off & on—Sue & I worked hanging pictures, with Deborah being director. This was fun. Homey.

Then, a big bouquet of flowers arrived. From Quincy. With a very sweet card. I was amazed. I said to D. & S. before opening the card: I smell a Peter Guber here. And I do think this is connected to the dream of making TCP a musical.

But it's true: this time I think I could enjoy everything.

Oct 4, 1996
Tonight Angela and I are going to hear Me'Shell Ndegeocello. I look forward to this. I enjoy Angela. I like to make her lighten up & laugh.

* * *

Rebecca just came into my room, using the back door! Tall & slender, like a young boy. She & Me'Shell[1] came last night & now she's taking her to an interview. Then they'll be back for breakfast. I haven't met her but I hope she slept well. Rebecca informed me she's staying. That Angel may come join her. Oy vey.

I'll keep the Xanax on standby.

My gray hair is very noticeable now. Sometimes I think it's glorious. Sometimes I'm not sure. Mostly I console myself that it is natural & therefore honest and that I love both naturalness & honesty. In fact, practicing both is my religion.

Oct 9 –

I long for the country! Lucky for me this house is large and I am able to disappear for hours. Rebecca & Angel are here. The fit between/among us is not a comfortable one. It is true to say that whenever Rebecca is around I walk on eggshells. But not as much as previously. I feel distant from her, actually, and she from me, obviously. This is regrettable but ok. I accept that we're not close anymore. I feel relieved not to still be grieving over it. She's not as sensitive a house guest as I would like, or as neat, but I console myself with the thought that she will be leaving soon. How soon? Well, at first she was staying one night. Then a week. Angel was coming. Not coming. For two days. Now maybe four days. Thank the Goddess I had sense enough to keep hold of my car. (Rebecca rented one).

Talked to Deborah about my feelings of uptightness, dread, lack of spontaneity around Rebecca. She's getting on with them both quite well. Sometimes I feel they've bonded & I'm left out. Which is silly. And if they have, & I am, so what? Since basically I just keep longing for them to leave.

I miss my family—which is more & more Bill's family. I feel easy and

---

1   Rebecca had become close to the acclaimed singer/songwriter Me'Shell Ndegeocello, with whom she would soon embark on a romantic relationship.

understood with Gregg & Monica, & with Gaynell. But I don't want to romanticize this either.

I think, of course, of Tracy. So far away in Australia. But in a way it is all nostalgia, since two years have passed since we were together. <u>Two</u>. And I have only memories, and the amazing number of gifts she's given me. No matter where I am or in which house, there's always a gift from her, silently reminding me that I was in her thoughts as much as she was in mine.

Not as painful, this, as a year ago. My heart seems healed. I realize too that I'm going through a long mid-life passage into the second half of my life. Soon I'll be 53. It still looks & feels youthful to me. But my bones do creak & my vision is blurred! So things are changing.

November & December I must dedicate to The Novel. January, too. In fact, the rest of my time & energy until it is done.

So –

Cheer up, my sweet girl. You and <u>your</u> mother are together again! There is hope for you and Rebecca. Tracy has left both scars & flowers in your heart. Love is what the world is made of. There will always be love for you.

Oct 24

I've had serious insomnia, waking at four & lying there! Partly this is hormonal. Partly though it is because Deborah & Rhyan & I had a talk that revealed R. is unhappy at her school & has also felt "I don't like her." It was a long talk that took place on & around my bed. Late at night. Next morning I told Deborah that I thought a good education for R. is more important than equity in the house, which it strains her each month to pay.

She eventually agreed & I have given her the money she put in—only about 5–6 thousand dollars over the year & a half we've owned the house.

Her house never sold; she rented it out.

So, I called my lawyer and asked him to re-draw the documents to reflect my sole ownership of the house.

I told D. that she & R. may stay as my guests.

But I'm not sure this will work for very long. I'm finding I miss the solitude of my house—& that, besides, I have many friends in Berkeley and they seem happy to visit me. I think hosting D. & R. & D.'s real estate office may prove to be too much for me. And it scares me that it doesn't seem to be doing that well.

Of course I berate myself for my selfishness. It's a huge house. Still, I notice I'm not crazy about D's art or her perfume. That it bothers me that she & R are junk food & TV addicts. That R's cottage is always messy & the TV on even when she's away at school.

So, I think I'll discuss the possibility of them going back to their house when the tenants' lease is up, next June or July. What do you think?

Nov. 3, 1996

I am in a mood that I recognize as my needing to be in the country mood. My needing space mood. However, no matter how much I look at my calendar, I won't be able to get away—except for an overnight—before the 12th.

This small funk or pique I'm in: that the bloom is off the rose with Deborah, Rhyan, the cat and real estate. . . . It's a strange thing: this longing I have for solitude, for privacy. I really don't like to see anyone in the morning before I'm ready. It really is odd trying to live with other people's scents and habits. D & R eat differently. They wash their clothes constantly.

But do I really resent the fact that I'm half a million in debt? It's not exactly debt; it's a mortgage. The interest is tax deductible. It's manageable. What I resent somewhat is D's inability to help with it—after I insisted she take her equity money & put Rhyan in a better school.

I think this funk is solely about not being able to go to Mendocino—everything else is manageable; everything else is even interesting.

I'm sad that I can't live with anyone, though. Apparently. But at least I'm observing myself: I'm so rigid. I notice stuff I wish was beneath notice. I'm critical. I'm a pain in the butt, really. Goddess, how did I get so tight? And I like to think of myself as generous. Not.

What smarts though is that I __am__ generous to Deborah & I feel it is, has become, one-sided. I know her resources, financially, are less than mine.

But she could offer a walk through an interesting spot she knows, or a movie on tv. Something. Or dinner.

But this is just muttering. It isn't important.

I shall try to let my mood elevate itself. Keep knowing that it is the country I need. Amazing what the beauty & solitude there do for me.

Great Spirit, continue, if it pleases you—& I hope it does—to bless this little weird part of You. I sometimes feel so puzzled. So strange to myself. So unsure. But lately I've begun to relax, to know that the days will go by and things will change.

There is a happiness, still, under all this.

Dec. 1,
A spectacularly sweet Thanksgiving. 18 or so of us. Deborah, Belvie, Joan & I began it by attending & being part of a sunrise ceremony on Alcatraz.[1] (I spoke to the gathering of 2700.) Came back from the island, had breakfast at Chester's in Walnut Square, then home to naps. Then guests! . . . Everyone brought wonderful food. And took home wonderful food.

December 4,
I've been gossiping so much about my home situation! Last night with Rebecca left a bitter taste. I really must sit & talk with Deborah directly.

I think I'm taking back a part of myself from my mother's shadow. Because she shared everything, space, time, resources, I feel I must. But, as Jean pointed out, you cannot share solitude. Especially not working solitude. It simply doesn't work. My mother did the kind of work that could tolerate interruptions—& eight children certainly primed her to <u>be</u> interrupted. She was a storyteller, not a novelist. I have wanted to emulate her wonderful generosity. And I've wanted to take care of others as she did. But the minute I feel I <u>have to do it</u> I

---

1 The sunrise ceremony was an alternative to Thanksgiving, a ritual to honor indigenous people and commemorate their histories and cultures.

begin to resent the people. They begin to grate on me. Get on my nerves. I find fault with them. And then I am upset with myself for not being better.

Well, I am no better than I am.

Anyway, something flashed as I was getting out of bed. That coming to the country is indeed like going off into the woods or into daydreaming when I was a child. A way to escape the squalor & violence & dullness of my home & family. At the same time, I must have experienced deep loneliness & feelings of abandonment. No one ever came to fetch me out of concern for my feelings or followed me to ask what was wrong. Somewhere in this pattern of flight to the peaceful solitude I grew to love & my sadness that I was not, apparently, missed, is at least part of the knot I am trying to untangle.

Dec. 9,

In short, I've now been in the country a week & have seen no one but my dog for six days. I've felt perfectly happy. Reading, writing, hauling in firewood, making fires & dinners. Napping. Walking in the rain. . . . This week the young woman who has agreed to let me attend the birth of her baby is coming with her mother & 2 midwives to do a sweat. They're Lakota. I am excited at the prospect of attending a birth. I've longed to witness this miracle.

Dec. 14, 1996

Had the dreaded talk with Deborah. She was extremely upset. Very angry & hurt. She cried a lot. I felt uptight giving her the letter, asking her to read it. I also felt relieved to be out of my silence. She said she was in shock. Had not noticed anything wrong except I had withdrawn from her. And had experienced no discomfort. I was amazed—but it just goes to show each of us lives in her own reality. Why did I expect her to be concerned that I was suddenly withdrawn, cool towards her? Why did I expect her to guess I was having a hard time adjusting to her & her child, her cat and her commercial enterprise? Was I dumb to expect her to wonder about me, to ask what was wrong?

She said she didn't inquire because if I needed to say something to her, well, she feels I should just say it.

The discussion was heated at times. I admitted being angry and spoke of feeling misled, misrepresented. That I lost trust. Stopped believing.

Basically, she doesn't want to go back to the house on Carleton St. I've given her 6 months, when I assume her tenants' lease will be up.

I feel shockingly distant. It really is true that I stopped believing D. cared about me a long time ago—the house, living in this area, I felt was more important to her than I was. As I felt that, my own affection dwindled.

Lakota, Teste, Odillia, Yeshi and Emma came yesterday & we did a sweat before the baby comes. They spent the night. I cooked a big dinner which we enjoyed. It was fun.

The baby, a boy, was born on the 17th of December. Sagittarius! I was there, holding the light for Yeshi[1] to see by. It was amazing. I will always love that baby. I will resist any attempt by the world to harm him. When women rule, one of our first laws will require fathers to be present to hold the light as their children are born. The father of Teste's child was not present, but a lot of the extended family turned up.

Now I must meditate. I'm <u>very</u> tired.

Dec. 24

Deborah apparently mentioned to Sue that she'd "gotten in over her head and now had to move." This is an accurate description, I think. She said she seemed devastated. I hope it helped her to talk with Sue.

Meanwhile, I'm sick with the flu. Missing <u>Mercedes</u>,[2] of all people. We spent the night together, the night the baby was born. The 16th. Passionate. Comfortable. Scandalous. Fun. Then off I went at 4 a.m. to witness the birth.

A couple of days later Yeshi called & she & I went to see a terrible Christmas thing at Davis. Left at intermission. Went to buy books. Later she told me she has a crush on me. We cuddled. Fell asleep. Very nice. She's to visit after Christmas.

---

1   A midwife, and a new friend.
2   AW's old friend and ex-lover.

Somehow, these two things, & knowing I will soon have free use of my house, have made me feel very balanced. Very calm. I know the companionship I've been longing for is very possible, perhaps even probable. I love my life!

Casa Paradise
Careyes
Jan. 10, 1997 Fred's birthday[1]
And I realize I've been insane about my eyes. They're beautiful! It is just that every time my life breaks down that is the weak spot that feels the stress. Or, rather, the weak spot on which I place the stress. Now I begin to see myself realistically. A firm 52 year old brown body of a wonderful shade—a leaf, pecan, earth—with graying hair & a graying eye.

Jan. 11, Saturday
Yesterday Gaynell, Mu & I went to La Fortuna beach, my favorite beach. We walked a couple of miles & then came back to Chee Chee's to have pescado frito & beer. Very pleasant. She is deep into the study of the Spanish language, using the Pimsleur tapes (Tracy's tapes) I brought. She is an eager, enthusiastic learner. She told me on the beach that the night before she'd found herself <u>not</u> fixated on Bill but rather on her lessons! This is a major turning point for her.

Our time together is pleasant and flying fast. She has only two more days here after today. Amazing.

Jan. 18, 1997
The month is flying. Soon, in two days, it will be time to go home!

I think of Yeshi. There, the conversation is deep and respectful. I can let my mind and my thoughts flow naturally. With her there's a natural understanding that grows out of the context of the Sixties. I respect what she does in the world. For me though there's no physical attraction, though I find her beautiful.

---

1 Fred was one of AW's brothers.

She's four years older than me. We could do some great travel together. Cuddling with her is also good.

Being with Mercedes is agony.[1] I just suggested that we go down the coast to shop. She was delighted. She must be bored also—we're on such different wavelengths. She is unfailingly on "body" and I on "spirit."

So, once again, Alicia, get a grip. It is <u>never</u> going to be ok with you & Mercedes. It is as if you're from different planets.

Jan. 25, 1997!

Careyes was, on the whole, very good. I studied & practiced my Spanish. I was present & non-irritable with Gaynell, although I slipped into moodiness once or twice with Mercedes. I was <u>mindful</u> of my behavior & tried to head bitchiness off at the pass! I love having learned the technique of "raising windhorse."[2] A Shambala training. Now when I feel I just can't do something that feels necessary I raise windhorse and get on with it.

So when I came home I talked to Deborah & as we officially entered the Aquarian age, at 12:56 Thursday, we were embracing. I've offered to help her get her own place. I just couldn't bear to see her suffer. I still feel—what can I call it that is accurate & not dramatic: Awake.

Thank you, Great Spirit. Por todo.

Jan, 26, 1997
Happy Birthday
Angela!

Who can understand how old we're getting!

---

1   Mercedes is visiting AW in Careyes for a few days.

2   "Raising windhorse" is a Buddhist practice for achieving liberation from self-constructed obstacles, and for building inner confidence, outlined by Tibetan meditation master Chögyam Trungpa in his 1984 book *Shambhala: The Sacred Path of the Warrior*. The image of a flying horse—representing strength, vitality, and energy that can meet and transform obstacles—is symbolic of the force that we can harness to face life's challenges, whether personal, communal, or societal.

Nonetheless, come to a birthday dinner on Feb. 9, at 5:30–6:00. In lieu of gifts bring food (a favorite dish). A story. A song. A new dance.

Casa Azul

Berkeley

Feb. 7 – Yesterday was Bob Marley's birthday. Happy Birthday, Beloved. Your very large photograph hangs over my bed. You are Mu's father & my soulmate.

—

I am having a birthday dinner on Sunday.[1] I'm hoping it won't rain! Twenty-odd people are coming & it should be fun. I can't believe I'm 53! But I have to say, it still feels quite young. I wonder if I'll feel old at 70? 80? Eighty, for sure. I'm beginning to understand what Mama meant when she said that inside, no matter what her age, she always felt sixteen. I don't feel sixteen but 35 or so.

March 25, 1997

Happy Birthday, Gloria

Written on the plane returning from the 3 Rivers Festival and after meeting Mumia!

Got up at the crack of dawn to visit Mumia[2] on death row. Had a great visit. Rushed to talk to high school students in Pittsburgh somewhere. Pre-signed books. Had a nap, then did my lecture before an audience (lovely) of 2,000. Signed more books, for over an hour. Then went to a reception then fell into bed around midnight.

Now on the plane headed home.

On 'a move!

---

1 AW's birthday was coming up soon, on Feb. 9.

2 Mumia Abu-Jamal is a political activist and journalist who was convicted of murder and sentenced to death in 1982 in the killing of a Philadelphia police officer. After numerous appeals, his sentence was commuted in 2011 to life imprisonment without parole. During his imprisonment Abu-Jamal has published several books and commentaries on social and political issues, including *Live from Death Row* in 1995.

May 1,

And I'm on the way to Austin, the last city on the East Coast part of the tour.[1] Last night at the Harold Washington library was wonderful. Overflow crowd. The night before in Boston also lovely. My family turned out! I was too thrilled. Jimmy & I walked arm in arm. He sat beside me as I signed books. Monica & Gregg got the Chinese dinner ordered. We sat in my suite & talked and ate. Like a real family! I can't get over the pleasure this gives me.

Amazingly, as I sat on the plane & thumbed through The American Way[2] I spotted my own face! My book. Silly review but what matters is the large numbers of people who will see it.

Can't wait to be home! Esp. with D & R gone.

May 12

The benefit for KPFA[3] at the MLK School was <u>too</u> wonderful! I sang! (My Anthem)

The crowd was immense—sold out. The welcomes genuine & warm. I was so happy to see I've found my people & my town.

I read & talked & smiled & laughed—& the community did too!

Then got up early to watch CBS Sunday Morning.[4] Very good piece. Brief. But packed with information.

———

I can see the end of the book tour. Always a lovely sight! On Wednesday I fly to Seattle → Atlanta → home → L.A. → home again until Pratibha & I go on the river. The Peacemaking Conference is the 9-11, which means I'll be home the 25-31 of May. Then the 1–8th of June, before the river trip! About 2 weeks for myself.

I thank you Great Spirit for all your support. For every tree, every bird-song, every bat, seen or unseen. Out my window are olive trees & a cork

---

1 AW was on tour to promote her new book of essays, *Anything We Love Can Be Saved.*
2 The in-flight magazine for American Airlines.
3 KPFA is a Berkeley-based, listener-funded public affairs and music radio station broadcasting to the San Francisco Bay Area.
4 The show featured an interview with AW.

tree. I hear birds. My friend in the next room is sleeping. My dog is also. I am awake, scribbling, counting my blessings and steadily loving you!

Tuesday the 5th!
My novel[1] remains very vibrant. I sat yesterday & read it through. It wants to go forward, as I promised it would, once off the tour. And so, even if I complete only 2 lines, I will turn to it now—offering my complete, grateful devotion.

June 14,
And that is what I did! <u>And</u> within the few days I had at TJ[2] I finished it! I'm shocked. I tried very hard to leave some for later—after the river trip. No dice. Finally I stopped resisting and sat down to write. It's a wonderful novel: I feel I've (with Daddy's amazing help from the other side) healed the wounds caused by——everything in our life. (No one to blame now, not even him, or me.)

So I came back happily to the city—though quite nervous about the Peacemaking Conference. Both my "workshops" were over 600 people. Anyhow, I studied & tried to bring something new into the program.

Met the Dalai Lama. Liked him. Thought about how interesting it would have been to have Fidel there. Made my statement. Listened to all the others.

Went every day. Had a <u>wonderful</u> time.

July 14, 1997
Yesterday, July 14, I really finished the novel, after working on it & feeling it wasn't quite done. I've gotten it back its original title & now contemplate whether to include a warning to parents (the ones who ban me) that it is scandalous. Apparently this is part of my nature. I think of what is scandalous as truth.

---

1   The novel-in-progress would become *By the Light of My Father's Smile*, published in 1998.
2   "TJ" refers to Temple Jook, AW's name for her country house in Mendocino on the Wild Trees property.

Anyhow, I've thought a lot about who the first reader should be and yesterday I realized it should be <u>Jean</u> B, if she is willing. I have now written six novels. I am amazed. I like all of them.

July 21, 1997

Trees that I planted here seven to ten years ago tower over me. Potatoes & beans I planted a few months ago are filling buckets & baskets. This abundance that seems nature's natural expression never fails to delight & startle me. Why is the earth so good? Also, how does this abundance happen, exactly? That one bean becomes a pot of soup?

I sent off the novel—<u>By The Light of My Father's Smile</u>—to Joan for proofing & on to Jean & perhaps to Wendy & Kate.

July 22

Last night I had my first relaxed, spacious dream about Tracy & me. We were in a public space, a dyke space clearly—lots of women with sweetness, attitude & short hair—and we were talking. About all kinds of things. Easily. We were aware that people—these women—were listening—it didn't matter for a while. And then we asked for a private space. (The place we were in looked like an art gallery or tea shop or combination space, maybe theatre.) Anyhow the first room we came to a white woman with a battered but healed face sat in a chair having her hair done—a pink cut with a pale blue streak. She said she & I were to appear on a program later, together. So there seemed to be some event coming up.

We didn't think we could find a private space. I suggested going to my place—not wholeheartedly. At that moment the women said they'd found an empty room. We went there. Some of the things we talked about I don't remember. I do remember talking about my hair.

Tracy always encouraged me to let it go gray. In her absence, I wore it graying for a long time. Last week I colored it. In the dream she felt my hair & said, oh, you're still coloring your hair! I said: after a while the gray hair made me feel tired & I was already tired. When I color it I feel less tired. She was not judgmental as I feared she'd be. And then I noticed the edges of her own hair (she has a few strands of gray in the top of her head) & that she'd colored <u>her</u> gray.

We seemed amused by our hair discussion.

This dream came after spending a delightful day and evening with a new friend from Hawaii.[1] A singer who sings traditional songs & who accompanies herself on the ukulele.

July 24,

The new friend from Hawaii, who is very beautiful, talented and is, among other things, a healer (& lives in an old house on the beach in Hawaii), asked if we might date each other—& I said yes.

She had come to my house many months ago with a friend. They'd stayed in the guest house. I invited them up to my house for tea & Zelie had offered to sing for me, once I knew she was a singer. She took out her tiny ukulele and sang away. In Hawaiian. I was charmed. Liked her. Was told by someone, or her, that she was in a relationship and forgot about being interested, except as a friend. A couple of months ago she arranged, via Joan, to visit me. I was surprised, but too busy with the book tour & peace conference to think much about it. But meanwhile, when Prathiba & I were on our way to Flagstaff to begin the Grand Canyon river trip, as we walked through the Phoenix airport, someone called my name. There was Zelie, on her way to study in the desert for 2 weeks with a shaman. She was alone, looking bright & self-possessed. Open. We were delighted to see each other.

So then, in Berkeley, she came to dinner. It was pleasant but, because she smokes, I thought even our friendship would be short lived. Still, I liked her, and was surprised to find I liked the smell of her tobacco—which turned out to be a traditional Native American Pow Wow blend that actually has sage in it! Ironically, while in Arizona, I bought two NA pipes.

Still, as we know, I've been exhausted and fixated. So I sent her on her way with a hug & went to bed.

After she asked if we might begin dating, she told me she'd been attracted to me the first day we met. This surprised me. And that she'd wanted to see me again & had been afraid I'd be too tired, which I almost was.

---

1 The friend was Zelie Duvauchelle.

Being with her though feels so easy. She doesn't know that much about me; she hadn't read my books. In the guesthouse she started reading <u>The Temple of My Familiar</u> & loves it. Her enthusiasm is lovely.

Before she went back to the city—where she will pick up at the airport the woman she's separating from, whom she hasn't seen in 3 months—we walked out to a bench that I've placed in the spot my mother most liked on my land. It overlooks the valley. We embraced & kissed. It felt very comfortable & easy & at home.

We are to see each other perhaps Monday before she goes off to Hawaii & before my nephews arrive for a visit. She'll be back in September & we've already arranged to see each other then.

July 29, 1997
Zelie left my bed in the wee hours of the morning. Her plane to Hawaii left at 8:50 this a.m. We had a wonderful two days.

Zelie & I went to the beach. Muir Beach. Then walked up the hill to Yeshi's house, sat on the deck waiting for her to return. She did. Fed us. Then took us on a tour of Green Gulch Farm. A magical place. Gardens, plants, fields! Truly sweet. Mu was in heaven.

Then Zelie & I, very tired, rambled on home to my house. Where Sue had cooked a wonderful chicken & rice & salad dinner. Joan had waited for us! The four of us sat down & had a great meal & time! Zelie fit right in and Joan & Sue were clearly happy for us.

I built a fire & somehow we agreed we'd like to lie together, to cuddle. Zelie wanted to be naked. So I took off my clothes as well & we cuddled in bed & talked & kissed for most if not all of the night. Very sweet.

She said she was awake much of the night, even while I dozed.

Anyway, this is how we ended up in the same bed & it was from this bed that we sallied forth to Muir beach, on Monday, by way of Vicky's—Zelie needed clothes—& I met Vicky. Victoria is Italian, but is very blonde, with cool gray eyes. Quite young, 33. Zelie says she, Zelie, is 38, but she seems older. Her (Zelie's) body looks 38, but her face looks 45. Anyhow, Victoria seemed very white indeed. But cordial & even caring. My sense was that she had helped connect Zelie to my work. They'd both been at the screening of Warrior Marks at the Castro. They'd sent me some earrings that said "Protect This Woman." When I said to Zelie that Victoria seemed cool she said: No, she's just in transition. She's just come back from Italy, met & became lovers with a German man; doesn't know what to do next. Is in culture shock.

Their separation seems faithful & without rancor. Their friendship seems strong. Zelie often speaks of the healing their 4 years afforded both of them.

It feels very good, this new relationship with Zelie.

It is a cool, foggy morning at Cazul in Berkeley. I've had my glass of Synergy & come back to bed. Mu is napping nearby.

My life has changed so much. And in the direction I prayed for. There are problems & will be more, but I feel I can meet and work with them. Zelie is open & loving. Thoughtful & generous.

She plans to be back in 3 weeks!

Great Spirit, Let me thank you for your unfailingness. Thank you for the great joy & beauty you quietly introduce into my life. Thank you for the newness and the old. For song. For sun & the setting of sun. Sunrise in life. Food and family. Love on the faces of my friends. And helpfulness. And the pleasure of naked bodies in a bed. Of hair & eyes and warmth & touch. For the sadness & pain that teaches us to let go. To survive the conquering of our stubbornness. I live in amazement on all levels, mirroring you, like a teeny twinkle or tear in your great eye.

All my love. Thank you.

August 5

Kate Medina[1] just called. She says she loves the novel. I'm so glad. That she & Wendy[2] are doing the "Publisher's Thing"—talking money. Timing. Etcet-

---

1   AW's editor at Random House.
2   Wendy Weil, AW's longtime literary agent.

era. Anyway. I welcome the support of her enthusiasm which is grounded in expertise, experience & competence.

The universe has sent me a lover. Someone who wants to love me <u>good</u> because I deserve it. Someone who herself has been loved well. Zelie.

Thank you, Great Goodness of Life. As we talk of meetings & visits and eating and making love.

August 22, 1997
In Molokai, having a very sweet time!

Aug. 26, 1997 7:20 p.m.
On the plane back from Hawaii.

It has been a most extraordinary week. Zelie is wonderful. Warm, loving, spontaneous, fun. And a <u>delicious</u> lover! She introduced me to the most intense, fun sex I've ever experienced. I never knew it was possible to laugh so much or to orgasm with such joy. And we also talk & walk & travel & eat together well. And swim & cook.

We love being together. Sleeping together. She is so natural. The most natural person—next to my daddy!—I've met. And she too has aches & pains, which I try to soothe. I love this—I get to take care of her.

August 31
Zelie & I are good, though she's in a lot of pain from a once chronic back & neck & shoulder dislocation. She once paddled completely around the Island of Molokai, her home, and probably damaged herself badly. I took her to see Dr. Lui who gave her herbs and acupuncture for toxicity of colon & liver. And to Sherry Ongh for an adjustment. And Joelle came to massage her. If we don't overdo it, she should begin to feel better very soon.

She, true to her word, left her tobacco in the Honolulu airport waste bin. And hasn't been drinking beer.

One of the things I wanted to do when I went to Hawaii was to visit Zelie's grandmother who has been in a nursing home, following a stroke, for four years. On our last evening we left Molokai and went to Honolulu to see her. There she lay, her long gray braid under her neck. Zelie immediately retrieved it and placed it on her pillow where it lay like a plume, as if she might fly. I brought 3 tiny flowers from her yard—Z lives in her house—and placed them along her body. These flowers have a special myth. They are naturally half-blooms and grow on the hedge that protects the house from the eyes of people walking on the beach. The story is that their "other half" went away for some reason & never came back, but can be found in the mountains. I was enchanted by this tale. Which is apparently true. Which is to say the upper part of the bloom does occur on the same plant in the mountains.

We talked to Grandma for half an hour or so. I told her how happy I was to see her. We rubbed her head and hands & feet. She did not seem to know we were there. I felt very glad to be with Zelie saying goodbye. Interestingly, the day before Z's aunt Paranani had called & said Grandma's nurse had asked if she was waiting for somebody.

The next morning before leaving Honolulu we went to visit Z's aunt. She & Z talked briefly about Grandma's condition. We soon left. The day after we arrived back in Berkeley, Grandma died.

Saturday, Sept. 6
Today we buried Grandma. At Our Lady of Sorrows Catholic Church, a church originally established by Father Damien of the Leper Colony. It is a beautiful small church, white with a red roof and small cathedral windows. Outside there is a spacious lawn, hedges, a huge cross & a fabulous view of the sea.

Zelie sang four songs for her grandmother. One of them Grandma's Song, from her new cassette. It was very moving. . . .

The days are so long! I noticed this the last time we were here. This time because there has been a houseful of people since Friday the days are two & three weeks long. Each day I've been frantic to get away. To walk, to sit by the ocean. Yesterday Zelie took me for a lovely walk & I did get to sit for five minutes by the ocean & let the wind blow through me.

Then we took a pineapple we'd bought and went back to visit Grandma. We sat on the grass by her grave & ate it. We also gave her a slice. Zelie pushed it into the small opening of the grave, underneath the flowers. I told her how in Mexico people celebrate the Day of the Dead & go to the cemetery and sit on & around the graves of the ancestors & eat picnic lunches. How they eat tiny skulls & skeletons made of sugar. It seems a wonderful pagan expression that comes naturally. We were "eaten," bitten by ants as we sat there.

I had a lot of tears. I was especially moved by the way the ceremony ended. After Grandma's ashes had been placed in the small hole, Zelie shoveled in the dirt. Her slight frame intent, focused, loving. It felt so true & right. And was so sweet and beautiful. I loved her very much as I watched her honor her grandmother in this way.

—

There is almost too much life to report. My novel is in Wendy's capable hands.

Zelie is a changeling. Endlessly fascinating, just her nature. In a lot of pain, unfortunately, but this morning she realized she threw her back out lifting a very heavy bag. She had a great massage last night & awoke in the night horny as anything. Our sex life is wonderful. Deep pleasure. Surprise. Yesterday I was feeling the need for solitude. I said hurtful things to her. She cried. I recognized my cruelty. Apologized. Held her. She forgave me, easily. Whew!

We talked & talked & talked. This cleared the air. This morning we're up early. The sun is shining. She's singing. I've meditated. We're trying to arrange our trip to Cuba.

So. Rebecca has disconnected from me. I don't know why. But I'm trying to bear it gracefully. She's at MacDowell[1] working on one of her books.

I can hardly believe the swiftness with which my life has changed. A very sweet & beautiful live-in lover/partner who spontaneously sings & makes other noises. The sexiest partner I've ever had. A good cook. A soulful communicator. A mature person! With lots of hair!

---

1 MacDowell is an artists' colony in Peterborough, New Hampshire.

Universe! You're amazing. I love you and thank you so much.

Zelie sees me. She loves my eye. She looks into it & sees a universe. She says things are moving, just like stars!

Sept. 29, 1997, Cincinnati, Ohio

It is late at night here though not so late in California where, thank Goddess, I live. I'm to do a seminar and a reading at Miami U. tomorrow. In Oxford, which is somewhere around here.

So far so good on the home front! Zelie & Mu drove me to the airport. Last night I initiated lovemaking. This is the best lovemaking ever, in my whole life—& I thought I was over the hill! So funny, life.

A tiny cloud is the way Z's old lover Victoria keeps insinuating herself. But Z seems to be slowly but definitely catching on.

The house is wonderful. Gradually reflecting the fact that Z lives there too. Her room's a mess, still, because she spends so much time in my room. I love to hear her singing or talking on the phone. Laughing, which she does a lot. I love her and always want her, a new feeling—a sort of constant turned on-ness.

Not much to report really. I enjoy all the simple things we do together. Walking. Eating. Driving around. Going to see films. All kinds of things. She is funny. Immediate. Present. Says what's on her mind. . . .

. . . I am as blunt as she is. I fear I hurt her at times. Goddess I hope not.

I encouraged her to write more. To spend more time alone. To enjoy the fruits of solitude: intimacy with her own mind, centeredness. Etc.

Rebecca, who finally returned one of my many calls, thinks my novel is about her![1] Amazing. And too bizarre even to comment on. Although I do recall that she introduced me to pomegranates.

Anyhow, she's as pissed as ever that I'm her mother. I don't know what happened to us, but <u>something</u> did.

Zelie is more mature than Tracy & can help me with her. This I know.

---

1 AW's new novel, *By the Light of My Father's Smile*, was to be published in 1998.

Sept 30th, 11:52 p.m.

The event(s) at Miami University went very well. 750 students inside, many more outside watching monitors. I felt very much in myself. Read poems, bits of essays. Talked. Read the FMH[1] essay & advised the audience to see the film. Henri's nephew distributed flyers. It all felt wonderful & the people were so sweet.

I'm really glad I came after all. I don't know if I should give up these lectures. It isn't really the money that's so compelling. It's the sense of fostering community.

On the way home I fantasized about making love with Z. It felt delicious just to think of her, of us, in bed & totally absorbed.

Great Spirit I thank you for this love. The making & remaking of which we do with so much joy.

Oct 19

The "charge" around T & her music & my memories is by now minor, though still present in an odd way. While on Molokai Zelie told me she listened to "New Beginning" to feel its effect on her. She became bored after a while—though she loves the CD—& turned it off. I decided to write T & to relisten to the CD. The best songs "The Promise" "Mother of Us All" "River" etc. she wrote while we were together. My favorite, "Give Me One Reason" I encouraged her to put on the CD. She didn't know or trust the deep blues feeling of that song or recognize its vitality, infectiousness or value. She clearly loved it though and always sang it with gusto. It's such a sexy song, too.

Trying to plan for my journey next week. Zelie & I ran through the Sesame St. script—which is about counting raindrops with the Count & Elmo the monster & teaching.[2]

---

1 *Follow Me Home*, the 1996 independent film starring Alfre Woodard and directed by Peter Bratt.

2 AW appeared on episode 3717 of the popular children's show *Sesame Street* to explain to muppet character Elmo why rain is important, and she counted raindrops with the character known as the Count.

Nov. 2

I can't believe I'm sitting in bed writing this in a hotel in Denver! Fortunately, I'm in a suite with lots of windows. And look out at the Rocky Mountains in the distance. I flew in yesterday morning, early. Got up at 4, the car came at 5, the plane left at 6:15 & I arrived at 9:48. Met up with Clarissa[1] in the convention center where the book festival was held & we proceeded to do our thing. It was slow, starting, but soon our conversation took on a wonderful slow-paced & thoughtful life. We were happy to be together & our affection for each other showed. At some point, after a comment I made, she reached for my hand and said I love you. I held her hand, squeezed it, & said I love you, too. I do love Clarissa. She's given so much that was suppressed back to the world. All women are in her debt.

Later we signed books together, very easy & matter of fact, shoulder to shoulder, & then went to the hotel for lunch.

Zelie & I had a wonderful time in New York. We both enjoyed Sesame Street. She & Gloria liked each other. Gloria & Hyun Kyung[2] had dinner with us at a restaurant called Bamboo.

Stopped on the way in Georgia to visit Mama's & Daddy's graves & to show Zelie our church & all the markers up & down Wards Chapel road. It was raining & seemed rather bleak. The church is falling apart. I think I'll offer 5,000 for its repair. New windows & doors, etc.

Had a wonderful time at the Harriet Tubman Museum. Met extraordinary people, including my 2nd cousin Edward, whom I like! So many family members came to the ceremony to see me accept the Shelia award—& I was

---

1 Clarissa Pinkola Estes, Jungian psychoanalyst and cantadora (keeper of the old stories) in the Hispanic tradition, author of the bestselling *Women Who Run with the Wolves: Myths and Stories of the Wild Woman Archetype.*

2 Chung Hyun Kyung is a lay theologian of the Presbyterian Church of Korea. She first came to international attention in 1991, when she made a now-famous speech—a feminist/Asian/Third World interpretation of the Holy Spirit—at the World Council of Churches in Canberra, Australia. She joined AW and her longtime friend, Gloria Steinem, for dinner during this trip.

delighted to see them, to see Polly! Ruth. Brandon. Kyle. Jimmy. On & on. And to see Zelie in the context of my tribe. Nice.

Then lovemaking in the 1812 white ante-bellum bed & breakfast. Sharing a room & more to the point a bathroom & doing ok with that. After the awards dinner we hung out with Cory & Rudolph Byrd & Henry & Valerie & Veta & Anita (Ponder) and Angie.[1] Very sweet. I felt so at home, very much in my body & spirit and happy to look across the room at Zelie who was glowing.

Back home! Both of us fell into a sink! Hers related to her cycle, which started. Mine related to the need for solitude. We suffered. Rehashed everything. Wept. Felt discouraged & misunderstood. Then slowly began to return to our senses.

I feel quite content to be here—since I'm here—looking out at the Rockies, waiting for breakfast, and accepting the fact that I have two events to do in Dallas before returning home.

I'll have about 2 weeks of being home before we all go to Cuba. A ten day trip. Then Thanksgiving. Birthdays. Then a free December. Careyes in January.

Zelie has told me two things that frightened me: A health problem she has & that she is about to lose her house! Kainehe, where she grew up & where she's lived all her life. This is a major loss for her & has upset her deeply.

I still have some "charge" around houses. I've resisted getting involved. But last night I thought (and after talking to Clarissa who told me she's invested her money in rental properties): Why not invest my

---

1 Carey Pickard, then executive director of the Harriet Tubman Museum in Macon, Georgia; Emory University professor Rudolph Byrd, cofounder of the Alice Walker Literary Society (AWLS) and artist Henry Leonard; AWLS cofounder, author/journalist (and now editor of this book) Valerie Boyd and dance-history scholar and Spelman College professor Veta Goler; Anita Ponder, then director of education at the Tubman; and Angie Brooks, operations manager. AW received the Shelia Award, an annual honor given by the Tubman Museum to an African American woman of distinction, on October 24, 1997.

350,000 B of A[1] thing in land in Hawaii, with Zelie? She'd get to keep her homeland, if not her homeplace, and we'd have a familiar warm place to hang out in. We could study Hawaiian culture which I have a feeling I'd really like. (Alicia, ever the optimist!)

It's true Molokai seems boring but that's partly because I'm such an outsider. Anyhow, this could be a wonderful solution to this problem that she feels of not having a home. (I can't seem to get away from this issue in relationships!) Soon I will discuss it with her. Maybe in Careyes. It would make more sense to study Hawaiian culture—more English—than Mexican anyway. And it would be so good for Zelie to maintain her roots. To have roots <u>and</u> wings.

Meanwhile, the nomadic life has to stop. It's too exhausting. And I miss all the <u>life</u> that goes on at home.

And so, I begin to bring this journal to a close—poor bespattered & bedraggled thing! Soon I must get up & dress, get myself on the plane to Dallas. It's this very evening that I talk!

I talked to Zelie last night. She said she misses & loves me. I asked her before I left what she'd miss most about not going with me. She said she'd miss being by my side. That is what I've missed too. Maybe in the future if there are places she'd really like to go she can come with me.

I love this feeling I have of my life being my own. Of being in love with a big "mo'o"—the lizard goddess/guardian of Molokai. The struggle to keep my own demons—hormonal & other—out of my intimate relationships continues. I've been hard on lovers. Not accepting that they love me perhaps because I did not truly love & value & accept myself. I <u>pray</u> this will change. That I will never turn on another lover, lashing out with hurtful words as I've done in the past.

Zelie & I talked about what needs to happen when we become tense & uptight & a danger to each other—we should, <u>must</u> give each other space. Luckily I can go to the country. Thank goodness & foresight.

*   *   *

---

1   B of A means Bank of America.

In the country (**Nov. 6.**) Z in the kitchen cooking oatmeal. She should be leaving soon, taking the Jeep back down to the city. So that we'll have two cars & Rebecca & Me'Shell can have wheels when/if they come for Thanksgiving.

Zelie wants to invite Victoria for Thanksgiving. I have mixed feelings about this. I've said it's ok but feel it's too soon, that we should have the tea beforehand that I've been trying to work my way toward. I'm amazed as well that Zelie is insensitive to my needs & timing on this. But, as she said this morning, she's extraordinarily self-absorbed. I've really noticed this since we've been together. She's lomi-lomied[1] me once—at my request—since we've moved in together. I mentioned knee pain on our walk the other night & she said: I don't want to hear about it. Meanwhile she inconveniences me (& Joan) regularly. . . . [And] she does very little. Her room in my house is still messy from when she moved in 2 months ago.

This morning after broaching the subject of V. & Thanksgiving she asked to look into my eye—just like that. I said no thanks. She got "hurt" & "went away." I explained it was poor timing. She said she'd wanted to look because the light from the skylight over the bed was so good, etc. etc.

I really don't think this relationship is going to work long term. It's pleasant most of the time now. The sex is very good. Conversation too, mostly. But I don't feel taken care of. I feel instead as if I'm doing it all. Plus I wasn't prepared for her almost constant illness/pains/etc. So many! I feel myself beginning to wonder about her mind, her state, etc. Emotional, psychological. Oh, Jesus! What a small mess!

What to do? She seems so often to feel empathy but perhaps it's always fake.

Anyhow. I don't want Victoria to come for Thanksgiving. I'll say so. And I'll continue to plan the tea for December.

Did just that. Told Z. I feel uncared for. She sat stunned by the information. Hurt, as I am also. We sat & ate oatmeal & then I got up to tend the fire & continue writing.

---

1   Lomilomi is a Hawaiian massage.

Who knows what will happen? I don't. But I said straight out that I want to be partnered by someone who makes me feel cared for. That I need to have their caring demonstrated. Wherever such candor leads I will no doubt see.

My hunch is that this will lead to much less angst around my period. What seems to happen is that I usually sit on feelings such as these & they make me sick around the week before my cycle starts. That's the truly suffering part of PMS. Unexpressed emotions meet hormones on the fritz!

Anyhow. She's gone. I'm alone, with Mu. Feeling clear, thoughtful. OK. Happy to have this refuge, this blazing fire.

And life without her. How would that be? What would I miss? I'd miss her. Lovemaking. Hanging out. But I'd be ok. Friends. Life itself. Besides, I dreamed of the Goddess again last night: a large dark woman who massaged me and laughed as she played with my arms.

Nov. 28, 1997

Yesterday we celebrated Thanksgiving. About 16 of us. Everyone around the large dining room table that is too small! Belvie suggested adding a board; Diana suggested adding another small table to make an "L." I will look into this for next year.

I was tired enough to faint but it was lovely.

Z. made a lovely altar with candles decorated with pictures from Cuba.

After eating lots of food we had show & tell. Most of us talked. Z sang. Beautifully. Arisika danced.

Today I'm recovering. The sun on my bed. Z off to find echinacea & golden seal, vitamin C.

We had an amazing visit to Cuba. So incredible I can't begin to describe it except to say I was embraced with love wherever I appeared. And Z too. Both of us appeared on Cuban television. We distributed presents wherever we went.

Tuesday, Dec. 9, 1997

In the country at last. In a freshly made bed with pink sheets. Feeling quite distant from Z. An odd feeling of: what if I've made a big mistake? Don't know why it's striking me so hard.

We went, the evening before we left, to see Victoria's show (of her handcrafted jewelry). I liked some of it. Bought a necklace. Z bought me another one.

It was pleasant after a few awkward moments.

Eventually embraced everyone & left. Went to Bucci's, an Italian restaurant that serves delicious food. Came home. Made love. Slept. Next morning came here.

It is super boring to relate but Z thought I should have consulted her before lending Rebecca the Jeep (for the 3 months she's in L.A.) I felt so tired talking to her.

What have I done?

I'm so critical, suddenly. Which I must stop!

Wed. the 10th—In bed listening to Bobby McFerrin. Something's there somewhere for us. Anyhow, he's singing "I can feel my body fully, yes!" So gorgeous.

Z called this afternoon & I was happy to hear her voice! Hadn't wanted to for two days. Hadn't called. Had no feeling for her, us, whatsoever. Thought I was out of love. But no, apparently. Now I want to see her, kiss. It's the death-life-death thing Clarissa talks about.

I'm much better. I slept for 2 days basically. Thank you Life!

So, here I am again. Climbing back to health. In love. Wanting to snuggle up & kiss. Dancing. Life. I must try <u>not</u> to exhaust myself as I've <u>been</u> doing!

Christmas Eve & green ink! Dec. 24

I am in bed at Cazul,[1] Mu outside my bedroom door, on her cushion, black & angelic. Such a little shadow. Always loving—even when I'm in a mood, as I've been. Quite mild because before she left for a week in [Hawaii] Zel talked me through and out of a sink I was about to fall into. My libido had been low and a plan of much anticipated pleasure failed to materialize. She

---

1 Cazul is AW's blue house, aka Casa Azul, in Berkeley. She also still owns the country house, Temple Jook/Wild Trees, in Mendocino County, and the house in Careyes, Mexico.

scolded me, out of her own disappointment, & of course I was bruised to the quick. Such a sensitive soul I am. Like my mother and like my brothers Bill & Bobby. We all cry easily although Bobby learned to hide his tears. I never could.

The horrible respiratory infection that started in Cuba—from irritants in the air on the road to Santa Clara but also from stifling my tears in Che's crypt—seems vanquished by the antibiotics I started taking 5 days ago. Tomorrow Mu & I will drive to the country for a couple of days returning probably Sunday. Zel returns then.

I am happy. Content. Pleased with my relationship with Zel. Delighted with Cazul. I've settled in here finally and love its spaciousness. Its beauty. The way the sun floods my bedroom in the afternoon.

Also I've rearranged things. My study is now upstairs next door to my bedroom, a major improvement. Downstairs is now a splendid guestroom. Zel & I went to Bed, Bath & Beyond in Jack London Square to get sheets. I'm not crazy about them but the room itself is fabulous. Big, open, inviting. Guests will love the fireplace.

Rebecca & Me'Shell are in Careyes. Can't seem to take a much needed break from each other. I feel sad for them. The going seems so rough. Rebecca is trying to write. Me'Shell trying to sing.

What am I trying to do?

Love Zel & Mu and stay home more!

We go to Careyes on the 6th: Stay there for a couple of weeks, then push off to the Yucatan and the Ethnobotany Conference. We come home. I welcome Howie & Studs on Valentine's day night & then speak in Chicago the end of the month. Then go to Hawaii for two weeks to the Dreamtime conference. In April we go to (Paris?) England for the book tour.

The contract with Random House has been signed. Kate has sent back the manuscript festooned with paper clips. Apparently a long list of queries is attached. I haven't looked & won't until I'm at Temple Jook. I'll take it to Mexico with me. Rebecca says there are mosquitoes. Hmmm.

My finances are excellent. My health is good. My hormones are causing migraines & lethargy, but not suicidal angst. Knock on wood. Major absentmindedness, though.

I'm reading an amazing biography of Che Guevara.[1] In many ways his life was shaped by his asthma. It was particularly moving to me to see that Celia, his oldest daughter, has asthma also & to know that as a pediatrician she treats babies with the disease. I like all four of Che's children.

I wish I'd met Aleida[2] after I read this book. I'm afraid I was very ignorant and awkward with her. Focused as I was on the children. I hope she forgives me.

What of Tracy? I still wonder about her and care. But the ache is gone completely. It is almost hard to remember her. I'd love to see her, actually. Her long, studied, determined silence is obviously calculated and meant to wound. It makes me know she's in pain, even if she can't feel it, and I worry about her.

Thank you Great Spirit for seeing me through the considerable pain of separating from her—the true love of my life.

I say that, and it amazes me. And yet I feel it is true. Didn't I think the same thing about Robert? I'm certain of it. Perhaps there are many true loves. Maybe Zel, coming home tomorrow, is one.

———

I've enjoyed a fabulous four days at Temple Jook. Drove up on Christmas Day, Thursday. Worked on SMILE[3] Friday morning.

Meanwhile Rebecca is in Careyes writing & having a wonderful time. Going to LA on the 30th to bring in the New Year with Me'Shell.[4] They may come north to Berkeley & the country while we're in Careyes in January.

Kate Medina's responses to the novel are not at all helpful. She's suggesting so much stuff I'm not able to trust any of it. I've added chapter headings, which I might have done anyway. But that's all. Perhaps she's feeling the shakeup at Random House and wanting to demonstrate how hard she works to the new head. Who knows.

---

1 Jon Lee Anderson's *Che Guevara: A Revolutionary Life* (1997).

2 Aleida March, Guevara's second wife, and a member of Castro's Cuban army.

3 The new novel, *By the Light of My Father's Smile.*

4 Rebecca was dating singer-songwriter and musician Me'Shell Ndegeocello.

I love looking around me at my beautiful house. . . . I feel so lucky! To have love & work and beautiful places to rest my soul. My only prayer these days is <u>Thanks</u>!

Jan. 9,
Sometimes there is just the feeling of dying. I feel that here[1] and marvel at the fact that I <u>always</u> feel it here. It feels like re-entry into failure. I sat on the upstairs patio & looked out into the lovely garden & it all left me cold. I started to weep, thinking of the relationships that have ended here. Or that have been badly strained. Robert & Tracy. Rebecca! Is it the coffee I've been drinking, strong, every day. The marijuana? The sugar? Yesterday the beer?

I've indulged in all these substances since arrival. Coffee overstimulates me. Sugar is the drug that most depresses me (I also had an ice cream before leaving Berkeley and another the first day at Playa Rosa!) Milk I can't tolerate at all. Beer makes me gassy and blurred and is always too much for my small bladder.

All of this over-indulgence in what is for me poison sent me to the bottom of despair. Zel and I talked and that helped but then I began to feel talking wasn't helping but making me feel more empty, hopeless. I craved silence. Solitude. I swam in the cold pool alone. Lay facedown in the sun. Crept upstairs & lay in the hammock naked. Hopeful that the sun would come from behind the clouds & warm me. It didn't. I couldn't move myself, even though I was very cold. After crying I felt better. Thank you Great Spirit for tears! And for teaching me once again that my way is not the way of strong coffee, sugar or ice cream or milk—the powerful drugs passed off to the gullible as "harmless" or "recreational."

I had a wonderful insight this morning about Casa Paradis which I have again been considering selling. Zel commented that the clothesline out back is a rope & not a clothesline. I said it was a clothesline & was in any case what we had used in my childhood to hang clothes on. But when I tried

---

1   At the house in Careyes, Mexico, which AW sometimes refers to as Casa Paradis, or Casa Paradise.

to fasten the towel I was hanging with a pin I discovered it <u>was</u> a rope & that the pin didn't fit around it! So I started thinking about the clotheslines of my youth.

Actually we rarely had clotheslines—if ever!—from the store. As I recall we used baling wire or we hung clothes on the garden fence. Usually both because there were so many children and my mother washed so many clothes.

Zel commented on my defensiveness. I <u>was</u> defensive. I felt as though she'd found yet another thing not to like about my house. And this led me to the revelation that I have a difficult time here because it reminds me of my childhood. Even the heat! I am back in a house in which many things are "wrong" or don't work properly. The city cousins are visiting, mocking our poverty, and we are desperate to offer them the best that we have. The best room, the best fire, the best food especially. We hope that if we feed them well and sleep them well they will not notice the holes in our walls or that the roof leaks or that we don't have a real clothesline.

My fascination with owning houses, which is in a way against my nature—I don't innately like owning things—comes from the desire to make where I live beautiful, comfortable; a place where everything works.

In Mexico because my Spanish is minor and because I'm here only once a year, and because there's so much culturally & politically I don't understand, it is impossible—or seems so—for things to work as smoothly as I might wish. (The whole <u>country</u> doesn't work!) (Not that ours does.)

And yet, when I'm here alone I focus on the good, the beautiful. Yet when others are here I seem to see only the faults. I tend to see my little house through their eyes and to judge it harshly. In fact, I <u>abandon</u> it, and this abandonment makes me feel divided, disloyal and sad.

I may have had this breakthrough before, but it feels new. It feels true.

This would explain why I sat crying on the patio—talking about feeling like a failure! After everything I've accomplished in my life, a word from a guest that something is amiss makes me feel nine years old, living in the worst shack of all the shacks we inhabited. I find this amazing. That it is in the encounter with <u>this</u> relatively small but pleasant house that so many of the tears of my childhood are stored.

And is that one of the reasons I bought it? To subject myself to an experience, as an adult, of a living situation that is "not quite right."

Now I begin to understand something else. That these "drugs"—coffee, sugar (most of all) milk—take me to the dark, heavy, oppressive corners of my psyche. Just as marijuana takes me to the place of mellow connection with nature and Ayahuasca[1] takes me to regions unfamiliar to me. And also introduces me to profound teachings—which are no less profound simply because I don't remember them.

The visit has turned around!

I feared the arrival of my friends Joan & Sue![2] Would they like what they found? Would the four of us be happy? They arrived laughing and whole. Admiring of everything. Sue especially is so appreciative. The flowers, the trees, the birds, the air! She lifted my heart. Joan as well. Soon I was—the nine year old—seeing my little "shack" through the eyes of love. And yes! I said. Isn't this wonderful! And that too. And come let me show you something else! I was incredibly happy that they were happy.

And so it has gone. Each day we rise late, eat fruit around the table (Sue goes off to have coffee at the hotel). We go to the beach in the afternoon. I swim. Zel creates beautiful sand sculptures. Joan & I fell asleep on the beach day before yesterday.

I slept well & then fitfully last night—the mota![3]—and lay long in bed this morning. Got up finally, trimmed the flapping end off the shower curtain, straightened out the room—Zel had gone downstairs, to write in her journal—and realized a feeling of contentment. Better than just muddling through. I love having Sue & Joan here. They are grownups and make things simpler, easier.

---

1   A plant-based brew that some Native communities use for divinatory and healing purposes.

2   Joan Miura was AW's longtime assistant and friend. Sue Sellars, AW recalls, "was not only my neighbor and friend but an extraordinary artist (painter) and lesbian separatist until she caved for Roberto!"—aka Robert Allen—with whom she developed a long-lasting friendship.

3   Mota is Spanish slang for marijuana.

And so, today, which I think must be the 14th of January, I am loving my little house again. Zel hates the bougainvillea because it's "messy" & she had to clean it up when she was a child. I love it for its color and magical "dry" blooms! Basically I am not abandoning my house—I am also learning to use & to enjoy our beach, Playa Rosa. And La Fortuna has never looked so fetching.

Such are mood swings! Like dark clouds in the sky of the spirit! Thank you Pema. Thank you to all my guides, teachers & esp. my loving friends.

—

My inner life is still unsettled from the radical changes occurring in my outer life. Namely the relationship with Zelie. She is a miracle & more interesting the longer I know her. . . .

Anyway. Life is fabulous. Isn't it always, really? I am here in my little white house on a hillside in Mexico knowing that my friends are enjoying themselves around me. It is sweet. Tomorrow Joan & Sue leave. I will miss them.

Jan. 27, 1998
Uxmal Mision Hotel, Uxmal, Mex.
Sitting on our balcony in Uxmal with its splendid view of the ruins a mile away. I've painted my nails "virtuous violet" and so my hands & feet seem to belong to someone else. We're up early. Zel is showering. I suspect it's going to be very hot for the rest of our stay—it's been rainy & overcast, often cold, since we arrived.[1] My body suffered, losing the warmth it had become accustomed to in Careyes.

Jan. 28, 1998
Enjoying this conference very much. Really like Terence[2] & Paul & Manuel and Peter. Also Jonathan Ott who is so smart. They all seem so familiar to

---

1 AW is accompanying Zelie—who, in addition to being a musician, is a traditional Hawaiian energy healer—at an ethnobotany conference in Uxmal.

2 Among those mentioned in this entry: Terence McKenna was an American ethnobotanist

me. Zel's crowd. Simpatico. I'm relieved. Happy. Learning new amazing things!

I've been distant from Z & from myself! for the past several days. Since Joan & Sue left (I missed them!) and this is due also to my never appearing, ever promising to come period. Which finally came. I seemed for many irritable, tight days, not to love Z. The old ice pattern where I think love has died and why am I with this person!? Isn't life better alone!? The answer is no. And so we struggled along together—Zel being very loving but holding her ground. Sure enough when I began to bleed my mood changed & I've been feeling very affectionate toward her. Tonight during Peter Furst's lecture we held hands.

It turns out Peter Furst is co-parent of the Modern Huichol Story Yarn paintings—a good friend of Jose Benitez Sanchez.[1] Over lunch he told Zel & me great stories of the Huichol early days.

Tomorrow is our last full day. We leave Friday.

It's been great. Going home feels great. Mexico has been entirely different this trip. More fun. More growth. More healing. Expansive.

I've found another part of my tribe.

Feb 3,

Soon I shall be fifty-four! Who can believe it! Not me. I feel my usual thirty-six or so, sometimes nine or ten. Occasionally 500,000. Anyhow, back from Careyes & the Yucatan. The seminar on entheogens was informative & so new for me: learning in a group like that.

*   *   *

---

and mystic who championed the responsible use of naturally occurring psychedelic plants. AW remembers him as "an extraordinary teacher to those who could be taught." Jonathan Ott is an ethnobotanist, writer, chemist, and botanical researcher who helped to coin the term "entheogen," which refers to a chemical substance, typically of plant origin, that is ingested to produce an altered state of consciousness for religious or spiritual purposes.

1   Peter Furst is the author of several books and essays on the Huichol, an indigenous people of Mexico, including *Visions of a Huichol Shaman*, which explores the visionary yarn paintings of the shaman-artist Jose Benitez Sanchez.

I'm sixteen years older than Zelie. Considering this, and much else, the miracle is that we relate so well. Sexually & otherwise.

I feel she is anxious about something. This concerns me.

Decided to leave her The Beamer & to ride up[1] with Sue. This turned out to be an epic ride & took 6 hours! Traffic, flooding, plus we stopped for food & gas. I bought a delicious Haagen-dazs chocolate bar, ice cream, & we cruised right along. Sue somewhat subdued but probably tired from the drive.

The monastery-like silence of Wild Trees is wonderful. There's a lull in the rain & I just hear a frog & the rushing of water down the hill.

I look out at the wet, wet landscape, & the eucalyptus tree and I feel very happy. (Amazing when I consider how wretched I felt at other times! Will I ever really get it that life is change & emotions are like weather?) This the Buddhists know and what a valuable lesson it is!

Both Tracy & Deborah seem gone from my life. The cords between us snapped.

I opened an envelope that was in my pile on return & in it discovered D. has cashed a bad check. And must now go to Bad Check Cashing School. I of course wanted to rush to her aid. But I received identical advice from Joan, Joanne & Zel. Don't. So I won't.

March, 1998

Lately Mamie has been more sisterly. She wrote a card recently saying she loves me & that they were all happy to greet me when I was born! Amazing.

—

1998 – Kaua'i

March 7, Saturday, Moore House, near Hanelei, Kaua'i. Brugh Joy Conference on Dreams.

---

1 AW rode to Wild Trees, her land in Mendocino, with Sue Sellars, her friend and neighbor.

My period came the day after the most magnificent massage by a Hawaiian man named Allen. 4 hours long and perfectly amazing. He found and dissolved knots I didn't know I had.

Though I felt exhausted and irritable last night & rather cool & distant even now, a fast & hang loose day, Zelie & I have been really good. She comes alive here in a way that moves me so much. I keep wanting her to have available all the energy she gets here, all the time. Berkeley has great energy too but the connection to the land here is still palpable. So precious!

I've been taking St. John's Wort & chaste tree berry for my moodiness. It seemed much less killer this month. Hoo-ray!

Maybe this morning I'll go for a walk on the beach, after putting a load of clothes in the washer.

Great Spirit, I need help! Don't I always? Help me to continue opening to Life. Help me to continue to see & to delight in people, events, everything. Sometimes, like now, I feel so awkward behind my attempts to grasp the newness of change. Help me. Which you do all the time, I know. And so,

Thank you.

March 25, Gloria's birthday:

Just looked up & noticed the sky is clearing & fog lifting. Mercy! I dreamed last night that I threw up some kind of cheese (white) onto a pile of Hillary Clinton's new clothes—still in a bag, neatly pressed. Something pink. When she came in I said: Just remember, I didn't cheat on you!

I'm really feeling for her & Chelsea, and him.[1] The media is relentless & it doesn't even matter that we don't care.

I came up on Sunday after a leisurely day in bed with Zelie. She's such a sweet lover! I'm so fortunate. She's so the young masculine to my Great Mother. I had this insight about myself: That I've always loved the young

---

1   For much of 1998, President Bill Clinton (along with his wife, Hillary, and their eighteen-year-old daughter, Chelsea) was embroiled in a political sex scandal. The forty-nine-year-old president initially denied having an affair with twenty-two-year-old former White House intern Monica Lewinsky. The scandal ultimately resulted in Clinton being impeached, only the second president to face that fate.

masculine. And have loved men who carried, embodied, it until they began to lose it. In their thirties & Robert in his forties, men seem (some of them) to begin a slide into the old feminine, which isn't the same energy as the Great Mother, perhaps because they're men. The Great Mother's attribute, like that of the Empress, is abundance, fecundity, plenty. Lush Life. Nurturing but in a reciprocal way, usually.

A sweet visit with Gloria who, at 64, looks adorable. She & I have been friends for so long! We just plug right back in and carry on. We're plotting a shopping trip when I come east in May. It'll be warm & sunny then, for sure!

I want to write poetry again. And feel I've earned the space after 6 novels and dozens of stories and essays. I like reading them when I lecture; it's wonderful to feel the response of the audience. People love poetry and they need it. Just as they need music. And they need and deserve the best of both.

So I am in bed, having meditated. . . . I'm lying before the fire in the evenings reading Angela's book on Blues Women[1] which is wonderful.

And so, Great Spirit, I thank you for all your blessings. How rich, varied & mysterious you are! How you play hide & seek with us and sometimes Hardball! Thank you for leaving me my houses standing. My health. My teeth. My eyes. My ability both to eat and to defecate with pleasure instead of pain. The list is endless. So, too, my gratitude & thanks.

You're the bomb! (As my daughter's generation says, strangely). Me Teamo.

May 6, 1998
Back from England. Very challenging 10 day trip.

Packed audiences—the largest at the Barbicon—1,900. Zel & I both pre-menstrual, jet-lagged, irritable. I said to her at one point "Fuck off & leave me be!"

---

1   Angela Davis's book *Blues Legacies and Black Feminism*—exploring the lives and art of Gertrude "Ma" Rainey, Bessie Smith, and Billie Holiday—was published in January 1998.

<u>Imagine!</u>

I felt so grown up!

Later we laughed & had a fabulous time in spite of my exhaustion.

Back at a Cazul that is literally crawling with flowers! Wisteria, jasmine, potato vine, roses.

I've been alternately energized and flat on my face/back. Today, just happy—which I stopped everything to record.

Thank you, Mama.

May 9, 1998

I seem to be dying to the life I've lived. I realize I don't care if I'm famous or even whether I'm remembered. Surely writers must be remembered partly because they've wasted so many trees. After this next tour I may well retire for real! I'd even buy back my stories/memoir from Random House.

What's more likely is that I'll wait a few years before publishing anything. At least 3. 6 would be ideal.

Zelie & I need a break from each other but in such a good way! We've been together constantly for weeks, months, and it's been so <u>real</u>. Now it is just time for solitude.

I'll drive to the country on Tuesday. Come down on Sunday for the picnic & to see her perform, then go back up on Monday & STAY until I have to go East. Back East I'll see Gloria & that will be fun. We'll shop & eat & talk. Then I'll fly to Chicago to talk to booksellers.

Zelie helps me realize I can live on very little & still be happy. And so I seem to be losing some of my <u>shack</u> fear.

Sat.
May 16, 1998

I've felt angry all day and want to suss out the roots.

First of all it is very cold. And has been raining off and on since I arrived on Tuesday.

I got myself together for the trip to England. Left home at noon, anticipating a 2:30 flight. Joan miscalculated. The flight was scheduled to leave at 4:30 & actually left around 5:00. I was really annoyed. . . .

England was a challenge. 5 lectures & several interviews & a signing each day—but with Zelie's help I rose to the occasion. The press was bad. Depressing. Left a bitter taste. Esp. <u>The Guardian</u> where the interviewer identified my Japanese gardener's pants as "combat" pants.

So, left Scotland in the wee hours, flew to London—excellent breakfast! I ate the sausage & all. Left London hours later. Got to SF hours after that! I'd asked Joan to hire a driver for us but no, there she was in her small car. A taxi would have been quicker.

Anyhoo—she <u>briefly</u> apologized for sending us off to the airport hours early before the long flight. Going through the basket later I left her a note asking if the repetition & tedium of the work wasn't getting to her. To which <u>she</u> responded that she needs more money!

We chatted. I said I was sure we could work something out, though I actually felt shocked. Later, I drafted a letter to her expressing my reservations about giving her a raise—"a cost of living increase," she said; her "rent was raised twice"—since I anticipate cutting back drastically on the work. I spoke of how frequently I've tried to get her to ignore the fax & phone. That I'm weary. Etc.

I went off for an Ayahuasca weekend with Zelie. When I returned, Joan's resignation was on my desk. Before I left for the weekend I'd written a follow up note and a check (bonus & celebration) for 25,000, so that she'd realize I wasn't trying to keep from paying her money—just not sure a raise made sense if her work is to be cut in half.

She left everything on my desk, files etc., and said her resignation was effective immediately.

I <u>felt</u> angry & jammed. Zelie came down & we talked, which helped. She asked to reread the letter—she'd read it on the computer before it was sent. <u>I</u> read it. Nothing on it seemed that bad to me. Zelie left Joan a message of support immediately. Next morning I called & left a message. Saying I was sorry she felt she had to resign, that I'd reread my letter & it seemed non-threatening & non-insulting. That I would add 11,000 to her 25,000 to give her a full year's salary as severance pay. (This was suggested by Gloria whom I called almost as soon as I could speak to another person about it.)

Later Sue told me Joan said she felt she'd been fired. That I wanted her to quit. She read parts of my letters to Sue. Those parts that, separate from the rest, seem to speak only of the past, not of the future.

I sent white Casablanca lilies & a note: To the light in us.[1]

I've spoken to several friends about it. And written up a job description. Feel <u>much</u> better & more balanced.

<u>However</u>, part of my anger is that this bombshell threw me. Suddenly I was very aware that I don't even know how to send a regular fax. I didn't sleep all night. <u>Cold</u>. Got up in the morning & went out to see that the rotten but beautiful avocado tree was being taken down, on schedule. I met, chatted with & paid the tree man. While noticing his whiteness (as he stood "overseeing") & the brown skin of his Mexican workers. He was pleasant enough. And the transaction was quite smooth. I felt—checkbook firmly in hand—quite ok.

Went upstairs to ask Zelie to show me how to fax something. She was still in bed, hugging my pillow, hoping to make love. <u>Now</u>? she asked. I said yes. Tersely. She grumbled a bit but got up & came downstairs. My first regular fax was very homemade. Handwritten. The bottom torn off. She was impatient with me. This hurt me deeply. Later she compounded the problem by saying she didn't want to have to show me every time I needed to fax something. No one has ever spoken to me in a tone that assumes I am stupid. I was very angry & told her so.

Our parting was tense and on my part icy.

All her talk about helping me, but when I most needed it she let me down.

So I said to her: I don't intend to ask you for anything! And I meant it.

I've been here since Tuesday—At this point Zelie called. She is upset

---

1   AW writes: "Joan Miura, my friend now for over thirty years, was also the best administrative assistant I've ever had. This painful severance led to a hiatus of connection that lasted several years—until, by accident, we met at an exhibit of Elisabeth Sunday's extraordinary photographs in a gallery in the Bay Area. I saw her before she saw me and said 'boo.' We have since continued our friendship and our work together, for which I am grateful."

I'm not coming tonight[1] as planned. . . . I read her parts of the above. She apologized. We agreed it's best that I stay here.

But then I went down after all. Starting while it was still light & arriving around 9:30. I waited & waited for her. Finally around 1:30 she came in—smelling of tobacco & beer. She'd stopped off at the pub. We had a so-so reunion.

And now we're both here, at Wild Trees. She is in the studio setting up her music; I've just planted Russian kale, Nicotiana & Japanese mustard greens. I am suffering from dearth of love and general out-of-sortness. Zelie's behavior re: the fax really did change how I view her. As someone, whatever her good points, who is selfish and lazy and self-centered. Ah! Skeleton Woman! I've felt very skeptical of her ability to love me. She takes everything she gets so for granted.

We discussed her laziness the other night. I don't think I've ever known, personally, a lazier individual. She says she has no energy. No motivation. She said her grandparents & stepfather always said she was lazy and "good for nothing." That Hawaiians were this way.[2] She asked if I thought it was depression. I said maybe. But really I've no idea.

Feeling relieved not to have an assistant. . . . Not to be tied to a greedy world through her feels free. Still I'm suffering from the loss. But something steely has entered me, too.

Yesterday Z & I went to Mendocino—to the beach. Had dinner at The Chocolate Mousse. I felt _so_ distant, as if I barely know her. I feel sad about this. She continues to smoke—so kisses aren't as tasty. She seems really into MJ. At least she's getting out of bed before noon. And making an effort to be helpful in a more conscientious way. I was bummed that she left me to buy the truck alone & to go to the ophthalmologist alone. Both things turned out ok—and the ophthalmologist turned out great.

---

1   Returning to Casa Azul in Berkeley.

2   Zelie's grandparents on her father's side were descendants of French settlers. Her mother was native Hawaiian. Zelie was hanaied (informally adopted) and raised by her grandparents after her father's untimely death. Their view of Hawaiians was typical of white colonizers of that era.

*   *   *

I'm premenstrual. I'm going to Philadelphia, NYC, Chicago in a few days—Goddess help me! And I need to write a 12 minute speech. I refuse to brood over this! The only answer is to change my life so that this doesn't happen!

Gloria says Wilma[1] is back in the hospital! That's a bummer. And a lesson/warning.

Great Spirit I am so low in my spirit—I've been in this place before. Help me. Just to have the grace not to hurt anyone around me.

I thank you.

June 9, 1998

Great Spirit, here I am again! Sitting in sun that I deeply thank you for. Hoping to improve my sour disposition. Which is with the sun, and sleep, & fresh fruit that Zelie bought before she left, improving. Thank you. I have felt like such a beast.

Joan's leaving the way she did was like a scorpion sting. Poisonous & lingering. I've felt angry over & over. And exhausted by it.

However, with the sun so bright and the breeze so soft, I really must let gratitude guide me.

After a day of small fights & sadness and all sorts of misery & eventual making up, Zelie drove off to Berkeley & from there she will go to Hawai'i. I was sorry to send her off alone but both of us need a break. And I'm not leaving here until I have to.

The sun is amazing! I must walk down soon just to feel it on my limbs.

It seems like this to me: That I was fine, Zelie & I fine, until we returned from our Ayahuasca weekend & found Joan's resignation. That I went into some kind of shock and panic—to be dumped so unceremoniously and after offering J. 25,000 in recognition of her work. Then I had only a week

---

1   Wilma Mankiller, a longtime friend of AW's, and an activist, social worker, community developer, and the first woman elected to serve as principal chief of the Cherokee Nation.

to regroup & then I was off to Chicago, New York & Philadelphia. Missed the flight to Philadelphia, due to rainstorm & heavy traffic. Got there just in time to be rushed before a gathering of rich white people who support The Free Library where I spoke. Speaking/reading went well. I was in a mood of "what the hell." Commented on one of the waitperson's biceps. He laughed. Woke next day at 8:08 & needed to make a 8:45 train to NYC. Got it by some miracle & fast foot work. Long drive up to Manhattan to Gloria's. She & I shopped all day & had a marvelous time. Then went to see The Lion King. The sets were stunning. (But the Young Lion King changed from young black boy to a white man without logic or warning.) Next day left her house at 12:30 to make 2:00 plane. Got there & was told that flight was cancelled! Got on United, after calling Corey limo. Waited at airport in Chicago. Driver arrived late. Took me on a hike to stand next to his car which he only then explained was broken & unable to move. Waited in parking lot for ½ hr. for replacement. One came eventually. On to my Spartan room & the Black Booksellers Association party. Then with Wendy & Carol to a dreadful noisy restaurant that I couldn't hear a thing in but noise. We were so early no table was ready. We left. Ate at my hotel. Wendy & I are old soldiers selling my books to publishers but time spent alone together passes slowly. Was relieved to go up to bed. Next morning up at 5:30—had to be in green room at 6:30. To wait & wait. Met the other speakers, Dava Sobel & George Stephanopoulos. They were warm & interesting. Also her publisher was with her & very cute. Carol sat with me. I spoke for 10 or so minutes. The others likewise. Spent 1 1/2 hours autographing books. Very long line. I was happy to get free. Back to the hotel. Packing. Off to the airport. A seat in first class but right in the middle of the floor! Horrid. So I read most of the way home. Got here. No driver. I called & while calling he appeared.

On to Cazul & Zelie & Mu! Which felt great. It had seemed a lifetime since we'd parted. I was so glad to see Cazul again I almost cried.

Coming here I think we were fine until Sue called & told me she'd had dinner with Joan the evening before & that Joan is out job hunting. I said but she doesn't have to be doing that yet. How silly of me to think she'd use the 36,000 to give herself at least a mini-break.

I had also felt annoyed because in my session with Jean Bolen Jean tried to justify Joan's quitting without giving notice.

I felt disappointed & annoyed with Jean for trying to justify what seems to me unprofessional behavior to say the least. Part of my agreement with Joan was that she'd help find & train someone before she left. The <u>least</u> she could have done it seems to me is give notice. She also refused to acknowledge my exhaustion, which hurt.

Zelie & I spent several days interviewing likely applicants. We've decided Kaiya is the right one. She struck us both as down to earth, smart enough. Motherly.

I called today & left the message that she has the job. She called back, delighted.

June 11, 1998

Yesterday I had more energy than I've had in a couple of months. My <u>own</u> energy, as opposed to that which I drew from the Universe (which I used in England & in Philadelphia & Chicago). With my <u>own</u> energy, then, I dressed, after writing checks (I enjoy this!) & tidying up my checkbook, and walked over to Angela's.[1] Picked greens. Sat on her porch. Enjoyed the sun. Walked back, knees creaking, puttered about the house. Eventually went down to the guest house & discovered that although there's no hot water in the shower, the hot tub was perfectly hot. I jumped in & had a great soak that eased the arthritic pain I've felt in my hips & lower back.

Zelie called. She's happy to be home & wearing few clothes. We're still rather easily irritated by each other's comments. Or I am. I told her I'd had a long talk with Rebecca who's coming on Saturday. Along with Trajal & his friend Kamron. I'd left a message explaining my exhaustion & end of my ropeness. She says she understands & is herself very tired. I said I felt I would have them from Saturday to Tuesday. She said fine. She & I must go to the DMV in Ft. Bragg to get the Jeep put in her name.

---

1 Angela Davis now owns a place in Mendocino, not far from AW's.

Anyway. The moon was full last night. I felt it in my ovaries. It woke me & I went out on the deck to see it—well I peeked out of the deck door. It's still cool.

My mood is much improved.

This time alone is precious.

When Zelie is around I talk too much. She has numerous health and emotional concerns & is constantly discussing them. It is as if my world is completely filled with another's static.

She's said some true things to me though. One is that I have no one to blame for my exhaustion but myself. That it is my problem/fault that I can't & don't say no. This is horribly true. I've worked under the assumption that work needed to be done & that my ancestors prepared me & sent me out to do it—but they didn't send me to do all these speeches. Which are draining when I schedule too many. And when they're added on to all the other things I'm interested in.

Zelie is ultimately good for me—no matter how meticulously I catalog her faults. She tells me I am unforgiving, hold grudges. Don't remember the good stuff. (Robert's complaint!) Etc. All true. And who else has the nerve to tell me?

What do I need to be happier in our relationship?

More time alone—   a minimum of 3 days a month. A maximum of 7.

This would give me a chance to meditate, hear my inner voice with clarity. Stay true to my inner sense of direction.

Wake up alone more often—
in my own bed   At least 1/3 of the time. I need to savor or recall my own dreams, meditate, feel at peace with my own rhythms.

Experience more silence while we are together. I am not a talker, by nature. I am essentially a contemplative. I <u>love</u> silence. I am refreshed by it. Too much conversation drains my creative energy & makes me feel irritable & empty.

Drugs:

I like marijuana but it hurts my eyes (dries them & leads to inflammation) & any kind other than Hawaiian makes me heavy & dull rather than light. I also suffer from hangovers. So I prefer to smoke ceremonially if at all.

The last MDMA experiences were wonderful. But the quality of the second batch was poor. I experienced little "truth" (the favorite place for me) & lots of residual aftermath: headache & general tiredness/out of sortness. So this is something I will probably not use again.

The Ayahuasca, last session, seemed to tell me clearly that I don't need it. Or in other words, what I got was "Go home & enjoy regular life!" I love regular life & so this instruction makes perfect sense to me. This means that I will probably not have "tea" after the coming 2 sessions.

More wilderness/outdoor/connection with Nature time. I would like to hike, go camping. River running. Bicycling. Etc.

June 13, 1998

Rebecca, Trajal[1] and Kamron arrived around seven last night. I love them all. Kamron is this tall, smart, quiet young man with warm hands and thoughtful eyes. They stayed at Cazul with Rebecca & slept in the guest room, which they enjoyed. Must get the closet in! Rebecca slept in my bed "deliriously" she said. We ate watermelon, cucumber & tomato salad & corn for dinner. Perfect. Trajal & I talked about joining a troupe, Kamron talked about his work with AIDS patients & the newest breakthroughs in the effort to stop cancer from devouring us. Wipe out capitalism, I thought. Wipe out the ability of some to gobble up others and to divert the rightful nutrients of others to themselves.

Rebecca spoke of her nesting instinct. The desire to have a settled life. A home & family. Having a nomadic childhood has been hard on her.

I was happy.

And so Great Spirit once again thank you for my incredibly wonderful blessings. I've lived half a century! I've seen sights! I've loved many & much! I've tasted everything! Even snails! I've been surrounded by beauty since birth!

Trees!

To die is to become you in another form. What fun!

6.29, 1998

In bed in Temple Jook. A cold, foggy morning. Yesterday the fog lifted by nine o'clock and I planted the front crescent garden: fava beans, squash, kale, mustard greens, salad mix. A few of the nicotiana plants have come up & two of the orig. kale and jap. mustard plants.

Zelie and I left paradise and went down to hear Me'Shell perform. I can't say I was overwhelmed, or even moved by her music, but I feel very protective of her & really moved by her courage, performing, since I'm aware (via R.) of her fragility. Zelie stayed to hear Indigo Girls & Natalie Merchant &

---

1   Trajal was a longtime friend of Rebecca's, and Alice's.

Sarah McLachlan (organizer of Lilith Fair). We went off to see High Art[1] at the Lumiere. I liked it a lot, but the ending is poor. They killed off the most interesting character without warning. . . .

The visit with Rebecca & Me'Shell was good. Me'Shell had a cold and was so exhausted I ached for her.

Zelie & I went for a lomi-lomi that was amazing. Done by two women who burped like frogs the whole time. Lots of stuff got stirred up. We went, afterward, for dinner at Thanh Long. Great! Then, on the way home, I asked if she'd fix the handle on the side gate. She replied it wasn't a priority of hers, in a tone of voice that made me cringe. I was stunned.

She lives in my various houses absolutely free, paying only her own phone bill. She also sometimes buys food.

This is so unsettling it's difficult to write about. Both her uptightness when asked to do something & my feeling of rejection/wrongness. I end up feeling it is emotionally unsafe to ask her for anything. This is a serious imbalance that will have to be consciously resolved.

July 8, 1998

I've been so irritable, I can hear the tightness in my voice. Annoyed with Zelie while she was here—distant, aloof. Annoyed while she's away—to V's birthday party & hanging out with her & other friends. I want her to have friends. She needs them, has lots of them. Well, only a few that are really close: Arisika, Victoria, Ehu & Nancy. Betty from Maui is in town. I'm still feeling the loss of Joan. Poor things! Both of us! She sounds, on the phone, as weepy as ever. I've written a long letter expressing my anger, etc. but haven't sent it. Today I cleaned out the closet in the little room. Yesterday I cleaned out the fridge. It's lovely to just be here day after day. With or without Zelie. Mostly with.

The younger generations are different. She reminds me of Rebecca

---

1   *High Art* is a 1998 Canadian American independent film, about a complicated lesbian relationship, directed by Lisa Cholodenko and starring Ally Sheedy and Radha Mitchell.

sometimes. I also feel the fact that she's never really had to work means a lack of fiber.

So in the middle of all the angst I've felt, I cut my hair. It probably looks ridiculous. I'm not sure I care.

—

Oppressed by Items! Stuff! Things! Houses!

August 24, 1998

In the country. Zelie is at the studio. . . . How do women live through menopause? I feel myself tipping over into craziness every five minutes.

We went to the Michigan Women's Music Festival. I read the 1st chapter of Light & Zelie sang. Rebecca & Me'Shell came—it was good to see them. Though later Rebecca remarked that being put in the position of being my daughter publicly was a strain. Poor Thing.

I have needed solitude desperately. Finally this morning—after sleeping in separate beds last night & resting superbly—I said to Z. I've got PMS & need to be alone. She was understanding. By telling her this I seemed to break the spell of my despair. I didn't blame her for some nonsensical or real offense. Didn't blame myself. Just owned my condition & its remedy. Later I helped her write up a Kainehe contract on the computer. Very funny. She's a novice. We temporarily lost the document. Etc.

We are buying Kainehe[1] together. She's trading property, I'm investing 300,000. This was/has been so scary for me. I'm just now about to get Deborah's name off my loan for Cazul. I'm refinancing the mortgage. Have felt very ignorant & like I don't have a clue what I'm doing. But really want to uncouple from her.

No word from Joan, beyond pleasantries. Nothing in response to my letters. So strange. I miss her; the Joan I used to enjoy.

Kaiya[2] seems ok, basically, but very spacy. I'm hopeful she'll "tighten up"

---

1 Zelie's childhood home in Hawaii.

2 AW's new assistant.

her phone persona, as I've asked her to. She tends to ramble on & on, as though disconnected from her own mind. It drives me crazy.

September 4, 1998

My handwriting is changing. More sloppy than ever. But at times, always a delightful surprise, it is graceful, too.

I've written nothing really in a year, since I finished the novel. Don't feel compelled to write anything. Content to live day to day.

Thankful for things like—for instance: today is not as hot as yesterday. The water tank is overflowing not draining itself empty.

My blessings in fact are as numerous as ever. I should count them:

Rebecca called last night & said she's packed up her house & rented it out. She's now on the West Coast—calling from L.A., beside the ocean. She & Me'Shell are having typical couple problems. R needs space. Just as I do. We commiserated with each other & laughed about our predicament.

Rebecca sounded good. I know she's got sound bones & teeth & a winning smile. Intelligence. Some compassion. She says she will call aunty Ruth.

Me. I am going through a rocky patch. Health and psyche. Since Joan left I've felt less stable. My hormones are causing me to feel odd. I went to see a homeopathist and am now taking lachesis and apis. Apis for eye pain, ear ringing, allergy to insect bites. Lachesis for mood swings & menopausal angst.

I'm hoping the cure won't prove worse than the illness.

Quiet. Solitude. Study with my teachers—Pema, Jack Kornfield, etc. will help. Also just <u>being</u>. Yoga, if I can bring myself truly to my senses. Meditation.

Is it work that I need? After each book I feel that I am finished. But— maybe not.

The book is beautiful.[1] I'm to go to nine cities on the tour. Manageable. <u>Three weeks</u>. I must rise right now & eat my Wheaties!

10.27.98

How delightful to report that I am home again, in the country, after a month away, on the road. Zelie gave me this notebook; I thought I would write in it on tour. How silly. I sent it home with a box of stuff picked up along the way & clothing that made no sense for the climate. Everywhere we went, except Toronto, was warm. We consistently brought sun and chased rain.

Zelie was a wonderful companion. Helpful, thoughtful, funny, sexy. Loving. We lit up rooms wherever we appeared. We shared the stage in Toronto & New York. Sweet.

In Atlanta & Boston we saw family & friends. In NYC Gloria took us to see "Ragtime" the musical. I liked it. Z was enthralled.

In L.A. Rebecca & I cozied up for dinner in my "plush" room at the 4 Seasons & later Bashir & Paul & Askia came to hear me read. Then I went with Rebecca to see her studio & the loft she shares with Me'Shell & Askia.[2] Her study is tiny. Simple. Very pure. She is proud of it.

En famille in the living room of the 4 Seasons we sat down to late tea with Scott Sanders & talked about TCP musical. I've been reading plays

---

1   *By the Light of My Father's Smile*, AW's new novel, had an official publication date of September 1, 1998.

2   Askia is Me'Shell's son. Me'Shell sometimes goes by the name Bashir as well.

by Pearl Cleage, Marsha Norman & Thulani Davis. Thulani gets my vote of who to write the "book" for the play.

———

My sister Ruth had colon cancer & surgery to have it removed, along with a long section of her intestine. She . . . has only the most tv shuttered distracted response to anything resembling Real Life. However, I think the cancer got her attention. She told me & Zelie, Invite me to Hawaii, I want to see a volcano.

It is a spectacular day. I feel grateful to be alive. I think I will find a place to lie in the sun.

I went on The Oprah Show. Oprah is in her prime. Very beautiful and admirable. Her eyes have a coolness I didn't remember but the interview went well. It was edited into 8 segments & has begun airing. I saw one of the segments & thought I looked foolish in makeup. I still don't understand makeup. It's a mask.

The tour was successful. Though not as well planned as previous tours. Also I'd made it clear I wasn't up to doing so much. Atlanta's event was poorly attended. Not my constituency. The same was true of D.C. where the event was held in the backwoods of Maryland. Bowie State.

Minneapolis was great. Philadelphia. Toronto. The 92nd St. Y.

The book[1] went on the NYT bestsellers' list a couple of weeks ago. It had started on both SF list & NYT's before I even began the tour. #15 I think. Then went on for real at #9.

I don't want to publish anything for a long time.

What I <u>do</u> want to do: Grow in my relationship with Zelie—who is on retreat in the Arizona desert for 11 days. (She called this morning; she's happy. I'm happy. Our love feels very peaceful). Pay down my mortgage! Spend time in Careyes and Hawaii—where Zelie & I are now the owners of her childhood home.

———

1   *By the Light of My Father's Smile* was AW's first novel since *Possessing the Secret of Joy* was published in 1992.

Life is good.

Thank You, Great Spirit OXO

Cazul 11.11.98

I let Kaiya[1] go and the new assistant, Barbara, seems competent & cheerful, with a life of her own, thank you very much! I've felt extremely lucky to have her.

I've been critical of Zelie. She cut her hair and I miss it so much. So does she. She seems male now, whereas before she seemed to have a strong masculine. It is as if the masculine overpowered the female in her. It bothers me. I love the feminine and like very much the masculine. I don't feel comfortable with one dominating the other.

My own hair is half in tiny pigtails. I'm slowly taking out my dreadlocks. As Angela said: It's time. That's the only correct answer. It feels good to get to know my hair again. So springy and so fine! Shocking. Like baby hair. Where does it come from? This soft, springy hair?

Dec. 4, 1998

Thanksgiving meant a wonderful visit from Rebecca & Bashir & Askia.[2] They'd like to buy land near us in the country. Pratibha & Shaheen would also.

Our community is growing nicely.

Zelie has taken a more domestic turn, now that her hair is so short! Making soup and muffins and pasta. All delicious.

We had a rough patch because at Thanksgiving Carmen, the friend she invited, took photographs. And she & Z disappeared like schoolgirls to have a toke—which took them out of the circle of family. I missed Zelie.

She apologized. Cried. Asked that I forgive her. At which point I realized she'd done nothing wrong.

---

1 Joan Miura's short-lived replacement as AW's assistant.

2 Rebecca's partner Me'Shell was now going by the name Bashir, among friends, and Askia was her young son.

That the offense, whatever it was, was minor, & not worth her tears. We made up and later made love, deliciously.

We're different now with our short hair—mine is in 200 or so <u>tiny</u> braids—than the ones we call "those two" of before our shearing. We are undergoing transformation. Have entered the unknown. Have made ourselves vulnerable, less attractive, more plain. I appreciate our undertaking of the journey though sometimes I feel adrift.

I've walked. Eaten. Made a fire. Started to read <u>The Light Inside the Dark</u>.[1]

I am aware that now there is nothing between me & life. I walk through it as if in a dense stream or river & it is as if I am immersed. I have caught up with Time.

Dec. 27, 1998
Kainehe, Moloka'i, Hawai'i

I am happy!

Zelie & I just returned to the house after an hour or so in the ocean, swimming & walking, meeting a couple of neighbors, Carole & Josh.

It is <u>amazingly</u> beautiful. The ocean just outside our door, Maui just ahead & to the left, Lanai off to the right. Peaceful, even with the folks cutting up tree branches in the backyard.

This is such a paradise. Zelie's house. It makes me happy to see her in her <u>placita</u>. She is so alive and into it.

Between us we now have 4 major houses! Ah, Life. You want my presence in 4 communities of the Earth & how better to tempt me than with gorgeous houses/locations. Zelie's house has such good soul/mana. From grandma & grandpa. And really wonderful ocean front.

And so—Thank you Great Spirit for the beauty you consistently present to my eye & heart & soul . . .

---

1   *The Light Inside the Dark: Zen, Soul, and the Spiritual Life*, by John Tarrant, is a 1998 book that explores how our darkest experiences can be the gates to wisdom and joy.

Jan. 5, 1999

Happy New Year, Alicita!

I stayed in my "mood spot"—good name for it—for quite a while. Also felt angry Z hadn't removed old photos of V. from her walls. Everything came to a head after we returned home. We discussed separating. Thanks to Z's greater maturity, I did not get left out on my habitual limb of alienation. Instead we talked & for New Year's Eve did Ho'o pono pono[1] with an ally and got to wonderful deep places of love! Made up.

Sat. Jan 15 or so, 1999

Zelie & I went to Cihuatlan[2] to shop for new mattresses . . . We couldn't get the mattresses, but we did get a boom box, a recorder for her, & a small radio for Marcos.

It was a great trip. Cihuatlan is about 1 hour & 15 minutes away, near Manzanillo. We managed to make our needs known & I loved using my Spanish.

Then, major magic happened. Yolanda[3] came to the house to give us massages. While she was here we decided to barter: The Nissan, which I was planning to trade in, for massages & Spanish lessons. While she was massaging Zelie the new refrigerator came: I asked her if she needed a refrigerator. She said Si. Zelie & I like her a lot. So now we've plugged the refrigerator in & the boom box. Zelie's been playing her ukulele & singing in her room. I've been in the dining room on the computer.

Now back in bed with doors & window open. Feeling happy.

Today is the **23rd of January**. Zelie left on the 20th. . . . She sounds happy to be in Kainehe & to be spending time with her familia.

I am having a <u>wonderful</u> time, after the usual bumps & grinds of Life. La Vida. Ai, yi, yi!

---

1 Ho'oponopono is a Hawaiian practice of reconciliation and forgiveness.

2 Cihuatlán is a coastal city in the Mexican state of Jalisco, a little more than an hour's drive from Careyes.

3 Yolanda is a friend, and massage therapist, in Careyes.

This morning at 9:30 I went to yoga. Blanca la maestra didn't appear until 10:15. I had time to check out the gym with its lovely view of the beach. Then in breezed Blanca & in trooped, eventually, four other women, & Yolanda. Blanca led us through an hour or so of energetic exercise. Then we showered & moved up to a vacant apartment patio & did yoga for another hour.

It was wonderful! I loved it as I was doing it. I <u>laughed</u>. I can still do almost everything except the Fixed Firm. Later the others went to La Loma, where we went last night for dinner—in Zapata—amazing food!—and I came home & had yogurt and juice. Juan Padilla came (Yolanda's brother) & picked up the refrigerator. At last!

Zelie & I had been in each other's company too much & needed a break.

As soon as she left I became attentive to a short story I'd started writing over a year ago.

Yesterday, in great happiness, I worked on it. On my tiny laptop, right at the kitchen table.

The solution for me, the only one that works, if I don't wish to inflict pain on others, is to embrace solitude. To simply disappear from the presence of anyone who could be hurt, even Marley.

And so. I've decided to paint the house blue. The wall ochre.

This is a lot like having a house in the South, living among people whose language I'm trying to learn, & loving them on some deep familial level while they remain mysterious.

Sometimes I shock myself by thinking: In 20 years I'll be seventy-five! But of course I could easily die before then.

For the moment I am very happy.

Thank you Great Spirit for all your blessings. For air & water & light & generous women. For the <u>sweet</u> Mexican men who so remind me of my neighbors & friends from childhood. So much tenderness, gentleness, liveliness. I cherish it the older I get.

Everyone treats me gently here. And today I connected again with Careyes & with why I choose to be here some part of every year.

My hair is still short. Each night I take out more of the ridiculous microscopic braids & rebraid it myself in uneven but more attractive, to me, braids. The braids of a little girl. Or of an old woman.

I seem shred of all pretense or aspiration. A monk. "Shred." Hmmm. Stripped? Looking at myself in the mirror today I could see I look less attractive. But I was laughing so much! Which means, I think, that my spirit is gaining strength.

Feb. 13, 1999

Goddess, el tiempo!

Halfway through the 2nd month of the year already. Savoring the one quiet day of the week—Sunday.

Overall we've had a wonderful time. Zelie loves people so much & is genuinely interested in them. Usually they respond to her. It's been great getting to know Yolanda & Blanca & Yolanda's boys. Such sweet boys. I hope they can grow into sweet manhood.

I spent my birthday[1] morning unbraiding & rebraiding my hair. Later we ate lunch at La Viuda & then went to Las Salinas for a swim—Yeshi[2] a marvelous guest. Then later to dinner (& after loving & a nap) at La Loma, which was a trip. Yolanda brought a huge cake, and everyone, including waitresses & restaurant owner, sang Happy Birthday in Spanish.

It was one of the happiest days of my life.

Feb 18

I'm fifty-five. I don't mind looking my age—it looks just fine, as far as I'm concerned. My hair is growing. I look like my little girl self, basically, except

---

1 AW had just turned fifty-five on February 9.
2 Yeshi is AW's midwife friend, visiting from the San Francisco Bay Area.

that sometimes I look like my mother. I look like Aunt Sally too. A kind of mystical, mischievous, <u>mad</u> look—Zelie says you can see the complete circle around the irises of my eyes.

I'm spending a lot of money but things, structural things, are getting done. The pond, for instance, the archive room, the sofas here, & this year, the bathrooms & the <u>kitchen</u>! Which is a disaster I never really noticed before. Although I do recall putting money in the account for a stove top.

Great Spirit I thank you for all my diverse blessings. For Marcos, who only completed 6th grade & is now 26 years old, working as my gardener, sweet & patient & respectful with me. A dancer.

For Yolanda, whose mother was pregnant 28 times & who is one of 14 living children. Such a brave sister. An artist.

And Blanca, so intense.

Thank you for Zelie.

Thank you for the women of our circle. For Joan, who was so good to me. For Belvie, who made me laugh so many times. For Diana who is so patient & loyal. For Evelyn who is so candid & protective. For Yeshi who loves me. For Sue who does too. For Arisika who wants to be closer.

For this time in Careyes that is filled with learning & laughter & food and getting things done. Flowers planted. Marcos & I made our first trip together, to the <u>Vivero</u>. For my Spanish which is improving.

For the quiet of this night—that is a blessing after the noise of the day. And for the sound of the waves crashing against the shore.

For this period of my life I shall wear lots of gray & sand & khaki & olive green!

April 27, 1999
Flying toward Pittsburgh.

I have been thinking of this strange emotional territory I've entered with Zelie.

We spent 2 wonderful months in Careyes. Time marred only by my neighbor's incredible noisiness. The only time I recall feeling really hurt or let down by Zelie was when I found Duccio's noise unbearable & woke her up to comfort and or just be with me, a witness. She said it wasn't bothering her that much & that she wanted to go back to sleep.

I felt very alone & oppressed. I didn't expect her to offer to duke it out with him, I did expect her to stay with me for a while, since it was a horrible experience for me.

I was <u>very angry</u> to be awakened in the middle of the night, to be kept awake.

Back home again we seemed ok—though something she'd said when we got home from Careyes disturbed me: That because I'm so "big," her "bigness" isn't seen. I <u>felt</u> exactly what she meant: I cast a large shadow & yet what can I do about it? Except what I've been doing. Spending lots of time together in places where who I am as "a personality" means nothing.

On the 15th of April Z left for Moloka'i. I was not sad to see her go. 2 weeks have gone by & I don't miss her. I feel numb, and as if, again, I don't know what happened.

I feel like bagging the relationship and going into a completely new one. With someone closer to my age, & closer to my own values.

I am due to go to Hawaii on the 5th of May.

4/29/99

I'm also loving my new short hair. I look butch, actually. Very interesting. I'm tempted to ask Raynetta to trim it for summer. When I left home I was thinking: it's time to put it back in dreads.

I have only a few minutes in Pittsburgh but perhaps I can pick up a pair of socks.

Talked to Zelie. She sounds bland and empty over the phone. I feel nothing when she says she loves me. I feel nothing when I say it to her.

There seems to be nothing left.

Which reminds me of what JoAnne[1] said: that it's time to begin again with a clean slate. Whether with Z or not is in a way beside the point.

Earthlyn's "The Changer"[2] says I'm losing friends because I'm changing so fast.

May 8, 1999

I have agreed to two readings in Northern NY—Buffalo & Rochester. I will arrange to be accompanied by Zelie or someone else _fun_. We will visit Niagara Falls and also the elders of the Onondaga people.

I will accept 2 more engagements, possibly, but why? There's no reason to accept any more unless I feel these events connect me to some crucial segment of the world. I wouldn't mind going back to the Southwest. Arizona or New Mexico. Southern Texas. Otherwise, No. Or, possibly someplace within easy driving distance. SF or Palo Alto.

4 speaking venues seems plenty. Financially it is excellent.

I have $ coming from RH for 2 more years. The Color Purple musical, royalties, etc.

<u>What</u> <u>ever!</u>

I want <u>all</u> my time. Something is trying to prepare itself in me. I need to keep quiet for as long as it takes. Go only with Spirit. (When I say this I see Wild Trees, the place Spirit, Ancestors, have provided me to do my work to benefit all.).

I asked Yeshi to think up a therapist for me. In Berkeley.

I've been feeling poetry coming. I'm not resisting exactly. Just not taking time. Letting the lines that come remain visible for a moment, then letting them sink. It's coming, though. It is in <u>that</u> direction that Soul wants to go.

My fear is that I see things so clearly—& do I want to share so sharp a vision. Especially, I do not wish to discourage the young, poor things!

---

1 JoAnne Brasil, writer and astrologer.

2 A set of oracle cards developed by Earthlyn Manuel.

5/10/99

And so. A bright, breezy morning at Kainehe. I've just returned from half an hour's walk on the beach. I walked as far as the fish pond & the blue roofed house that is so beautiful.

The beach is lovely.

Zelie prepared the outer bedroom for my private domain & I am very comfortable there.

When I saw her waiting at the airport, bearing leis her mother made, I felt so happy to see her. At first she seemed almost a stranger. And I savored that impression. Her hair is so curly & she is so brown! I thought she looked very attractive. And her look is that of fieriness.

She was immediately warm and attentive to me. . . . She is <u>so</u> beautiful. Such a good, strong spirit. We drove to the market & then to the fish house and then to Kainehe.

We were shy, careful, with each other. But attracted, too. We went to my room, at long last, and made love very sweetly.

Yesterday, Mother's Day, we went to visit her mother.

Z & I discussed being lovers & not partners. Having other lovers. Having male lovers. We were open and honest.

What will happen? What will Life actually have us do?

We learned, during our recent separation, that we are each capable of contentment in our own worlds.

May 23, 1999

> There is nothing
> to say
> I am content.
> Zelie
> on her blue bike
> has gone off
> to feed
> the dogs.

6/7/99
Back from Moloka'i. A fascinating time. More later. No sleep last night.

June 30, 1999
Zelie and I began couples counseling last week. A wonderful woman named Jane Ariel who is Jewish, gay, once lived in Israel. White hair. Warm eyes. I like her a lot. We all liked each other I felt.

It felt great to dive into our problems with someone so smart, savvy, thoughtful and dressed in such a neat outfit. Black pajamas, Chinese style, & green shirt & green Jade earrings.

Zelie & I have had incredible loving & a couple of big fights. However, the last fight blew up, she exhibited her volatile & vulgar anger & I laid on the couch thinking about why we were fighting. Realized it had something to do with my disappointment that Rebecca & Bashir are not very thoughtful house guests. I've felt put upon. Barbara's[1] been sick. Etc. Etc. We didn't run off—our mode of behavior—but sat on the couch talking & then hugging & kissing. Yeah! Breakthrough!

July 16, 5:05 a.m.
Zelie & I drove past Deborah's house on Carlton[2] last week. She has a fence around it that looks like plywood. I felt very sad seeing it. So desolate & as if she's hiding from the world.
Joan, Tracy, Deborah, Mercedes, Belvie. Old Life.
Zelie, Diana, Yeshi, Evelyn, Arisika. New Life.

How to proceed?
The Motherpeace[3] says The Sun will shine again soon. That there's a

---

1   Barbara is AW's excellent, and still fairly new, assistant.
2   Deborah, AW's former housemate, had moved back into her old home, which she wasn't able to sell.
3   The Motherpeace Tarot is a deck of tarot cards inspired by the Goddess movement and second-wave feminism. Created in the 1970s by Karen Vogel and Vicki Noble, it has never been out of print.

chance to be lovers in a way that heals old wounds. That I can handle complexity. (Except when I'm tired.)

I want a simpler life. Fewer things. More quality time with people I love.

Rebecca informed me she thinks I'm not enthusiastic enough in my response to her writing. I told her I've seen little of it. I don't read the magazines she's published in. Am never told when something is coming out. Have assumed whatever she writes about me will basically be an attack. Etc. But actually I don't care that much anymore & I'm glad. She's got a right to her feelings & her view. I feel I have been very praiseful of what I've seen & heard. But she thinks not.

Otherwise, our time together has been fine. I've enjoyed having her & Bashir around. I must try not to overdo, though.

This <u>complete</u> exhaustion I feel is not good. So empty I feel weak in the knees.

Blessings to all sentient beings including myself!

August 14, 1999

I have been feeling intensely sad. Probably since, at least, the death of John Kennedy, Jr.[1] There is as well the escalating violence of everyday life in the US, and an upsurge in hate crimes—primarily against Black people & Jewish ones. Closer to home I am feeling that the longer part of my life is over. Finished. As if a long row of doors just back of my neck slammed shut with an incredible finality. I sent off what may well be my last book: The Way Forward is With A Broken Heart. I may never write another book & that feels ok. What feels awful is the place betwixt & between where I find myself. The old life is over. The new one has not begun. I don't know even if there is a new one.

---

1   On July 16, 1999, John F. Kennedy Jr. died when the airplane he was piloting crashed into the Atlantic Ocean off the coast of Martha's Vineyard, Massachusetts.

August 17, 1999

1:02 am

Life, New Life, has begun. Thank you Jesus. Thank you Buddha. Thank you Isis. Thank you Life, yourself!

Z came back from Hawaii "on fire" with a new, expanded vision of her life. It includes wanting an "open" relationship & moving out. At first I was upset. Angry. Hurt. We talked & talked. Went to see Jane Ariel, our wizard therapist. Had a great & funny session. I feel (after being miserable & then crying ten pounds of tears) great. It is so astonishing. I'd had no real energy for months. Now I have plenty. Waking early; meditating.

I feel we're giving each other freedom & its foundation is unconditional love. She went out last night with old friends. I went out with Susan Griffin. We both had fun. Earlier Evelyn & I had gone walking & later to the walk shop to buy me shoes.

Who knows what will happen? Z says she'd like to start her 6 months of "open relationship" i.e. availability to potential other lovers as soon as Sept. 1 when her house becomes vacant. There is a Hawaiian woman she's attracted to/she has 3 children & a husband.

Z is such a unique creature. It is a trip being with her.

On the horizon is more meditation, yes! Walking. Yoga. And some new clothes. My clothes seem <u>too</u> tatty. I've thrown out lots.

8.30.99

Rebecca & Bashir and Askia[1] are here. The house holds us all very well. Yesterday was Bashir's birthday. We celebrated by going to see Fanny at Chez Panisse, a musical based on Alice Waters' book—followed by dinner at Chez Panisse. Very sweet evening. Zelie & I held hands through much of the performance.

*   *   *

---

1   Rebecca had come to visit with her partner, Bashir (singer/songwriter Me'Shell Ndegeocello), and her son Askia.

Zelie went out to look at a place to move into. She found one maybe: a room & bath in a black woman's house. I will miss her—but realize by now that Life just goes on . . . no matter who's coming & going. I feel a distance between us. Today I mourned what isn't to be. Felt the tears behind my lids.

But I also feel deeply okay. Myself. There's a wonderful scent of jasmine from the flower covered fence outside.

I will slog through the rough parts—after Porter, after David, after Mel, after Robert, after Tracy. . . . I've been here before.

"Love Don't Stay Gone Long . . ."

Goddesses help me. Ancestors.

—

Z is moving out tomorrow. I am going to Georgia for a school reunion. I'm looking forward to seeing old friends and classmates.

9/7/99

Evelyn[1] & I went to Eatonton for my high school reunion—wonderful to see everyone. Folks I would never see, otherwise. I danced with Porter.[2] . . . He's fat and balding. Looks short. Oy vey!

I didn't see any teachers to recognize them. But lots of classmates. Murl & LeRoy, & Doris & Mozelle & Edith & Eunice. It was great. Almost all the men not only hugged me wholeheartedly but lifted me off the ground and held me in the air!

Then we went to visit my brother Bobby who showed me the largest melons I've ever seen. One weighs 101 lbs. He gave us a little one that bumped along in the back of our car, split, & which we opened up at Ruth's & ate. Delicious!

—

I returned from Eatonton to find a note from Zelie saying she'd like to spend the evening with me.

---

1   AW's biographer, Evelyn C. White.
2   AW's high school boyfriend.

She came & we went to Breads of India for dinner. The owner gave me a hat he'd brought back from India! So sweet.

At home Zelie asked to sleep in my bed. We lay cuddled close until we fell asleep. Then she was up & gone by 7:00.

Ah, Life!

Sept. 17, 1999

An emotional session with JB[1] yesterday. Jean, I said, I've run out of steam! This admission made me teary. I talked about my insomnia, lack of motivation for writing. Told her about my series of big dreams. She, like ME, encouraged me to paint. I will get paper today. Although it occurs to me I probably don't need anything special.

Anyway, a muddling, draining session. I was tired & disoriented leaving SF. Missed the right freeway turn. Headed to San Jose.

Made it home to my family in one piece. Rebecca had bought soap, a shower curtain for the studio, & sushi. She & I had had a wonderful walk around lake Anza earlier.

Took a nap!

Then, Yeshi returned my call. She reminded me to use my PROGEST! I'd stopped. I can't believe it. So I took a hot bath and slathered it on. I slept very well last night.

Thank you Goddess Yeshi!

Today I look out on, yes, the fog.

But I shall get up anyway & buy some more Progest. Take Mu to the marina.

Since walking early in the morning with Evelyn I am seeing these mornings as lovely.

Thank you Great Spirit for all your blessings. For Jean Bolen who is wise. For Yeshi who is generous. For Zelie who awakens me in all my shadowy

---

1   Jungian psychiatrist Jean Bolen, AW's longtime therapist.

parts! For Rebecca who is caring. For Bashir who is gentle and so sweet. For Askia who is a delight. For Mu who is loyal. For Frida who is a queen.

For this blue house that shelters us all, expanding & contracting at will.

For Barbara who is funny & real. For Evelyn who loves truth. For Belvie who rises to the top! For Mercedes who taught me I can't base a friendship on guilt while subjecting myself to manipulation. Yeah! For Pema Chodron who has blessed my life with wisdom.

For Bobby who grows 101 lb. watermelons & peanuts for me, special! For loving me.

I am so thankful & so blessed. Let me now get out & encounter your wonder in all its forms!

—

Great Spirit, Life Rolls On!

Sept. 19,
At the Buddhist Retreat for People of Color at Spirit Rock.

I need to report meeting Russell Brown from Santa Fe. A black man, a psychiatrist. Plays the didgeridoo. A handsome, beautiful man. Deeply sensitive. Smart. Knowledgeable & wise. I loved him almost—well, after I'd heard him speak once or twice in council.

I wrote him a note: "I just love you. Let's be friends."

He wrote back: "Your note made me weep. Thank you! We are already friends."

This has been an astonishing experience. I've never been happier. I love everyone. I love Spirit Rock.[1]

Jack Kornfield has said he'll mentor me in the Dharma. After trying to steer me toward Gandhi & King.

---

1   Spirit Rock is a meditation center in Woodacre, California, that focuses on the teachings of Buddha as presented in the Insight Meditation tradition. It was founded in 1987 by a group of meditation teachers including Jack Kornfield, a bestselling American author and teacher in the Vipassana movement.

I am very happy at the possibility of learning the Dharma well enough to teach it.

And so tomorrow I go back to my world. To Cazul. What it will be like I can only guess. It will be good to see Rebecca & Bashir & Askia & eventually Zelie. I hope they are all safe & well & happy.

Life!

Oct 2, 1999 **Temple Jook**

I returned to Cazul to find Rebecca escorting a photographer to the gate. The woman who does those Women at 40, 50, 60, 70, books. It had been a difficult meeting for R. but she was very present & interested in my retreat experience. Which I shared as fully as my afterglow permitted.

For the next couple of days I caught up on mail, went into the city to see Jean B. (who says I'm ok & don't need to come again!) & to go to Bob Burke's office to sign trust documents. Then finally to Hilltop to buy bras!

Yesterday, after a lot of housecleaning, washing, etc., I came here. The drive was a bit long because of traffic, but still: I left at a quarter of two & by 5:30 I was preparing collards. From the plant I'd dreamed about since my last visit. It is so healthy I can feel it speaking to me. Such good greens!

Unfortunately I overate. Tossed & turned all night. Dreams of fried potatoes!

Today started cold & foggy. Now it's turning warm & sunny.

October 13,

I went with Zelie to therapy yesterday, which was good. Then to visit her room in Oakland. Which was also good. Her room is neat and restful, aesthetically pleasing. I lay on her bed while she gathered a few things to bring over. She's been staying here with me.

We are still very much in relationship. We've agreed that I am to own 2/3 of Kainehe rather than continue the "loan" of 345,000. We've been thinking of making some kind of center there for ourselves & other women. We could then stay there longer each year.

We're excited about going to Oaxaca on the 22nd & on to Careyes later. Life is abundantly good.

Rebecca is wonderful. Bashir is wonderful. Askia is divine. I love having them near. Such precious, brave souls! I feel so lucky!

And so, in my 55th year I find myself blessed. Ancestors present and helpful. Earth & plant spirits beckoning. (Forgot to mention that 8 shamans from Colombia came to tea on Sat.!)

Life!

Blessings to all Beings, Everywhere!

31 Octubre O El primero dia de Noviembre
Oaxaca, O. Mexico

On the 14th of October Zelie, Maria Elena & yo went to visit grandmother Ayahuasca & her helper, Jose. It was the first time I was in ceremony with a mixed group, men & women, & except for Ricci, I was the only black person. It felt very different & at first was really hard to relax into the experience. I had also worried that grandmother had already told me to go home & live ordinary magical life. I thought this meant not to take Ayahuasca anymore. I asked <u>the 8 Shamans who came to tea</u> about this. They seemed to think I shouldn't take the message as definitive & for all time.

So then I thought: Maybe I'm supposed to be Ayahuasca's friend & am supposed to learn more about it/her.

This is what I said to Jose on the first night. That I felt called to be a friend to Ayahuasca & to be a friend as well to the people who traditionally use her medicine, i.e., the Shamans.

That same day word arrived that Thomas Ridge, governor of Pennsylvania, had signed a death warrant for Mumia—Dec. 2 is the date set for his execution. I was feeling anger & grief & sorrow & helplessness which I pushed away all day. When I took the medicine, however, the full impact of Ridge's action hit me. I sat weeping & rocking, with my shawl over my head.

The next night, having shown me this deep grief, grandmother answered me:

I found myself in a forest filled with large trees & empty spaces. I was calling "Grandmother! Grandmother!" Looking everywhere. I realized after awhile that she wasn't there! I felt intensely bereft, lonely. Then I realized, after saying to myself "she's not here!" that I was there & that I am grandmother! Very patiently she said: Right. We are the same.

It was quite an insight. That I am now grandmother. That there is no higher authority. I had a deep sense of the power of Grandmother. Of her trustworthiness. Wisdom. No nonsense caring for all. I felt baptized into the next phase of my life.

Through all of this Jose is singing icaros. Zelie, Maria & I are bonding with him. Our hearts became completely attuned to each other. We realize our kinship. It is amazing.

The next night Jose gives us a different Ayahuasca that cleanses the blood. He sings to us of opening the heart:

"Now is the time
Ya es el tiempo
Now is the hour
Ya el la hora
To open the heart
Para abra el carazon"

He tells us many wise things:

A good teacher is always learning
The moment he thinks he knows
He has gone wrong

My "trip" this time is to remain in the present. With Jose, with Zelie, with Maria Elena.

I sit for 4–5 hours in contemplation, purging (as I have each night) once. I experienced a feeling of mellowness, kinship, happiness & ecstasy.

I felt quite close to Jack & Ricci. And closer to one or two of the white people. However several of them were very disrespectful of the medicine. One of them vomited on the floor & took forever to clean it up. Others tried to make the medicine erotic. And the most obnoxious of all kept making rude condescending comments & mocking Jose. I was really disgusted. It felt like a pack of vicious ghosts inhabited one corner of the room.

The bonding with Maria Elena was intense. I've never experienced anything like it.

So after this <u>incredible</u> experience of being initiated into authority as grandmother, the same as Nature (!) we came home to pack for our journey to Oaxaca.

November 8, 1999

I've no desire to write anything. And don't care in the least. I am aware of having emptied myself of my old life. I can barely bear to speak of it, it seems so distant and unattached to me. This self feels new, fledgling, but is getting stronger. Filling itself with new dreams, realizations, desires.

Dec. 23,

Almost too much life to report!

We're all here at Kainehe: Me, Zelie, Rebecca, Bashir, Askia! Tomorrow Pratibha & Shaheen arrive. How did this happen?

Last night Zelie taught the boys, Askia & Todo, how to build a fire on the beach. It was wonderful. We gathered sticks (they even "gathered" & burned my walking stick!) for the bonfire in anticipation of a large full moon which didn't appear—because of clouds!

Zelie's stepfather, Ah Yong, and her brother, Clinton, came down to join us. As did Ian and Kumau. It felt sweet. I had a beer, which tickled Ah Yong. I said I want a strong one, not a "lite" one!

Rebecca was taking pictures with her old fashioned camera. The night before had had wonderful moonlight.

It is early in the morning, overcast & chilly. My locks are finally in place—it has taken a year! And my scalp needs washing. Esp. because sparks from the bonfire & ashes fell on my head.

It is so <u>different</u> being with family. I love it. I'm amazed by this. I went for a walk with Askia & the dogs last week. We went to Lake Anza. At some point he wanted to stop, jump the creek & climb up the opposite hill. To play. I sat down on a rock & watched. Grateful & content. A grandmother! How happy I was! How simple the cause!

Zelie is moving back here, to Molokai. To be with her family more. To work on her music more. Whatever. We've agreed to own Kainehe in equal partnership, which feels fine to me, though I'm tempted to give her my share. Something stops me, though. Partly I love Kainehe. I may still give it to her, though, because it is her home.

Dec. 27, 1999

Dearest Zelie,

This is to let you know I have decided to give my share of Kainehe to you. I actually decided a few weeks ago, while we were still in Berkeley; the night I cried so much!

Anyway.

It is your home & my joy to make this gift to you.

I will also provide the agreed upon support. The key is to begin, to persevere. Work.

The motivation darling will be love of your people, of the earth, and gratitude for your having been offered a role and a tool in healing both.

Sing!

With love,

Alice

This is a record of my intent in the event anything unexpected & final happens to me!

I trust Rebecca to see that this is done.

Jan. 4, [2000]

On the first day of the year I called & left a message for Bob Burke (my lawyer) asking him to prepare transfer documents from me to Zelie of Kainehe. So, it's done! Then, yesterday morning, I told her about it.

She wept.

I told her I would also support her for 1 year.

I don't know if this is the right thing; it <u>feels</u> right.

I could not hold on to something so precious to her & her family & sit back while she tried to sing her way out of the debt.

Who knows what will happen with us. Whatever happens we've had an amazing 2 ½ years!

<u>And</u>, on the 30th of Dec. Tracy called! I got her message a day or so after. Amazing. I'm so happy for her. She sounded so sweet. I called & left a message saying I'd be back on the 9th, which I will—Goddess willing.

Jan. 8, 2000

Tomorrow I head home to Berkeley & Mu.

*   *   *

And yesterday, my guides came back! I was sitting up in bed looking at the window curtain blowing in the strong wind. I wanted to see out. I got up, pulled back the curtain, looked out to the ocean. Soon I realized there was a little face in the tree (made of leaves) that was very animated by the wind & quite expressive. And then I realized it was talking to me! It was like an Ayahuasca experience, really. I can't remember word for word but the gist was: Oh stop muttering about. You're full already. Just begin. Anywhere! A full lecture, bashing my hesitations, running roughshod over inhibitions. Amazing. Urgent.

And sure enough, I picked a line from this very journal & soon it expanded into—the beginning of something! I was amazed. As usual.

I was so thankful I got down on my knees before the tree, which lives outside my bedroom, & in tears I thanked it for the message that now I can begin the dance again.

The world is so magical it frightens some people. Hence repressions of all sorts. I'm so thankful the magic of it feels delightful to me. If this is being crazy, what unending joy!

POSTSCRIPT

BY ALICE WALKER

A few days ago I celebrated my 77th birthday. I did it with friends, and a niece, in a tiny fishing village on the central coast of Mexico. During these past few years I have lived an almost monastic life, mostly in the countryside in Northern California in a Zen-like house on a hillside overlooking a valley that is often, most mornings, covered completely in mist, so that looking out it is as if my house and I, and my beloved dog, Ede, are drifting in a pearl-gray sea. I love this. It is as if every fairy tale I was told, or read for myself as a small child, somehow came true.

I keep in touch with my writing life, which appears to be an intrinsic part of me, by occasionally placing my thoughts—poems, essays, observations, encouragement to the young—on my blog, AliceWalkersGarden .com. There are, for other parts of my nature: walks in the forest around my dwelling, gardening, though not as much as earlier in my life, swimming in a rain-filled lake, and seeing the occasional friend who might wander up my hill. It is a life primarily lived in solitude, which I have always deeply enjoyed and from which, as this journal attests, I was often distracted by the entreaties of a world that I imagined I could help. Whether I was actually able to do so is something I occasionally ponder. At any rate, most of my activities in that direction seemed like a good idea at the time. I have no regrets.

That Valerie Boyd appeared to help me edit, shape, and publish my journals is a dream come true. *Wrapped in Rainbows*, her perfect biography of Zora Neale Hurston, whom we both love and admire, was all the evidence I needed that she could be trusted to trim away hundreds of pages of my runaway journals and offer readers a form more easily transportable, and understood.

Though I miss some of the dreams, visions, conundrums explored in the pages that rest now only in the archives of Emory University library, it is a relief to see that caring eyes and a feeling heart, connected to a resourceful mind and sharp editing scissors, found a way to comply with an editorial demand that, in *Gathering Blossoms Under Fire*, we offer about five hundred rather than a thousand pages. And, of course, there will be a volume two.

What sorts of things were left out? you might wonder, if you are as curious a person or reader as I have been. I considered this, and decided that if I were to write an afterword, for which at first I saw no need, it would offer a sample.

A few outtakes from *Blossoms*, and my comments on them:

I find myself in a not esp. delicious dilemma: The middle of a triangle comprised of Robert & Mercedes & me. My overall feeling is one of tiredness. Robert & I very comfy together, generally, though experiencing a certain roughness when he called & I said I was in bed with Mercedes. I was. Though she was sound asleep.

Did I enter the relationship with Mercedes out of frustration with Robert's slowness? His male inability to passionately comprehend women's lot?

What is striking about some "romantic" intrigues is that they consume so much energy! But also, journaling through such periods can be an aid to understanding one's own motivations, frequently lost in the emotional rush of running away from a perplexing situation and trying something new.

—

Rebecca called. We have made up. She hurt my feelings by saying she doesn't feel at home in our house and that W's family is "normal," etc. I asked her to stop comparing. Anyway, now she thinks W is gay. . . . She says "Is everybody gay?" I say no, but I suspect everybody's bisexual. She says she's sure she's not. I say there's no surety in life & even when you're dead you might come back as bisexual saplings.

Try to see the larger picture, I urged. And then she told me white men are planning to colonize Mars. We muse: who else would think of this? They're not planetarians, I say. Not of Earth, anyway. And I think: I <u>never</u> want to leave Earth. It is not even a thought I have. But now I have another thought about *"the white man" as child: Does he feel so homeless & unwanted that he is always seeking farther & farther away to be?*

My daughter and I, thank every Goddess and God ever imagined, are as close today as we ever were, and we have been plenty close. Life for whatever reason gave us grief for a number of hard-to-bear years. This conversation, so typical of us, reminds me of us at our most "deep into the stuff of it" days.

Dream, Dec. 1990

Lying in Robert's arms one afternoon, sleeping, I dreamt:

A square church congregation nothing much happening. Then a young black man arises & magically organizes a circle of dancing people. There is a crippled woman who makes astonishing moves with her cane, including lying prostrate on the floor, & springing up again. There is another woman, or the same woman, a wonderful brown, dancing gracefully in a short split dress/skirt. This is all done joyously & these are all people of color. And then, surging into the church/circle comes the bluegrass contingent, white Americans filled with love & music, & the plangent sound of the banjo. I woke up saying, as I had in the dream, it is so wonderful to know who we are & what we look like & <u>are</u> like! Happy.

I could not bear to leave this dream out of the book! In fact, what will America look like when—if ever—it is united and happy!? I will not live to see that day, but the dream of it must be planted—hence this dream—in the hearts of our multicolored tribe. I was fortunate, after being bruised to the core by life in the South and especially after years of strife in Mississippi, to find myself at last in a community of hippies in a back-to-the-land community in Northern California where I could shake my shekere alongside the bluegrass folks' violins, banjos, and horns. I saw us then as a seed of sanity and fun; ah, I would muse, it isn't impossible after all! America *can* be free.

Aug. 16, 1985

There was a dream the other morning that was wonderful: I was in my mother's house, which, as usual, was filled with visitors. She was lying in a large room

*by a window & I was in & out looking at and talking to her. But I was really an-
noyed with the people & wanted them out. This I expressed to her, sitting beside
her on the bed. But she explained that having the people around her, old friends &
newer ones, made her feel remembered. And sure enough, as she said this, her face
became younger and younger, until she was younger than she was when I was
born—& I realized that yes, many of her old friends <u>remembered</u> her that way!
And that to them, there was <u>that</u> still, in her, which I could never know. This was
a great lesson for me and changed, I hope, forever, my annoyance at her visitors.
In the dream I actually sat down in a corner & started to work on myself.*

Beware of anything that destroys or distorts your dreams! This was one of
the clearest dreams I ever had. Most if not all dreams might be like this,
I believe, having dreamed much in this life. Dreaming is the source of the
first knowledge, in my view.

———

*Now I must stop & just look at the way the wind, invisible, moves everything,
especially the branches of the trees I see from all 7 windows!*

My house at the time was a wooden teepee with seven windows! Built by
a back-to-the-land hippie who believed humans could make do with less,
it stands today as a testament to our ability to make beauty out of castoff
wood, glass, doors, and window frames, and lavender doorknobs!

Oct. 22, 1980

*Some wonderful experiences with Robert. Great lovemaking & even greater
ability to love through touch. I said to him one night at his place, Why is it that
now your touch is all pleasure, there is no longer any pain (sometimes his pressure caused soreness in my breasts) and he said, "Because I am loving you more."
Then tonight when I told him I was feeling out of it, he called back to remind me
it is the night of the full moon. He said: I love you. And I said "Well, maybe, I
think . . . maybe."*

But I felt love for him too. And anyway, whether I say it or not my touch says it.

*He said in the car when we were driving to the park to walk & have lunch in
the hills: You know what? I love your touch, and your touch loves me.*

He is much handsomer now than even a year ago. Tall & lean & the color of copper, with nice deep dimples.

This is a relationship that had many trials! And yet, it held so much tenderness and beauty, and, above all, growth. I could not let go of us, as we were in so many of our moments together. Growing. Savoring. Wandering. Loving. Usually while going somewhere!

———

We went to Cambridge together & I did a benefit for Oxfam. We raised 10,000. Quincy sent lovely tulips—he's so thoughtful and <u>present</u> wherever I go. Then there was a telegram from him & Harry Belafonte. From USA Africa. I feel Quincy really seriously becoming my brother/father/friend and I love it. The story "Cuddling"—writing it—seems to have cured my lovesickness.

I had a crush on this wonderful soul mate. But got over it when I realized it was his spirit, expressed in music, that mostly attracted me.

———

We are no longer struggling in our relationship. Or at least not in any of the old ways. I am aware of trying to help him in his struggle to liberate himself, his psyche, and this is rather joyous too, since the person emerging is beautiful and engaging. It is almost exactly like seeing someone be born, and that they are 6 foot 2 is irrelevant. Sometimes I see in his eyes the bewilderment and hurt & trust of a child and I just have to take him in my arms, as I would a small child, and hold & rock him. I <u>love</u> the person he's becoming. I would love him even if I didn't know him.

Relationships are ideally suited for this kind of work. Helping to rebirth each other.

April 1983/after winning Pulitzer for *The Color Purple*

My dear this is the end of the line for almost everyone. But be encouraged. Have no fear. Things are going to be ok. If not for human beings, then for our planet, which is much more in tune with the refinements of eternity than we are.

*   *   *

Such tedious work is this. I'm amazed. Is this "Fame"? The tiredness and the effort to make what is long succinct?

———

The directive from the camera person was that I "write something" while being filmed.

———

Phone rang: Miss Sue from up the street wants to get some "healing water" from a spring she has heard about. This spring used to be for whites only. Now, integrated. It is a trickle as big as a finger.

She comes to the door & Mama lets her in. She collects gallon size plastic jars. 4 of them. I go in, hug her. She tells me I look good, thin & <u>happy</u>. She says "What you doing? Marrying again?"

I say "I don't believe in marriage." She stops. Then laughs.

I like her.

She says they say this mineral water will make you feel 16. But she doesn't want to feel 16. It would get her in trouble. She & my mother have been tight friends for 50 years.

I love knowing that I come from a mother who had staunch women friends her whole long life. That they shared adventures and tribulations and jokes. That they understood the history, social and otherwise, of something as odd as this segregated, now integrated, "healing water."

———

Ruth and I struggled through the rough periods of our relationship as we've done for years now. She made a real effort not to talk so constantly about herself. I intend to have a bracelet made for <u>myself</u> that spells <u>Silence</u>. Because I think there is a real danger in talking too much. I think talking robs us of potency the way perfume is robbed of scent when the bottle is left open. I always feel bad, almost nauseous, when I've talked too much. I guess that's where the expression "spilled her/his guts" comes from.

My sister and I were very different, which is often true of sisters. I see now that talking a lot, like writing for me, was a way to validate herself in a family that rarely listened. I am such a lover of silence, I used to joke, it will no doubt be a pleasure to be dead.

—

Tomorrow, Robert, Carole Ellis (new friend), Rebecca, Casey & I are giving a small party. All day I shopped & cooked (eggplant lasagna & curried chicken; Robert made pies) and I am feeling happily in love? With Robert. It is different, somehow, now. More like puppies, really. Two puppies rolling about blissfully together in a warm, bright spot. That's us.

When we made love last night I looked at his face as I was coming—usually I close my eyes & imagine his face & him. This time I looked. I prefer looking. His face was so intent on serving me. All of his will was into pleasing me, bringing me to climax—and I felt as if we were on opposite sides of a river with our arms out, straining toward each other.

And then—the river, the distance, vanished.

Such is the gift of trust. And why it should never be broken.

—

Some random thoughts: my life with Mel always had a quality of unreality about it, as if something in me was asleep throughout the relationship. I felt great peace but a peace constantly sabotaged by longing.

With Robert—when I'm with Robert—I feel at rest, as if my spirit, not just my mind or body, has found rest. But interestingly I "rest" by moving with him. I said to him on our desert trip that—since we do not wish to offer each other symbols of the fetter, i.e. bracelets, rings, etc. I think a perfect gift to ourselves would be matching moccasins. And if we should ever have a ceremony, that's what I'd like to exchange. Matching moccasins.

We never had a ceremony other than, as I recall, washing a large crystal in the ocean under a full moon. Robert's son, Casey, carrying crystal and flashlight.

—

It is hard to write. I begin to feel somehow that the act of writing separates me from Being. The bliss of giving myself up to wind sounds and the way the leaves look as they blow. There is no question, following my heart & the Spirit of the Universe I've found my place. My little round house with its new yellow floor, its sleeping loft & skylights.

* * *

When we find our place, we know. Everything else can seem a distraction. We settle in to enjoy the beauty of Life itself.

—

And so on!

I close by offering a short poem by a beloved teacher, Buddhist monk Thich Nhat Hanh.

The present moment
Contains past and future.
The secret of transformation
Is in the way we handle
This very moment.

I have kept a journal all my adult life, since I was in my teens. I've kept it partly because my memory is notorious, among my friends, for not re-membering much of what we've shared. The journal gives me back some of what I have lost. The conversations, psychic discoveries, and journeys of all kinds.

And yet, I have lived constantly in another present. The present mo-ment of creation. While I was writing the journals I was also writing, in another realm, worlds that I discovered in my imagination. Novels, poems, short stories, etc. This means this journal is, in many ways, my attempt to hold moments I have savored, with friends and others, as also unforgettable and dear. And it is, therefore, truly dedicated to them.

February 12, 2021

ACKNOWLEDGMENTS

A book of this size and scope—more than eight years in the making—requires an intentional community of good actors and well-wishers to bring it to life. I have so many people to thank for their general good will, as well as for specific acts of kindness and grace. At the risk of leaving someone out, I will attempt to name names here. But even if your name isn't mentioned, please know that I am thankful for all the little moments that led to this big one. I am grateful to every librarian who retrieved an archival box for me; to every barista who painstakingly poured a sweet oat-milk design atop my chai tea latte; to every friend who, despite the seeming setbacks, kept the faith.

I must start with my two graduate assistants, Stephanie Blount and Nicole Morris Johnson, who, over the years, helped me to transcribe every word of Alice Walker's handwritten journals. That summer in the archives with you, Steph, is one of my treasured lifelong memories. And, Nicole, I will always be thankful for your unwavering, years-long commitment to the enterprise.

I also thank the archivists and administrators—especially the late Rudolph P. Byrd, Yolanda Cooper, Courtney Chartier, Gabrielle Dudley, Jennifer Gunter King, Rosemary Magee, Randall Burkett, Kevin Young, Clint Fluker, and the late Pellom McDaniels III—at the Stuart A. Rose Manuscript, Archives & Rare Book Library at Emory University, which lovingly houses the vast and wide Alice Walker Collection.

Huge thanks to our original editor on this book, Dawn Davis, who held fast to the vision, even through the haze of a thousand pages and a big career move. And to our current editor, LaSharah Bunting, who stepped in to see it all through—with robust support from her assistant, Maria Mendez, and our excellent, exacting senior production editor, Mark LaFlaur. All of this was made possible by the generous support of Dana Canedy, senior vice president and publisher of the Simon & Schuster imprint, and her impressive team of bookmakers.

I offer deep gratitude to Joy Harris, the devoted literary agent whom Alice Walker and I share, and to her team, Adam Reed and Alice Fugate.

I am privileged to offer never-ending thanks to my lifesavers: Dr. David Kooby, Dr. Walid Shaib, P.A. Sujata Kane, and the many nurses and other health-care professionals who have gotten me through challenging times. Three deep bows to you.

I have so much gratitude for my little family of strivers: my parents, both now ancestors, Roger and Laura Boyd, who always supported my literary ambitions, despite not being "book-reading people" themselves, as my dad once put it; my niece Kaylisha Lewis Boyd; my brothers Mike and Tim, and my sister-in-law Regina.

Finally, it brings me great joy to thank the many friends and colleagues, old and new, who have simultaneously held me down and lifted me up—or, as Zora Neale Hurston might say, who've "propped me up on every leaning side." Thank you, beloved companions on the journey: Veta Goler, Gina Breedlove, Mignon Goode, Linda Blount, Monica Pearson, Kelley Alexander, Miriam Phields, Shay Youngblood, Ellen Sumter, Boston Fielder, Annette Lawrence, Aunjanue Ellis, Nina Revoyr, Valerie Woods, Craig Seymour, Nivea Castro, Beverly Guy-Sheftall, Ti Walker, Monimala Basu, Eileen Drennen, John T. Edge, Janice Hume, Jeff Springston, Elena Grant Napper, Swasti Oyama, Marcia and Daniel Minter, Lois Hurston Gaston, Charlayne Hunter-Gault, Jamilah Shakir, and dozens more.

None of these thanks would be possible, of course, without the original thank you: *To Alice Walker, for being you, the freest person I know, and for choosing me.*

—VB

* * *

I thank all those—many now in the spirit world—for whom I have stayed alive.

And those—in this and in the Spirit World—for whom I would have died.

—AW

ILLUSTRATION CREDITS

163   Be Nobody's Darling. Photo by Nan E. Park. Alice Walker Collection, Stuart A. Rose Manuscript, Archives & Rare Book Library, Emory University.

171   The handwritten first page of *The Color Purple*, from a 1980 journal. Alice Walker Collection, Stuart A. Rose Manuscript, Archives & Rare Book Library, Emory University.

195   AW illustration of her newly purchased land, which she dubbed Wild Trees, in Mendocino County, California. From a 1982 journal. Alice Walker Collection, Stuart A. Rose Manuscript, Archives & Rare Book Library, Emory University.

217   AW in 1984 with her "reconstituted family, going strong," as she put it: her partner Robert Allen, her daughter Rebecca, and his son Casey. Alice Walker Collection, Stuart A. Rose Manuscript, Archives & Rare Book Library, Emory University.

231   AW working at Wild Trees, 1984. Alice Walker Collection, Stuart A. Rose Manuscript, Archives & Rare Book Library, Emory University.

293   AW photo by Dwight Carter for *Essence* magazine, September 1989. Alice Walker Collection, Stuart A. Rose Manuscript, Archives & Rare Book Library, Emory University.

294   AW and Rebecca. Photo by Jean Weisinger, July 1991. Alice Walker Collection, Stuart A. Rose Manuscript, Archives & Rare Book Library, Emory University.

377   AW photo by Sydney R. Goldstein, City Arts & Lectures, San Francisco. Alice Walker Collection, Stuart A. Rose Manuscript, Archives & Rare Book Library, Emory University.

471   AW in her fifties. Alice Walker Collection, Stuart A. Rose Manuscript, Archives & Rare Book Library, Emory University.

494   AW dancing. Photo by Jean Weisinger, 1992. Alice Walker Collection, Stuart A. Rose Manuscript, Archives & Rare Book Library, Emory University.

INDEX

ABOUT THE AUTHORS

Alice Walker, winner of the Pulitzer Prize and the National Book Award, is a canonical figure in American letters. She is the author of *The Color Purple, The Temple of My Familiar, Horses Make a Landscape Look More Beautiful, The Way Forward Is with a Broken Heart, Now Is the Time to Open Your Heart,* and many other works of fiction, poetry, and nonfiction. Her writings have been translated into more than two dozen languages, and more than fifteen million copies of her books have been sold worldwide.

Valerie Boyd is the author of the critically acclaimed biography *Wrapped in Rainbows: The Life of Zora Neale Hurston,* winner of the Southern Book Award and the American Library Association's Notable Book Award. She is the founder and director of the MFA Program in Narrative Nonfiction and the Charlayne Hunter-Gault professor of journalism at the University of Georgia. In 2017, she received the Georgia Governor's Award in the Arts and Humanities. She is editor-at-large at the University of Georgia Press and senior consulting editor for *The Bitter Southerner.*